The Siege of Washington

The Siege of Washington

The Untold Story of the Twelve Days that Shook the Union

JOHN LOCKWOOD AND CHARLES LOCKWOOD

OXFORD
UNIVERSITY PRESS

OXFORD
UNIVERSITY PRESS

Oxford University Press, Inc., publishes works that further
Oxford University's objective of excellence
in research, scholarship, and education.

Oxford   New York
Auckland   Cape Town   Dar es Salaam   Hong Kong   Karachi
Kuala Lumpur   Madrid   Melbourne   Mexico City   Nairobi
New Delhi   Shanghai   Taipei   Toronto

With offices in
Argentina   Austria   Brazil   Chile   Czech Republic   France   Greece
Guatemala   Hungary   Italy   Japan   Poland   Portugal   Singapore
South Korea   Switzerland   Thailand   Turkey   Ukraine   Vietnam

Published by Oxford University Press, Inc.
198 Madison Avenue, New York, New York 10016

www.oup.com

Oxford is a registered trademark of Oxford University Press

Library of Congress Cataloging-in-Publication Data
Lockwood, John, 1951–
The siege of Washington : the untold story of the twelve days that shook the Union / John Lockwood and
Charles Lockwood.
p. cm.
Includes bibliographical references and index.
ISBN 978-0-19-975989-7 (cloth : alk. paper)
1. Washington (D.C.)—History—Civil War, 1861–1865. 2. United States—History—Civil War, 1861–1865.
3. Scott, Winfield, 1786–1866. 4. Andrew, John A. (John Albion), 1818–1867. 5. United States. Army.
Massachusetts Infantry Regiment, 6th (1861–1864) I. Lockwood, Charles, 1948- II. Title.
E472.1.L66   2011
975.3′02—dc22
2010040078

1 3 5 7 9 8 6 4 2

Printed in the United States of America
on acid-free paper

To our mother, Allison Lockwood

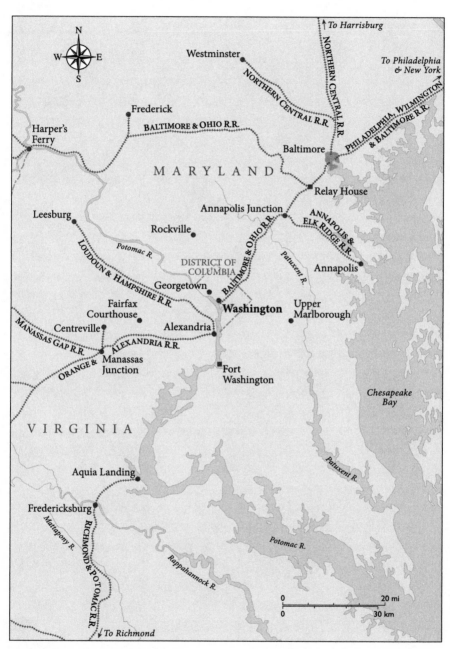

Washington and vicinity, April 1861.

We meet here again after another week of deep, intense, heartfelt, wide-spread and thrilling excitement. I have never spent days so restless and anxious. Our mornings and evenings have continually oscillated between the dim light of hope, and the gloomy shadow of despair. We have opened our papers, new and damp from the press, tremblingly, lest the first line of the lightning should tell us that our National Capital has fallen into the hands of the traitors and murderers who have bound themselves as with an oath to break up our National Government.

    Frederick Douglass, "Hope and Despair in These Cowardly Times" (April 28, 1861)

On the 12th day of April, 1861, the insurgents committed the flagrant act of civil war by the bombardment and capture of Fort Sumter. . . . Immediately afterward all the roads and avenues to this city were obstructed, and the capital was put into the condition of a siege.

    Abraham Lincoln, Message to Congress (May 26, 1862)

CONTENTS

PREFACE

When Major Robert Anderson, the commander of the Union garrison at Fort Sumter, surrendered to Confederate Brigadier General Pierre G. T. Beauregard on April 13, 1861, many Americans in both North and South expected that the first real battle of the war would soon be fought over Washington. Surrounded by the slave states of Maryland and Virginia, the nation's capital was largely bereft of defenders, lacked any fortifications within its borders, and seemed an easy target for Confederate attackers. "From the 15th to the 25th of April the nation held its breath in anxious suspense," wrote journalist and West Point graduate Edward D. Mansfield in 1862. "All eyes were upon the capital . . . with enemies within and advancing armies without, the fearful trembled for its safety, and the most sanguine were held in doubt."[1] Even President Lincoln feared that Washington might be captured: on April 15, he startled his cabinet by telling them, "If I were Beauregard, I would take Washington."[2]

For the twelve anguished days between Sumter's surrender and Washington's rescue, the city's fate hung by a thread. When Lincoln recalled these days one year later, he stated simply that Washington was in the "condition of a siege."[3]

In the end, the city was not attacked, and the first battle of the Civil War would occur at Bull Run, two months later and some thirty miles from the capital. Washington's escape from near-certain Southern capture appeared a miracle, and many Northern leaders could not understand why the Confederacy had not attacked the lightly defended city. In his book *The War of the Rebellion*, published in 1884, General Theodore B. Gates called it "one of the unsolved riddles of Confederate policy."[4] General Benjamin F. Butler, who played a central role in the drama, noted his own puzzlement in his 1892 autobiography: "Why Washington was not captured within ten days after Fort Sumter was fired upon has always since been a subject of careful consideration on my part, and a thing which I have been entirely unable to understand."[5]

The capture of Washington might have ended the war before it started, as financier Henry Villard observed. The young Villard had served as the *New York Herald*'s Washington correspondent in April 1861, and the question of why the South had failed to act still vexed him four decades later as he composed his autobiography: "I did not understand then, nor could I ever understand, why the rebel hands were not stretched out to seize so easy a prey—a seizure that might have resulted in the immediate triumph of the insurrection."[6]

As they grew older, government officials and Washington residents who had lived through the siege of Washington regretted that this pivotal event at the start of the Civil War had been eclipsed in national memory—quite understandably, given the awful bloodshed of the next four years of war, and the subsequent turmoil of Emancipation and Reconstruction. When Washington seemed doomed to fall to the Confederacy during those bleak days in April 1861, Lucius Chittenden, the register of the Treasury, had watched the army's preparations to make a last stand against the expected attack from the Treasury building. Shortly before his death in 1900, he observed: "No account of the isolation of Washington has yet been written."[7] A century later, Chittenden's statement still rang true. This book, at long last, offers that account.

The Siege of Washington

Prologue

"On to Washington!"

On April 12, 1861, only hours after Confederate guns opened fire on Fort Sumter in the Charleston harbor, Confederate Secretary of War Leroy P. Walker appeared before a jubilant crowd in Montgomery, Alabama. "No man can tell when the war this day commenced will end," Walker thundered from the balcony of the Exchange Hotel, at the heart of the Confederate capital, "but I will prophesy that the flag which now flaunts the breeze here will float over the dome of the old Capitol at Washington before the first of May"—less than three weeks away.[1]

The cry "On to Washington!" already resounded across the South.[2] Earlier that year, on January 3, Maryland's governor, Thomas H. Hicks, had warned that "secession leaders in Washington" had "resolved to seize the federal Capitol and the public archives, so that they may be in a position to be acknowledged by foreign governments."[3] Later, on March 4, Abraham Lincoln had taken the oath of office in Washington amid rumors of a secessionist conspiracy to interrupt his inauguration and seize the capital. Now, with the first shot of the Civil War fired, the Confederate States of America seemed ready to make a dash at Washington, drive out or imprison Lincoln and his cabinet, and move the Confederate capital north of the Potomac.

Jefferson Davis planned to be living in the White House by May 1, according to the plans of his wife, Varina. On April 17, New York insurance executive William Holdredge wrote Secretary of State William H. Seward in exasperation, informing him that the "wife of the Rebel President Davis has had the impudence to send cards to her lady acquaintances at the Saint Nicholas"—a favorite New York hotel for visiting Southerners—"inviting them to attend her reception in the White House at Washington on the first of May!"[4]

JEFF, DAVIS

IN THE WHITE HOUSE.

AIR—"Ye Parliaments of Old England."

Ye Northern men in Washington,
    Your administration, too—
Consider well what you are about,
    And what you are going to do.
Yankees gained the day with foreigners,
    Yet I am sure you'll rue the day,
When you meet the sons of Southern blood
    In battle's proud array.

JEFF. DAVIS in the White House,
    What glorious news it will be;
Abe Lincoln in an inglorious flight,
    In a baggage car we will see:
With Seward as conductor,
    Gen. Scott as engineer,
Old Hicks, our traitor governor,
    Following, *panting in the rear.*

Take my advice, ye Northern men,
    Throw off old Lincoln's yoke;
Hurl down the tyrant from his seat,
    Who dares this war evoke.
Recognize the Southern Confederacy,
    Be brothers in heart and hand—
Peace, happiness and prosperity,
    Will shower its blessings on our land.

A popular song from the early months of 1861, "Jeff Davis in the White House," imagined the Confederate president driving President Lincoln out of Washington and taking residence in the executive mansion himself.

Many Southerners, however, believed that Washington was not worthy of occupation and should instead be left to decay. "With a new Republic, we should have a new Capital, erected in the heart of the South," wrote the *Richmond Examiner* on April 23. "Let Washington remain, with its magnificent buildings crumbling into ruin—a striking monument to future ages of the folly and wickedness of the people of the North. It would teach a lesson, in its silence and desolation, all the nations of the earth could learn and understand."[5] Other secessionists called for the outright destruction of Washington. As John William Draper recounted in his 1868 *National History of the War for the Union,* one of the early histories of the Civil War, secessionists in Washington planned to "blow up the Capitol and the Treasury Building, to burn the President's house and other public edifices, and to leave in the blackened wreck of the ruined city a proof to the world that the Union was ruined."[6]

Seizing Washington and transforming it into the Confederate capital, however, would have numerous advantages, foremost among them the Confederacy's gaining instant legitimacy as an independent government. "The capture and occupation of Washington," remembered General Benjamin Butler, who led the Eighth Massachusetts Volunteers to defend the capital, "would almost have insured the Confederacy at once a place by recognition as a power among the nations of the earth."[7] Former Louisiana Senator John Slidell wrote to Jefferson Davis on April 24 that it was "difficult to exaggerate the importance of the prestige of early successes in a struggle like this." The Confederate government would need diplomatic recognition from European nations and lines of credit from their banks, both of which would be far easier to secure with Washington in their control. "If the war is to be prolonged, our great difficulty will be the financial one, if we are in possession of Washington we can negotiate our loans in Europe," Slidell wrote to Davis. "But if reduced to the defensive," the Confederacy would find securing foreign credit impossible.[8] Of course, the possibility of a prolonged war would itself be greatly reduced with Washington in Confederate hands: the North might be so humiliated by the loss of the capital and the capture of the president that it might capitulate to a negotiated peace without fighting.

"Can there not be found men bold and brave enough in Maryland to unite with Virginians in seizing the Capital?" the *Richmond Enquirer* had demanded on Christmas Day, 1860.[9] Rumors of a plot to take Washington had spurred a congressional investigation in January 1861 to gauge whether there was an active conspiracy by secessionist groups within the city. After interviewing numerous witnesses, the committee issued its report on February 14, 1861, concluding that there was no secret plot to capture Washington, though many pro-Southern political clubs drilled there openly. The committee found that these clubs "sympathized strongly with secession," but uncovered "no proof that they intend to attack either the Capitol or the District," unless the surrender of Washington "should be demanded" by

Virginia or Maryland, if either or both states seceded. The committee's report also concluded that there was no secret plot per se, because Washington secessionists were open in expressing their sympathies and did not consider secrecy necessary.[10]

Washington was undoubtedly easy prey. The Union capital was located 60 miles south of the Mason-Dixon Line, in slaveholding territory. The city's main transportation link to the North was the Baltimore & Ohio (B & O) railroad line, a single track that served both north- and southbound traffic, with telegraph lines running alongside. Both the telegraph and train lines could be torn up by a handful of men, severing Washington's physical and communication ties to the rest of the Union.

Washington's natural defenses were nonexistent, and in early 1861 its chief manmade fortification was Fort Washington, a decrepit structure built in 1809, located seven miles down the Potomac River and defended by exactly one soldier. Washington proper was scarcely better protected: only 1,500 soldiers, marines, and militia were stationed in the city. "A long period of profound peace had made every [U.S.] military organization seem almost farcical," recalled Union general Jacob Cox a quarter-century later.[11] Obtaining the necessary additional troops for Washington from the U.S. Army was unrealistic, given that at the start of 1861 nearly all of its 16,000 troops were scattered on the frontier west of the Mississippi River. Within several months, that number quickly dropped by one-third, as Southern officers and soldiers departed for home when their states joined the Confederacy.

The U.S. Navy was "as weak and unavailable as the army," wrote General Gates in *The War of the Rebellion*.[12] Of its ninety vessels—most of them antiquated—only a handful were either in U.S. waters in April 1861 or dry-docked at the Gosport Navy Yard in Norfolk. The remaining ships were at sail in foreign waters on the order of the previous Secretary of the Navy Isaac Toucey, a Southern sympathizer. The Navy Department in Washington, which stood on the east side of Seventeenth Street at F Street, was as old-fashioned as the fleet. The building had no gaslight for nighttime illumination. If clerks and officials wanted to work past twilight, they had to light candles or lamps.[13]

As states in the Deep South seceded, led by South Carolina on December 20, 1860, their militias seized federal installations within their boundaries—typically small, lightly defended fortifications in out-of-the-way locations. Some of these installations held newly manufactured arms, which

Secretary of War John B. Floyd, a secessionist, had ordered shipped to the South . These fortifications often fell without a fight, as Union commanders saw no reason for their men to be killed or wounded in a hopeless battle. Besides, many of their troops' sympathies lay with the South. Before Fort Sumter, the Southern victors usually let the vanquished Northern men go home. In early February 1861, for example, the Texas militia allowed the 200 men of Companies D, H, and I of the Second U.S. Cavalry to return to the North after their surrender. The Texans, of course, kept the unit's horses, so the Northern men had no choice but to march 600 miles from Texas's western frontier to the port of Galveston, where they caught ships to New York, and from there took the train to Washington, arriving on April 13 and 14. To one reporter writing in Washington's *National Republican*, the "soldiers look very much worn down by their march."[14] Nonetheless, with invasion expected within days, these defenders, however bedraggled, were an unexpected godsend.

General Winfield Scott, the longtime commander of the U.S. Army, along with a handful of leading Northern politicians and military leaders, had begun calling for greater reinforcement of the U.S. Army's southern fortifications in late 1860, along with stronger defenses for Washington. These proposals had gone nowhere, because Floyd—given his sympathies—did not support them. President Buchanan was so ineffectual that he refused to affirm or reject Scott's suggestions for Washington's defense. Only after Floyd had resigned his cabinet post on December 29, 1860—he had been indicted by the District of Columbia grand jury for conspiracy and fraud—and was replaced by Joseph Holt, who was pro-Union, could Scott begin work on his long-overdue defensive plans.

After his inauguration, Lincoln was aware that the capital was weakly defended and that the U.S. Army was far too small to fight a civil war. Nonetheless, he was reluctant to issue a call for volunteers, lest it fail to raise enough men and thereby make a mockery of the North's military credibility and of his own administration. Although many Northerners followed the secession crisis with rapt interest, Washington's plight was largely ignored, even after the formation of the Confederate States of America in February 1861 and the seizure of over 20 Union military installations in the South after the New Year.

U.S. Army Colonel William Tecumseh Sherman, who resigned as superintendent of Louisiana's state military academy after the state's secession on

January 26, 1861, was struck by the contrast between Northern and Southern attitudes on his journey from New Orleans to Washington to visit his brother, Senator John Sherman of Ohio, in mid-March. "In the South, the people were earnest, fierce, and angry, and were evidently organizing for action," he wrote after the war, "whereas, in Illinois, Indiana, and Ohio, I saw not the least sign of preparation."[15]

In Washington itself, Sherman was shocked to see "but few signs of preparation, though the Southern senators and representatives were daily sounding their threats on the floor of Congress, and were resigning and leaving to join the Confederate Congress at Montgomery, Alabama."[16] He was appalled that even in the War Department "there was open, unconcealed talk, amounting to high-treason." Nor was Sherman impressed by President Lincoln after meeting him at the White House with his brother. During the conversation, Lincoln downplayed the many warnings about the South's overall military efforts. Before leaving Washington to rejoin his family in St. Louis, Sherman somberly told his brother that "the country was sleeping on a volcano that might burst forth at any minute."[17]

Why did Lincoln not awaken the Northern states to the rising peril after taking office? First, his administration's first days were disorganized and ill-managed. Lincoln's Washington experience consisted of a single two-year term as a congressman from Illinois from 1847 to 1849, and as newly inaugurated president he was often forced to focus on administrative matters, particularly dealing with endless entreaties from job seekers. Second, the new administration had to fix the damage that secessionists in the Buchanan administration and in Congress had done to the Army, Navy, Treasury, and other departments. Insufficient funds had been appropriated to maintain fortifications, buy the latest weaponry, and increase the size of the army to guard these installations more effectively. Finally few Northern leaders, including Lincoln, "appreciated the serious, deeply seated hostility of either the chiefs or the rank and file of the secession movement," recalled Colonel Charles P. Stone, inspector general of the District of Columbia Militia. They thought that "all violent opposition to the United States Government would soon melt away before the power of official patronage. 'There will be,' said they, 'a vast deal of bluster, but when it comes to a question of actually fighting against the Government of the United States, there will be none of it.'"[18]

Many federal leaders, however, were pessimistic that Washington could be held if Confederate troops launched an attack. "The Federal Government,"

Gates remembered, "could scarcely have been less prepared for war than it was on the day the Confederate batteries opened their fire on Fort Sumter."[19] "We have war upon us," wrote Edwin M. Stanton to James Buchanan on April 12, the day the bombardment of Fort Sumter began. "The impression here is held by many: 1st, that the effort to reinforce [Fort Sumter] will be a failure; 2d, that in less than twenty-four hours from this time, [Major Robert] Anderson will have surrendered; 3d, that in less than thirty days Davis will be in possession of Washington."[20]

The fall of Fort Sumter on Saturday, April 13, and its official surrender the following day transformed public opinion throughout the long-slumbering North. "All its [the South's] high-sounding talk of war was obstinately regarded as empty gasconade," recalled Mary Ashton Livermore, an abolitionist and suffragist in Boston. "When, therefore, the telegraph, which had registered for an astounded nation the hourly progress of the bombardment, announced the lowering of the stars and stripes, and the surrender of the beleaguered garrison, the news fell on the land like a thunderbolt."[21] For Frederick Douglass, the attack on Sumter clarified the meaning of the conflict for the North and the South. "Our rulers were ready enough to sacrifice the negro to the Union so long as there was any hope of saving the Union by that means. The "attack upon Sumter," however, finally made clear that "insatiate slaveholders not only mean the peace and safety of slavery, but to make themselves masters of the Republic," Douglass wrote. "It is not merely a war for slavery, but it is a war for slavery dominion."[22]

On Sunday, April 14, Northern ministers delivered sermons they hoped would instill both patriotic fervor and a sense of a moral mission. "The pulpits thundered with denunciations of the rebellion," recalled Livermore. "Congregations applauded sermons such as were never before heard in Boston, not even from radical preachers." One of the nation's most famous ministers and abolitionists, Henry Ward Beecher, whose sister Harriet Beecher Stowe was the author of *Uncle Tom's Cabin*, delivered one of his most stirring sermons, "The Battle Set in Array," to 2,800 devoted followers who filled his Plymouth Church in Brooklyn Heights. From his pulpit, Beecher orated: "And now our turn has come. Right before us lies the Red Sea of war. It is red indeed. There is blood in it.'"[23]

Outrage in the North over the attack on Fort Sumter ignited a mass outpouring of support for the Union. Northerners were, to be sure, angry about the success of the Confederacy in real military terms. But they were also releasing months of pent-up rage over Southern taunts—for example, that 10 Northern men were not worth one Southerner in the field—and exasperation over constant threats against the President and the Union government in Washington. "Mr. Cox, the people have gone stark mad!" Senator Thomas M. Key of Ohio said to Representative Samuel S. Cox when they met in Cincinnati in mid-April. "I knew they would if a blow were struck against the flag," Cox replied.[24]

Lincoln worked to harness this rage into support for the Union cause. That Sunday, he returned through the wind and rain to the White House after services at the New York Avenue Presbyterian Church and then commenced an all-day meeting with his cabinet and General Scott, which started at 11 a.m. and lasted into the evening.[25] The main topics were the surrender of Fort Sumter, which had taken place that afternoon, the measures needed to protect Washington, and the raising of an army to counter the rebellion. Without strong public support across the North and the enrollment of tens of thousands of volunteers, the Union cause was nearly hopeless.

The cabinet was unanimous in supporting an immediate call for volunteers, whom the Army would order to Washington's defense, recalled Frederick W. Seward, who served as undersecretary of state for consular affairs under his father, Secretary of State William H. Seward. "The time had manifestly arrived to call for troops. . . . Nor was there any delusive hope that a small force would suffice. Each of the Cabinet realized that the contest would be gigantic."[26] The draft proclamation required state governors to raise volunteer militias to suppress the rebellion of states that had seceded from the Union. Congress had adjourned in early March, and Lincoln had to wait until legislators reconvened to formally appropriate the funds for a larger professional army. Until then, Washington's—and the nation's—defense would rely on the responses of state governors and their ability to quickly enlist volunteers. The cabinet reviewed the wording of the proclamation, which sought volunteers for three months of service. Amid debates over the number of volunteers to call forth, Lincoln chose 75,000 troops. He wanted a number large enough to sound impressive yet not so large as to set a goal that might not be met. Lincoln also knew that arms and materiel were in short supply, and that it would be difficult enough arming and outfitting 75,000 soldiers, let alone 100,000 or more.

The recent adjournment of Congress complicated Lincoln's actions considerably. Congress had "put forth no preparation for the coming crisis, had made no extra appropriations, had not authorized the enlistment of any additional seamen," wrote Gideon Welles, the secretary of the navy, in his diary.[27] Yet only Congress had the legal authority to increase the size of the nation's army and navy and to approve new expenditures, loans, or tax increases. Lincoln carefully weighed the desirability of carrying out policies without congressional approval during this unprecedented crisis. "It became necessary for me to choose whether, using only the existing means, agencies, and processes which Congress had provided, I should let the Government at once fall into ruin," recalled Lincoln a year later, defending the actions of his administration, "or whether, availing myself of the broader powers conferred by the Constitution in cases of insurrection, I would make an effort to save it, with all its blessings, for the present age and posterity."[28]

Thus, the question of the right time to call the House and Senate back into session was a critical topic at that Sunday cabinet meeting. Some cabinet members urged Lincoln to do so at once. Secretary Seward, however, cautioned Lincoln that Congress would interfere with his actions during this critical time. Said the shrewd Seward: "To wait for 'many men of many minds' to shape a war policy would be to invite disaster." Seeing the merit in Seward's advice, Lincoln decided that the proclamation would contain a provision calling the House and Senate into session on July 4. He would have to hope that the returning Congress's "patriotism to sanction the war measures taken prior to that time by the Executive" would exonerate any overreach of presidential authority, recalled Frederick Seward.[29]

Until Congress reconvened, the Secretary of the Treasury, Salmon P. Chase, would gain necessary funds by obtaining loans from New York banks and issuing government bonds. An early leader of the new Republican Party in Ohio in the 1850s, Chase was fiercely opposed to slavery and promoted progressive ideas such as widespread public education and greater rights for women. He did not have an extensive financial background, however, when Lincoln appointed him. Fortunately, Chase was smart, hardworking, and a quick learner, and he successfully managed government funding through the difficult first months of the war.

While they waited for the returning Congress to authorize a large expansion of the U.S. Army, the cabinet agreed that General Scott would have to rely on volunteer militia from Northern states—the 75,000 men to be called for in the proclamation—to safeguard Washington and the remaining Northern states. Most, but not all, of the cabinet members welcomed General Scott's command of the defense of Washington and the Northern states. Scott had been a national military hero for decades and was known as the "Grand Old Man of the Army." Born in 1786, one year before the drafting of the Constitution, Scott had won several U.S. victories during the War of 1812 and secured his fame in the Mexican-American War (1846–1848) with the conquest of Mexico City. Some of Scott's other accomplishments, much praised at the time, are now considered to be disgraces in U.S. history, the most prominent of them the forcible removal of Cherokees from their homes and extensive lands in Georgia and Tennessee to Oklahoma, along the Trail of Tears, a policy Scott had questioned but carried out under orders during the administration of President Andrew Jackson. Scott had been the Whig Party's presidential candidate in 1852, but lost the election to Democrat Franklin Pierce.

By 1861, Scott had served for almost half a century, under 14 presidents, from Thomas Jefferson to Lincoln, and the defense of Washington would be one of the last great challenges of his long and distinguished career. John Sergeant Wise—son of Henry A. Wise, the rabidly secessionist governor of Virginia—recalled Scott's imposing figure in his memoir *The End of an Era*: "What a monster in size he was! Never was a uniform more magnificent; never were feathers in cocked hat more profuse; never was sash so broad and gorgeous. He was old and gouty, keen for food, quick for drink, and thunderous of voice, large as a straw-stack, and red as a boiled lobster."[30] Scott was proud of his appearance in uniform, all the more imposing because of his six-foot, four-inch height. Because of his insistence on strict discipline, military appearance, and esprit de corps among his men, he earned the nickname "Old Fuss and Feathers." In 1858, when Scott left a reception in Richmond held by Governor Wise, "a characteristic incident occurred," recalled the younger Wise. "In the great hallway, he called for his wraps and his galoshes. The servants were quick to hurry forward with them. Several cadets had been invited to the entertainment, and were standing about awestruck in the presence of the commander-in-chief. As the servants offered him his cloaks and overshoes, he waved them away imperiously, and in his commanding voice thundered out, 'No, no! Let the cadets attend upon me. Here, you cadets. Help me with my overshoes and wraps. It is not every day that I can get such orderlies, and it is not every day that you can wait upon the general of the armies.'"[31]

By early 1861, the 75-year-old Scott was suffering the effects of age, a severe wound received in 1814 at the Battle of Lundy's Lane, and his decades-long love of good food and drink—not to mention rudimentary mid-nineteenth century medical practices. He weighed more than 300 pounds, and because of gout and rheumatism, walking had become increasingly painful for him. During a conversation with Secretary Seward, Scott shared his frustration at his physical condition and displayed his determination to serve the Union as best he could. "'If I could only mount a horse," Seward remembered Scott complaining before "checking himself, with a shake of his head," then adding, "but I am past that. I can only serve my country, as I am doing here now, in my chair."[32]

Scott's critics focused on his physical ailments, but they were off target in claiming that he was the relic of another era. Scott's acumen proved decisive in the protection of Washington, and no member of Lincoln's cabinet worked harder than he did during the perilous early days of the capital's defense, or displayed greater courage.

On December 2, 1860, President Buchanan had requested that Scott move his New York–based military offices—and himself—back to Washington. The general lived in a brownstone on fashionable West Twelfth Street off lower Fifth Avenue, ate at the best restaurants, and attended lavish parties and fashionable performances at the Academy of Music. His wife spent most of her time in Europe. When he arrived in Washington on December 12, 1860, he took a simple room at a boarding house on Sixth Street owned by a famed French caterer, Cruchet. Scott moved the headquarters of the U.S. Army into the Winder Building, which still stands at 600 Seventeenth Street NW, just one block west of the White House.

While the ineffectual Buchanan administration sputtered to an end, Scott took measures to protect Washington with the pitifully few troops at his disposal, and supervised security measures to protect both the Electoral College delegates who met at the Capitol in mid-February and Lincoln's inauguration several weeks later. Stanton, who had served as attorney general near the end of the ex-president's term of office, wrote to Buchanan: "General Scott seems to have *carte blanche*. He is, in fact, the Government, and if his health continues, vigorous measures are anticipated."[33]

Scott, whose responsibilities of course extended to the whole army, needed an officer to supervise Washington's defensive measures in the waning days of the Buchanan administration and the expected trouble at

Lincoln's inauguration. On December 31, 1860, he invited Charles Stone, who had served as a colonel in the U.S. Army until his 1856 resignation, to his office. Stone had spent the summer and autumn of 1860 in Washington, and when Scott asked him about local loyalties, Stone could knowledgeably reply, "It is my belief, General, that two-thirds of the fighting stock of this population would sustain the government in defending itself if called upon." "But," he added, "they are uncertain as to what can be done or what the government wants done, and they have no rallying point." Scott had already decided that Stone was the man he needed. He told Stone, "Make yourself that rallying point!"[34]

The following day, January 1, 1861, Stone again assumed the rank of colonel as inspector general of the District of Columbia Militia. His immediate responsibility was the security of Washington. He stationed armed guards at the bridges over the Potomac and Anacostia rivers, and at major routes leading into and out of the city, such as the road (now known as Wisconsin Avenue) that went from Georgetown to Frederick, Maryland; Seventh Street, which turned into Georgia Avenue three-quarters of a mile north of Pennsylvania Avenue and ran through today's Silver Spring; and the Bladensburg Road, which started northeast of the Capitol and led into Prince George's County, Maryland.

If the city was attacked, Colonel Stone would rely on three defensive "centers," which he believed could survive under siege for at least 10 days, by which point relief would have already arrived. The first fortified site would be the Capitol, because it was solidly constructed and 2,000 barrels of flour would be stored in the basement. Major Irvin McDowell would camp out each night in the Capitol with 200 or 300 members of the local militia. The second defensive location was the Old City Hall area, including the Patent Office and the General Post Office, with guards placed there each night. The third was the "Executive Square," comprising the White House and the nearby buildings housing the War, Navy, State, and Treasury departments. Each would have soldiers stationed inside at night. As Colonel Stone phrased it: "The citadel of this center is the Treasury Building." Like the Capitol, the fortress-like Treasury would also have 2,000 barrels of flour in the basement, and "perhaps the best water in the city is to be found there," where defenders would attempt to hold out if the rest of Washington was overrun with Southern attackers.[35]

Despite the North's outrage over the attack on Fort Sumter, President Lincoln feared that his proclamation might not generate adequate enthusiasm for 75,000 men to enroll for 90 days of service. Indeed, support for the Union was not always assured in free states. Eleven years earlier, California had entered the Union as a free state as part of the Compromise of 1850. In early 1861, however, Senator William Gwin, a Southern-born advocate of slavery, urged California to secede from the Union and form its own nation. Over the short term, the secession of California would prevent its gold from funding the Union war effort. Over the long term, California's secession would shatter the dream of an ocean-to-ocean nation, and might trigger the secession of Oregon and Washington to join California in a Pacific republic.

Worse, Lincoln was aware that the nation's most populous city, New York, was a hotbed of pro-Southern sentiment. Many New York merchants and bankers could not be trusted to support the Union and boost Washington's defenses, since they had played dirty to prevent Lincoln's election and avert war. Before the election, Wall Street tycoons staged a short-lived financial panic, and then informed the press that it had been caused by fear of Lincoln's victory. James Gordon Bennett, Sr., publisher of the *New York Herald*, cautioned workingmen that "if Lincoln is elected, you will have to compete with the labor of four million emancipated negroes." The *New York Daily News*, whose editor was Benjamin Wood, brother of the city's anti-Lincoln mayor, warned New Yorkers that if Lincoln won, "we shall find negroes among us thicker than blackberries swarming everywhere."[36]

Many leading New Yorkers not only supported the Confederacy but wanted secession for the city itself. In January 1861, Mayor Fernando Wood proposed to the Common Council, the city's governing body, that if the Southern states seceded from the Union, "New York be, and from henceforth forever hereafter shall be and remain, a free city of itself."[37] Many leading bankers and merchants favored an independent and neutral New York, fearing the loss of the highly lucrative trade with the South, particularly in cotton, which they shipped to European textile manufacturers. New York merchants took 40 cents out of every dollar that Europeans paid for Southern cotton. War threatened to disrupt their livelihoods and the city's economy.

Keeping New York in the Union was absolutely essential for the North's war effort. It was the richest city in the United States by any measure, "the locomotive of these United States," wrote businessman, author, and adventurer George Francis Train, "transporting the nation and its people into the future with increasing speed, "twenty miles an hour—thirty—forty!" New York was also a critical source of tax revenue for the federal government. In 1860, ad valorem taxes—tariffs on imported goods at U.S. ports—provided $56 million of the $64.6 million of all federal revenues, and more than two-thirds of imports, as measured by goods' value, passed through New York.[38] If New York became "a free city of itself," the Union war effort would probably collapse immediately: the government would lose its primary source of financing the war at a time when the Treasury was already nearly empty.

President Lincoln's draft proclamation calling for 75,000 volunteers, formally issued on April 15.

To achieve the maximum impact on Northern public opinion, the proclamation for 75,000 volunteers would have to be rushed to newspapers for publication the following day. Would the sudden wave of patriotism translate into a firm resolve to fight the war? Or would the sentiment crest and then just as suddenly ebb? Southerners, of course, hoped for and even expected the latter. Beauregard told William Howard Russell, correspondent for the *Times* of London, that Northern public opinion "belongs to that washy sort of enthusiasm which is promoted by their lecturing and spouting." He asserted that the Southerners, by their nature, would prevail: "Southern men had more physical strength, owing to their mode of life and their education, than their Northern brethren."[39]

As soon as Lincoln had made the final changes on his handwritten text of the proclamation on April 14, his secretary, John Nicolay, rewrote it in to a more readable copy. Secretary Seward took the document to the State Department, where a formal copy was "duly perfected in form and engrossed" by the clerks, who then affixed the Great Seal of the United States to the document.[40] At the Washington City Telegraph Office, a telegraph operator tapped out the proclamation in Morse code, transmitting it to the rest of the nation.

After the cabinet meeting had broken up, Nicolay walked upstairs to the second-floor bedroom he shared with John Hay, Lincoln's assistant secretary. Official Washington had been stunned to learn that Lincoln had given such important positions to these two young and unknown men; Nicolay was twenty-nine, Hay twenty-two. Together, they set President Lincoln's schedule, decided which letters reached him and who he would see. While Washington Society was always polite to Nicolay and Hay in person—they had no other choice—some insiders leveled scathing criticism at these "mere boys from the West" behind their backs.[41] "The President is affable and kind," wrote Noah Brooks, journalist and Lincoln confidante, "but his immediate subordinates are snobby and unpopular," in particular singling out Nicolay as "the grim Cerberus of Teutonic descent who guards the last door."[42] Nicolay and Hay's access allowed them an unparalleled view of the Lincoln presidency. Their biography of Lincoln, first published in the *Century* from 1886 to 1890 and later in 10 volumes as *Abraham Lincoln: A History*, was so exhaustive that it contains detailed accounts of events not recounted elsewhere at such length, including the precarious twelve days after the fall of Sumter in Washington.[43] Since Lincoln himself, of course, left no memoirs, Nicolay's and Hay's account, if veering toward hagiography—influenced by Robert Todd Lincoln,

John Nicolay (above) and John Hay (below).

who controlled many of his father's papers—is one of the key accounts of the events in the White House.[44] Hay, moreover, also began a diary on April 18, providing a contemporaneous view of the inside workings of the White House during these tumultuous days.

In Washington, Nicolay and Hay quickly proved indispensable to the day-to-day functioning of the president's office. They had already demonstrated their skill in handling correspondence, visitors, and the press in Springfield after Lincoln's election and proved equally adept in the White House. They had the physical strength to keep up with Lincoln's seemingly boundless energy, were unswayed by flattery, did not accept gifts, and were completely devoted to Lincoln, and, it seemed, he to them. When speaking to each other about Lincoln in private, they nicknamed him "The Ancient" or "The Tycoon." "If they were especially moved," described Nicolay's daughter Helen in her book *Lincoln's Secretary*, they referred to him as "The American." In public, they always called him "Mr. Lincoln." In return, Lincoln addressed Nicolay as "Mr. Nicolay," just like most of his friends. Hay, whom Lincoln regarded "almost as a son," according to Helen Nicolay, he called "John."

Nicolay was "thin almost to emaciation," wrote Helen Nicolay. "Never in his life did he weigh more than a hundred and twenty-five pounds." He had immigrated to the United States from Bavaria with his father at the age of six and had been orphaned at fourteen. He was the printer's devil, then the editor, of the *Free Press* of Pittsfield, Illinois, an antislavery weekly, when he met Lincoln after an 1856 political rally there. In late 1857, Nicolay decided to become an attorney so that he could earn an adequate income to marry Therena Bates, his fiancée. As luck had it, he moved to Springfield so that he could read law in the state capitol's library and serve as a clerk in the law office of Ozias M. Hatch, who happened to be attorney general of Illinois and a good friend of Lincoln.[45] In the next few years, Nicolay got to know Lincoln by playing chess against him. Still a journalist in his spare time, Nicolay also wrote favorable articles about Lincoln for Illinois newspapers, including the *Chicago Tribune* and Springfield's *Illinois Journal*. Nicolay prepared a pro-Lincoln political pamphlet, *The Political Record of Stephen Douglas*, during the epic 1858 debates between the two men. He also found time to gain admission to the Illinois bar in early 1859. Soon after Lincoln won the Republican nomination for president on May 18, 1860, he hired Nicolay to be his private secretary at $75 a month.[46]

After Lincoln won the election, Nicolay could not keep up with the surge in letters. Late that month, he asked his friend John Hay, who was bored studying the law at a Springfield attorney's office, to help out. Hay said yes.

Six inches shorter than Nicolay, Hay was handsome and well-educated, was skilled in foreign languages and poetry, and could play the piano well, which got him invitations to the best parties. Moreover, he had a "sweet, true tenor voice," according to Anna Ridgely, one obviously smitten admirer during his Springfield years. Hay was the son of the well-to-do physician Charles Hay of Warsaw, Illinois, a small town on the Mississippi River. Seeing great potential in his son, Hay taught him both Greek and Latin. He proved an excellent pupil. In 1851, the doctor sent his son, then 13, to a small school in Pittsfield, Illinois—the home of the 19-year-old printer's devil Nicolay. Hay could speak German, and the school's headmaster introduced him to Nicolay so that they could converse together, and this was the start of their lifelong friendship.[47] A year later, however, Hay moved to Springfield to attend a larger prep school so he could go to Brown College in the fall of 1855. Nicolay had also wanted to attend Brown, but he lacked the educational background and money. In 1858, Hay returned to Springfield, after graduating (in only two years) from Brown, where he had been a great academic and social success. A few months later, when Nicolay came to Springfield to study for the law, the two men renewed their friendship. Hay was admitted to the Illinois bar on February 4, 1861, though he was less than enthusiastic about practicing law and spent his spare time writing poetry.[48]

Lincoln originally had no plan to bring Hay to Washington. As Lincoln's departure from Springfield neared, however, Nicolay asked Lincoln if Hay could come to Washington and serve as an assistant secretary, the role at which he had been so successful after the election. "An odd expression crossed Mr. Lincoln's face," wrote Helen Nicolay, "turning all its ruggedness into lines of perplexity, as he answered: "But I can't take all Illinois with me!" Nonetheless, Hay was on board the special train that departed from Springfield on February 11 and stopped at many of the North's leading cities on its nearly two-week-long journey to Washington for Lincoln's March 4 inauguration.[49]

That day, after being sworn in as president on the steps of the heavily guarded Capitol, Lincoln had returned to the White House with James Buchanan. The departing president told his successor, "If you are as happy, my dear sir, on entering the house as I am in leaving it and returning home, you are the happiest man in this country." Going upstairs to his office, scarcely more than an hour after being sworn in, Lincoln was immediately reminded that he had assumed the presidency amid the greatest crisis the nation had faced. "The first thing that was handed to me after I entered this room," Lincoln recalled several months later, "was a letter from Major Robert Anderson, Union commander at Fort Sumter, saying that their provisions would be exhausted before an expedition could be sent to their relief." General Scott had already read the letter. He added an ominous note, "I now see no alternative but a surrender."[50]

Five weeks later, with Scott's grim prediction fulfilled, hopes that the secession crisis might be brought to a peaceful resolution were now dashed: the nation had entered the uncharted territories of war. In Washington, the rumors of a secessionist conspiracy within the city were now amplified by the prospect that a Confederate force was on its way from the South. The enemy army, many worried, would be on the banks of the Potomac in days. For many, however, the sudden rush of events trumped fear, at least for the moment.

At midnight on April 14, Nicolay wrote to Therena Bates, who remained in Illinois, as he often did late at night. "I shall not write much. The news you will of course read before you could possibly see it in this letter—that Fort Sumpter [*sic*] has been taken by Southern rebels—that the President has called out 75,000 men to put down the rebellion, and that Congress is to be convened in July." The day's events had clearly moved him, as he realized his own role in the broader history unfolding before him: "All these things will make stirring times. I can hardly realize that they are so, even as I write them."[51]

Monday, April 15

"The Capital Can't Be Taken"

BY THE PRESIDENT OF THE UNITED STATES A PROCLAMATION

Whereas the laws of the United States have been for some time past, and now are opposed, and the execution thereof obstructed, in the States of South Carolina, Georgia, Alabama, Florida, Mississippi, Louisiana and Texas, . . . I, Abraham Lincoln, President of the United States, in virtue of the power in me vested by the Constitution, and the laws, have thought fit to call forth, and hereby do call forth, the militia of the several States of the Union, to the aggregate number of seventy-five thousand, in order to suppress said combinations, and to cause the laws to be duly executed.

I do hereby, in virtue of the power in me vested by the Constitution, convene both Houses of Congress. Senators and Representatives are therefore summoned to assemble at their respective chambers, at 12 o'clock, noon, on Thursday, the fourth day of July, next, then and there to consider and determine, such measures, as, in their wisdom, the public safety, and interest may seem to demand.

In Witness Whereof I have hereunto set my hand, and caused the Seal of the United States to be affixed.

Done at the city of Washington this fifteenth day of April in the year of our Lord One thousand, Eight hundred and Sixty-one, and of the Independence the United States the Eighty-fifth. President Abraham Lincoln.[1]

On the morning of Monday, April 15, 1861, newspapers across the North published Lincoln's emergency proclamation word for word. In many newspapers, the call for troops appeared next to the late reports of Fort Sumter's surrender on Saturday, April 13—some papers did not have a Sunday edition—and the juxtaposition was not lost on readers.

Unlike the fall of Fort Sumter, however, the proclamation came as a surprise to nearly everyone. News of the Union attempts to resupply Fort Sumter had played in newspapers for weeks, and a Southern attack had been expected. Lincoln's bold, swift response to the bombardment, however, had not been anticipated. In fact, few outside Lincoln's inner circle knew that the United States was prepared to respond to Southern military action at all, let alone that it would issue a massive call for volunteers.

Lincoln had known that his proclamation was as much a mobilization of Northern spirit as of military might. "Public sentiment is every thing," he had stated in a speech several years before. "*With* it, nothing can fail; *against* it, nothing can succeed. Whoever moulds public sentiment, goes deeper than he who enacts statutes, or pronounces judicial decisions. He makes possible the inforcement [*sic*] of these, else impossible."[2]

Many of the headlines about the proclamation declared the Union cause in dramatic, staccato terms. The cascading headline in the April 15 *New York Herald*, for example, read:

Highly Important News from Washington

A WAR PROCLAMATION

Seventy-five Thousand Men Ordered Out

Preparations for the Defence of the National Capital

The Great Free States Arming for the Conflict[3]

The high stakes were equally obvious on one recruiting poster, where a fierce-looking American eagle brandished a banner that bore the two most important dates in the nation's history:

1776! 1861!

VOLUNTEERS WANTED!

An Attack Upon Washington Anticipated!

A REGIMENT FOR SERVICE
UNDER THE FLAG OF THE UNITED STATES
NOW IS THE TIME TO BE ENROLLED![4]

Frederick Seward remembered that "the response to the proclamation at the North was all or more than could be anticipated."[5] "The lion of the North was fully roused," remembered Nicolay and Hay. "Betrayed, insulted, outraged, the free States arose as with a cry of pain and vengeance." The fall of Fort Sumter, though a tactical defeat, would allow the ultimate triumph of the Union, many Northerners believed. "Fort Sumter is temporarily lost," wrote General John A. Logan, "but the Country is saved. [Long] Live the Republic!"[6]

Washington's excitement over Lincoln's proclamation was intense, but patriotic response there was muted. Washington was foremost a Southern city, one that also happened to be the capital of the Union. A substantial portion of the city's residents favored the Confederacy. Though some loyal businesses and households displayed the American flag, patriotic bands did not march at all hours as they did in other cities, and the accompanying crowds were also absent.[7] Even those residents whose allegiance remained with the Union had eyed the new Lincoln administration with suspicion, for the months since his election had only brought trouble to the city. Local real estate values had collapsed, as many Washingtonians were planning to depart for the South, particularly longtime residents of means. The price of slaves declined at the markets across the Potomac in Alexandria, Virginia, because many people expected Lincoln to outlaw slavery outright in the District of Columbia, where trading in slaves had already been banned since 1850. For superstitious residents, the discovery of the Thatcher Comet just prior to the attack on Fort Sumter was an ominous omen.

But with war now unquestionably imminent, all Washingtonians—both loyal and secessionist—could no longer fail to recognize that the city's defenses were threadbare and that the threat of Confederate attack was real. The younger Seward noted that "suspicion supplied the place of information. The community was torn with conflicting emotions and interests."[8]

Waves of rumors threatened to set the tinderbox of the city's emotions ablaze. On April 14, a prankster had posted a fake dispatch from "Cape Hatteras Light" in the lobby of Willard's Hotel, the city's most popular hostelry and a center for exchange of gossip. Now that Fort Sumter had fallen, the dispatch read, the Confederacy was using a newly invented ship—the Charleston floating battery—to drive away the U.S. Navy, and it was heading north, perhaps to Washington. The news provoked a minor panic until accurate word spread that the dispatch was a hoax.

Looking back on that moment from the distance of 1873, Reverend C. H. Hall, rector of the Church of the Epiphany (who later read the Episcopal burial service at Lincoln's funeral) recalled, "Men went mad with fear or rage. Old sores broke out, and cords of amity that seemed eternal were burst. Men were here disloyal, and then suddenly and violently loyal."[9] Those tensions were felt across Washington's population: "There is an apparent calm throughout the City," observed the *New York Times*, just prior to the release of Lincoln's proclamation, "but a deep feeling of suspense exists."[10]

That morning at the White House, at 10 a.m., another marathon cabinet meeting commenced and lasted into the early evening.[11] Like most Americans, the cabinet members wanted to hear the latest news about the Union force that had surrendered Fort Sumter. Major Robert Anderson and his 85 men were headed north at that very moment. The previous day, they had marched out of the ruined fort with their drums beating and flags flying and boarded ships for New York. Anderson had said soberly: "Our Southern brethren have done grievously wrong, they have rebelled and have attacked their father's house and their loyal brothers. They must be punished and brought back, but this necessity breaks my heart."[12] Beauregard had let Anderson—his artillery instructor at West Point—return north by boat with his force, but many now expected Beauregard himself to travel north with a hostile army in tow: his troops could travel by rail from Charleston to the opposite banks of the Potomac in three or four days. That morning, the *New York Times* reported that the administration had "satisfactory information that the Confederate States have proposed, immediately after reducing Fort Sumter, to march on Washington with their army of twenty thousand men," since the force now had "nothing else to do."[13]

The true extent of the danger Washington faced from Beauregard was the subject of a heated exchange between General Scott and the Pennsylvania

Republican political leader and journalist Alexander Kelly McClure, who attended the meeting with Pennsylvania Governor Andrew Curtin. Scott told the meeting's attendees that he had only 1,500 trained and experienced troops in Washington at his command, although that number would rise significantly as volunteer troops arrived in the city from the North in the coming days. Seizing on that figure, McClure asked Scott how many men Beauregard commanded. "General Beauregard commands more men at Charleston than I command on the continent east of the frontier," Scott answered. To the general's annoyance, McClure pressed Scott several times more about the reliability and skill of the forces already in the city. Each time, Scott's reply was the same: "Sir, the capital can't be taken; the capital can't be taken."[14]

During this exchange, Lincoln was silent, staring at Scott and twirling his spectacles in his hands. Finally, he spoke: "It does seem to me, general, that if I were Beauregard I would take Washington." Scott straightened himself up in his chair, and said once more, this time with unmistakable resolve, "Mr. President, the capital can't be taken, sir; it can't be taken."[15]

Accompanying Lincoln's proclamation were Secretary of War Cameron's formal requisition orders to the governors of the states that remained in the Union. The requisition request spared a handful of distant western states but included all the slave states that had not yet seceded, and read:

> Under the act of Congress "for calling forth the militia to execute the laws of the Union, suppress insurrections, repel invasions," &c., approved February 28, 1795, I have the honor to request Your Excellency to cause to be immediately detached from the militia of your State the quota designated in the table below, to serve as infantry or riflemen, for the period of three months, unless sooner discharged.
>
> Your Excellency will please communicate to me the time at or about which your quota will be expected at its rendezvous, as it will be met as soon as practicable by an officer or officers to muster it into the service and pay of the United States. At the same time the oath of fidelity to the United States will be administered to every officer and man. The mustering officer will be instructed to receive no man under the rank of commissioned officer who is in years apparently over forty-five or under eighteen, or who is not in physical strength and vigor.[16]

New York was ordered to provide 17 regiments (a total of 13,280 men), Pennsylvania 16 (12,500 men), and Ohio 13 (10,153 men). The numbers for other states ranged from one to six regiments, with roughly 780 men per regiment.

Responses from the Northern governors flooded back immediately. Indiana Governor O. P. Morton wrote, "On behalf of the State of Indiana, I tender to you for the defense of the nation and to uphold the authority of the Government 10,000 men."[17] The governor of Maine, Israel Washburn, cabled back, "Your dispatch is received, and your call will be promptly responded to. The people of Maine of all parties will rally with alacrity to the maintenance of the Government and of the Union."[18]

Lincoln was aware that some governors were making unrealistic claims about how many men their states could provide. Pennsylvania Governor Curtin boldly promised "one hundred thousand Pennsylvanians in Washington within forty-eight hours, if required." Senator Zachariah Chandler of Michigan wired: "We will furnish you the regiments in thirty days if you want them, and 50,000 men if you need them."[19] Lincoln and his cabinet wondered how many troops each state could actually raise, how well equipped they would be, and how soon they could arrive in Washington. Would enough volunteer regiments actually reach Washington within a few days, giving the South only a narrow window in which to make an attack? Or would the days stretch into a week, or two, leaving Washington virtually undefended as Southerners dispatched an army to take the city?

Fortunately, the governors of New York, Massachusetts, and Pennsylvania—the states called on to provide most of the troops—had planned for this emergency soon after Lincoln's election by designating militia regiments to be sent to Washington first. Once the Southern states had begun seceding from the Union, these governors ordered the commanders of the first-response regiments to start daily training and to alert the men about a probable sudden departure. In March, for example, most men of the Sixth Massachusetts Volunteer Regiment had been issued their uniforms and new Springfield rifles. John A. Andrew, who became governor of Massachusetts on January 3, 1861, had the most foresight in planning the reinforcement of Washington. With South Carolina out of the Union and other Deep South states weighing secession, Andrew sent prominent state officials to other New England states "to propose a military combination in support of the Government, first in defending Washington City from seizure by the insurgents". In addition, without waiting for replies, he ordered the

5,000 men in the various Massachusetts militias to start nightly drilling at their armories, and he sent one of his advisors to Washington to meet with civil and military leaders, including General Scott, to plan the men's immediate departure to the capital "in event of insurrectionary movement against it," as Benjamin Lossing described in his *Pictorial Fieldbook of the Civil War.*[20]

Lincoln and Secretary Cameron frequently communicated with the three governors in early April. On April 8, for example, Lincoln had written Governor Andrew Curtin of Pennsylvania: "I think the necessity of being *ready* increases—Look to it."[21] The next day, Governor Curtin spoke before the Pennsylvania legislature and asked for funding to purchase additional uniforms, weapons, and camp equipment so that the state's militias would be fully ready.[22]

Equally gratifying was the near-unanimous support for Lincoln's proclamation coming from Northern newspapers, the primary organs of public opinion. Thousands of men across the North were already enlisting for the ninety-day volunteer service. Many businesses had closed for the day. Everybody wanted to talk about the upcoming war or participate in the outpouring of loyalty for the Union. Spontaneous marches and demonstrations—complete with flags and bands—swept through towns and cities. Beyond the widespread pledges of support and the enrollment of thousands of new volunteers, the proclamation had spurred deep patriotic feeling, and many who were not likely soldiers were determined nevertheless to assist the Union. "I long to be a man," novelist Louisa May Alcott exclaimed.[23] She soon set off for Washington to serve as a nurse. A 15-year-old boy from Newburyport, Massachusetts, wrote Governor Andrew: "Sir, They won't let me enlist because they say I am not old enough. I think that I am old enough to whip a secessionist; at any rate, I should like to try."[24] Ninety-three-year-old Mrs. Greene of East Greenwich, Rhode Island, began knitting socks for Union volunteers; she had done the same thing for soldiers in the Revolutionary War as a girl. Across the North, women started making clothes and bandages for the volunteer troops. In Washington, local women opened an office at 427 Pennsylvania Avenue NW, where they collected handmade bandages, and other items, like socks, shaving supplies, and sewing kits.[25]

Politicians who had been Lincoln's rivals put aside differences and rallied to the Union cause. On April 14, Senator Stephen A. Douglas had visited the White House between 7 and 8 p.m. on short notice. "Being privately received by the President, these two remarkable men sat in confidential interview, without a witness, nearly two hours," recalled Nicolay and Hay.[26] "Douglas waived all party rivalry, and assured Lincoln, without questions or conditions, of his help to maintain the Union."[27]

The timing of Douglas's early evening visit was impeccable; afterward, the White House had enough time to telegraph a report about it to the nation's newspapers before their deadline for their Monday morning issues. The next day Douglas's statement that he was "prepared to sustain the President in the exercise of all his constitutional functions to preserve the Union, and maintain the Government, and defend the Federal capital" was widely published.[28] Shortly thereafter, Douglas left Washington to undertake a series of speaking engagements across the Midwest, which ended with his unexpected death on June 3 from pneumonia at his Chicago home.

The reaction of Southern governors from states that had not yet seceded to Lincoln's proclamation and Cameron's accompanying requisition order was as angry as the response of the Northern governors was enthusiastic. These governors, not surprisingly, sent dismissive rejections back to Washington. Governor John W. Ellis of North Carolina put a wry twist on his reply. "Your dispatch is recd. and if genuine, which its extra ordinary character leads me to doubt[,] I have to say in reply that I regard the levy of troops" as a "violation of the Constitution, and a gross usurpation of power."[29] Governor John Letcher of Virginia, who had previously opposed secession, sent an angry telegram to Cameron responding to his request for 2,340 men from the state, which was widely republished in the North and South. "The militia of Virginia will not be furnished to the powers at Washington for any such use or purpose as they have in view," he wrote. "Your object is to subjugate the Southern States." Letcher concluded: "You have chosen to inaugurate Civil War."[30]

Jefferson Davis's April 16 public response to Lincoln's proclamation was derisive. "Fort Sumter is ours, and nobody is hurt. With mortar, Paixhan, and petard, we tender 'Old Abe' our *Beau-regard*," he was reported to have said.[31] The same day, the following classified advertisement appeared in the *Mobile Advertiser*:

75,000 COFFINS WANTED

Proposals will be received to supply the Confederacy with 75,000 Black Coffins.

No proposals will be entertained coming north of Mason and Dixon's Line.

Direct to JEFF. Davis, Montgomery, Ala.[32]

Across the South, public outcry greeted Lincoln's proclamation, and it served to raise Confederate troops, just as the surrender of Fort Sumter had sent thousands of young Northern men to recruitment stations. On the day of Fort Sumter's fall, the virulently secessionist *Richmond Enquirer*, which repeatedly called for the occupation of Washington, had written:

> ATTENTION, VOLUNTEERS!—Nothing is more probable than that President Davis will soon march an army through North Carolina and Virginia to Washington. Those of our volunteers who desire to join the Southern army as it shall pass through our borders, had better organize at once for the purpose, and keep their arms, accoutrements, uniforms, ammunition, and knapsacks in constant readiness.[33]

Now, with the Union actively raising troops for war, the mobilization of Southern volunteers to seize Washington seemed inevitable. On April 15, former U.S. Navy officer Edward C. Anderson wrote to Jefferson Davis from Virginia: "Much excitement. The Confederate flag flying all over Richmond."[34] Similar telegrams reached Confederate leaders in Montgomery from slave states that had not yet joined the Confederacy. A Richmond correspondent wrote to Confederate special agent D. G. Duncan, who was about to depart the Confederate capital on a reconnaissance mission to Washington: "Virginia in a blaze of excited indignation against Lincoln's proclamation. Ordinance secession [to] be passed sure."[35]

Across the South, many voices asserted that the South was ready to subdue Northern enthusiasm with military action. The *Atlanta Confederacy* wrote: "We still hope we shall be spared the calamity of a bloody war; but if the fanatical Nigger Republican North is resolved to force it on us, we are ready to meet it."[36] Indeed, a few Southerners were so eager to seize Washington that they dared to ridicule the Confederate leadership for not launching an immediate attack on the capital in the wake of the surrender of Fort Sumter. The *Southern Argus* of Norfolk, Virginia, thundered, "When will that collection of political dwarfs in Richmond cease their garrulity, and relieve us from the intolerable burden of an administration that is now about to inaugurate a war upon our social institutions?"[37]

The Washington of April 1861—also commonly known as "Washington City"—was a compact town. Due to the cost of draining marshy land and the lack of reliable omnibus service, development was focused around Pennsylvania Avenue between the Capitol and White House. When the equestrian statue of George Washington was dedicated at Washington Circle in 1860, its location—three-quarters of a mile west of the White House, where Twenty-Third Street intersects Pennsylvania Avenue—was described as out of town. Several blocks north of the White House, at L Street, the land was countryside. "Go there, and you will find yourself not only out of town, away among the fields," wrote English novelist Anthony Trollope in his travel account, *North America*, after his 1861 visit, "but you will find yourself beyond the fields, in an uncultivated, undrained wilderness."[38] A writer for the *Atlantic Monthly*, writing in January 1861, deemed Washington a "paradise of paradoxes," foremost because it was both "populous" and "uninhabited" at once. Noting another paradox, he observed that the capital was '[d]efenceless, as regards walls, redoubts, moats, or other fortifications"—though the only party to "lay siege" to the city of late was the unyielding onslaught of politicians and office-seekers, not soldiers.[39]

Travelers arriving from northern cities caught a glimpse of the city's grandeur and squalor as their train pulled into the B & O Station at the foot of Capitol Hill. "I looked out and saw a vast mass of white marble towering above us on the left . . . surmounted by an unfinished cupola, from which scaffold and cranes raised their black arms. This was the Capitol," wrote *Times* of London correspondent William Russell, who arrived in Washington at the end of March 1861. "To the right was a cleared space of mud, sand, and fields, studded with wooden sheds and huts, beyond which, again, could be seen rudimentary streets of small red brick houses, and some church-spires above them."[40]

From the B & O Station, most carriages and hacks headed westward down Pennsylvania Avenue, the city's main artery. The Avenue was the traditional route for grand parades between the Capitol and the White House, and by the mid-nineteenth-century, its north side was the location for the city's finest hotels and shops. Yet many visitors, particularly those from leading cities like New York or London, were unimpressed by its pretensions to grandeur, and found the cityscape a formless jumble. Pennsylvania Avenue, observed Russell, was "a street of much breadth and length, lined with ailanthus trees . . . and by the most irregularly-built houses [and commercial buildings] in all kinds of materials, from deal plank to marble—of all heights."[41]

At the corner of Fourteenth Street, one block before Pennsylvania Avenue made its northward turn at the Treasury before continuing west past the White House, stood Willard's Hotel. The hotel, favored by Republican Party leaders, was the center of Washington's social and business life under the new administration. Willard's contained "more scheming, plotting, planning heads, more aching and joyful hearts, than any building of the same size ever held in the world," according to Russell.[42] Because Willard's attracted Washington residents and guests at other hotels, every public room was thronged—the "smoking room, the bar, the barber's, the reception-room, the ladies' drawing room"—while 2,500 people dined there each day.[43] Nathaniel Hawthorne observed that Willard's could be "much more justly called the center of Washington and the Union than either the Capitol, the White House or the State Department."[44]

For all the magnificence of the government buildings like the newly enlarged Capitol and the grand private homes north of the White House, Washington was a surprisingly backward city, even by the standards of its day. Unlike Boston, New York, and Philadelphia, Washington lacked an up-to-date municipal water supply and sewer system, and residents were plagued by cholera and yellow fever. Municipal garbage collection was infrequent, so in wet weather streets became a noxious stew of mud, manure, and garbage. In dry weather, the streets were dusty rutted pathways. If there was a wind up, the dust would be blown into people's faces, clothes, homes, and lungs. The garbage-filled canals, within a few blocks of Pennsylvania Avenue and the White House gave off a stench in warm weather, and were the breeding grounds for the flies and mosquitoes already all too common in the marshy landscape. Thus, for many, the capital was at best a pestilential swamp, dotted with signs of a future grandeur that never seemed to take hold—the "City of Magnificent Intentions" of Dickens's famous description.

The threat of an attack on Washington was not an alien feeling to city residents who had lived through the British army's sack of the city in 1814. One such resident was Peggy O'Neal Eaton, widow of John Henry Eaton, Andrew Jackson's secretary of war. At age 15, she had witnessed the burning of the Capitol and White House firsthand, because her parents owned the Franklin House hotel and tavern on I Street between Twenty-first and Twenty-second streets just off Pennsylvania Avenue. Those conflagrations had lit the night-time sky around the city for miles.

The young, intelligent, and very pretty Peggy Eaton had been the primary cause of the so-called Petticoat Affair, which had upended Andrew Jackson's first administration of 1829–1833. After her first husband died in 1828, she and John H. Eaton were married with undue haste by the day's standards. When Eaton became secretary of war, Peggy was blocked from joining the cabinet wives' social circle. She was, after all, the daughter of an innkeeper, and, contrary to a lady's expected behavior, was considered too outspoken. Worse, she had supposedly carried on an affair with John H. Eaton before their marriage. When the scandal remained a constant source of gossip, Jackson realized that his political opponents were behind the newspaper articles and rumors. He demanded that every cabinet member submit a letter of resignation and then appointed other men in their places. No wonder that a popular toast among Jackson supporters was: "To the next cabinet—may they all be bachelors—or leave their wives at home."

One afternoon in early 1861, Mrs. Horatio Nelson Taft, whose husband was an examiner at the Patent Office, and her 16-year-old daughter, Julia, met Peggy Eaton in Lafayette Square opposite the White House. "She gave me peppermints from her black reticule, and I was secretly mortified," later recalled Julia Taft, who thought she was "was too old to be given peppermints by a peering, near-sighted old lady."[45] "'These are troublous times,'" said Mrs. Eaton in parting. "'We need a firm, determined leader, one who is not afraid to use armed force.' And she looked up at what Tad Lincoln called the 'tippy toe' statue where General Jackson gallantly rides a horse rearing back on its hind legs. There could be no question as to the kind of a leader she felt was needed." The inscription on the base of the statue, which was dedicated in 1853, carried the words Jackson had spoken to John C. Calhoun in 1830 against the South Carolinian's doctrine of nullification: "Our Federal Union. It Must Be Preserved."[46]

In the five decades since the attack on Washington in 1814, the burdens of office for the president had greatly increased, yet the machinery of government and the size of the president's offices had scarcely been expanded. The

United States had more than quadrupled in population since 1810, to more than 30 million, and the country's physical boundaries had moved west from the Mississippi River all the way to the Pacific Coast. The bureaucracy that was supposed to run the government was fairly small. Despite great leaps in technology since the 1810s, the government had not kept pace. For example, though the telegraph had become essential for businesses and railroads in the 1850s, no federal office, not even the presidential office, had this essential equipment. All federal telegrams had to be sent from public telegraph offices.

Government offices were not only outdated but also badly run. Some, including Lincoln's presidential offices at the start of his administration, were managed on an ad hoc basis, depending on the official in charge. "There were no set hours for beginning or ending work in the national business office," recalled William O. Stoddard, a 28-year-old journalist who became Lincoln's third secretary, after Nicolay and Hay. "Mr. Lincoln kept no hours, and never once asked what his assistants were doing with their time."[47] One of Nicolay and Hay's most important—yet unofficial—tasks was minimizing the waste of Lincoln's time and keeping him on schedule during their customary Monday–Saturday work week. Hay found Lincoln's ever-changing office practices quite frustrating.

Whatever the season, the president typically arrived at his desk between 5 and 6 a.m., when he could review dispatches, write occasional letters without interruption, and review policies before meeting with other government officials. "He was an early riser and was apt to be at his toil before the humblest clerk on the national pay-rolls had eaten his breakfast," recalled Stoddard. "That of the Chief Magistrate was very frequently brought to him in his office that he might lose no time."[48] Occasionally, Lincoln got to his desk so early that the White House staff had not yet put the day's newspapers on his desk. That April, one of Lincoln's acquaintances was walking past the White House early in the morning, and he was surprised to see Lincoln standing behind the gate. "Good morning, good morning," he said to the passerby. "I am looking for a newsboy. When you get to the corner, I wish you would send one up this way."[49]

Around 9 a.m., Lincoln usually read his mail, which "came to the White House by the bushel," wrote Helen Nicolay in *Lincoln's Secretary*. All the letters had been sorted and organized by Nicolay or Hay, who set aside fewer than one in fifty of them for Lincoln's personal review. Many letters that

should have been addressed to a government department had to be forwarded to their proper destination. Hate mail or an assassination threat "were
assigned to their obvious destination, the wastebasket."[50] If Lincoln had to
respond to a letter, he usually asked Nicolay or Hay to write up the responses
under their own signatures, which started with "The President directs." At 10
a.m., Lincoln commenced what John Hay called "office hours." The "visitors
presented their cards to guards," Hay recalled, "and the president selected
whom he wished to see," starting with cabinet members and congressmen,
who waited in the nearby Office Reception Room, separate from the mob of
job-seekers in the hallway.[51]

At noon, Lincoln left his office for the family quarters, where he ate lunch:
typically some fresh fruit, a roll, and a glass of milk (in winter, water the rest
of the year). He soon returned to his office to review more dispatches and
correspondence or hold one of the day's many meetings. At 2 p.m., he
resumed his office hours. At 4 p.m., he liked to ride in an open carriage with
Mary, provided he wasn't too busy and the weather was good. Sometimes, he
took his two sons on the carriage ride, and Hay was asked to join them.
Between 5 and 6 p.m., Lincoln returned to the family quarters for dinner,
usually a soup, followed by meat and potatoes, and a dessert like apple pie,
his particular favorite. At the same time, Nicolay and Hay headed to Willard's
Hotel for dinner, where they were welcomed as Lincoln's two secretaries,
learned the latest political and military gossip, and, despite constant entreaties, refused to convey White House secrets. After dinner, Lincoln might
join Mary and some friends in the Red Room, which served as their parlor to
receive guests. Or he would head for his office, where he met "with a few
friends in frank and free conversation," recalled Hay. Often, he caught up on
his work in the early evening hours, with Nicolay, Hay, or both young secretaries on call.

On April 1, Lincoln had written to General Scott to "make short, comprehensive daily reports to me of what occurs in his Department, including
movements" as well as "orders, and the receipt of intelligence."[52] Each day,
usually in the evening, Scott handwrote a brief dispatch on military affairs on
simple blank paper addressed "To The President" and put it into an envelope,
which might be plain or instead have "War Department Official Business"
printed on its upper right-hand corner. A messenger then carried the envelope to the White House so that Lincoln could review its news at the end of
his working day.

Between 10 and 11 p.m., Lincoln usually went to bed, which gave Nicolay and Hay the opportunity to read, write, or talk with friends without being interrupted by one of his evening tasks. Often, they would join friends for a late night drink at the Willard's Hotel bar and then return to write letters until late in the night. Their room had two windows overlooking the front driveway and north lawn, was large but "sadly need[ed] new furniture and carpets," Nicolay wrote.[53]

Lincoln's offices, which consisted of five rooms on the eastern end of the White House's second floor, were surprisingly shabby and outdated. In his own office, Lincoln sat at a well-worn writing desk. Inexpensive oilcloth covered the floor. In addition, the total space devoted to the presidential offices was surprisingly small: just 1,800 square feet, or the equivalent of two floors in a middle-class Washington rowhouse.[54] To reach them, visitors climbed a staircase to the left of the main entrance foyer. Reaching the second floor, they entered the large square room officially named the office vestibule but generally referred to as the anteroom. To the right were the closed double doors to the Lincoln family's private quarters. Straight ahead was the doorway to the office reception room, overlooking the South Lawn, where cabinet members, senators and congressmen, and visiting celebrities waited in comfort for their appointments with the President. Most visitors, however, turned left once they reached the office vestibule and walked down several steps into the 42-by-16-foot hallway known as the office waiting room, which was jammed with office-seekers during the early months of the administration.

Four doors opened onto the office waiting room hallway: the first on the right led into Lincoln's private office, which overlooked the half-built Washington Monument; the first on the left led into Nicolay and Hay's bedroom; the second on the right led into Nicolay's office at the southeast corner of the White House; and the second on the left led into Hay's office. At the end of the hallway, a large semicircular window overlooked the Treasury and provided the only natural light and ventilation in this long, narrow, and often stuffy space. From the time of Andrew Jackson's administration, the president's offices occupied this end of the White House second floor. Prior to Jackson, several presidents kept their offices on the first floor, while Thomas Jefferson rented offices nearby.

Jonathan Elliott, who wrote *Historical Sketches of the Ten Miles Square Forming the District of Columbia* (1830), had visited President Jackson's private office and described the room in detail. "The center," he wrote, "is occupied by a large table completely covered with books, papers, parchments, etc. and seems like a general repository of every thing that may be wanted for reference; while the president is seated at a smaller table near the fireplace, covered with the papers which are the subject of his immediate attention; and which, by their number, admonish the visitor to occupy no more of his time ... than necessity requires."[55]

Subsequent presidents made few changes in the Jackson offices. Thirty years later, the abolitionist politician and biographer Isaac N. Bright, who had known Lincoln since his early Illinois days, and who frequently visited him at the White House, provided one of the best descriptions of Lincoln's office; the room was largely as Elliott had described it, including the furniture, during the Jackson Administration:

> The furniture of this room consisted of a large oak table covered with cloth, extending north and south, and it was around this table that the Cabinet sat when it held its meetings. Near the end of the table and between the windows was another table, on the west side of which the President sat, in a large arm-chair, and at this table he wrote. A tall desk, with pigeon-holes for papers, stood against the south wall.
>
> The only books usually found in this room were the Bible, the *United States Statutes* and a copy of Shakespeare. There were a few chairs and two plain hair-covered sofas. . . . There was an old and discolored engraving of General Jackson on the mantel and a later photograph of [British reformer and politician] John Bright [no relation].
>
> Doors opened into this room from the room of the Secretary [John Nicolay] and from the outside hall, running east and west across the house. A bell cord within reach of his hand extended to the Secretary's office. A messenger sat at the door opening from the hall, and took in the cards and names of visitors.[56]

The arrangement of the executive offices was inefficient by even the most charitable measure. Because the door into the president's office lacked a private vestibule off the hallway, the noisy mob of job-seekers could look into the room and even see Lincoln at his desk whenever the door was opened. Because Nicolay and Hay's offices—and not Lincoln's office—were located at the end of long hallway, both men had to battle their way through the crowd to bring Lincoln a note, or struggle another thirty feet through the crowd to reach the reception room, and then move back through the mob to bring a dignitary to Lincoln's office for a scheduled appointment.

The government had a handful of modern and impressive new buildings, the Treasury, Patent Office, and Post Office among them. Yet most government departments' buildings were woefully outdated, and soon proved too small to accommodate the increasing number of government workers needed during the war.

The War Department itself, occupying a two-story building one block from the White House at the southeast corner of Seventeenth Street and Pennsylvania Avenue, was hardly ready for the logistical challenge of directing a conflict involving hundreds of thousands of troops. The *Philadelphia Inquirer* of April 20, 1861, made the department sound like little more than a college building: "It is a substantial two-story brick edifice, oblong in shape, with cross-passages running through the centre each way. In the upper story is a library, rich in rare military works, which are arranged in alcoves, and on the walls of the long passage are oil paintings and lithographic sketches, representing scenes in the war with Mexico."[57]

The building was only one impediment to effective military actions in the weeks after the surrender of Fort Sumter. Secretary Cameron catalogued the magnitude of this problem best: "Upon my appointment to the position, I found the department destitute of all means of defence, without guns and with literally no prospect of purchasing the *material* of war." According to Cameron, there was no one in whom he could place any degree of trust. "The Adjutant-General deserted; the Quartermaster-General ran off; the Commissary-General was on his death-bed; more than half the clerks were disloyal."[58]

Brigadier General James Wolfe Ripley, who had been head of the large Springfield armory in Massachusetts, experienced the same conditions after he was appointed head of the Ordnance Department on April 14. The department was so entangled in needless rules that Ripley had to wait until ten days later to officially start his job, despite the threat of Confederate attack. Once in command, he learned why the department could not supply the newest and best weapons for the army quickly from its own armories. Record keeping was virtually nonexistent, and nobody had ordered systematic standardization for equipment. Riley, aghast, found over six hundred ammunition varieties and calibers, with no evident logic for uniformity.[59] Despite the magnitude of his task, he was undaunted. As he was passing through New York City on his way to Washington, a New Yorker said to him, "Your country needs you," to which Ripley answered, "It can have me, and every drop of blood in me."[60]

As both Scott and Cameron discovered, apart from frustrating rules and inept management, the loyalty of the men working in these government offices was a serious problem. General Scott was often heard muttering, "Treason. Damnable treason"—directed at many of his staffers still at their jobs. In the weeks after Lincoln's inauguration, hundreds of government workers had resigned their positions or simply walked off the job and headed south. Others had remained at their posts, but only so that they could draw their government salaries while continuing to send the latest information to the Confederate government. Disloyalty extended beyond the cabinet and government workers to the Supreme Court. Associate Justice John A. Campbell was not only a secessionist but the highest ranking Southern informant in Washington. He regularly sent letters about Washington's defenses and other critical matters to Jefferson Davis until he belatedly resigned at the end of April and returned to Alabama.

When the governors of Massachusetts, New York, and Pennsylvania received Cameron's requisition request for troops on April 15, they immediately sent orders to the commanders of their state's regiments, which had trained for several months in expectation of such a call to service. Massachusetts Governor Andrew's prompt response to Cameron's dispatch for troops didn't waste words: "Dispatch received. By what route shall we send?"[61] In the late afternoon of April 15, Andrew then dispatched an urgent order to Colonel Edward F. Jones, commander of the Sixth Massachusetts regiment, to assemble his troops in Boston by the following evening, April 16, so they could depart for Washington on the morning of April 17:

> Commonwealth of Massachusetts
> Adjutant General's Office, Boston, April 15, 1861
> Col. Jones:
> Sir,—I am directed by his Excellence the Commander-in-Chief [Governor Andrew] to order you to muster your regiment on Boston Common, forthwith, in compliance with a requisition

made by the President of the United States. The troops are to go to
Washington.
By order of His Excellency the Commander-in-Chief
Wm. Schouler, Adjutant General[62]

This directive meant that Colonel Jones and his fellow officers had to notify
all soldiers in the regiment. The late-afternoon arrival of Governor Andrew's
order meant that Jones would have only a few hours of light; the moon was
several days away from its first quarter. In the finest Paul Revere tradition,
Jones rode through an icy sleet storm late that afternoon and throughout the
dark evening to order his men to Boston by the following night.

The men of the Sixth Massachusetts came from towns and villages in the
four counties of Essex, Middlesex, Suffolk, and Worcester, which included
some of the same communities on the route of Paul Revere's ride in 1775.
Many troops came from the busy mill towns of Lawrence and Lowell. Often,
these young men had never been to Boston, much less a city as distant as
Washington. All that they knew was their mission: to leave Boston early the
morning of April 17 in order to reach Washington by April 19. Because of the
tightness of the schedule, the men had virtually no time to prepare for their
departure. "Sacrifices were made by men and officers," recalled John Wesley
Harrison in the official regimental history. "Not only, like their revolutionary
ancestors, did they leave the plow in the furrow, but business and professional
men, without a moment's hesitation, abandoned every prospect and engage-
ment." One of the officers, Major Watson, had only two hours' notice, "but he
locked the door of his law office, leaving a large docket to look out for itself."[63]

Harrison's "leave the plow in the furrow" remark was no exaggeration.
While the Sixth Massachusetts volunteers were later waiting to leave New
York for Washington on April 18, a well-dressed man asked one soldier: "Is
there anything I can do for you, sir?" After a moment's hesitation, the soldier
raised one foot and showed a hole in the boot. He explained: "When the
order came for me to join my company, sir, I was plowing in the same field at
Concord where my grandfather was plowing when the British fired on
the Massachusetts men at Lexington. He did not wait a moment, and I did
not, sir."[64]

The gravity of Washington's situation was reported in the official communi-
qués from the city's diplomatic corps to their home governments. On April

15, Lord Richard B. P. Lyons sent a dispatch to London, identifying the protection of Washington as the government's primary objective, underscoring that point in his dispatch:

> Civil War is now imminent, or, rather has already begun. The loss of Fort Sumter is not, of itself, of much importance, in a military point of view, to this government. As the beginning of the Civil War, it is a most serious and a most unhappy event. It seemed calculated to arouse feelings of resentment and humiliation in the North, which will overwhelm the party of peace, and throw the people, with bitter eagerness, into the war.
>
> *The immediate apprehensions of the government are for this city.* The chiefs of the Southern Confederacy of the city loudly declare their intention of attacking it immediately if the border states join them. This government, previously to the issue of the proclamation this morning, were already making arrangements with the governors of the Northern states to obtain volunteers and militia to defend it.[65]

Lincoln was aware that getting troops to defend Washington immediately took precedence over the longer term plans to suppress the Southern rebellion. At the cabinet meeting that day, Scott assured Lincoln that Washington would be reinforced before Southerners could mount an attack. He informed the president that he agreed with Colonel Charles Ferguson Smith, commander of the military Department of Washington, that "our means of defence, with vigilance, are sufficient to hold this till reinforcements arrive."

Washington would have to be saved by Union troops that were still hundreds of miles away, or it would fall to the South. By April 15, one overriding question was now evident to all in Washington, as well as leaders across the Union and Confederacy: whose forces would get to Washington first, Northern defenders or Southern attackers?

Tuesday, April 16

"The Uprising of the North"

From the early morning to the late evening of April 16, a steady stream of messengers brought telegram after telegram to the White House, Secretary of War Cameron, and General Scott from Northern governors and mayors, pledging their support for the Union and promising to provide volunteer troops to defend Washington. As the Washington correspondent for the *New York Times* described that day: "Dispatches continue to reach us from all parts of the North and West, giving the most conclusive assurances that the Government need entertain no fear that it will not be fully sustained. Volunteers are being offered, not only by thousands, but by ten thousands."[1]

Patriotic fervor was sweeping the long-passive Northern states. "An enthusiastic outburst of patriotic feeling—an 'uprising of the North' in town and country—was reported by telegraph" to Washington, remembered Frederick Seward.[2] The phrase "uprising of the North," was widely voiced by elected officials and the public, and soon afterward became the title of a popular poem, by J. C. Hagen, which appeared in the *Boston Transcript*; its first eleven lines read:

> *The northern men are up in arms,*
> *To wage no servile fight;*
> *They've risen at their Country's call*
> *To battle for the right.*
> *The city echoes with their tread;*
> *Their hosts the valleys fill;*
> *Their shout is born on every stream.*
> *An hundred thousand men are out;*
> *A word has called them forth;*

A million more, if need be
Are ready at the north![3]

The raising of volunteer Northern regiments to protect Washington inspired the song "Abraham's Daughter," which was published around late April or early May. Set to the refrain "I'm goin' down to Washington to fight for Abraham's daughter," the spirited song was about a New York Fire Zouave "volunteer who's goin' to fight for glory" on his way to Washington along with his colorfully dressed regiment:

> *But let us lay all jokes aside, it is a sorry question;*
> *The man who would these States divide, should hang for his suggestion.*
> *One Country and one Flag, I say, whoe'er the war may slaughter,*
> *I'm going as a Fire Zouave, and don't you think I oughter;*
> *I'm going down to Washington, to fight for Abraham's daughter.*[4]

Some Northern leaders and newspapers predicted that the response to Lincoln's proclamation would total far more than the 75,000 volunteers he had requested. A representative response came from the *New-York Courier and Enquirer*: "To the simple, dignified, calm but firm Proclamation of the President of the United States, the loyal States of this Union will respond, 'In the name of God, Amen;' and not only 75,000, but five times 75,000 men will be ready to come forward to meet this rampant insolent Rebellion in arms of South Carolina and the States confederate with her in Treason, and put it down."[5] The defense of the Union was now a common cause for many who had sat silent during the Secession Crisis. In Camden, New Jersey, for example, the "intense" Union feeling was not "confined to persons of any particular creed, every one seeming to consider that the question was not one of partisanship, but of nationality," observed the *Philadelphia Inquirer* on April 16. "Many who never handled a gun, offered themselves gratuitously for the defence of the flag of our Union."[6] The same day, the *Inquirer* editorialized that the divisions of politics were now erased: "There is from this hour no longer any middle or neutral ground to occupy. All party lines cease. Democrats, Whigs, Americans, Republicans and Union men, all merge into one of two—patriots or traitors."[7]

Such reactions were not universal in the Northern press, of course, and the more vociferous pro-Union newspapers singled out less-than-enthusiastic transgressors for public scorn. Under the banner headline "The Voice of Treason," the *New York Tribune* reprinted reactions from newspapers that did not support the proclamation or the coming war, like the *New York News*. "Let not this perfidious Administration invoke the sacred names of the Union and the Constitution," the *News's* editorial had trumpeted, "in the hope of cheating fools into the support of the unholy war which it has begun."[8]

Among the Northern public, the response to the proclamation was raucous enthusiasm. In most cities and towns, flags and bunting covered downtown business buildings, local officials gave rousing speeches to crowds that spontaneously filled public squares, and the streets resounded with the noise of bands and patriotic songs. So many men flocked to hastily arranged recruitment offices across the North to sign up for 90 days of volunteer service that some state militias achieved their initial quota in a matter of days. State legislatures and city councils went into emergency sessions to appropriate large sums to support their state's military companies and to fund the purchase of new guns, uniforms, and camp equipage like tents and cooking equipment, so the men could set off to Washington quickly. On April 19, for example, the City Council of Philadelphia "appropriated $1 million to equip the volunteers and support their families during their absence from home."[9] Civic organizations and leading businesses made loans or outright contributions to support the volunteer militia and, occasionally, made a direct gift to the U.S. Treasury. Many communities matched their patriotism with pragmatism by raising money to provide the troops' families with an adequate income during their absence, given that the volunteers' 90 days of service would be unpaid. Some businessmen promised to hold the men's jobs for their full three-month term. In Massachusetts, one Quaker businessman told his employees, "If thee will enlist, not only will thee have thy situation [job], but thy salary shall go on while thee is absent. But if thee will not serve thy country, thee cannot stay in this store."[10]

In New York City, elected officials and business leaders, who had recently flirted with secession because they feared the halt of Southern trade, moved to provide loans and outright contributions to the Treasury. Many secessionists were stunned by New York's immediate allegiance to the Union despite its long-time financial bonds with the South. "New York will be remembered with especial hatred by the South to the end of time," raged the *Richmond Whig*. Boston we have always known where to find; but this New-York, which has never turned against us till the hour of trial, and is now moving heaven and earth for our destruction."[11]

The prevailing mood in the North was equally bellicose. One common target of Northerners' anger, of course, were Southerners who lived in their communities. These residents were taunted in public, told to leave town, and sometimes attacked on the streets. In the ten days following the surrender of Fort Sumter, ardent Unionists in Pittsburgh hung nooses from lampposts and beat up a dozen supposed secessionists.[12] On April 16, a rumor circulated in Philadelphia that General Robert Patterson, commander of the Philadelphia militia, was planning to head south to serve the Confederacy. A mob marched to his mansion on Thirteenth Street, and its leaders rapped on the front door. The frightened servant who answered slammed the door in their faces, further inflaming the mob. Fortunately, General Patterson was at home. He appeared at a window with the Pennsylvania militia flag and proclaimed his loyalty to the Union. The crowd dispersed.[13]

Even a clerical collar did not protect a suspected Southern sympathizer from harassment. The junior Henry Wise, son of the former Virginia governor, was an Episcopal minister in West Philadelphia. "Hoping against hope, he had clung to his charge, thinking that possibly something might happen to avert hostility," recalled his brother, John Sergeant Wise. "Meanwhile, the feeling there had become intense." One day, Reverend Wise had gone to the barbershop at the Girard House, a hotel on Chestnut Street between Eighth and Ninth streets. "The barber by some means discovered who he was," recalled his brother, "and, seeking from him some assurances of loyalty to the Union which he could not conscientiously give the barber threw down his razor, and refused to finish shaving a rebel." Leaving the barbershop as a crowd started gathering outside, Wise went home and discovered that a mob had arrived there earlier. His home had been spared, because a quick-thinking young boy who worked for the family had shown a Union flag to the crowd. On the advice of several friends, Wise and his family fled Philadelphia later that day for his father's plantation, Rolleston, near Norfolk, while the elder Wise was in Richmond, plotting Virginia's secession.[14]

The enthusiastic response to the proclamation—however cheering to Lincoln, Secretary Cameron, and General Scott—meant little if Washington could not be defended against attack. Ever since his return to Washington in late December 1860, Scott had undertaken defensive measures that represented the first steps in the city's transformation from a sleepy capital into the command post for a vast military enterprise. On April 12, the day Confederates attacked Fort Sumter, Washington's military atmosphere had already been unmistakable, as the *New York Tribune* reported: "For two or three days past, this city has seemed like a military camp." This transformation was shorn of pomp: there was a "marching to and fro of troops, in small squads, at short intervals, without any excess of martial music, and with a business-like air and mien, as if earnest work was in preparation, if not in close proximity."[15] On the morning of April 16, the scene was very much the same, as a procession of twenty wagons proceeded up Pennsylvania Avenue to provide a full supply of ammunition to the U.S. Army troops and District Militia guarding the bridges and main roads into the city. The wagons were laden with cartridges, grapeshot stored in iron jars, and artillery rounds.[16]

Orchestrating the defense of the city—a monumental task under the best circumstances—was made vastly more difficult by logistical obstacles that could not quickly be overcome. The most glaring difficulty, of course, was the lack of trained men in Washington to protect the city until the Northern volunteer regiments arrived in large numbers—and they would have no place to lodge when they arrived. The city had no fortifications, no barracks or mess halls, no sizable warehouses to store the soldiers' provisions, and few hospitals to care for the inevitable casualties. The *New York Herald* summed up the lack of preparations: the "city is woefully unprepared for its defense, and equally unprepared for its defenders."[17]

The defense of Washington was also compounded by long-standing logistical problems, particularly the government's obsolete and inadequate communications infrastructure. At first inspection, Washington did seem well-connected to the rest of the country: hundreds of telegrams went daily from telegraph offices in Washington to Northern officials and then back to General Scott and Secretary Cameron. Messengers, who stood ready at every government office for their next errand, rushed these dispatches among the various departments and to the White House all day and into the night.

The sight of messengers racing from one government office to another created a sense of drama, but the system wasted time and, worse, gave Southern sympathizers ample chances to intercept dispatches. Government officials had no other options. No direct telegraph lines ran between government offices and the North; to send an official telegram to New York or Philadelphia, for example, a messenger had to take the message to one of the public telegraphic offices and wait in line. This situation was totally impractical for dealing with the surge in telegrams to and from Washington, but the Treasury had no money to pay for the installation of an up-to-date telegraph system for the government.

In a show of patriotism, Edward S. Sanford, president of the American Telegraph Company, stepped forward. In mid- to late April, the company started installing telegraph service between the War Department, the Navy Department, the Arsenal, and Chain Bridge, as well as to the North, forgoing immediate payment.[18] In late April, the first telegraph line was opened, connecting the War Department with the Washington Navy Yard—a logical choice, given that the Navy Yard was over a mile from the government offices near the White House.[19] The commander of the Navy Yard, Lieutenant John A. Dahlgren (who invented many naval ordnance devices and later organized defenses to keep the ironclad *Merrimack* from steaming up the Potomac River), seemed underwhelmed by the newly installed telegraph there. This was his only comment: "There is also a telegraphic communication established with the office and the Departments, which works pretty well."[20]

The threat of invasion was growing by the day, whether or not Washington's defenders were ready. The most direct, immediate danger to the city's security was Virginia. Since Lincoln's election the previous November, Unionists had managed to retain the balance of power in the state, which included the heavily pro-Union northwestern counties that would become West Virginia in 1863. The Virginia Secession Convention, which had convened at the state capitol on February 13, 1861, and afterward met at the Virginia Mechanic's Institute at Ninth and Franklin streets, across from Capitol Square in Richmond, had voted several times to stay in the Union. Less than two weeks before, on April 4, the convention had decisively voted 80 to 45 against secession. The surrender of Fort Sumter on April 13, immediately followed by Lincoln's call for 2,340 Virginia volunteers on April 15, transformed Virginia public opinion in favor of secession, and former Union supporters like Governor John Letcher moved to support the Confederacy. With the political mood in Richmond changing fast, and anger toward the North on the rise, Virginia secessionists knew that the moment had come to seize control of events.[21]

On April 16, the Lincoln administration suspected that secessionists would attempt to secure a new vote by the convention, but how soon was still in question. That day's *New York Times* reflected the concern, reporting, "Much anxiety prevails in Washington as to the course which Virginia is likely to pursue in the present crisis, and opinions appear to be pretty equally divided." If Virginia's delegates voted to remain in the Union, the critical federal military installations of Harper's Ferry, the Norfolk Navy Yard, and Fort Monroe were safe, at least in the short term. If Virginia seceded, its militias would try to seize these lightly defended installations immediately.[22]

Virginians were most likely to attack Harper's Ferry Armory and Arsenal, and its loss would pose an immediate danger for Washington's defense, given that Harper's Ferry was only 65 miles northwest of the capital and held over 15,000 stand of arms. (A "stand" consisted of a musket, bayonet, and cartridge belt and box.) In his dispatch to Lincoln that day, Scott wrote that the president had undoubtedly "been informally made acquainted with the reply of the officer commanding at Harper's Ferry yesterday . . . that he wants no reinforcement."[23] A month earlier, on March 20, Scott had met in his office with Harper's Ferry garrison commander Lieutenant Roger Jones about plans to reinforce the arsenal. Jones had assumed command of the defense of the arsenal in January, and his already small force had dwindled to fewer than 50 men. At their March meeting, Scott had told Jones that he could not send any additional troops to Harper's Ferry. Lieutenant Jones had replied, "I don't expect to need any more, unless Virginia should pass an ordinance of secession. Then they will be needed."[24]

On the evening of April 15, with Virginia now on the brink of secession, Scott telegraphed Jones, asking whether "80 or 100 men and an officer from Carlisle would be of any service" to him, referring to the small Pennsylvania town whose barracks, first built in 1757, functioned as the second oldest active military base in the nation. Jones replied in the negative. As Jones testified in a congressional hearing about the defense of Harper's Ferry later that year: "I knew if any demonstrations were made against the place it would be by a very large force, probably numbering thousands, and that 80 or 100 men added to my small force of less than 50 would contribute nothing towards the defence of the place."[25]

Still, Scott intended to reinforce Harper's Ferry and all other federal installations in Virginia as soon as he had enough troops to do so. In his dispatch to Lincoln that day, Scott laid out his plan to send troops to the Norfolk

Navy Yard in order to divert attention away from Harper's Ferry and gain time for an adequate reinforcement there. "As soon as the Capital, the railroad to the Delaware, at Wilmington, & Fort Monroe are made secure, my next object of attention will be the Security of Harper's Ferry." In the meantime, Scott proposed dispatching Marines from Navy installations in Northern cities to the Norfolk Navy Yard to shift the attention of Virginia secessionists to that point, winning time to "send a regiment of volunteers" to Harper's Ferry "in advance of any formidable attack, upon it."[26]

Apart from the threats from nearby Virginia, Cameron and Scott were also anxiously watching Confederate plans to raise an army, in advance of their own. On April 8, a proclamation ordered the seven Confederate states to raise 21,000 volunteers, and Confederate Secretary of War Walker would soon issue a second proclamation calling for 32,000 additional volunteers the following day, April 17.[27]

As the South hurriedly raised its volunteer army, units responding to Lincoln's proclamation were assembling across the North. The Sixth Massachusetts Volunteers were the first troops to leave for Washington. By midday April 16, those men started arriving in Boston, either individually or in their companies, so that they would be ready to depart the next morning, in accordance with the orders of regiment commander Colonel Edward Jones. Some men had only enough time to leave their work, go home and get their uniforms and rifles, and say goodbye to their wives and families. "I was working in the machine shop at the time," recalled a man from Lowell, the thriving mill town. "I got my notice at the armory that we were going in the morning. I hired a horse and buggy at a livery stable and drove to Pelham, N. H. where I bade farewell to my sister. I then drove to Tingsboro [Tyngsborough, Massachusetts], as I wanted to see my brother who . . . came with me to Lowell." There, the mill bells rang to mark speeches by city officials, a benediction from Reverend Amos Blanchard of the First Congregational Church, and music by the regiment band. The men then departed for Boston on a special train.[28]

Despite the inclement weather that afternoon, Bostonians welcomed the Sixth Massachusetts men as heroes. "During all the heavy rain the streets, windows, and house tops have been filled with enthusiastic spectators, who loudly cheered our regiment," wrote one man. "The city is completely filled with enthusiasm; gray-haired old men, young boys, old women and young, are alike wild with patriotism." Some troops stayed overnight at the third floor of the Boylston Market building, overlooking Boston Common, which usually hosted lectures and concerts. Others went to Faneuil Hall, the setting for a number of important gatherings at the outbreak of the American Revolution, and later a key meeting place for the abolitionist movement. "We have been quartered since our arrival in this city at Faneuil Hall," wrote one volunteer enthusiastically to his family, "and the old cradle of liberty rocked to its foundation from the shouting patriotism of the gallant sixth."[29]

Other soldiers were less exuberant. "My heart is full for you, and I hope we may meet again," one corporal from Lowell wrote his wife. "I shall believe that we shall."[30] One woman in Marblehead, Massachusetts, was so determined that her husband not depart for Boston that she did not pack anything for him. He left anyway. She immediately had second thoughts and filled a valise with necessities and then headed for Boston. She managed to reach the city before the Sixth Massachusetts men left and found him at Faneuil Hall. "In less than a minute," a newspaper recounted, "she was the most delighted of wives, and he the most surprised of husbands."[31]

In April 1861, Washington remained filled with secessionists, who could serve as spies against the Union government or rise up to support Confederate attackers who reached the city. Colonel Stone, inspector general of the District of Columbia Militia, had estimated that at least-one third of Washington's residents supported the South. Others were less charitable in their estimates. "The population of the city was largely and bitterly opposed to the administration," remembered General Gates. "The city of Richmond, itself, could hardly have been more hostile."[32]

Despite the wave of pro-Union patriotism that had swept the North in the wake of the proclamation for troops, Washington's secessionists continued to flaunt their beliefs in public, just as they had done in the months before the fall of Fort Sumter. Even the White House had not been off limits. At President Buchanan's reception on New Year's Day of 1861, a number of guests had worn secessionist cockades, typically a circular knot of blue ribbons. Some refused to go through the receiving line to be greeted by President Buchanan and his niece, Harriet Lane, who served as First Lady. Others went through the line, reported the *New York Herald*, and the women, in particular, walked past them "with an effort at display of lofty disdain."[33] The same display occurred on March 8, 1861, when the Lincolns staged their first levee at the White House, when "anybody and every body who felt so inclined were at liberty to call, to see and to shake [the hand] of the representative of the people," reported the *New York Times*.[34] Once again pro-South guests wore their secessionist cockades, and a few stood in the long receiving line in the East Room but snubbed the president by refusing to shake his hand. (This mobbed reception, nonetheless, was "the most successful ever known here," wrote John Nicolay to Therena Bates. The main entrance and hallway were so crowded that "many climbed in at the windows.")[35]

Even some of Mary Lincoln's Kentucky relatives—who had come to Washington to witness the inauguration and then stayed to seek patronage jobs—could not resist expressing their true sympathies outside the normal boundaries of etiquette. When Mary's cousin John C. Breckinridge, former vice president and a presidential candidate on the split Democratic ticket in 1860, visited the White House before he headed South, he joked with Elizabeth Todd Grimsley, another one of Mary's cousins, "Cousin Lizzie, I would not like you to be disappointed in your expected stay at the White House, so I will now invite you to remain here as a guest, when the Confederation takes possession." Overhearing this exchange, Mary frostily replied, "We will only be too happy to entertain her until that time, general."[36]

By mid-April, tensions in Washington had escalated to occasional violence, and many expressed their anger and anxiety with their fists. James W. Nye, the 45-year-old former president of the New York City Metropolitan Police Board, gleefully attacked several secessionists on Pennsylvania Avenue.[37] He had just been appointed governor of the Nevada Territory (he appears in Mark Twain's 1872 semiautobiographical novel *Roughing It* in that role). In another incident, a Washington policeman named Bowers showed his true colors for the South. Standing near Pennsylvania Avenue, he loudly started to proclaim his allegiance to secession, shouted that he wanted to kill all who opposed it, and repeatedly cursed the city and federal governments. As an angry crowd of Union supporters gathered around the screaming, red-faced man, Chief of Police John H. Goddard went up to him and told him to go home unless he wanted to be locked up complied went home.[38] Goddard was not finished with Bowers; he filed charges against him and suspended him from the force. Bowers, however, did not care about his job or the looming charges; instead, he soon enlisted in one of the Confederate companies stationed in Alexandria.[39]

Amid the rising anxiety, Washingtonians began engaging in a new pastime: trying to catch sight the Confederate flags flying above rooftops in

Alexandria, six miles downriver. Most people went to the city's highest elevations, but others used field glasses to gaze at Virginia from the roofs of their homes. Mary Henry had one of the best vantage points in the city: the 140-foot tower of the original Smithsonian Castle, which still stands on the Mall. Her father, the eminent physical scientist Joseph Henry, was the first secretary of the Smithsonian Institution, and the "Castle"—the institution's only building—contained living quarters for the secretary and his family. The inquisitive Mary climbed to the top of the tower, a difficult undertaking. Each floor of the tower had an office or storage room—some seven in all, piled one on top of another—and the only way to get to the next floor above was by climbing a straight-up (not angled) ladder through a narrow hole in the ceiling. When Mary got to the top, she recorded in her diary, she saw Confederate flags fluttering across the river in Virginia.[40]

Despite such ominous signs, Washington's white residents could still convince themselves that the war was little more than a fraternal conflict writ large, one that would be over in a few months. For black Washingtonians, there could be no such sentimental formulation of the nature of the conflict. From Rochester, New York, Frederick Douglass eloquently noted that the fall of Sumter and Lincoln's proclamation meant that the stakes of the coming war—freedom or slavery for the nation's blacks—were evident to all Americans, even if some, including the Lincoln administration itself, chose to ignore that reality for the time being:

> Any attempt now to separate the freedom of the slave from the victory of the Government over slaveholding rebels and traitors; any attempt to secure peace to the whites while leaving the blacks in chains; any attempt to heal the wounds of the Republic, while the deadly virus of slavery is left to poison the blood, will be labor lost. The American people and the Government at Washington may refuse to recognize it for a time; but the inexorable logic of events will force it upon them in the end; that the war now being waged in this land is a war for and against slavery; and that it can never be effectually put down till one or the other of these vital forces is completely destroyed.[41]

Washington counted 10,983 African Americans in the 1860 census, or 18 percent of the total population of 61,122. Of those, 1,774 were slaves, who naturally feared that they would be sold if their owners moved back South permanently or suffered financial reverses during the attack. They did not want to be forcibly separated from their family members or lose their tightly knit social networks of friends, churches, and social services.

Worst of all, Washington slaves feared being sold "down the river" to one of the dreaded Mississippi River sugar and cotton plantations, where thousands of slaves toiled under brutal conditions in the 1850s, as the wealthy planters built lavish columned mansions and their wives purchased linens, lingerie, and House of Worth gowns in Paris. (A few wives insisted that their garments be sent back to Paris to be washed and pressed, or to be cleaned by the new cleaning process for the most delicate fabrics—*nettoyage à sec*, or dry cleaning.)

Washington slave owners made buying trips to northern Virginia and Maryland. "NEGROES WANTED," ran one Washington newspaper advertisement. "The Subscriber wishes to purchase, for his own use on his cotton in Rapides parish, Louisiana, a stock of from twenty to fifty good Negroes, in which there shall be a fair proportion of serviceable men. Any person having such to dispose of will please to address me, enclosing fully descriptive list, care of Box No. 282 post office, city of Washington. G. Mason Graham."[42] While slaves could not be legally bought or sold in Washington as part of the Compromise of 1850, Graham hoped to reach slave owners in nearby Virginia and Maryland and then consummate the sale in jurisdictions like Alexandria, which had a large slave market. Afterward, he could bring the slave back to Washington, where ownership was still legal, until he departed for Louisiana with his new property.

Many of Washington's slaves did not work in their owners' homes or businesses, but were instead leased as laborers. This system was commonplace throughout the South, but featured a special twist in Washington, given the presence of many Northerners. Many Washington families, who might abhor the idea of slavery, did not recognize the incongruity of renting somebody else's slave to work in one's household. "We were accustomed to the convenience of having Negro servants," recalled Julia Taft, "and a good many Northern people like my parents, hired such servants from their masters, though they would have been horrified at the idea of actually owning slaves."[43]

Of all Washington's residents, the ones with the most to lose if Confederates overran the city were its 9,209 free African Americans—15 percent of the city's population. They lived throughout the city, from the Anacostia River (then known as the Eastern Branch) to Rock Creek near the eastern edge of Georgetown. Like many other mid-nineteenth century American cities, Washington did not yet have rigorously segregated neighborhoods. Nonetheless, though a few enterprising and thrifty free families purchased homes on the main residential streets, most lived in cottages or dirt-floor shacks in the alleys, which bisected many of the city's blocks, or in areas like Swampdoodle and Murder Bay. Despite bad living conditions, they were living in centrally located neighborhoods, close to work, shops, schools, and churches, not as squatters in broken-down shacks at the furthest edge of the city, as did many poor blacks and immigrants in most U.S. cities.

Despite their freedom, Washington's free African-Americans suffered countless indignities. A curfew law barred the city's "colored population," both slave and free, from the streets after 10 p.m., except for hack and wagon drivers.[44] If free blacks wanted to settle in Washington, they had to pay a tax for a license, show proof of their freedom, and provide letters of recommendation about their "good and orderly conduct."[45] Such rules were endemic in the ostensibly free North, not just Washington, where slavery was legal. In 1858, the Philadelphia, Wilmington, & Baltimore Railroad posted a "Notice to Colored People," both free and slave, that they would be "required to bring with them to the ticket office . . . some responsible white person . . . to sign a bond to the company before they can proceed" and purchase a ticket.[46]

Even Washington's churches excluded free blacks and slaves from their congregations and Sunday schools. In the early nineteenth century, Methodists and Baptists—outsiders in the city's Protestant hierarchy—had welcomed, or at least tolerated, free blacks in their congregations. Methodists in Georgetown, for example, had allowed black members in the 1810s and 1820s, and maintained a list of slave churchgoers who had been sold to owners in other states. By the 1830s and 1840s, however, the city's Methodists, and then Baptists, prospered and entered the city's mainstream society, and in turn adopted prevailing discriminatory policies. Black parishioners were required to sit in segregated pews or balconies, as established Episcopal and Presbyterian congregations had insisted for decades. Often, white pastors would refuse to touch or hold a black child during their baptism.

In response to these insults, the city's steadily growing free black population formed their own congregations to serve their families and the city's slaves. Some groups worshiped in vacant stores and workshops, empty school buildings, or members' homes, while others built new churches, typically little more than frame buildings. More prosperous congregations purchased churches that white parishioners had outgrown. The First Presbyterian Church near the Capitol, for example, became the Bethel Colored Methodist Episcopal Church. White ministers from Northern states often served these new African-American congregations, since some black parishioners specifically did not want a preacher of their own race. By the 1850s, however, leaders of the city's free black community were advocating churches "for Negroes and by Negroes."[47]

Free blacks in Washington still found more toleration there than in other Northern cities, according to Gamaliel Bailey, founder and publisher of the antislavery *National Era* weekly, which had published Harriet Beecher Stowe's novel *Uncle Tom's Cabin* in installments. The free blacks were largely ignored by white Washington residents, who overlooked "the thrift and industry of the great mass" of the city's free population and the "dignity, decoration and good taste that they display."[48] Guidebooks like the influential *Appleton's Companion Hand-Book of Travel* elided the free community in their Washington entries, and most European visitors who published accounts of their American travels did the same.

Nevertheless, Washington's free black men and women were an integral part of the city's workforce, and found jobs as waiters, barbers, mechanics, laborers, teamsters, and particularly as servants, where a position at the White House was particularly coveted. Other free blacks became clerks or laborers at government offices, though such appointments were few, due to prejudice. A coveted job was as a teacher for the 1,100 black children who attended private schools, because they were barred from the District of Columbia public schools until 1862. Due to these schools, Washington's free blacks had a high literacy rate over 42 percent.[49] Although the city did not have its own African-American newspaper, black residents could read the *Weekly Anglo-African*, the monthly *Anglo-African Magazine* of New York, and the *Douglass Monthly*, published out of Rochester, which served a national audience.

Washington's free community could also admire its success stories, such as James Wormley, who was born free in a two-room house on E Street off

Fourteenth Street in 1819. Originally working for his hack driver father, Wormley wanted to serve well-to-do Washington residents and travelers as a proprietor of his own business. By 1861, he owned a small fashionable hotel on I Street and a private boarding house across the street. That year, English novelist Anthony Trollope visited Washington and stayed in what he called Wormley's "private lodging house." Trollope was obviously delighted with his accommodations. In his 1862 *North America*, he wrote: "I found myself put up at the house of one Wormley, a colored man, in I Street, to whose attention I can recommend any Englishman who may chance to want quarters in Washington."[50]

Another one of Washington's most successful free African Americans was Elizabeth "Lizzie" C. Keckley, a dressmaker to prominent Washington ladies like Varina Howell, a.k.a. Mrs. Jefferson Davis. Born a slave in 1818 and put to work as a servant and seamstress at an early age, Lizzie gained a chance for greater opportunities after her master, Hugh Garland, and his family moved in the late 1840s to St. Louis, where she displayed her extraordinary skill in dressmaking. Soon, some of the city's leading women were asking her to make their gowns. Hugh Garland retained all her earnings, however, and that kept her from achieving her greatest dream, freedom. Garland had agreed to grant Lizzie and her son George manumission for $1,200. Lizzie could not hope to save that amount, because she worked long hours on dresses whose profits went directly to the Garlands. Some of Lizzie's St. Louis clients knew that she wanted to buy her freedom, and a Mrs. LeBourgeois collected the $1,200 among her friends. "Like a ray of sunshine, she came, and like a ray of sunshine she went away," Lizzie wrote. "At last, my son and myself were free. Free! Free! What a glorious ring to the word. Free!"[51]

In 1860, the skilled and ambitious Keckley moved to Washington, while George attended Wilberforce College near Xenia, Ohio. At first, her dressmaking business was slow, but she had one loyal client, a Mrs. Rheingold, and that was all she needed. During a fitting at the Rheingold residence, Anna Custis Lee—Mrs. Robert E. Lee—met Keckley, saw her work, and asked her to make a gown for an upcoming dinner party at the White House. That evening, women wanted to know where Lee had obtained the distinctive gown, and soon Keckley had many clients, including the wives of cabinet members, congressmen, and senators. Through her work as a sought-after seamstress, Lizzie Keckley also became a confidante to some of her clients. When the Davis family was preparing to move to Mississippi following

Jefferson Davis's resignation from the Senate in January 1861, Varina urged Keckley to come with her. Keckley, however, feared that she might lose her freedom, no matter how powerful her patron. Besides, Keckley wanted to make dresses for a client who would outrank any senator's wife in Washington's social firmament: Mary Lincoln. Keckley got her wish after the president complimented his wife on one of her new Keckley gowns. She soon became both Mary Lincoln's dressmaker and confidante, and many photographs of the president's wife wearing a fashionable gown show Keckley's work.[52]

Lincoln's 1860 candidacy provoked great enthusiasm in the free community, along with threats and outright violence from white Washington residents. In October 1860, some free black men had joined the end of a 500-man parade of the city's Republican Association. Onlookers threw rocks and shouted, "Damn Niggers! They oughtn't to be allowed in the streets."[53] By April 1861, the leaders of the city's free African-American community planned for a Southern attack, as more secessionist troops surrounded Washington and telegraph service to the rest of the U.S. was threatened with disruption. Like white Washingtonians, they stockpiled food and purchased guns—an illegal act for any blacks in the city. They not only were ready to relocate their families to rural parts of the District of Columbia, but wanted to raise an all-black regiment to support the fighting men in Washington's local militias.

Southern victory at Washington would threaten the reenslavement of the city's free population. Free blacks, usually men, already were regularly kidnapped on the streets by slave traders. If captives protested that they were free, the slave dealers simply whipped them. A chilling 1853 book, *Twelve Years as a Slave*, had described how free Solomon Northrup had been kidnapped in Washington by one of the city's most notorious slave dealers in 1841 and sent to Louisiana, where he toiled at various plantations for 12 years. Only a chance encounter with a Canadian businessman at a plantation where he worked led to his release in 1853 and return to his wife and family.[54]

The sale of slaves had been prohibited in the District of Columbia since 1850, so the city's free blacks were at least spared from the sight of slave auction pens that had been located less than a mile from the Capitol, where auctioneers shouted their pitches above the stench of human bodies. The pens were now located just across the Potomac in Alexandria, however, and slave's cells were prominent at the luxurious St. Charles Hotel at the northwest corner of Pennsylvania Avenue and Third Street, a longtime favorite of rich Southern visitors and slave dealers. None of the city's other hotels could match the

St. Charles in its accommodation for one category of guests: masters traveling with their slaves. The St. Charles proudly promoted this feature and offered a money-back guarantee. "The Proprietor of this hotel has roomy underground cells for confining slaves for safekeeping," read a flyer posted in the lobby, "and patrons are notified that their slaves will be well cared for. In case of escape, full value of the negro will be paid by the Proprietor."[55]

Washington, if captured, could serve as the capital of the Southern slave empire. In 1860, Edmund Ruffin, a Virginia secessionist often ascribed as firing the first shot at Fort Sumter, wrote *Anticipations of the Future: To Serve as Lessons for the Present Time*, a book that imagined a future civil war through a series of letters penned to the *Times* of London from an English traveler observing the war between North and South.[56] Ruffin envisioned that Washington would be captured by Southern troops, allowing the city to "again" become the "seat of federal government for the South."[57] In Ruffin's speculation, Northerners had already abolished slavery in the District of Columbia by the time Southern troops took the city, and its capture allowed slavery to be reinstated and trouble-some free blacks there expelled—or better, voluntarily reenslaved. "All the free negroes of the District of Columbia were banished," imagined Ruffin, and forced to move north of the Mason-Dixon Line to Union states. Still, "the greater number preferred, and adopted, the alternative course . . . to re-enslave themselves to masters of their choice." Ruffin's slaveholder fantasy saw Washington as the seat of a slave nation "cleared entirely and permanently, of its former dangerous nuisances of northern abolition agents and free negro population."[58]

On April 16, a prominent New York merchant, James Henderson, sent President Lincoln a confidential letter in which he warned Lincoln of plots against Washington of which he claimed special knowledge. Henderson, a trade and collection agent with many Southern contacts, would have been well supplied with intelligence from the South. Henderson wrote that he had "important communications just received from Charleston and Montgomery" dated April 10 that described the "intention of the conspirators to march on Washington, rendezvousing at Richmond" after the fall of Fort Sumter, already considered a certainty. Further, Henderson wrote, the Confederates saw "rapidity of movement" by the Southern forces and "expected demoralization" on the Northern side as the key "element of success" if they were to "secure Washington city and perhaps force Border Slave States into Secession." As for the number of available Southern troops, Henderson wrote that there were "5000 men in Virginia, 3000 in Maryland, and 1000 in Washington city (several hundred [in the] employ of [the] government) who are ready to assist in [the] movement contemplated by the conspirators."[59]

Against these rumored numbers, General Scott had at his command on April 16 only 900 U.S. Army troops and several companies of District of Columbia volunteers under Colonel Stone totaling around 600 men—many of questionable loyalty and limited military experience—to hold Washington until reinforcements arrived. In Scott's daily dispatch to the president, written as the day was coming to an end, he expressed his confidence that the city's defense was secure: "With the authority of the Secretary of War, we are engaged in mustering into the service eight additional companies of District volunteers," he wrote Lincoln. "These, I think, place the Capital a little a head of impending dangers & we will maintain, at least, that advantage, till by the arrival (in a week) of regular & abundant volunteers our relative advantage, will, I trust, be more than doubled."[60]

Wednesday, April 17

"Independence or Death"

On the morning of April 17, the Lincoln family's new open carriage rolled out of the White House gates, drove past the Treasury building, and headed slowly up Pennsylvania Avenue toward the Capitol. The coachman and footman wore their splendid mulberry livery trimmed with silver lace. Mary Lincoln was taking her sons, Tad and Willie, out for a ride along the city's busiest thoroughfare. Hundreds of Washington residents saw the Lincoln carriage as it moved along the avenue and then turned around several blocks before the Capitol to head back down the same route toward the White House. The Lincoln family, as many rumors claimed, had not fled Washington for safety, a fact that gave a measure of comfort to the many onlookers.[1]

The same morning, government clerks unfurled a flag at the monumental Greek revival Patent Office building, which spanned the two blocks between Seventh and Ninth streets on the north side of F Street. The Stars and Stripes, an unmistakable symbol of Union loyalty, was visible from many blocks away. The Patent Office was taller than the surrounding buildings, and its impressive Doric portico, which stood on the axis of Eighth Street, could be seen all the way south to Pennsylvania Avenue. As the Patent Office workers spontaneously hoisted the flag, a group of District of Columbia volunteers passing by gave three cheers each for "the Flag of the Union!" and "the President!" and "General Scott!"[2]

In contrast to the muted reaction to Lincoln's call for volunteers only two days earlier, Washingtonians now displayed a burst of Union sentiment. Pro-Union government workers, who had endured months of pro-Southern bravado and anti-Lincoln banter from colleagues, felt secure in whistling "Hail Columbia," at that time the unofficial national anthem. Outside the government, "many private citizens of Washington . . . raised the American flag over their residences," reported the *New York Times*, and "the National Hotel was the first to raise the colors permanently."[3] Open expressions of Southern support began to fade from public display, although Washington's many secessionists merely cloaked their anti-Union views for the time being. "The feeling here in favor of the Federal flag and of sustaining the Administration, is intense, and daily increasing," noted the *New York Tribune's* Washington correspondent in his April 17 report. "Where four months ago a true Union man would have been looked on with suspicion, it would now be unsafe for a Secession badge to be seen."[4] A new badge appeared: red, white, and blue pro-Union cockades, often sewn at home by women who had started organizing sewing circles to make bandages and clothing as well.[5] Like their counterparts across the North, Washington's mothers and daughters also began decorating writing paper and envelopes with American flags and patriotic expressions, such as "Union Forever." Such homemade stationery was so popular that printers soon began producing dozens of variations on Union themes. Whatever their personal sentiments, Washington shopkeepers began displaying what William Seward described as "patriotic devices" in their windows, and some merchants seized on the demand for bellicose advertisements.[6] One envelope, printed for Anderson & Colt's Cathartic Pills, featured an American flag, below which was a firing cannon and the caption "Our Compromise for Traitors."[7]

This newfound expression of Union sentiment was tempered by the expectation that the city would soon face attack. Indeed, many expected Washingtonians' sentiments to swing back to the South if Confederates overran the city. "The people of Washington are strongly Southern in sympathy, and have for years been ruled and fed by embryo traitors," wrote one Northern businessman who was in Washington during the ten days following the fall of Sumter and whose observations were published in the *New York Times*. "They are for Washington," he continued, "and whichever Government proves strongest. They don't want the city destroyed, and will fight for its defence; but when the struggle comes for its possession they will divide, and I shall be surprised if the traitors do not get the larger moiety."[8]

The signs of preparation for a Southern assault were everywhere. "Soldiers are now met with at every turn and the drum and bugle are heard almost all the time from some quarters of the city," wrote Horatio Taft in his diary that day. At the same time, fewer Washingtonians and visitors were out at night, even along usually busy Pennsylvania Avenue and adjacent blocks. "Went down to the Hotels after dinner . . . the crowd not so great tonight," wrote Taft. "All the papers from the North indicate but one feeling in reference to the coming contest."[9]

In addition to these preparations, many longtime residents were leaving the city, for fear of being caught in a block-by-block battle. If Confederates crossed the Potomac, street skirmishes could easily branch out from obvious targets such as the Capitol and White House into residential neighborhoods, and an errant artillery shell meant for a government building might strike a residence instead. Although Washington had slowly been losing residents for several months as secessionists had departed for the South, residents of all political persuasions now realized that they faced immediate physical danger, especially women. "It is said that a large number of ladies are leaving Washington, and it is certain that among the arrivals there are very few, except those accompanied by men," reported one Washington correspondent.[10]

Washingtonians heading north filled the Baltimore & Ohio trains for the one-and-a-half-hour ride to Baltimore. There were four a day, departing at 4:25 a.m., 7:10 a.m., 2:45 p.m., and 5:45 p.m. (Trains left Baltimore for Washington at 4:00 a.m., 8:10 a.m., 3:45 p.m., and 5:00 p.m.)[11] Once a train reached the Relay House junction, 25 miles from Washington, the passengers could disembark to take a B & O train west or stay aboard for the final journey to Baltimore, where they could switch to different railroad lines heading to Union states to the north and west.

Washingtonians heading for the South crossed the Long Bridge over the Potomac River to catch trains for points south in Alexandria. A familiar sight was heavily laden wagons waiting in front of the better Pennsylvania Avenue hotels—with the exception of Willard's, a Republican stronghold—since well-to-do families would decamp to a hotel while their belongings were being packed up and removed from their homes before departing Washington for good.

Attendance at the city's popular theaters plummeted, and fewer guests patronized restaurants and bars. Business at the brothels—from the elegant "houses" within blocks of the White House to the hovels in dangerous Swampdoodle—dropped off, though the slump was of course also due to recent adjournments of the House and Senate. All forms of entertainment were affected: even "gambling-houses" were "nearly all deserted," reported the *New York Tribune*, a sign the paper offered "as proof of the great excitement in

Washington."[12] Rumors swirled throughout the city—of Virginia's impending secession, of Beauregard's movement northward from Charleston, of the army of Texan Confederate General Ben McColloch lying in wait just across the Potomac, of Baltimore's secessionist militias planning their own attack. Washingtonians expected their city to be a battlefront in a matter of days. This was the "great excitement" referred to by the *Tribune*, the thrill and fear of the unknown in the face of imminent attack.[13]

The U.S. Army and the War Department scrambled to strengthen the city's defenses with the limited resources available. Colonel Charles Stone, the inspector general of the District of Columbia since the beginning of the year, worked virtually nonstop. Each day and continuing late into the night, he left his office to visit the guards stationed at the main roads leading into Washington from its Maryland border and to inspect defenses at the five bridges over the Potomac and Anacostia rivers. Should they attack, the Confederates were expected to storm over the Long Bridge, which ran from the foot of Maryland Avenue, half a mile southeast of the Washington Monument, to the Virginia shoreline just south of where the Pentagon is now located. Stone ordered that the bridge be "patrolled by dragoons" and that artillery be stationed there "so as to sweep the passage," reported the *New York Tribune*'s correspondent, who visited many of these fortifications on April 17. With his forces spread thin, however, Stone could spare only 50 men at this critical crossing.[14]

Meanwhile, all the major government buildings were guarded at night by District Militia and U.S. Army troops under the command of career officers, including Captain William B. Franklin at the Treasury, Lieutenant-Colonel Julius V. Garesche at the War Department, and Colonel Dallas Bache at the State Department. Major Irvin McDowell commanded the defense of the Capitol. Thomas Morris Chester, a reporter for the *Philadelphia Press*— and the only African-American correspondent for a major newspaper— described his accidental breach of the perimeter around the building. As he and a friend walked past the Capitol, deeply engaged in discussing the state of affairs, a voice from under one of the arches shouted out the command "Halt!" he recalled. "Not supposing that the order was addressed to us, we walked on. 'Halt!' shouted the voice a second time, but with a similar result. We continued to go forward until we heard the command uttered in a still more emphatic tone; and on looking up, we found ourselves face to face with a sentinel, armed with a disagreeably long, sharp-looking bayonet, at the end of a rifle, pointed within a foot of our noses!"[15]

At their morning meeting on April 17, General Scott's and Lincoln's main strategic concern remained the three endangered U.S. military installations in Virginia—the Harper's Ferry Armory and Arsenal, Fortress Monroe, and the Gosport Navy Yard at Norfolk. General Scott reported that the enormous Navy Yard, which repaired ships and manufactured arms, was expected to be prime target if Virginia seceded; later that day he wrote in his dispatch to Lincoln: "As soon as one of the four [Massachusetts regiments] reaches Fort Monroe, it, perhaps, may be safe to detach thence, for the Gosport Navy Yard, two or three companies of regulars to assist in the defence of that establishment."[16] In the meantime, little could be done to secure the installation with the lack of defenders at his disposal. He said he expected to be fully apprised of the threat to Harper's Ferry by the following day, and that if troops moved quickly, it could be reinforced: "One of three [Massachusetts regiments] may, I think, be safely spared for Harper's Ferry—If the danger there (& I shall know tomorrow) shall seem imminent."

Scott remained hopeful that reinforcements would soon arrive in Washington. He expected a total of six volunteer regiments: the four from Massachusetts, and one from both New York and Pennsylvania. The Third Massachusetts Volunteers, who left Boston by boat on April 17, were scheduled to arrive at Fort Monroe on April 20. The Fourth Massachusetts Volunteers also left Boston by boat on April 17, and would arrive the following day in New York before proceeding further south to reach Fort Monroe on April 20. Meanwhile, the Sixth Massachusetts Volunteers would leave Boston by train that afternoon and were expected to arrive in Washington on April 19, with the Eighth Massachusetts Volunteers following the next day along the same route. Meanwhile, the Seventh New York Regiment was planning to leave New York on April 19 and reach Washington the following day. The First Pennsylvania Volunteers, who had gathered in Harrisburg, would depart for Washington on the morning of April 18 and arrive in Washington late that same afternoon.

The volunteer soldiers in these regiments heading to defend Washington had little idea of what they would face. With the exception of the Seventh New York Regiment—which was considered polished because of the intensive training of the recruits—many volunteer regiments had only commenced daily military practice when war appeared an inevitability as the secession crisis dragged on. Before that, most units had only drilled once a month, and their only other training consisted of an annual encampment and a parade in uniform on the Fourth of July, earning the men such epithets as "weekend soldiers" or "holiday soldiers." In the First Pennsylvania Volunteers, most of the men "regarded the journey" to defend Washington from Confederates as a "pleasant change from daily occupation," regiment member Private James Schaadt remembered. The journey would be little more than "a picnic and agreeable visit to the Capital."[17]

The First Pennsylvania Volunteers was composed of five companies, all ready for a quick departure for Washington: the Washington Artillery, National Light Infantry, Ringgold Light Artillery, Logan Guards, and Allentown Guards.[18] On the early morning of April 16, Captain James Wren, head of the Washington Artillery of Pottsville, telegraphed Governor Andrew Curtin that they were "full and ready for service."[19] Governor Curtin ordered the five companies to gather at Harrisburg the next evening, April 17, so they could depart on the following morning and arrive in Washington the same day. The trip was a relatively short one: 80 miles from Harrisburg to Baltimore, where they would change trains, and another 40 miles from Baltimore to Washington. By midday on April 17, the 530 men of the First Pennsylvania Volunteers were already streaming into Harrisburg. Their overnight accommodations were their first wake-up call to the hardships of military life. The men from Pottsville stayed at the Lager Beer Saloon, "the dirtiest place" imaginable, in the words of Private Curtis Pollock. "After a person was done [eating], they took the plate and threw what was left on it on the floor and then wiped the plate with a dirty towel." Still, the men remained enthusiastic about their departure the next morning. In the words of an early regimental history: "All were impatient to move to the defence of the Flag."[20]

In Boston, meanwhile, on the morning of April 17, the 700 men of the Sixth Massachusetts Volunteer Regiment filed out of the Boylston Market building and Faneuil Hall, where they had slept, and marched uphill to the State House to receive new rifles. As the men passed through Boston Common, cheers from thousands of onlookers filled the air.

After the troops received rifles, Governor John Andrew and Ben Butler, who had been appointed the militia's commanding general earlier that morning—rather than the more experienced expected choice—delivered impassioned speeches in front of the State House to both the troops and the crowd on the Common. Afterward, Andrew ceremoniously presented the regimental standard to Colonel Edward Jones. "This flag, sir, take and bear with you. It will be an emblem on which all eyes will rest, reminding you always of that which you are bound to hold most dear." "Your Excellency," replied Jones with obvious emotion, "you have given to me this flag, which is the emblem of all that stands before you. It represents my whole command; and so help me God, I will never disgrace it!"[21]

To the sound of more cheers and the pealing of church bells, the Sixth Massachusetts men—looking every inch like soldiers in their new gray over-coats and bearing their new, polished rifles—marched the half mile to the Boston & Albany Railroad station, followed by onlookers and family members who wanted to see them off. A large crowd was already waiting at the station, and when the men arrived, "the excitement burst out into a frenzy of shouts, cheers, and ringing acclamation," recalled Mary Livermore. "Tears ran down the cheeks not only of the women, but those of men; but there was no faltering." A long train slowly entered the station while the men said their final goodbyes to their wives, families, and friends. The cry "Fall into line!" pierced the air, and the men marched onto the train company by company in two columns. As the train pulled out of the station, the locomotive "'whistled' a shrill goodbye," according to Livermore, and "every engine in the neighborhood shrieked back an answering farewell."[22]

In Boston, as in other towns and cities across the North, the send-off of volunteer regiments struck a profound patriotic and emotional chord rarely experienced in America's history as a nation. "Future generations will find it difficult to imagine the excitement that pervaded all classes and conditions of this portion of the people of the old Bay State," recalled the Sixth Massachusetts Regiment's chaplain, John W. Hanson, in 1866. "The fires that burned at Concord and Lexington, in the days of '76, had only been smouldering, and they flashed with all their old brightness at the first demonstration of armed rebellion."[23]

In Washington, residents did not have such spectacle to grasp onto for catharsis. Instead, they experienced bouts of anticipation and panic as the city was buffeted by news that shifted every few hours. "The city has been made wild to-day by rumors, and great excitement has resulted," reported the *New York Tribune* on April 17. "The feeling aroused was not easily quieted, and the feverish state of the public mind showed how deeply interested in the events of the day."[24] Moods oscillated wildly. On April 14, Horatio Taft had recorded in his journal: "Think[ing] of sending my family out of the City immediately." The following day, he and his wife had changed their minds. "My wife is not so much frightened today. I think we will not *hurry* in getting the family off."[25]

Washingtonians had, of course, lived with apprehension since Lincoln's election, which had thrown the future of the seat of national government into doubt. At Christmas 1860, the widowed Elizabeth Lindsay Lomax, a descendant of a distinguished Virginia family, who lived on G Street near Lafayette Square, felt little of the traditional holiday joy. I have a "terrible feeling of uncertainty—and fear," she wrote in her diary. "Fear of separation, fear of danger to those we love, fear for our beloved country. God grant us peace." Lomax's anxiety was increased because of differing political views within her family. "After much thought and deliberation," she was "definitely for the Union"—with "some amendments to the Constitution." Her three children—daughter Victoria, daughter Anne, and her West Point-educated son, Lieutenant Lunsford Lindsay Lomax—favored the South.[26]

Some tried to deal with uncertainty by maintaining their everyday routine. Taft liked to "take a little cherry whiskey every morning, about half a wine glass full" before he ate breakfast and left for work. After dinner with his family, he often took evening walks in pleasant weather with a friend or colleague from the Patent Office. He stopped at hotels if one of his acquaintances was visiting Washington, and before heading back to his family he usually "got the NY newspapers and came home to read them."[27]

Once war became a near certainty after the fall of Fort Sumter, government officials and Washington residents worried about possible shortages of food. The U.S. Army would have to feed the thousands of volunteers headed to the city, a great logistical challenge. Worse was the possibility of a long siege. Should Southerners block the roads into the city or halt river traffic, the city's residents would struggle to put food on the table, as would the city's hotel dining rooms, which served hundreds of meals a day. Most residents went to the public food markets almost daily. Although large hotels and some households had iceboxes in which some provisions might be stored for a few days, everybody wanted the freshest possible meat, fish, milk, eggs, and other perishables. These came from the surrounding countryside, and Confederate troops could easily stop deliveries by halting farm carts crossing bridges to Washington and preventing fishing boats from sailing up the Potomac River to deliver their catch.

As threats escalated, residents of means stockpiled foods, such as beans, rice, flour, and dried fruit, in the event that deliveries were cut off, and purchased supplies of salt pork and preserved fish. While well-to-do families would not go hungry, everyone else would not fare so luckily. Merchants instituted strict new payment policies, creating immediate hardships for some families. Many market vendors and neighborhood grocers refused to offer credit except to their best accounts. Most refused to accept paper money issued by Southern banks. Other vendors would only accept specie—silver or gold coins—as payment. Or they discounted the value of paper money, so that a $5 bill issued by a Washington bank might buy only $4 worth of food.

With fears of military attack and food shortages spreading, Washington residents also worried that the uncertainty would spark a wave of crime that the city was equally ill-prepared to defend against. Even in more placid times, criminals from dangerous neighborhoods such as Swampdoodle and Murder Bay were always a threat to pedestrians on nearby Pennsylvania Avenue and middle-class residential streets. Washington's residents had little confidence in the ability of the local police to maintain safety, and had long complained about the police as being on the take or inept. One of their constabulary duties was rounding up stray hogs, which ate spoiled food and garbage thrown into the streets. On April 2, 1861, for example, the police had launched one of their periodic hunts for wandering hogs and gathered enough to fill four wagons, which were sent to the Government Hospital for the Insane (later known as St. Elizabeth's) in the then-undeveloped southeast portion of the city. Residents delighted in and sneered at the spectacle of police officers chasing down hogs and then loading the squealing animals into the wagons. "The appearance of the officers with their wagons and dogs never fails to kick up a row," reported the *Evening Star*. "In a moment they are surrounded by a crowd eager to see the sport, and men and women, owners of the offending animals, are seen driving in their hogs in hot haste, to save their bacon."[28]

Less humorous was the possibility of mob violence. A riot on June 1, 1857, had left 10 people dead after trainloads of Baltimore ruffians from the gangs the Plug Uglies and the Rip Raps came to Washington to influence that day's municipal elections, as they had done in Baltimore during the previous few years. President Buchanan ordered the U.S. Marines at the Navy Yard to maintain order, and the men shot and killed 10 people in the resulting altercations. Lucius Chittenden, the Vermont-born lawyer, banker, and politician, witnessed the lurking gang members as soon as he arrived in Washington on April 17 to become register of the Treasury at Salmon P. Chase's repeated urging. Once war seemed certain, Chittenden recalled that the Plug Uglies had returned to Washington's streets spurred "by the hope of possible plunder when the rebellion should break out." An ever-changing group of the men gathered near the National Hotel at the northeast corner of Pennsylvania Avenue and Sixth Street, where they were a frightening presence and often taunted passersby. Chittenden described them as "idle, vicious, muscular, sensual brutes, who subsisted upon whiskey and crime."[29]

In this atmosphere of doubt, many Washington residents armed themselves. Shops selling guns and ammunition rapidly ran out of their stock, and there was a brisk trade in second-hand weapons. Horatio Taft noted on April 20 that he had his pistol "put in better performance" by a gunsmith.[30] Even President Lincoln practiced his marksmanship, using the White House's South Lawn to maintain his skills, often trying newly invented guns that had been submitted to the Patent Office. One evening, a clerk working late at the Navy Department heard footsteps in the hallway, followed by a man saying "I do wonder if they have gone already and left the building all alone." The clerk stepped into the hallway and found President Lincoln standing there. "I was just looking for the man who goes shooting with me sometimes," Lincoln said. The clerk knew the man, told the president that he had gone home, and offered to assist instead. Together they headed to the South Lawn, where Lincoln made targets out of congressional stationery and then grabbed his rifle for shooting practice.[31]

In early April, a 39-year-old woman started practicing with her pistol at the city's shooting ranges and empty lots near the Washington Monument, much to the amusement of men nearby. She was quite skilled with a pistol, and could easily hit the bull's-eye of a target 50 feet away, thanks to training by her father and brother. She was Clarissa "Clara" Barton, later the founder of the American Red Cross, and the first episodes of her devotion to caring for wounded soldiers would occur during these tense days in Washington.

To casual observers, the slender and diminutive (she was five feet tall) Barton appeared shy, but when she set her mind on a goal she was resolute and determined.[32] Born and raised in Oxford, Massachusetts, Barton had taught school in other Worcester County towns located west of Boston in the 1850s. She had been one of the few women to get jobs in the federal government, joining the Patent Office during the Franklin Pierce administration, and she regained her position after Lincoln's inauguration. By 1861, she was an experienced clerk in the Patent Office, where she copied out patent applications and regulations in her precise longhand script. When she had started the job, she had written one friend that her "situation" was "delightfully pleasant." Soon, however, she admitted that her walk to work had become a "weary pilgrimage."[33] As the only woman in the office and an unmarried one at that, she was an easy target for misogyny. She was an even likelier target because she was intelligent, honest, and hardworking and did not conceal her antislavery, pro-Lincoln views from her many secessionist coworkers.[34] She regularly had to deflect snide comments and outright derision from the men in her office. She was a "slut" who had illegitimate children with "negroid" features."[35] Some mornings, they lined the hallway that led to her desk, and as she passed they spat tobacco juice at her and blew smoke in her face. They spread false stories of her sexual promiscuity. Nonetheless, the job paid well. She found Washington an exciting city, even if it was a difficult place to live because of the uncomfortable summers and appalling sanitation, and chose to endure the harassment.

Even without it, her work at the Patent Office would have been arduous enough. The overcrowded office was overwhelmed by applications for patents, so Barton and her colleagues worked from early morning until late at night. "My arm is tired," she wrote Julia Barton, her sister-in-law, "and my poor thumb is all calloused holding my pen." The clerks worked in the basement of the Patent Office building under conditions that were enough to make anyone ill, and Barton suffered recurring attacks of malaria, a common sickness in Washington at the time. In winter, the offices were cold and damp. In summer, they were so hot that the workers, most of whom wore the dark, heavy clothing of the day, tied handkerchiefs around their wrists to prevent them from dripping perspiration on their paperwork. Somehow, Barton put up with it all. "It wasn't a pleasant experience, in fact, it was very trying," she recalled years later, "but I thought perhaps there was some question or principle involved, and I lived through it."[36]

Even as the Lincoln administration struggled to defend Washington and prepare for war, it expended vast amounts of time and effort on awarding thousands of federal patronage jobs—from the prized position of collector of the Port of New York (in charge of levying taxes on imports) to that of postmaster in countless towns and villages. Lincoln himself, not just his

assistants, devoted precious hours to spoils appointments. In a detailed cri-
tique of the young administration, Secretary Seward wrote Lincoln that the
task had "prevented attention to other and more grave matters"; they had
little choice, however, but to spend critical moments on these appointments,
since there was no comprehensive civil service legislation. Lincoln's election
as the first Republican meant that the turnover in spoils jobs was even greater
than usual, and much effort was spent in rewarding Republicans with patronage positions. The most prestigious and lucrative jobs were allocated
through private correspondence or personal meetings between Lincoln and
high-level Republican Party officials, such as General James Wadsworth and
New York businessman George Opdyke. Lincoln took a personal interest in
many of the higher level appointments. He often ignored the requests of his
cabinet members so that he could reward his own friends and political allies.
On April 16, he took the time to write Secretary Cameron, "I especially wish
Robert A. Kinzie to be appointed a Pay Master. This is not a formality, but an
earnest reality."[37]

What attracted thousands of job-seekers to Washington—and nearly
paralyzed the administration in its first weeks—were mundane but well-paid
federal jobs, from clerkships in the various departments' offices to the coveted postmaster positions. Beginning in the days leading up to the inauguration on March 4, the streets had been swarming with these hopeful
candidates. "Office-seekers abound in untold and seedy looking multitudes,"
wrote William Stoddard. "They roamed the streets, seeking introductions,
button-holing great men." Stoddard could be disdainful, because he had
come to Washington from Illinois to serve as an assistant at Lincoln's
request.[38]

The number of seekers for midlevel jobs far outnumbered the number of
positions available. To be considered for such jobs, candidates not only had
to be active members of a president's political party, but also ideally needed
letters of recommendation from government officials, congressmen, and
senators. And to boost their chances, they flocked to the White House in the
hope of making a direct appeal to the president in person, who made himself
astonishingly accessible to such entreaties in his White House offices. "At
any hour of the day one might see at the outer door [of the White House]
and on the staircase, one line going, one coming," recalled John Nicolay. "In
the anteroom and in the broad corridor adjoining the President's office,
there was a restless and persistent crowd,—ten, twenty, sometimes fifty,

varying with the day and hour,—each one in pursuit of one of the many crumbs of official patronage." He continued: "They walked the floor; they talked in groups," he continued. "They scowled at every arrival and blessed every departure; they wrangled with the door-keepers for the right of entrance." The hallway and anteroom reeked with smoke from cigars. The floor was covered in oilcloth to protect the carpet from tobacco spittle, and wet gobs of tobacco juice were spat everywhere, while the walls were marred by stains from job-seekers who missed the spittoons on the floor.[39]

By April 17, however, all but the most determined job-seekers were preparing to leave the city, not only because of the growing risk to their safety, but because many had run out of money in the six weeks since Lincoln's inauguration. "Applicants for office are less *pertinacious* than they were and many have left for their homes," observed Horatio Taft in his diary. Some men had already checked out from their hotels and boardinghouses and were starting to sleep in parks, still clinging to the hope of landing a patronage job. The national illustrated weekly magazines published engravings of disappointed job-seekers, with images of the men in their best suits, looking dour and worn out in their desperate hope to get government jobs as the threat of an attack on the capital loomed.

As Washington residents fled the city after the surrender of Fort Sumter, a select group flocked to the city instead: reporters sent by leading Northern newspapers to cover the unfolding national crisis. Nearly all of them young men, these correspondents sought assignments in Washington despite the threat of a Southern attack, as they placed their careers and the chance to witness history-making events ahead of their personal safety. For their readers back home, these youthful newspaper correspondents' accounts offered compelling coverage, in part because they often gained easy access to leading administration officials. By virtue of their age, they would be ready companions to fraternize with the soldiers who had come to Washington and whose experiences Northern readers wished to follow with rapt interest. New York newspaper articles were syndicated via telegraph nationwide, so their coverage determined the national perspective on the conflict. Even in Washington, the New York papers were the favored source of up-to-date news, since the *Tribune, Herald,* and *Times* were all available in same-day editions delivered by railroad, and all three were more widely read there than the city's own dailies.[40]

For newspaper owners, the crisis meant profits from increased circulation. Everyone wanted the latest news. Some newspapers, like the *New York Tribune*, launched Sunday editions so that readers could have coverage seven days a week. While the crisis boosted revenues, it also now constrained expressions of editorial opinion. Some Northern newspapers had originally supported portions of the South's demands. Likewise, some opinion-makers in border states had earlier adopted a cautious stance on secession, or were skeptical about the idea altogether.

All this changed following Fort Sumter. Northern newspapers adopted an all-Union, all-the-time stance, while Southern newspapers were solidly pro-Confederate. The *New York Herald*, the largest circulation newspaper in that city, owned by James Gordon Bennett, Sr., had opposed Lincoln and the Republican Party, and often expressed pro-Southern opinions. On December 29, 1860, soon after South Carolina voted for secession, the *Herald* predicted a dismal fate for the nation's capital if the Union were dissolved. Washington would become the home of "bats and owls."[41]

Such pronouncements of doom were out of the question for Northern newspapers after April 13. On the evening of Monday, April 15, thousands of New Yorkers packed City Hall Park to protest the *Herald*'s editorial policies. The next day—when every Northern city and town was covered in red, white, and blue bunting and thousands of men answered Lincoln's call for volunteers—Bennett's newspaper dared to advocate more concessions to the Confederacy. An angry mob of several hundred men surrounded the newspaper's offices at Nassau and Ann streets in lower Manhattan. The mob gathered around the ground-floor windows of the counting room and shouted at the frightened employees or screamed up at the windows of the editorial department: "Beauregard and Bennett. Heroes of the South!" A *Herald* worker started to display a hurriedly acquired American flag from the third floor, but this did not seem to mollify the seething mob. One man in the crowd shouted, "His head [Bennett's] ought to be swinging there!" Only the arrival of the police and a rainstorm broke up the crowd.[42]

The same afternoon, the newspaper sent an urgent telegram to its war correspondent in Washington, Henry Villard, a twenty-six-year-old who had emigrated from Bavaria in 1853 and rapidly learned English. "Come to New York immediately," the telegram said. Villard left for New York on the night train. On the morning of April 17, he arrived in New York and headed straight for the *Herald*'s offices. Reading the morning's paper, he saw that Bennett had made a dramatic shift in editorial policy: he now supported Lincoln's preparations for war.

When Villard got to the *Herald*'s office, he found an invitation to accompany Bennett to his Washington Heights home that afternoon, spend the night, and return to the office the next morning. "As was my host's regular custom, we drove from the office up Broadway and Fifth Avenue and through Central Park to the Heights," wrote Villard in his autobiography.[43] Villard did not know what Bennett had in mind for him. He had recently thought of leaving his job because of "the sneaking sympathy of his [Bennett's] paper for the Rebellion, and its vile abuse of the Republicans for their anti-slavery sentiments." After dinner, Bennett "disclosed his true purpose in sending for me," recalled Villard. "He wanted me to carry a message from him to Mr. Lincoln that the *Herald* would hereafter be unconditionally for the radical suppression of the Rebellion by force of arms, and in the shortest possible time, and would advocate and support any 'war measures' by the Government and Congress." Villard knew that Bennett did not have a choice; the angry mobs that had threatened to burn down the *Herald* building for several days had brought about "this complete change in its attitude."[44] On April 18, Bennett returned to the *Herald*'s offices with Villard. Shortly thereafter, Villard was told that he was getting a raise. Eager to return to Washington, he booked a ticket on the night train for the following day, April 19.

Throughout the day on April 17, Lincoln administration officials waited for news from Virginia's Secession Convention in Richmond. "Great interest is felt here today as to the course which will be taken by Virginia in the present crisis," wrote Lucius Chittenden, who was serving his first day as register of the Treasury. "The general impression is that she will secede, and if she does our country seems inevitably destined to endure the horrors of a long and bloody civil war."[45]

Late that afternoon, a fresh wave of rumors seemed to confirm the news that Virginia had seceded. Lincoln discounted the rumor until it could be corroborated, as he was "not prepared to believe that one of the founders of the Union, and the mother of so many of its rulers, was yet ready to break down her own work and blast her own glorious history," reported the *New York Times* the next day. Still, nothing definitive arrived that day in Washington.[46]

The majority of the Virginia Convention's 152 delegates were Unionists, but the fall of Fort Sumter and Lincoln's proclamation calling for troops had transformed public opinion in the state, giving secessionists the upper hand in deliberations. The convention, which had moved back into the state capitol in Richmond the week before, voted on April 16 to move into secret session. At this juncture, former Virginia governor Henry Wise, who had been viewed for months as on the radical fringe of the convention, now took firm command of Virginia's destiny.

Wise had served as Virginia's governor from 1856 to 1860, and during his term of office had ordered state militia to suppress John Brown's 1859 raid on Harper's Ferry. After leaving office, Wise had become the outspoken leader of Virginia's secessionists and immediately after Lincoln's election had called for the capture of Washington. He had demanded the seizure of Fort Monroe as early as December 1860 and threatened to depose newly installed moderate Governor Letcher if he did not comply.[47] Indeed, Wise's son, O. P. Wise, the editor of the firebrand *Richmond Enquirer*, had repeated the call to depose Letcher in the days immediately following Sumter, while the elder Wise was already devising a more effective—and radical—scheme. Without any legal authority to do so, he ordered military action himself.[48]

At the time of Fort Sumter's surrender only a few days earlier, Wise had appeared to be "worn out, and prostrated by a distressing cough which threatened pneumonia," wrote journalist John Beauchamp Jones in his book *Rebel Clerk's Diary*, a compilation of diary entries from Richmond during the war. "But ever and anon his eagle eye assumed its wonted brilliancy."[49] With the opportunity of leading Virginia into secession, Wise was soon at peak form again. He "thrilled every breast with his intrepid bearing and electric bursts of oratory," according to Jones.[50]

Wise had two immediate targets: the Navy Yard at Norfolk, with its ships and munitions, and Harper's Ferry, with its large supply of newly manufactured arms. The plot to raid Harper's Ferry was "organized at the Exchange Hotel in Richmond on the night of April 16, 1861," with Wise "at the head of this purely impromptu affair," wrote one of the main conspirators, John D. Imboden, who had served in the militia that put down John Brown's insurrection in 1859.[51] Wise, Imboden, and Alfred M. Barbour, the still-serving ordance superintendent of the arsenal, along with a host of other Virginia militia members, assembled in the hotel that night. There they decided that the attack would be launched the following day—as soon as the convention voted for Virginia's secession—and won the support of Virginia's railway directors to move troops north along the various railroad lines.

With their course of action set, a delegation of Wise's men went to Governor Letcher to secure his approval for raids on Norfolk and Harper's Ferry. Letcher, who had opposed secession over the past months, declined to support the plan, stating that he was pledged not to take military action against the federal government until Virginia had voted to leave the Union. Wise's men returned to the Exchange Hotel. Wise asked if them if they were willing to act without official sanction, and all agreed to do so. Then Turner Ashby, a cavalry officer, said to Wise, "You have been governor of Virginia, and we will take orders from you, sir, as if you were now governor." Wise quickly drew up a plan of attack and orders for the men.[52] The following morning, with the plot in motion and after meeting with Wise in private, Letcher had no choice but to give his full support for the raid.[53] Letcher appointed Major General Kenton Harper as commander of the attack, telling him to expect orders en route, though wise's men were moving ahead of him, apparently following wise's own orders.[54]

If captured, of course, the Harper's Ferry arsenal would bring the prize catch of 15,000 stand of arms. Virginia's soldiers were desperately lacking military weapons, a problem that all secessionists within easy reach of Washington faced, because the Confederacy's weaponry had largely come from U.S. Army installations in the Deep South and remained there. Speaking at the secession convention on April 16, Wise had stressed the lack of arms in Virginia, saying that "it was needful, *pro salus populi*," to obtain them. The *New York Times'* reporter interpreted Wise's statement to mean that "Virginia has no guns, and if she means to secede she should preface the public expression of the intent by a seizure of Harper's Ferry."[55]

On the morning of April 17, the convention met to weigh the final decision. The remaining Unionist delegates mounted a final effort to halt secession by postponing the decision until a statewide referendum, to be held in May or June. By that time, they hoped, cooler heads would prevail. Secessionists defeated that measure by a vote of 77 to 64.

All eyes turned to Wise, who "rose in his seat and drawing a large Virginia horse pistol from his bosom, laid it before him, proceeded to harangue the body in the most violent and denunciatory manner," according to John Marshall Hagans, a pro-Union delegate from western Virginia. Wise told delegates that the Harper's Ferry arsenal was now controlled by Virginia soldiers and that the Navy Yard at Norfolk was soon to be captured.[56] That news was a fabrication, but it won the desired raucous reaction. Secessionist members erupted into sustained cheering and yelling of Confederate slogans. The convention then voted 88 to 55 for immediate secession. According to the resolution, the state's voters were to ratify or reject that decision on May 23. That vote, however, would function as a mere formality. Virginia was out of the Union.

That evening, Wise appeared before a rapt audience at the separate "Spontaneous People's Convention" in Richmond. He entered the hall arm-in-arm with former president John Tyler, "amid a din of cheers," noted John Beauchamp Jones, who attended the event.[57] This convention, formed at Wise's instigation on April 16 and headquartered close to the state capitol, was intended to pressure wavering delegates at the official convention into following a more radical course. Before a boisterous crowd, Wise "lamented the blindness which had prevented Virginia from seizing Washington before the Republican hordes got possession of it." It was now time, Wise said, for "Independence or Death."[58]

After Wise's electrifying address, Governor Letcher appeared; having made a quick switch to a strong secessionist stance, he was now "loudly cheered by the very men who, two days before, would gladly have witnessed his execution," Jones recorded. After brief remarks in favor of secession, Letcher urged the attendees to remember that the vote "should not be divulged at present" so that "the enemy should not know it before certain preparation[s] could be made to avert sudden injury on the border."[59]

That evening, former Virginia Senator James Murray Mason, who had been expelled from the U.S. Senate on March 28 because of his support for the Confederacy, cabled Jefferson Davis that he had arrived at Richmond the night before and that Virginia's secession was now assured. "Harper's Ferry Arsenal to be seized at once. You shall hear as things advance. If you have anything to reply, telegraph to me here."[60] At this point, the decision to attack Harper's Ferry was Virginia's to make, not the Confederacy's. In the secret meeting with Wise the day before, Mason had apparently argued against Wise's call for the Virginia militia to continue from Harper's Ferry to Washington. Nevertheless, with Virginia seceded, the borders of the Confederacy were now on the opposite banks of the Potomac from Washington, and the city appeared be the logical destination for Confederate troops streaming northward.

Jefferson Davis likely had the capture of Washington on his mind when the telegram from Mason reached him, as his other correspondence hinted at such a course of action. Davis forwarded to his secretary of war an April 17 letter about a proposal to enlarge a Virginia militia based northwest of Washington, adding in his own hand, "A good point from which to pour men on Baltimore & D.C."[61] In a confidential letter dated the day before, April 16, South Carolina's governor, Francis Pickens, had written to Davis that he hoped that the capital be taken immediately: "You see the news from Washington, Richmond & Baltimore—I have it from Va. & from high authority from my old friends in Maryland that they will both be out of the union certain. I really do think if Virginia moves as she certainly will, that the true course is to take Washington city immediately."[62]

Pickens then offered Davis some shrewd advice: "I would prefer Virginia & Maryland to do it, than to involve our Confederate Govt. in it yet unless we are called on by Va. & Md. In that case it would do our cause no harm."[63]

Now that Virginia was out of the Union and Maryland appeared to be close to secession, the idea that the Confederacy's logical course of action was to take Washington was understood across the North and South. In an editorial on April 17, the *New York Tribune* concisely laid out the Confederacy's strategic position. The Confederacy "must hurry matters or succumb, and . . . must make an immediate dash at our weakest point, the Federal Metropolis."[64] Time was of the absolute essence if the Confederacy wished to seize the capital, the paper wrote, since the Union held the upper hand: "They cannot wait; we can; and they will show that they cannot by a speedy advance on Washington, unless they shall despair of success, and desist from serious effort altogether."

By the evening of April 17, anxiety over the immediate future—the "great excitement" often described by Washington correspondents—now dominated the mood in the capital. The city had not received any definite news from Richmond. Had the Secession Convention voted to leave the Union? If so, would the Virginia militia attack? Or place guns on Arlington Heights and bombard the city? "It is certain," the *New York Tribune's* correspondent observed, "that the minds and eyes of all frequently turn toward the Virginia hills, as if in expectation of a sudden attack from that quarter."[65]

With events moving so quickly—and often in unexpected directions—residents, including top administration officials, wondered whether their plans to safeguard the city from attack would be successful under the ever-changing conditions. It suddenly seemed possible that the secessionists could attack their city that night.

On April 17, Confederate vice president Alexander Stephens wrote in his diary that "events happen so rapidly now that it is useless to speculate two days ahead." His entry mentioned false rumors that Jefferson Davis intended to "head an expedition to Washington" and leave Stephens to manage the government in Montgomery.[66] In fact, Stephens was scheduled to depart for Richmond in two days to confer with the newly seceded Virginia government and to negotiate "offensive and defensive" coordination between Virginia and the Confederacy.[67]

Yet the window of time in which to take the nation's capital might narrow considerably in the two days before Stephens's scheduled departure, because Northern volunteers were on their way to Washington. The time to act decisively was now. North Carolina's Governor Ellis cabled Jefferson Davis on April 17 about military actions already under way in his state, which had not yet officially left the Union, including the seizure of federal installations and weapons. "I am in possession of forts, arsenals, &c. Come as soon as you choose. We are ready to join you to a man." Throughout the day, Ellis sent telegrams back and forth to officials across the state to organize a North Carolina militia. Ellis's telegram to Davis concluded with the essential question: where should those new volunteers be ordered to assemble? He supplied his own answer. "Strike the blow quickly and Washington will be ours."[68]

Thursday, April 18

"Between Many Fires"

"This day has been more exciting than any of its predecessors," observed the *New York Tribune*'s Washington correspondent about the turmoil in the capital on April 18.[1] "What with authentic reports, probable theories, and most absurd rumors," the report continued, "every hour has furnished food for the conversation which fills the city with its hum." No firm news had yet come from Richmond about Virginia's decision to leave—or stay in—the Union since the Secession Convention had gone into secret session on April 16. Many reports suggested that Virginia had already seceded and that it would immediately launch military actions against Washington and U.S. fortifications in the state. Some rumors, such as the sudden movement of Virginia militia forces toward Harper's Ferry, Virginia, were based on known facts, yet administration officials had a "strange difficulty in having authentic intelligence from Richmond," exacerbated by periodic outages in telegraphic services between Richmond and Washington.[2]

The uncertainty tore at the already weak fabric of trust in Washington. "Rumors were flying thick and fast; some probably true, others certainly not so," reported the *Washington National Intelligencer*, "but almost all showing the doubt and distrust which everybody feels of the purpose of those our heretofore most trusted friends and neighbors and fellow-citizens."[3] Many residents believed that an invading army was lurking just across the Potomac. "A body of 5,000 armed men are on the way to attack this city from Richmond," wrote Lucius Chittenden in his diary on April 18.[4] Other reports were even more alarming. One rumor, widely published in leading Northern newspapers, claimed that 20,000 troops from the South were only a few days march away from Washington. Yet another claimed that Confederate gunboats would soon sail up the Potomac River and shell the city.[5] In absence of verified facts, observed one newspaper correspondent, the cascade of rumors "threw the city into a terrible turmoil, and at Willard's Hotel one would have thought an invading army were at the very gates."[6]

Based on facts or not, Washington's citizens had plenty of evidence to believe that calamities would occur. For the past few days, they had looked through spyglasses and seen the first Confederate flag, the "Stars and Bars," flying above Alexandria, Virginia, just seven miles down the river. At night, they could pick out the menacing glow of campfires over the hills, rumored to be the staging ground for thousands of troops soon to arrive.

On April 18, while residents grew increasingly worried about an attack from Virginia, U.S. Army Colonel Robert E. Lee left his Arlington estate, which stood on a hill overlooking Washington, rode across the Long Bridge over the Potomac, and arrived at Francis Preston Blair's home—now known as Blair House—on Pennsylvania Avenue diagonally across from the White House. At this private early morning meeting, Blair, who was a founder of the Republican Party and an unofficial Lincoln advisor, had been entrusted with an important task: to unofficially offer Lee the command of the U.S. Army. From Blair's house, Lee rode around the corner to U.S. Army headquarters in the Winder Building at the northwest corner of Seventeenth Street and F Street. There, reportedly, General Scott also offered Lee command of the Union armies, this time officially. That proposition would have come as no surprise to Lee, given that Scott had described him in 1857 as "the very best soldier that I ever saw in the field" and the army was short of leadership at the top ranks.[7] Just after the proclamation for volunteers, Secretary Seward had complained to Scott, "What are we to do for generals?"[8] When Scott met with Lee, he urged him to make up his mind quickly. Otherwise, as a colonel in the U.S. Army, he might be assigned a duty in conflict with his beliefs. After leaving General Scott's office, Lee rode back home to make his decision.

Though Lee's subsequent rejection of the offer and his decision to fight for the Confederacy later became celebrated as a pivotal event of the Civil War, his deliberations had an immediate effect on Washington's security. In the days after the fall of Fort Sumter, Southern-born U.S. Army and Navy men in Washington and elsewhere were wrestling with the question of whether they should serve the Union or return home to fight for the Confederacy. As soon as the Southern states had begun seceding from the Union, starting with South Carolina on December 20, their senators and congressmen had left Washington for home. Government officials and military officers in Washington had also resigned their positions and headed south. Many men had left hurriedly, having heard a rumor that the U.S. government would force all males over 16 years of age to join the Union army. Some wives of Southern officials, however, did not want to leave Washington for an isolated plantation or small town. Anna Lee, wife of Sydney Smith Lee and sister-in-law of Robert E. Lee, was "dragged" out of their Washington home. Matilda Emory, the Philadelphia-born wife of federal army officer William Emory, got her way about staying in Washington—her Maryland-born husband submitted his letter of resignation and left the army, but she managed to retrieve the letter and get him reinstated. Still, many had not made a decision by April 18, and some, like Joseph E. Johnston, quartermaster of the U.S. Army, agonized for days in Washington before electing to go South. Because Lee was such an admired and popular officer, his decision was a bellwether of how many wavering men would act, and his arrival in Richmond several days later would serve as compelling propaganda to abandon military service in Washington for the Confederacy.

By late morning the administration had finally confirmed the actions of the Virginia Secession Convention. Two "unconditional Union delegates from western Virginia," John S. Carlisle and Marshall M. Dent, who had fled Richmond the previous night, fearing for their safety, "informed Mr. Seward and the President how irretrievably eastern Virginia was committed to rebellion"—that is, that Virginia had voted to secede from the Union.[9] By midday, news of Virginia's secession had spread around Washington, as John Dahlgren, commander of the Washington Navy Yard, recorded in his diary that night: "It has now leaked out that Virginia seceded on Tuesday, in order to secretly grab the public property that is within her borders."[10]

The confirmation of Virginia's secession was a crushing blow to the Union. The home of so many of the country's founding fathers—George Washington, Thomas Jefferson, and James Madison—Virginia lent legitimacy to the Confederate cause, and many believed that its secession would push the other slave states—Arkansas, Missouri, Kentucky, Tennessee, North Carolina, Delaware, and Maryland—out of the Union. At a strategic level, Virginia was the most populous state in the South, and Richmond's Tredegar Iron Works—which manufactured steam engines, circular saws, and "plantation machinery" in peacetime—was one of the few Southern foundries capable of producing heavy armaments. The significance of Virginia's exit was not lost on Confederate leaders. In his diary that day, Confederate vice president Stephens wrote, "The news came that Virginia is out. Great rejoicing—firing cannon, etc. The day is brilliant."[11]

General Scott's optimism about the city's defense underwent a dramatic turn over the course of the day, and by nightfall he had grown far less confident that the city could ward off Confederate attack, that volunteers from the North would arrive in time, and that he could successfully defend U.S. military installations in what was now the hostile territory of Virginia. At the beginning of the day, Scott's strategy for the reinforcement of Washington and federal military installations in Virginia was the same as he had laid out to Lincoln the previous day. In the morning, he issued an order to the Army quartermaster in Baltimore at Fort McHenry, advising him that "Two or three Massachusetts regiments may reach Baltimore in the next three days, and one New York regiment. Hasten the latter to this place"—that is, Washington.[12] Scott still hoped that two of the expected four Massachusetts regiments moving southward could be diverted to defend government installations: "One of the Massachusetts regiments must be turned off to Harper's Ferry, unless it be known that the establishment has been captured. If a fourth Massachusetts regiment by mistake arrive at Baltimore by rail instead of Fort Monroe by sea, send it down the bay to that fort."[13]

By that afternoon, Scott had grown frustrated and pessimistic, because he no longer knew when the necessary reinforcements to secure Washington would arrive. His exasperation was evident in his daily dispatch to Lincoln later that day: "I am (placed between many fires—Fort Monroe, Harpers Ferry, Gosport Navy Yard, &c &c—) much embarrassed by the non arrival of troops."

While writing this longer-than-usual dispatch at his office, Scott was continually interrupted by the arrival of new telegrams. Rather than starting over and rewriting his remarks to correspond to the latest news, Scott left his earlier comments in place, adding new information to the dispatch as it arrived. This handwritten dispatch is a remarkable record of the changing course of Scott's thinking, and is marked with such interruptions as "At this instant the War Department has a telegram . . ." and "Here a report reaches me . . ." The rapid rush of events is evident, for example, as Scott added the latest information about the problem of bringing various regiments of

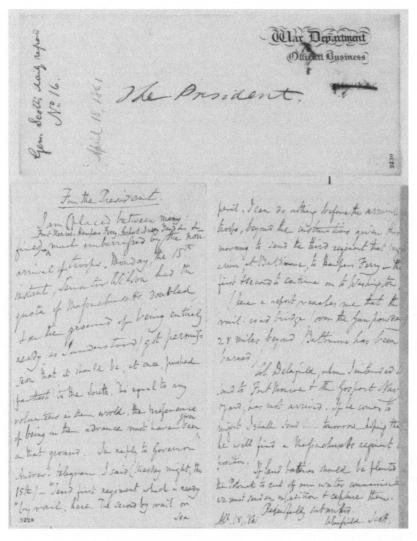

General Winfield Scott's April 18 dispatch to Lincoln.

volunteer troops to Washington on schedule. At 2:30 p.m. he wrote, "I have not heard anything farther respecting the Massachusetts quota," and then immediately corrected that information with a new telegram laid in his hand "from Philadelphia, saying that 'the Massachusetts troops are here, this afternoon. Leave tomorrow (friday) [*sic*] early.'" (The telegram did not report how many Massachusetts troops had arrived, leading Scott to believe that three regiments had reached Philadelphia instead of only one.)

Despite this heartening report about the Massachusetts men, Scott was galled about the lack of news from the Seventh New York regiment, after receiving a telegram the night before reporting that the regiment was ready to move out from New York. He had "instantly replied" with the order that the regiment should be sent by rail and the "hour of departure" be telegraphed to him. Yet he wrote to Lincoln on the afternoon of April 18: "I have, as yet, heard nothing." Nor, he wrote, had he received any word about the First Pennsylvania Volunteers, who had left Harrisburg for Washington via Baltimore earlier that day and whose men were badly needed for the defense of the capital.

Scott next turned to the defense of the inadequately defended federal installations in Virginia. He suspected that Virginia militia soldiers were already on their way to seize Harper's Ferry and the Gosport Navy Yard at Norfolk. "In respect to Harpers Ferry & the Gosport Navy Yard, both of which are in great peril," he wrote, "I can do nothing before the arrival of troops, beyond the instructions given this morning to send the third regiments that might arrive, at Baltimore, to Harper's Ferry—the first & second to continue on to Washington." He expressed the hope that the Third Massachusetts volunteers would arrive by boat at Norfolk by April 19.

Finally, Scott was concerned that Confederate forces were ready to place artillery at two positions along the Potomac south of the capital. If positioned at Fort Washington, a battery would control shipping; the other guns would be located directly opposite Washington and could bombard the city itself. "If land batteries should be planted on the Potomak [sic] to cut off water communications we must send an expedition & capture them." Those batteries opposite Washington would likely be placed on Arlington Heights—the site of Lee's mansion, Arlington House—and shells fired from there could easily reach the White House.[14]

During the afternoon of this discouraging day, Lincoln granted an interview to the well-known journalist Bayard Taylor of Horace Greeley's influential *New York Tribune*. With daily, semiweekly, and weekly editions, this newspaper had the largest circulation in the country, and its various editions were widely read outside New York. Greeley had asked Taylor to interview the president while Taylor was making what he called "a flying visit" to Washington to get a new passport.[15]

Taylor arrived in Washington that morning and stopped first at Willard's Hotel. "The most exciting rumors were afloat," he wrote. "Harper's Ferry was taken—Virginia had secretly seceded—Wise was marching on Washington—always winding up with the impatient question, 'Why don't the troops come on?'" Indeed, the excitement had reached such a fever pitch that Taylor was "obliged to look more than once at the sunny street and the building trees to convince" himself that shells were not even at that moment "whizzing across from the Virginia shore." When he met with Lincoln at the White House, he was obviously impressed with the president. "I was very glad to notice the tough, enduring vitality of his temperament—he needs it all." Lincoln "does not appear to be worn or ill, as I have heard, but, on the contrary, very fresh and vigorous. . . . I came away from his presence cheered and encouraged."[16]

On his departure from the White House, Taylor encountered General Scott in front of the Treasury building, "erect and firm as ever, but walking slowly, with his head slightly bent, and apparently absorbed in thought." Taylor observed that Scott appeared "resolute and self-reliant" and wondered "what chapters of unwritten history may take their coloring from the schemes of that 'good, gray head.'"[17]

Earlier that day, at 8:10 a.m., the First Pennsylvania Volunteers in Harrisburg had boarded two trains of the Northern Central Railroad for their trip southward to York, Pennsylvania, through Baltimore, and on to Washington, a total of 120 miles. The trains had passenger cars for some of the men and cattle cars outfitted with rough benches for others. As the men marched to the trains, crowds of well-wishers gave them food and money, promising to look after their families in their absence.

The First Pennsylvania Volunteers did not look the part of troops who would later be accorded the distinction of "First Defenders" as the first soldiers to reach Washington in response to Lincoln's proclamation. Some wore the mismatched uniforms of their own local volunteer militia; others were in their everyday clothes. Very few carried any weapons, because they had been ordered to store their guns at their respective armories before leaving for Harrisburg, where they were to receive new weapons. The Harrisburg armory, however, had no available rifles. Most of the volunteers quite rightly were angry that they would be unarmed while traveling through Maryland and the secessionist stronghold of Baltimore on their way to Washington. Fortunately, on board with them were 40 men from Company F of the Fourth United States Artillery, under the command of Lieutenant John C. Pemberton. These trained, professional soldiers—who were fully armed—had been

stationed in Carlisle, Pennsylvania, when they had received the order to reinforce Fort McHenry in Baltimore.

The fears of the First Pennsylvania Volunteers were justified. Baltimore was
not only heavily secessionist; it was known as "Mob City" for the fierce riots
there on the election days of 1856, 1857, 1858, and 1859. Moreover, secessionists there had allegedly plotted Lincoln's assassination as he traveled to Washington on February 23 for his inauguration. Learning of the plot, Lincoln had
at the last minute secretly taken a much earlier train to foil the conspiracy. Baltimoreans, including some of the city's few Lincoln admirers, resented his
hasty and unheralded passage through their city. Moreover, both Mayor
George W. Brown and Chief of Police George P. Kane, who had wanted to
greet Lincoln, had been embarrassingly stood up at the station. Kane himself
was a well-known secessionist, and after Lincoln had issued his April 15 proclamation, many Baltimore residents had expected him to lead opposition to
the passage of any Northern troops through the city. The "rumor is current
that Marshal Kane has written to Governor Hicks, notifying him that if Pennsylvania troops should attempt to march through Baltimore to the Federal
Capital, their progress will be resisted by the whole force of the Police Department," wrote the New York Tribune's Baltimore correspondent in an article
datelined April 15.[18] The next day, Samuel M. Felton, president of the Philadelphia, Wilmington & Baltimore Railroad, had forwarded to Secretary of
War Cameron a letter from Kane himself to railroad officials that suggested
that he planned to stop any Northern troops in transit along that rail line.[19]

On April 18, with more and more credible reports arriving in Washington
about secessionist plans to attack Northern troops traveling through Baltimore, Secretary Cameron telegraphed Hicks to remind him that it was his
duty to prevent any possible mayhem. "The President," he wrote, had been
"informed that threats are made and measures taken by unlawful combination
of misguided citizens of Maryland to prevent by force the transit of United
States troops across Maryland on their way, pursuant to order, to the defense
of this capital." Cameron reminded Hicks, who was known for changing
his positions, that he had been "warned in time" to "take immediate effective
measures" against any attack on Northern troops. Otherwise, the "most
deplorable consequences" for Maryland would result.[20]

The impending passage of Northern troops through Baltimore placed
Governor Hicks in a vexing political knot. He was a pro-Union man, but
many Baltimoreans disliked—or outright loathed—Lincoln and the newly

founded Republican Party's political principles. Lincoln had received 40 percent of the vote nationwide in the 1860 election, almost all of it in free states in the North; he had received only 2.5 percent in Maryland and 3.6 percent in Baltimore—a mere 1,087 votes out of the city's total of 30,151. One resident, refusing to identify himself, had written directly to Lincoln on April 11 to warn him that a mob was forming to "seize the Capitol and yourself and . . . they say that they will tar & put cotton on your head and ride you and Gen. Scot [*sic*] on a rail."[21]

While most residents did not share such violent intentions, the many rumors circulating in the city suggested that the Lincoln administration looked on them as enemies: that Northern militias would strike their city, that abolitionists would arm Maryland slaves to attack it, and that federal gunboats would shell it. In Washington, Maryland-born Admiral Franklin Buchanan, superintendent of the U.S. Navy Yard, was so concerned about his Baltimore relatives that he wrote to a nephew that "every Marylander should be at his post." Shortly thereafter, he resigned his commission and left for Baltimore "to render the assistance in [his] power."[22]

Baltimore was also enduring a deep recession with unemployment at an estimated 25 percent. Homeless men and families slept outdoors or inside police station shelters. "No one has any idea of the distress in Baltimore," Edward Spencer, who lived near the city, wrote his longtime friend Anne Catherine Harrison on in March 1861. "If there should occur any disturbance," he added, presciently, "it will be awful, for men become fiends when bread is lacking."[23]

No trains from the North ran directly through Baltimore to Washington. Like other cities, Baltimore had outlawed the passage of noisy, smoky steam engines through its central business district. As a result, the city had two main railroad stations, the President Street station and the Camden Street station, located a mile and a half from each other, as well as the smaller Bolton, Calvert, and Mount Clare stations. Southbound trains headed from Philadelphia to Washington on the Philadelphia, Wilmington & Baltimore line stopped at the President Street station, while trains on the Northern Central from Harrisburg stopped at the Bolton station. Train cars were decoupled from the engine in the inbound station's train shed and moved one by one along rails at the front of the terminal, where a team of horses pulled each car on rails to the B & O's Camden Street station. The cars were then connected to another engine and resumed the trip to Washington.

Passengers could either stay in the cars or walk between the two stations. The transfer took thirty minutes, if all went well—ample time for an ambush.

The First Pennsylvania Volunteers knew that their train had crossed the Mason-Dixon Line at midmorning on April 18 when they spotted girls cheerfully waving the Stars and Bars along the trackside. Still, John W. Forney, a Pennsylvania Volunteer who later served as clerk of the House of Representatives and secretary of the Senate, recalled that "few people were willing to admit that the pro-slavery mob of the city would dare to attack the soldiers on their way to the immediate scene of peril"—that is, Washington.[24]

That morning, Baltimore's large contingent of secessionist militias held rallies. One of the largest was that of the Maryland National Volunteers, some 700 strong, who gathered in Monument Square. Hundreds roared their approval for calls to stop any Northern troops from moving through the city.[25] Early that afternoon, secessionists staged another rally on Federal Hill, a favorite public gathering place overlooking Baltimore from the south side of the harbor. Several men raised a Confederate flag, while others started a 100-gun salute in honor of Virginia's secession from the Union the day before. The rally infuriated pro-Union workers at a nearby foundry, who charged up the hill, drove off the Confederate supporters, and tore down and ripped up the flag. They went on to smash the cannon's wooden gun carriage, haul it down the hill to the harbor, and with a loud cheer, toss it into the water.[26]

Twenty miles outside Baltimore, the trains carrying the Pennsylvania men unexpectedly slowed down, pulled onto a siding, and abruptly stopped. "We were informed by telegram that a mob was formed in Baltimore to stop our passage through the city," recalled Captain James Wren, who commanded one of the five militias on board.[27] The Pennsylvania Volunteers' officers held a hurried meeting. Was the news of the Baltimore mob merely a ruse to frighten the Pennsylvania Volunteers into returning home? Nobody knew. Wren wrote that "it was resolved unanimously to go through Baltimore to Washington, let the result be what it may. We thought if we stopped for reinforcements, it would make the passage through Baltimore more difficult and would be an acknowledgement of rebel strength."[28] The regiment's officers hoped that their arrival at the Bolton station might win them time to transfer trains without incident, since the Pennsylvanians assumed that many Baltimore secessionists would gather across town instead, expecting a train arriving from Philadelphia at the Camden Street station.[29]

When the trains reached Bolton station at 2 p.m., the Pennsylvania men were shocked to see an angry mob waiting for them. "A throng of several thousand persons" had gathered, manifesting "strong symptoms of a riot," as the *Baltimore Sun* described the scene.[30] Fortunately, Police Chief Kane brought 120 policemen to protect the men on their way along Pratt Street to the Camden Street station. The mob "came up the street like a lot of wild wolves," recalled Captain Wren. "There were many desperate-looking characters among them, armed with clubs, stone, and brick-bats, all yelling like Indians. They cheered for Jeff Davis and the Southern Confederacy."[31]

As soon as the Pennsylvania Volunteers disembarked from the trains and formed ranks to march to the Camden Street station, the crowd shouted "Fight! Fight!" Those soldiers were ordered back on the train, and the 40 armed professional soldiers of the Fourth United States Artillery held off the furious mob. Some of the police showed their displeasure at their duty, smiling, joking among themselves, even breaking into laughter over the "discomfiture and anxiety" among the Union troops, recalled Edmund Smith of the Ringgold Light Artillery, one of the companies of the Pennsylvania Volunteers.[32]

Screened by the Fourth Artillery, the Pennsylvania Volunteers again disembarked from the train and marched along formation, flanked by the police, with the now-furious mob following closely, screaming threats: "You will never get back to Pennsylvania!" "Let the police go, and we will lick you!" "Stone them! Kill them!"[33] The mob had now swelled to 2,500 people. At the intersection of Charles Street, the men of the Fourth Artillery left the marching column and headed toward Fort McHenry, which itself could not hold back a sizable mob. The Pennsylvania Volunteers were now defenseless and greatly outnumbered. "The mob lashed itself into a perfect fury," recalled the company's historian, James Schaadt. "Rough and toughs, longshoremen, gamblers, floaters, idlers, red-hot secessionists, as well as men ordinarily sober and steady, crowded upon, pushed, and hustled the little band [of men] and made every effort to break the thin line."[34] They even jostled the police in their determination to split the Pennsylvania men into small defenseless groups that could be more easily attacked. The determined Pennsylvanians kept marching forward without fighting back, as they had been ordered, but the 34 members of the Logan Guard, who had smuggled their old-fashioned flintlock muskets onto the train when they left Harrisburg, were now told to half-cock their guns as if they were ready to fire. A few men used these muskets as clubs to beat back the crowd.

When the Volunteers reached the Camden Street station, the mob spotted 65-year-old Nicholas Biddle, a freed slave and longtime orderly in the Washington Artillery. Out of gratitude for his 20 years of service, the men had given him a uniform before they left Harrisburg. Biddle was not only a black man—he was also in uniform. The crowd went wild. "Nigger in uniform! Nigger in uniform!" the crowd chanted over and over again. "Poor Nick had to take it," Wren later recorded, as the mob closed in. Biddle "was hit full in the face by a stone," according to one Volunteer's recollection. "Blood spilling on his uniform, he stumbled but was helped by one of his officers" onto the train. Biddle, the Pennsylvania Volunteers claimed, had shed the "first blood" of the Civil War, as the first casualty caused by enemy hands.[35]

Biddle was not the only Pennsylvanian to sustain serious injuries. A brick hit Private David Jacobs in the mouth, knocking out teeth and leaving him briefly unconscious on the street. As Private Henry Wilson Derr got onto the train, a brick struck him on the side of his head, rendering him deaf in one ear for the rest of his life. Derr spotted the man who threw the brick at him in the mob, ran over with his flintlock rifle, and beat his assailant to the ground, leaving the man bruised, bloodied, and missing one ear.[36]

Now that many of the Pennsylvania Volunteers had reached the Camden Street station, the mob made a last-ditch effort to stop them. They pelted them with eggs, rotten food, and dead animals, and next hurled bottles, rocks, bricks, and paving stones. From the second-floor windows and roofs of nearby buildings, screaming men and women hurled more bottles, more bricks, and stones. Amid this deafening chaos, the Pennsylvania Volunteers boarded the train, while some among them cleared the debris from the tracks in front of the engine. To keep the mob at bay, a few of the Logan Guards leaned out of the passenger car windows and once again cocked their muskets as if getting ready to shoot. As the train pulled away from the station, finally heading to Washington at 4:00 p.m., the exhausted Pennsylvanians listened as "the demonic yells of the crowd" became quieter and quieter until the only sound was the locomotive's engine and iron wheels on the tracks.[37]

On April 18, as on the previous day, Colonel Charles Stone continued to strengthen the city's defenses with the few men under his command, though he expected the number to quickly swell as volunteer regiments arrived. He inspected the troops stationed at the main roadways entering the city and the five bridges into Washington: the Benning and Navy Yard bridges over the Anacostia River, the Chain Bridge, several miles upriver from George-town at Little Falls, the Aqueduct Bridge linking Georgetown to today's Rosslyn, and the all-important Long Bridge. Several dozen U.S. soldiers were guarding the bridge, and they had placed a cannon near the river's edge that could fire on any invaders or, if necessary, blow a hole in the bridge, making it impassable.

Late that afternoon, the Department of the Treasury assigned its clerks an additional role: they became the Treasury Guards, and their job was to supplement the limited number of U.S. Army soldiers and local militiamen. The clerks were divided into several companies but not given weapons. If they lived within earshot of the Treasury and heard the night alarm, they were ordered to run to the building, where they would be issued arms. Colonel Stone did not know who was loyal to Union and who was not. If a Treasury clerk showed up to protect the building in an attack, he would likely be a loyal Union man, Stone reasoned, and could be handed a weapon.[38] To give the new Treasury Guards a semblance of military identity and to weed out secessionists, Colonel Stone told the clerks to assemble in front of the building at 5 p.m. to renew their oaths of allegiance to the United States. The oath was the same one used by the U.S. Army: "I, [Name], do solemnly swear that I will bear true allegiance to the United States of America, that I will serve them honestly and faithfully against all enemies or opposers whatsoever, that I will obey the orders of the President of the United States, and of the officers appointed over me, according to the rules of the armies of the United States, so help me God." (The U.S. government still referred to the United States as "them" rather than "it.") General Scott was well aware that these clerks—who were more skilled in wielding pens than weapons—offered limited protection.

On April 18, two other much-needed groups of volunteer troops were ready to serve, both of them led by prominent public figures, Cassius Marcellus Clay of Kentucky, an early member of the Republican Party whom Lincoln had appointed minister to Russia, and Senator James H. Lane of Kansas, another founding Republican.[39] On April 15, Scott had asked the two men to organize private guard forces immediately, and both men had agreed to do so without hesitation. Lane's men—the Frontier Guards—would protect the White House, while Clay's men would patrol the downtown streets near Willard's Hotel at Pennsylvania Avenue and Fourteenth Street. Scott could scarcely have found two more dissimilar men for these tasks. Rough-hewn, outspoken, and volatile, Lane had been born and raised in Indiana, where he had become, in succession, an attorney, a member of the state legislature, a lieutenant governor, and a congressman in Washington. In 1855, he had moved to the Kansas Territory, known then as "Bloody Kansas" because of the violence taking place there between proslavery and antislavery forces. Under the terms of the Kansas-Nebraska Act of 1854, residents in these two territories would vote on whether they were to enter the Union as free or slave states. Proslavery people (nicknamed "Border Ruffians" by Horace Greeley, editor of the *New York Tribune*) had streamed into Kansas from Missouri and Arkansas, while truly fervent antislavery easterners made the long trek to settle there to tip the vote in their favor. As tensions mounted over the future of Kansas, each side attacked the other's homes and settlements. Each faction shipped weapons to their Kansas adherents. Boxes of weapons from the East intended for the antislavery settlers were often labeled "Bibles" or "books." On May 21, 1856, proslavery forces carried out the "sack of Lawrence," an antislavery stronghold that had been founded by the New England Emigrant Aid Company two years earlier. Three days later came the Pottawatomie Massacre, in which John Brown and several comrades hacked five proslavery leaders to death with broadswords.

Lane—who became known as the "Grim Chieftain"—had thrived in this tumultuous and dangerous arena. He organized the defense of antislavery communities like Lawrence and launched attacks on proslavery communities closer to Missouri and Arkansas. His charismatic personality, organizational ability, and stirring oratory rallied Kansas's antislavery forces. As John Holloway wrote in his *History of Kansas* (1868), Lane "immediately became a terror to pro-slavery men. The mere mention of his name would cause them to quake, and news of his approach would create a stampede of the citizens in every pro-slavery town."[40] When Kansas entered the Union as a free state on January 21, 1861, Lane had become one of its first two senators. He had attended Lincoln's inauguration and offered to provide a contingent of experienced Kansas men to protect the event, an offer Scott had refused.[41] Now, many of the same men—who had not left Washington because they expected patronage appointments—would patrol Washington. What better way, these men thought, to gain the support of the high-profile Senator Lane for a federal position than to serve in his volunteer guard?

Cassius M. Clay was Lane's opposite in upbringing, appearance, and demeanor. Born to one of Kentucky's leading families, Clay was rich, vain, and something of a paradox. A cousin of the famed senator Henry Clay, his family wealth had come from a Kentucky plantation and its slaves. But Cassius Clay had become an ardent abolitionist while an undergraduate at Yale in the 1830s. Still, if the occasion called for it, this six-foot-tall Kentucky aristocrat could be just as savage as Lane. When a man shot him during one of his antislavery speeches in 1843, Clay grabbed his Bowie knife, lunged at his assailant, and cut out one of the man's eyes and his nose. In 1849, Clay was nearly killed by a furious proslavery mob after giving an abolitionist speech. Recovery was slow, but he dared to run for governor of Kentucky on the controversial emancipation ticket in 1851. He lost. By the late 1850s, Clay had become an active Republican and harbored ambitions of running for president in the 1860 election.

When Clay and his family arrived in Washington early on the morning of April 18, the formation of a volunteer guard was the last thing on his mind; he had come to Washington to receive his diplomatic instructions before leaving for St. Petersburg as an ambassador to Russia. Once General Scott told Clay of Washington's perilous situation, he sent his wife and family to Philadelphia for safety. Then he visited Secretary Cameron and offered his services "as an officer to raise a regiment, or a private in the ranks." Cameron replied, "I don't believe I ever heard of where a foreign Minister volunteered in the ranks." "Then, let's make a little history," Clay replied, it was said. Clay—jokingly nicknamed "Cash" because of his wealth—enlisted many of his Washington friends to join his battalion and lured other volunteers to his force with money or promises of political favor.[42]

By afternoon of April 18, just three days after General Scott made his urgent requests to Lane and only hours after he asked Clay for help, Lane's Frontier Guards and the Clay Battalion were ready to defend Washington. Other unlikely volunteer guards joined the effort. The "Fossil Guard" consisted of 51 members who were 40 years old or more—and the nickname was chosen by the men themselves.[43] Even local veterans of the War of 1812—men who would be over 60 years old—formed a small company that became known as the "Silver Grays."[44]

The leaders of Washington's free African-American community wanted to do their part—and to defend their freedom against the Confederate slaveholders—by raising an all-black regiment. One of the community's leaders, Paul Jennings, had seen how an invading army could wreck havoc on Washington, since he had witnessed the burning of the Capitol and White House in 1814. Five years earlier, Jennings—then 10 years old and enslaved—had come with James and Dolley Madison from their Virginia plantation to be a footman in the White House. Within a few years, Jennings had become Dolley Madison's page. When British troops advanced on the city on August 24, 1814, and a breathless horseman arrived at the White House with James Madison's urgent message "Clear out! Clear out!," it was not Dolley Madison who saved Gilbert Stuart's famed 1797 full-length portrait of George Washington from British troops, as many versions of the story recounted. That tale was "totally false," recalled Jennings in his 1865 book *A Colored Man's Reminiscences of James Madison*. The White House doorman, a gardener, and Jennings "took it down and sent it off on a wagon, with some large silver urns and such other valuables as could be hastily got hold of."[45]

A year after her husband's death in 1836, Dolley Madison returned to Washington with Jennings, who was forced to leave his first wife, Fanny, and their children back at Montpelier. In 1846, three years before her death, the nearly destitute Madison sold Jennings to Pollard Webb, a local insurance agent. The 46-year-old Jennings feared that he might be sold again, this time, in his words, "to the traders." At this critical juncture, fate intervened in Jennings's favor. Senator Daniel Webster of Massachusetts knew Jennings from his many calls on the widow Madison at her home on Nineteenth Street. Webster purchased Jennings and promptly gave him his freedom. Jennings paid off the debt as a servant in the Webster home in a little more than a year and then worked for a salary there for several more years. In 1851, he had secured a job at the Pension Office as a laborer, one of the few positions open to an African-American man in the federal government at that time. He saved enough money to purchase his children, who still lived in Virginia, and paid $1,000 in 1854 for a newly built frame house at 1806 L Street NW, a racially mixed neighborhood near the outskirts of town. Jennings, as one of the most prominent free blacks in the city, was one of the logical organizers of a regiment from Washington's free black community in April 1861.

Another prominent free African American made a direct offer of troops to the Lincoln administration. On April 23, Jacob Dodson, a servant in the

Senate Chamber of the Capitol, wrote to Secretary of War Cameron that he knew of "some 300 reliable free citizens of this city who desire to enter the service of the city." He signed the letter, "Jacob Dodson (Colored)."[46] Dodson, in his early 30s, had been a member of the celebrated Western expeditions of John C. Frémont, later the Republican Party's first presidential candidate. In 1856, Congress had granted Dodson compensation for his service under Frémont, since Dodson had never been mustered into the Army because blacks were wholly barred from military ranks.[47] Cameron's reply to Dodson's offer affirmed that policy: the War Department had "no intention at present to call into the service of the Government any colored soldiers."[48]

On the afternoon of April 18, Lincoln and Gideon Welles, secretary of the Navy, held a "very lengthened interview" with General Scott to attempt to organize a force and dispatch a "competent military officer" to defend the Norfolk Navy Yard.[49] Woefully undermanned, the sprawling facility was hard to defend even with an adequate force. Commodore Charles S. McCauley, who was in charge of the installation, was indecisive at best and incompetent at worst. A week earlier, Welles had ordered McCauley to sail the Navy's prize ship, the steam-powered, 40-gun *Merrimack,* out of the Navy Yard to Philadelphia without raising "needless alarm," so that it would not fall into Confederate hands. On April 17, McCauley—after being pressured by two of his officers—had finally ordered the departure of the *Merrimack.* Just as the ship was getting ready to leave, however, McCauley changed his mind. "Draw the fires on the *Merrimack,*" he told his men, meaning that they should shut down the steam-powered boilers. The prized ship would not be able to escape an attack. By April 18, Welles had so little confidence in the Navy Yard's defenses that he started to prepare plans for the dry docks to be destroyed, buildings to be burned, and ships to be scuttled in the event of an attack in the next few days.

Only the arrival of several hundred soldiers might keep the installation under Union control. Scott's reply to Lincoln and Welles's entreaty was forthright, essentially repeating what he had already stated numerous times: "he would send troops for the shore defence [of the Navy Yard], as was his duty," but only "if he had them." He, of course, did not; as Scott lamented, "Congress had provided neither men nor means for this great and terrible crisis," which had compelled him to abandon the Norfolk Navy Yard and Harper's

Ferry and its "armory and arms to destruction." Both installations, said Scott, had to "be sacrificed" in order to keep Washington safe.[50]

Scott expressed similar frustrations that day when he had confided to New York Republican Party leader Thurlow Weed. "What can I do?" Weed recalled Scott telling him. "My effective force, all told, for the defense of the capital is twenty-one hundred. Washington is as much in danger as Harper's Ferry. I shall repel any attack upon this city, but I cannot hazard the capital of the Union, as I should do by dividing my force, even to save Harper's Ferry."[51]

At 9 a.m. that morning, Scott had telegraphed Lieutenant Roger Jones, the commander of just under 50 men at Harper's Ferry, that "three trains of troops had passed from Manassas Junction up the Manassas railroad for the supposed destruction of Harper's Ferry." Scott concluded his telegram to Jones with the simple message, "Be on your guard." That afternoon, at 5 p.m., Jones sent Washington a telegram, reporting that he had "received intelligence confirmatory of his [Scott's] morning despatch." An attack on the arsenal was imminent.[52]

Even by the early evening of April 18, cabinet members were still not aware of the Baltimore mob's assault on the First Pennsylvania Volunteers. Otherwise, one of the nation's best-known politicians, Senator Charles Sumner of Massachusetts, would never have stopped in Baltimore on a social visit that very day, on his way home to Boston from Washington, and unwittingly risked his life. Sumner was one of the nation's most famous—and outspoken—proponents of equal rights for all blacks, slave or free. While most abolitionists merely wanted an end to slavery, Sumner insisted on full racial equality. He had played a major role in the Massachusetts legislature's 1855 enactment of the first law banning racial segregation in the state's public schools. He was most famous for almost having been murdered in the U.S. Senate in 1856 in response to his incendiary speech "The Crime of Kansas," in which he mocked Senator Andrew Butler of South Carolina and "his harlot, slavery." Listening to Sumner's speech, Senator Stephen A. Douglas told a colleague, "This damn fool is going to get himself shot by some other damn fool."

Two days later, while Sumner was sitting at his Senate desk, Congressman Preston Brooks of South Carolina, a relative of Senator Butler, walked into the Senate chamber with two men and started beating Sumner with his cane. After Sumner fell, the enraged Brooks tore the bolted-down desk from the floor and struck him repeatedly with the cane. Congressman Laurence M. Keitt of South Carolina, who had accompanied Brooks to the Senate, kept the other senators from rescuing Sumner by brandishing a pistol and threatening to shoot them. "Let them be!" he screamed at the horrified witnesses. Only after Brooks had broken the cane over Sumner's blood-covered body did he calmly walk out of the Senate. Severely injured, Sumner eventually returned to the Senate, although his recovery took four years.

When Sumner arrived in Baltimore on April 18, he checked into the luxurious Barnum Hotel, located at the southwest corner of Fayette and Calvert Streets and named for its builder, Zenus Barnum, a distant cousin of P. T. Barnum. Sumner signed his full name in the hotel register. Later, he walked across the street for an early dinner alone at Guy's Monument House, which was "always famous for its good fare and a favorite resort of the celebrities when they visited the Monument City."[53] Afterward, he walked over to a family friend's home. On the way, he was startled to see several people staring or pointing at him, but he did not understand why. The explanation was that news of his arrival had already spread among secessionists. One Baltimorean sent the following telegraph to the *Philadelphia Inquirer*: "Senator Sumner, who is now stopping at Barnum's Hotel, causes much excitement. There is a great indignation felt among all parties at his presence among us."[54]

At his friend's home, Sumner talked for several hours and ate a light meal with the mother and her children. Returning to Barnum's at 9 p.m., he noticed a huge, noisy crowd in the square in front of the hotel and fortuitously entered through a private side door some distance up the street. Once inside the hotel, he met a man who recognized him and was dumbfounded to see him there. "That mob in the square is after you!" he excitedly told Sumner. "Their leaders have been to the hotel and demanded you. They were told that you were out,—that nobody knew where you were, and that you had probably left town." The mob, still agitated over the escape of the Pennsylvania Volunteers that afternoon, had not accepted this explanation. They stayed, threatening to burn the building unless he was handed over and chanting, "Bring him out! Bring him out!"[55]

Shaken, the hotel's proprietor, Andrew McLaughlin, told Sumner that his return to the hotel not only risked its destruction, it could lead to injury or death for both of them. When the mob leaders had first entered the hotel looking for Sumner, it was McLaughlin who had told them that the senator was not at the hotel, despite his signature on the guest register. McLaughlin had technically told the truth; Sumner was still visiting his friends. McLaughlin insisted that Sumner leave the hotel and then begged him to. Sumner argued that he could not be turned out and pointed out that he had nowhere to go, unless he hid at his friends' home and put them in danger instead. McLaughlin relented and gave Sumner a small, out-of-the-way third-story room where he could look out the window, out of which he could still see the surging mob and hear their cries. Repeatedly asked whether Sumner was staying at the hotel, McLaughlin continued to deny it. At 5 a.m. the next morning, he took Sumner to the railroad station for a train to Philadelphia and safety.[56]

Elsewhere in Baltimore the evening of April 18, secessionist meetings were underway, plotting the disruption of the train and the slaughter of any "foreign" troops who passed through the city. That night, a group of anti-Union plotters, the States Rights and Southern Rights Convention, had convened in their usual gathering place, Taylor's Hall on Fayette Street, which had been a magnet for the city's secessionist militias over the past several months.[57] Overflowing crowds attended the meeting.[58] Inside the hall, arms manufacturer Ross Winans, one of the city's richest citizens, introduced a resolution urging Marylanders "to repel, if need be, any invader who may come to establish a military despotism over us."[59] The resolution passed unanimously.

Those words echoed the secessionists' call to arms earlier that day. One of the most vocal Baltimoreans, Wilson C. Carr, had proclaimed on the morning of April 18 that even if some soldiers escaped Baltimore and made it to the capital, they would meet their fate when Maryland's and Virginia's armies seized Washington: however "many Federal troops are sent to Washington, they will soon find themselves surrounded by such an army from Virginia and Maryland that escape to their homes will be impossible." He said that the South would "exterminate and sweep them from the earth" the 75,000 volunteers Lincoln had called for before they had a chance to further "pollute" Southern soil.[60]

By the late afternoon of April 18, the Lincoln administration was completing its final defensive measures across the city. For the first time, with news that the Virginia militia was closing on Harper's Ferry, an attack on Washington seemed unquestionably imminent. Major David Hunter personally went to Senator Lane's rooms at Willard's Hotel and told him that his Frontier Guard was needed at the White House no later than sundown. Lane sent out runners to gather his men immediately at the hotel, where "Cash" Clay had already started gathering his. Meanwhile, Secretary Cameron planned to sleep in his office in case of emergency.

At around the same time, U.S. Army soldiers arrived at the Treasury. Some stood guard around the building; others were stationed at the Riggs & Company bank directly across the street. Other soldiers took up positions inside the Treasury building. Henry B. Stanton, an attorney and the husband of the feminist Elizabeth Cady Stanton, who was in Washington on a business trip, saw the soldiers arrive at the Treasury late that afternoon. Returning to his hotel, he wrote a letter home the same evening, addressing her as "my dear love":

> A sense of danger makes me wish I was with you. I am surrounded by soldiers on all sides; the report comes to us, seemingly well founded, that the Virginia troops are rallying at Alexandria, a dozen miles away.
>
> I was at the Treasury Dept. tonight, when coming down the stairs to leave it, I had to step aside to let eighty armed soldiers go up who were going to be on guard there tonight. The same is true of all the other departments—War, Navy, Post office, &c. &c.[61]

That evening, at 7 p.m., the First Pennsylvania Volunteers, whose whereabouts had been unknown for much of the day, finally arrived at the B & O Railroad station, several blocks from the Capitol. By then, the men's morale had improved markedly. "We arrived in fine spirits," wrote Private Benjamin Franklin Jones in a letter to his brother the next day. They had earned a place in history, "because we were the very first volunteer company that are here."[62]

Several hundred men and women greeted them with cheers, but the crowd had expected a large contingent of armed fighting men, more than enough to safeguard their threatened city that night. Instead, the tired and battered men had disembarked from the train wearing their motley assemblage of uniforms and work clothes, dirty from the long train ride and the attack in Baltimore. The only weapons they had in sight were the 34 old-fashioned flintlock rifles carried by the Logan Guard.

Because Washington had no available barracks, the Pennsylvania Volunteers were lodged in the Capitol building, as both the House and Senate were out of session. As the men trudged up Capitol Hill in the twilight, they gazed at their surroundings in near disbelief. Until a day earlier, most of them had never left rural Pennsylvania, where the grandest building was a courthouse or a church. Now, they saw the Capitol with its white marble walls gleaming in the twilight. Gaslight glowed behind dozens of windows, where lamps had been lit for their arrival. Only the jarring contrast of the partly completed dome and the construction debris littering the grounds detracted from the Capitol's grandeur. The men marched up the steps of the East Front, where the wooden platform for Lincoln's inauguration had stood only six weeks before, and into the rotunda, an impressive 96 feet in diameter, a stirring sight even if it lacked its dome. At the rotunda, they turned left and walked down a wide hallway toward the arched doorway of the House of Representatives, their opulent temporary quarters. The House chamber and nearby members' lounges were "magnificent," wrote Captain Thomas Yeager to a friend two days later, with "[l]ooking glasses as large as a door, Brussels Carpets, sofas, lounges, [and] drawing tables."[63]

Soon after the arrival of the Pennsylvania Volunteers, James B. Gay, a member of the Ringgold Light Artillery, had a bold idea. He headed to Willard's Hotel to spread the news that the newly arrived Pennsylvania Volunteers totaled 2,000 soldiers. As he later recalled, "the first man I met as I entered the doors was Lieutenant-Colonel Magruder," a suspected secessionist who would resign from the U.S. Army a few days later and become a Confederate general. Gay told Magruder to step out the front door of the hotel, where he said, "Do you see that?" pointing up Pennsylvania Avenue to the Capitol, where dozens of windows gleamed from the lights inside.

"Yes," Magruder replied, "but what of that?" The building should have been dark that night, Gay reminded Magruder, because Congress was not in session. "Two thousand soldiers have marched in there this evening, Sir, armed with Minie rifles," Gay replied. "[Is it] possible? So much!" Magruder replied, in what Gay remembered as an "excited manner." Later that evening, Gay told his comrades, "Of course, what I told him was not true, but I thought that, in the absence of sufficient troops, this false report might save the city."[64]

John W. Forney had the same brainstorm about spreading exaggerated rumors of the Pennsylvania Volunteers' numbers, and he embellished his version with even greater zeal. Leaving his comrades at the Capitol, "our own John W. Forney spread the news of this arrival through the corridors of Willard's Hotel," recalled Oliver C. Bosbyshell of the Washington Artillery, a

22-year-old private at the time, "and being anxious to make the most of it added an additional naught to the sum, saying 5,000 Pennsylvania soldiers had arrived, when 500 was the figure, but the mantle of night had shielded the arrival, so that numbers could not be known."[65]

That evening, three unexpected visitors walked into the House of Representatives: Abraham Lincoln, Secretary Seward, and Secretary Cameron. "Imagine the scene," remembered Bosbyshell, who never forgot this moving event—his fellow militia members "spread out on the hard marble floors of the Capitol of the Nation, in an effort to secure some rest from the fatiguing journey just completed, when every man is brought to his feet by the announcement of the presence of the one man in the United States each one most desired to see."[66]

"Profound silence for a moment resulted, broken by the hand clapping and cheers of the tired volunteers," he continued. "Yes, here, towering over all in the room was the great central figure of the war. I remember how I was impressed by the kindliness of his face and awkward hanging of his arms and legs, his apparent bashfulness in the presence of these first soldiers of the Republic, and with it all a grave, rather mournful bearing in his attitude."[67]

Secretary Cameron, "highly elated and proud," introduced President Lincoln to the awestruck men. Cameron was a familiar name to these men, as he had served as a senator from Pennsylvania before becoming secretary of war. "I did not come here to make a speech," Lincoln told them. "The time for speech-making has gone by, and the time for action is at hand. I have come here to . . . shake every officer and soldier by the hand, providing you will give me the privilege."[68] Lincoln greeted each man, paying particular attention to injured men like Nicholas Biddle. As the president moved among the Volunteers, recalled Bosbyshell, "a kind of awe seemed to come over the boys, and many for the first time realized the peril brought upon the Nation. . . . It was a kind of baptism of responsibilities."[69]

At the other end of Pennsylvania Avenue, the executive mansion had undergone a transformation since the afternoon: "the White House is turned into a barracks," wrote John Hay in the first sentence of his new journal that evening.[70] Senator Lane and his Frontier Guard had arrived to protect the White House and were "stationed" in the East Room, the only room large enough to accommodate all the men. One of the Frontier Guards, Clifford Arrick, a lawyer who worked as an examiner in the Patent Office, also began a diary that evening. An Ohio native in his late twenties, Arrick made an invaluable record of the guard's service at the White House. In his first entry, Arrick described the formation and arming of the Frontier Guard. Lane "received from the Secretary of War in the presence of the President his Sword, and at once proceeded to arm his Company.[71] The battalion's members, who wore their everyday clothes rather than uniforms, opened up ammunition boxes to pass out supplies of cartridges and stacked their guns in the hallway outside. Major David Hunter, who supervised security at the White House, bestowed a special honor on John Hay. "The Major has made me his aide," Hay wryly noted in his diary, "and I labored under some uncertainty as to whether I should speak to privates or not."[72]

The arrival of the Frontier Guard soon turned into a social event. As elegantly dressed guests arrived to greet the men, "the scene [became] a medley of bizarre contradictions,—a blending of masquerade and tragedy, of grim humor and realistic seriousness,—a combination of Don Quixote and Daniel Boone altogether impossible to describe," recalled Nicolay and Hay.[73] The rotund Senator Samuel C. Pomeroy of Kansas could not find a belt long enough to go around his waist, so he spliced two belts together, much to the amusement of onlookers. Senator Lane "walked proudly up and down the ranks with a new sword that the Major had given him," wrote Hay in his diary.

Shortly after the Frontier Guard reached at the White House, Lincoln wanted to introduce his wife and several cabinet members to the men. As Lincoln reached the doors to the East Room, one of Frontier Guard stopped him, because he had orders to admit no one unless they had the password. Lincoln, however, had not been told what it was. "Even the President," one newspaper recorded, "when he attempted to enter the hall, accompanied by his lady and some members of the Cabinet, was pricked with the sharp steel of the sentinel, and told,—perhaps jocosely—that *he could not possibly come in!*" The president "was forced to beat a retreat, to the no small amusement of the company."[74]

Meanwhile, Cassius Clay, on "leave of absence" from his men at Willard's Hotel, wore his improvised uniform with three pistols and his "Arkansas Toothpick" (Bowie knife) at his waist. In Hay's opinion, Clay looked "like an admiral vignette to 25-cents-worth of yellow-covered romance." The evening ended "in an exceedingly rudimentary squad drill under the light of the splendid gas chandeliers."[75] By then, Lincoln had already gone to bed at his usual early hour.

"That night, Kansas had Supreme possession of the White House," wrote Hay in his diary, describing the force now guarding the executive mansion from within. "Two long rows of Kansas ex-Governors, Senators, Judges, Editors, Generals, and Jayhawkers were dozing upon each side, and the sentinels made regular beats around them."[76] Those who were not on patrol "slept by their guns," Arrick recorded.[77]

At 9 p.m., while the Frontier Guard were showing off their military prowess in the East Room, Lieutenant Jones, the commander of the U.S. Army force at Harper's Ferry, sent a telegram to the War Department: "Up to the present time, no assault or attempt to seize the Government property here has been made, but there is decided evidence that the subject is in contemplation. . . . [A]t sundown this evening several companies of troops had assembled at Halltown, about three or four miles from here, on the road to Charlestown, with the intention of seizing the Government property, and the last report is that the attack will be made to-night."[78]

For the last four hours, Jones and the new superintendent of the arsenal, Captain Charles Kingsbury, had worked to prepare the destruction of the installation before Virginia militia arrived. General Scott had appointed Kingsbury chief ordnance officer on the previous day, immediately after Alfred Barbour—who was among the Virginia secessionists plotting the seizure of the arsenal—had submitted his formal resignation. Scott had expected Kingsbury "to act, a few days, as Superintendent—that is, till a new appointment (of a civilian) can be made," expecting that Harper's Ferry would remain in Union hands.[79]

To ignite a conflagration, Jones's men placed small kegs of gunpowder in their bed sacks, which they filled with straw and then distributed around the arms, along with other combustibles, including a large quantity of timber. By 6 p.m., the arsenal was ready to be set ablaze with the strike of a match on lines of gunpowder leading to the explosives. In the confusion of fire and explosions, Jones and his men hoped to cross the nearby bridge over the Potomac River and retreat north through Maryland toward Carlisle, Pennsylvania. With night approaching, blowing up the armory offered the only chance of preventing its large cache of weapons from falling into the Virginia militia's hands.

After sending his 9 p.m. telegram to the War Department, Jones wrote another telegram to the adjutant general's office in Washington: "I have taken steps which ought to insure my receiving early intelligence of the advance of any forces, and my determination is to destroy what I cannot defend, and if the forces sent against me are clearly overwhelming, my present intention is to retreat into Pennsylvania."

As Jones wrote the telegram, a courier informed him that the Virginia militia were on their way from Halltown. Once the first fires had been started, Jones wrote the last lines of the dispatch: "The steps I have taken to destroy the arsenal, which contains nearly fifteen thousand stand of arms, are so complete that I can conceive of nothing that will prevent their entire destruction."[80] With that, Jones and his men fled through the bridge over the Potomac and headed for Pennsylvania. Washington would not know of Harper's Ferry's ultimate fate until morning—unless the attacking Virginia militia swung southward to attack Washington itself.

As Hay got ready for bed around midnight, he wrote the last sentence of the day's diary entry, describing the "tempest of great excitement" that all felt in a Washington on the brink of the expected invasion.[81] Across the city, other Washingtonians expected the assault that night. "There seemed to be a great anxiety to fight manifested all round," wrote Horatio Taft in his diary that night. "[A]n attack is expected upon the City from Virginia." Yet Taft remained sure that an attack could be checked: "The City is apparently pretty well prepared. Wo[e] to the invaders."[82]

His confidence was not universally shared. Despite these preparations, Washington did not have nearly enough men to ward off a large Virginia force from across the Potomac. That day, Lieutenant John Dahlgren estimated the then-current number of available men for the city's defense: 1,000 men from the U.S. Army and Marines, 1,200–1,500 men enrolled in the District of Columbia militia, and the 600 to 700 men of the Pennsylvania Volunteers, who, he observed, had arrived in "poor order."[83] Late that evening, Dahlgren appended his entry: "Every one believes . . . that a body of men are on the way to take Washington, and the alarm is intense." It was, he wrote, "the critical night, and *the* chance for the South."[84]

Friday, April 19

"Minute Men of '61"

On the morning of April 19, Washington residents awoke relieved. No attack had come from Virginia during the night. Signs of war, however, were still everywhere. At the Capitol, the newly arrived First Pennsylvania Volunteers were at work fortifying the building's west façade overlooking the mall with barrels of cement and thick sheets of iron previously destined for the half-finished dome.[1]

At the other end of Pennsylvania Avenue, the Treasury building "seemed singularly metamorphosed," recalled Lucius Chittenden. "Armed men guarded its entrances, and excluded all but officers and employees. Stacks of rifles and boxes of cartridges occupied the halls. . . . barricades, from floor to ceiling, closed the way to the vaults, and the sharp notes of the bugle rang out at intervals."[2] Outside, workers stacked sandbags between the columns of the Treasury's grand south portico. Next door at the White House, John Hay conferred with Major David Hunter about stronger defenses at the executive mansion. As they met, news came that the Harper's Ferry Armory had been destroyed by Union officers late the previous night—before Virginia militia had seized it. The report "delighted" Hunter, recounted Hay, since he viewed it as a "deadly blow at the prosperity of the recusant Virginia."[3]

Details of the armory's destruction did not arrive until 1 p.m., when Lieutenant Jones telegrammed General Scott from Chambersburg, Pennsylvania, where he had fled with his small force. Recounting his actions since the previous night, Jones wrote: "Finding my position untenable, shortly after 10 o'clock last night I destroyed the arsenal, containing 15,000 stand of arms, and burned up the armor building proper, and under cover of the night withdrew my command almost in the presence of twenty-five hundred or three thousand troops."[4] Jones, who left Harper's Ferry before he could evaluate the full extent of what had gone up in flames, concluded the telegram: "I believe the destruction must have been complete."[5]

This modestly worded dispatch belied the importance of what Jones had accomplished, because the destruction of the weapons at Harper's Ferry was critical to Washington's safety and may have forestalled an imminent attack on the city. On April 22, when the event's significance had become clearer, the New York Herald's editorial page declared: "who can estimate the value of that timely little conflagration at Harper's Ferry? We consider it a greater victory than that of Waterloo; for we believe that it has saved the capital of our country." Had they been seized by secessionists, the weapons at Harper's Ferry could have been used for the "deliberately contrived seizure of the authorities, the magnificent buildings and their archives, the treasury." Washington might have fallen, the paper speculated or at least an attack on "the seat of the government of the United States, would, perhaps, have been attempted several days ago."[6]

Was the New York Herald correct in its estimation? Henry Wise, the architect of the raid on Harper's Ferry, called for Washington's capture on the very day the raid was launched. However, Governor Letcher apparently opposed a run on Washington and authorized only for Virginia militia to seize federal military instillations within the state. On April 17, Wise had urged Letcher to press the Confederate government at Montgomery to order a direct attack on Washington, an entreaty Letcher rebuffed after former Virginia Senator James Mason told him it was folly.[7] The same day, South Carolina's Governor Pickens—who on April 16 had secretly written to Davis to call for Maryland and Virginia to capture Washington—rejected Wise's special appeal for troops, because the nominal authority, Governor Letcher, had made no request himself.[8] Thus, in the struggle for leadership with Wise in Richmond, Letcher believed that he had checked plans for an immediate march on Washington.

Nevertheless, Letcher was aware that his authority was weak. He had assented to the seizure of Harper's Ferry only after Wise had made clear that the raid would be launched with or without Letcher's approval, and the men who had planned to lead the attack had already sworn to act under Wise's command—"without official authority" from the Virginia government.[9] An insider's account of the Harper's Ferry raid written by John C. Imboden, Wise's chief subordinate in planning the attack, does not mention any designs on Washington.[10] Imboden's account, however, makes clear that the plot was hatched in a tightly knit group who made every effort to prevent any rumors of the attack from becoming known and, in particular, to keep their destination secret to all outsiders, including the militia who would carry out the attack. The false destination of the Portsmouth Navy Yard was "indicated in all our dispatches, to deceive the Government at Washington in case there should be a 'leak' in the telegraph offices."[11]

Indeed, Wise and his fellow plotters knew to be careful of leaks, for they had their own source in Washington providing secret information: Wise's son-in-law, Dr. Alexander Garnett, identified earlier that year as a member of a secessionist militia in the capital.[12] (He later left Washington with his family and served as Jefferson Davis's personal doctor in Richmond.) As the conspirators were meeting in Richmond, Garnett contacted Wise to warn him of General Scott's plan to divert Washington-bound Union troops to protect Harper's Ferry: "Early in the evening [of April 16] a message had been received by ex-Governor Wise from his son-in-law Doctor Garnett of Washington, to the effect that a Massachusetts regiment, one thousand strong, had been ordered to Harper's Ferry," recalled Imboden.[13] Wise's men were able to formulate their attack plans in open communication with secessionists in Washington, who appeared to have had access to orders within the War Department, either directly or through sympathetic colleagues.

Evidence that the Harper's Ferry plotters intended to seize Washington also comes from the only Union officer to meet the attackers face to face, Captain Charles Kingsbury, the chief of ordnance, who believed that the Virginians intended to use the arms to take the capital, in collaboration with secessionists in Baltimore. Although Lieutenant Jones and his small company fled Harper's Ferry before the Virginia militia arrived late in the evening of April 18, Kingsbury chose to remain at the arsenal to see the attackers firsthand. He was briefly captured and witnessed a train standing ready, he believed, to transport arms to Baltimore. As he later described the scene, an "extra locomotive of the Baltimore and Ohio Railroad, with steam on was in waiting at the Harper's Ferry bridge," along with "a mysterious party from Baltimore" that was present, apparently working in coordination with the Virginia plotters.[14]

After his release, Kingsbury walked along the rail line on foot to Monocacy, Maryland, 20 miles to the northeast, and telegraphed Washington the next day. He later fleshed out the details of the attack and its relation to a wider conspiracy against Washington when he testified before the U.S. Senate on November 26, 1861, together with Jones, during an inquiry into the destruction of the Harper's Ferry arsenal. Kingsbury's testimony was unequivocal:

> There is hardly a doubt that the object of the attack was to secure the arms at the armory for an ulterior purpose. The Richmond secession ordinance was adopted . . . and this force [the militia organized by Wise to take Harper's Ferry] was immediately organized and put in motion.
>
> Arrangements had been perfected for a demonstration in Baltimore, which came off at the prescribed time, but not altogether in the manner which had been agreed upon. It was doubtless supposed that the arms would reach Baltimore on the morning of the 19th, (the day on which the Massachusetts regiment was fired upon) and with these and the reinforcements from Virginia, an attack upon the capital could hardly have failed of success.[15]

In sum, Kingsbury held that "the plot was ingeniously contrived as to time and means; but the sudden and unexpected interference [the destruction of the arms] with the latter baffled the conspirators, and Washington was saved."[16]

At the hearing, Kingsbury maintained that the waiting B & O train he saw at Harper's Ferry was ready to carry arms to secessionists in Baltimore, enough arms to launch a coordinated attack on any Union soldiers changing trains in the city on April 19 and thereby preventing reinforcements from reaching the capital. Meanwhile, the Virginia militia in Harper's Ferry, who would have now been well armed, could have taken the B & O train east to the Relay House and caught southbound trains to Washington. The *New York Herald* offered a similar version of this scenario: "The main body of the insurgents would follow [into Harper's Ferry] as rapidly as possible; all would be supplied with arms from the arsenal, and, thus equipped, the railroad leading to Baltimore and Washington would be pressed into service, and within a few hours this invading revolutionary force would be discharged at the foot of Capitol Hill"—at the city's B & O station, where the unarmed Pennsylvania Volunteers would have been the only Union reinforcements to have reached Washington.[17]

Kingsbury also credited an unlikely accomplice with helping to destroy Harper's Ferry: John Brown, who had seized the arsenal in 1859 in his short-lived attempt to incite an armed slave rebellion and who had been hanged for the crime in December of that year. When Jones and Kingsbury were preparing the arsenal for destruction, they did not want to send their men to fetch barrels of explosives from the main storage building, because secessionist arsenal workers and townspeople living on nearby hillsides could see what they were doing. Fortunately, they found small kegs of gunpowder left behind from Brown's raid, which they used to ignite the blaze. In Kingsbury's estimation, John Brown had helped save Washington, because his gunpowder was "admirably adapted to the holy and patriotic purpose for which it was now wanted."[18]

Long before Kingsbury's testimony, officials in Washington recognized the importance of the destruction of the weapons at the arsenal. On April 22, just three days later, Secretary Cameron promoted Lieutenant Jones to the rank of captain for his "gallant" conduct at Harper's Ferry and conveyed special thanks from President Lincoln to him and his men.[19]

On the morning of April 19, however, news of the destruction of Harper's Ferry was only beginning to circulate in Washington. Most of the attention was still focused on Virginia's secession, which had been a rumor the day before and now was confirmed in newspaper headlines in the capital and across the country. Now, the nation now knew that Washington was the new front line of the war. A headline in the April 19 *New York Herald* read: "Stirring and Decisive News—Virginia Seceded—Washington and the Line of the Potomac to be the Battle Field."[20] This article was the *Herald*'s first definitive report that Virginia had left the Union, and it offered a glimpse of what might soon happen in Washington. "Virginia has seceded. She has taken this dreadful leap in the dark, and terrible to her, we fear, will be the consequences. A revolutionary army, under Governor Wise, is supposed to be moving upon Washington."[21]

Another epochal event of the first days of the war swiftly followed the thunderclaps of Harper's Ferry and Virginia's secession: the Sixth Massachusetts Volunteer Regiment's bloody passage through Baltimore. At 8 p.m. the night before, they had arrived in Philadelphia, after leaving New York earlier that afternoon, following their grand parade down Broadway. Upon arriving in Philadelphia, the regiment had marched amid cheering crowds and fireworks to the imposing Girard House, where a large banner over the front entrance carried the famous pledge of Massachusetts's late senator Daniel Webster: "Liberty and Union, now and forever, one and inseparable." The hotel had recently closed so that hundreds of Philadelphia women—from seamstresses to society matrons—could make uniforms, blankets, and bandages for the Pennsylvania Volunteer regiments. That night, several hundred rooms were available at the Girard House for the troops, but all the beds had been taken from the rooms to provide more space for the workshops, so the men planned to sleep on the carpeted floors.

After cleaning up in one of the half-dozen marble bathrooms on each floor, the Sixth Massachusetts Volunteers had marched across Chestnut Street for dinner at Philadelphia's newest and grandest hotel, the mammoth Continental, where Lincoln had stayed while traveling to Washington for his inauguration. Like so many volunteer regiments whose members came from small towns and farms, these Massachusetts men had never entered such a grand hotel lobby, with marble floors, Corinthian columns reaching to richly decorated ceilings, and huge mirrors on the walls that made the light from the gas-lit chandeliers seem even brighter and the already vast lobby even larger and more luxurious. They gawked at the steam-powered "vertical railroad"—or elevator—that noiselessly carried hotel guests up or down at the rate of one floor every 15 seconds.

Writing to his family back home, Private Luke Robbins described their dinner that night. "An awful good supper and the dining room was large enough for the whole 1,000 [with] 50 negro waiters to wait on us at the tables." Rank had its privileges. The officers sat at smaller tables, where they were served by local political and business leaders. Continuing his letter, Private Robbins wrote: "Philadelphia is all union. . . . Have shaken hands so much with those that have congratulated us, both ladies and gentlemen . . . that I would not give a cent to shake hands with the President."[22]

During dinner at the Continental Hotel, P. S. Davis, one of Colonel Edward Jones's fellow officers, informed him of a disturbing rumor. Baltimore secessionists were planning to attack the Sixth Massachusetts men as they changed trains in Baltimore the next day, either to force them back northward or simply to slaughter them in the city's streets.[23] Several "prominent Philadelphians" believed the rumors to be true, recalled regimental Chaplin John W. Hanson, and feared "that there would be a stormy time of it when the regiment should reach the Monumental City."

Despite trepidation on the part of some of his officers, Colonel Jones insisted that they go ahead at once, for two reasons. First, Washington's safety required the arrival of the Sixth Massachusetts Volunteers the following day, no later. "My orders are to reach Washington at the earliest possible moment," said Jones, "and I shall go on."[24] Second, Jones believed that if his men left ahead of schedule, they would arrive in Baltimore early enough in the morning that the rumored mob might not yet have assembled. His men, hopefully, could change trains and head to Washington unscathed. Colonel Jones immediately met with Samuel M. Felton, president of the Philadelphia, Wilmington & Baltimore Railroad, whose railroad would carry the Sixth Massachusetts to Baltimore. Felton believed the rumor, based on his own latest intelligence reports, and arranged for the predawn departure of the regiment's train.[25] Both Felton and Colonel Jones suspected that Baltimore's Mayor Brown and Police Chief Kane were party to the secessionist plots against the Massachusetts men, and did not inform them about the new train arrival time. Having finalized the new arrangements, Colonel Jones hurried back to the Girard House.

At 1 a.m., the sound of drumbeats resounded through the hotel and woke the Massachusetts Volunteers, who had recently fallen asleep on the floors of the empty guestrooms. The original plan had called for getting up at 4 a.m. and resuming travel shortly before dawn. Now the men were ordered to dress in their uniforms and overcoats, put on their regulation blue caps, assemble in the lobby, and prepare to move out immediately.

Before leaving the Girard House, the men ate a breakfast of thick hardtack crackers and salt pork.[26] Afterward, only half-awake, they trudged through the deserted streets to the Philadelphia, Wilmington & Baltimore Railroad's handsome, brownstone-front station at South Broad Street and Washington Avenue. The gaslights had been lit, turning the station into a beacon in the darkness, and several company officials, workers, and policemen stood to greet the men at the entrance.[27] The Massachusetts men walked through the empty lobby, past the ticket windows and waiting rooms, and into the vaulted train shed where their train sat ready for departure. The train consisted of 10 carriages: nine regular passenger cars for the soldiers and one freight car that had been outfitted with benches for the 24-member band and their instruments. As they boarded the train, some of the men spotted a shipment of beer kegs, piled high on another platform. Several of the policemen saw the men's envious glances, and they good-naturedly hauled a single keg up to the train.[28]

Colonel Jones's goal of an early morning arrival in Baltimore, however, was complicated by a last-minute change of plans at the station. Pennsylvania was sending 1,000 additional volunteers—once again, unarmed—to the nation's capital on the same rail line. Instead of connecting their 25 railroad cars to another locomotive, they were coupled to the back of the Sixth Massachusetts Volunteers' train—meaning that the locomotive had to pull 35 cars, more than three times the weight of the original ten. The train would now arrive in Baltimore at midday rather than in the early morning.[29]

At 3 a.m., the overburdened train pulled away from the station.[30] At their recent meeting, Colonel Jones had told Felton that his greatest fear was an obstruction on the tracks that might derail the train or a sabotaged bridge that could cause the drowning of hundreds of his men in a river. Felton arranged for a pilot engine to verify the condition of the tracks all the way to Baltimore. Jones also decided to wire ahead from every station along their route to Baltimore for word on the conditions there, a sensible step except that it further delayed the train's progress. At each stop, the railway officials in Baltimore replied to Jones that all was quiet in Baltimore and that no violence was anticipated unless the Sixth Massachusetts started it.[31] Jones was skeptical of these repeated assurances and expected that the Sixth Massachusetts's now-delayed "passage through the city of Baltimore would be resisted," he later told War Department officials. In anticipation, he "caused ammunition to be distributed and arms loaded." Each man was issued 20 rounds of ball cartridges, and they loaded and capped their rifles.[32]

After the train departed Havre de Grace, Maryland, 30 miles from Baltimore, where the cars were floated on a ferry across the Susquehanna, Colonel Jones walked through each of the 10 train cars carrying the Massachusetts regiment and issued orders to the men: "The regiment will march through Baltimore in column of sections, arms at will. You will undoubtedly be insulted, abused, and, perhaps, assaulted, to which you must pay no attention whatever, but march with your faces square to the front, and pay no attention to the mob, even if they throw stones, bricks, or other missiles; but if you are fired upon and any one of you is hit, your officers will order you to fire."[33] His final order: "Do not fire into any promiscuous crowds, but select any man whom you may see aiming at you, and be sure you drop him."[34]

As their train neared Baltimore, many of the volunteers thought of their families they had left behind so abruptly only two days earlier. Because virtually none of these men had ever been under fire, their thoughts were filled with anxiety about what lay ahead and knew that they would face the greatest challenge of their young lives that day. "You can imagine my feelings when I left Boston without even bidding you good bye; but forgive me for I had no time," one man had written his brother during the regiment's brief stop in New York. "Should you write and I should be shot, say to father and mother that I died in defense of the 'stars and stripes.'"[35]

Despite Samuel Felton and Colonel Jones's best efforts to keep the trip through Baltimore a secret, the city's secessionists learned of the regiment's arrival by telegraphs dispatched from the B & O stations north of the city, giving them plenty of time to gather and carry out their plan. The attack on the Sixth Massachusetts would be a more coordinated effort than the previous day's violence against the First Pennsylvania Volunteers, reports of which the *Baltimore Sun* had relegated to the last page in that day's edition.[36] For months, secessionists had talked about preventing the passage of Northern troops for the defense of Washington, and in the words of one Pennsylvania Volunteer, the city was a "vortex of seething madness."[37]

As the train slowed down at the city's outskirts, people began running toward the tracks, gesturing wildly, shaking their fists, and screaming taunts. When it finally pulled into the President Street station at 11:20 a.m., the city's fire stations started ringing their alarm bells as a signal.[38] Now Colonel Jones had another rude surprise. He had intended for his men to disembark from the train and march in close formation the one and a half miles to the Camden Street station, where they would board their train to Washington. No railroad official had alerted Jones that his troops would be transported in separate horse-drawn cars on tracks to the Camden Street station, a process that would take far longer than covering the transfer distance on foot, as the First Pennsylvania Volunteers had done the day before.[39]

As the Sixth Massachusetts disembarked from the train, railroad workers detached the now-empty cars from the engine and moved them one by one to the tracks in front of the station. From there, each car would be hauled by four horses to Camden Street. Meanwhile, a large, noisy crowd had already gathered outside the station, and shouts filled the air: "Cheers for Jeff Davis!" "For South Carolina and the South!"[40]

As workers pulled each of the railroad cars out of the station's train shed and to the front of the terminal, a group of Massachusetts men walked from the building and boarded the carriages, whose window blinds had been lowered to screen them from the crowd. At the same time, police prevented the ever-growing crowd near the station from mobbing the train cars or blocking the tracks. One by one, the horses hauled the cars northward along President Street to Pratt Street, where they turned west to run along the waterfront to end up at the Camden Street station, two blocks south of Pratt Street.

As the carriages carrying the men passed through downtown, "the entire community was perfectly wild with excitement," recalled Baltimore historian and journalist John Thomas Scharf, who was 18 when he witnessed the events that day. "In less than 15 minutes, hundreds of people were rushing in crowds toward the railroad track on Pratt Street, with the intention of preventing the passage of troops."[41] As the teams of horses slowly pulled each railroad car down Pratt Street, the boisterous crowd—which grew to several thousand—hissed and shouted their favorite pro-Southern and anti-Union taunts. Still, nine of the cars reached the President Street station safely. A few rocks shattered windows on the fifth and sixth cars, but all of the Sixth Massachusetts troops inside arrived unharmed. Now these men anxiously awaited the tenth and final car, which carried the last of their comrades, so they could all leave on the train to Washington that was waiting at the station.

That, however, was the end of the Sixth Massachusetts men's luck. One block after the tenth carriage had turned onto Pratt Street, its wheels ground to a halt, and the car jumped the tracks. The mob had "dumped a car load of sand on the bed of the track, placing also four or five large anchors" onto them, causing the carriage to derail.[42] As the troops wondered what had brought the car to a stop, one of the windows in the carriage shattered, spraying the compartment with glass. A man in the crowd had thrown a rock—a "signal to all assembled," recalled Scharf, "and in an instant the stones were flying thick and fast."[43] Some Massachusetts men were wounded by the breaking glass, and their comrades wanted to shoot at the assailants, but were ordered to hold their fire and lie on the floors of the carriage, now strewn with shards of shattered glass.

The railroad car's driver, understandably terrified, hitched his team of horses to the rear of the car and started to head back to the President Street station, as the crowd hurled more stones and bricks. Meanwhile, some men arrived with picks, crowbars, and shovels and started ripping up 150 feet of track along Pratt Street, while others blocked portions of the rail line with piles of paving stones that had been set out earlier that morning, as well as a load of sand from a passing wagon.[44]

At the Camden Street station, William P. Smith, superintendent of the B & O Railroad, informed Colonel Jones that because so many of the rails along Pratt Street had been ripped up, any further transfers by horse-drawn rail cars were now out of the question. "If you will send an order for them to march across," he told Jones, "I will deliver it." On the back of a railroad notepad, Jones wrote, "To the officer in command of detachment of the Sixth Massachusetts Regiment:—You will march to this place as quickly as possible; follow the railroad track."[45]

In the chaos, the order never reached the Massachusetts troops at the President Street Station. The remaining Massachusetts men hesitated whether to try fighting their way through the angry crowd, and remained in the rail car at the station. Likewise, the regiment's band and the Pennsylvania Volunteers in the two dozen subsequent cars did not make a move. Meanwhile, a rumor swept the mob that troops in another railroad car, which had by now been pulled back to the station, were planning to march to the Camden Street station. Within 15 minutes, an estimated 2,000 men gathered around the railroad car, while the Massachusetts men sat inside, frozen in fear. "The crowd became furious with excitement," according to Scharf, and they were "about to force an entrance into the cars, when a large detachment of police . . . made their appearance and rushing forward . . . succeeded in preventing the attack upon the cars."[46]

The police told Captain Albert S. Follansbee, who commanded the troops, that they would accompany them to the Camden Street station. Lacking any other option, the Massachusetts men got out of the car and, with help from the police, formed a double-file line. "Here they come! Here they come!," shouted secessionists in the crowd, and soon the volunteers were hemmed in on all sides. The police did their best to open up a path so that the men could march down Pratt Street.[47]

The mob in the streets consisted mainly of men; the onlookers on the sidewalks included some women and youths, including the teenaged Ernest Wardwell, whose classes at the Adams School had been dismissed when the Northern regiments arrived that morning. Young Wardwell was fascinated by the military—he often played soldier with his friends—so he and some classmates headed for Pratt Street, where he saw some of the rail cars being hauled to the Camden Street station. "The mob was very violent and shouted all manner of vile names and kept up a steady flow of missiles at the car windows," according to Wardwell, years later. "It was an awful scene . . . the crowd following like a coniferous pack of howling wolves." Soon, the young man "caught the mad fever, and yelled and shouted with the best of them." He did not throw any objects at the cars "simply for the want of something to throw."[48]

Soon, Wardwell spotted the last group of Massachusetts Volunteers, who were marching to Camden Street station. Near the Marsh Market, the crowd was so large and "wedged in" that the surrounded troops could not march further. Lieutenant B.F. Watson climbed up a pile of paving stones and urged the mob to let them pass. "Men of Baltimore," he shouted, "we have no quarrel with you. We only ask the right of transit through the city to obey our orders." The officer immediately received his answer. A thick piece of lumber flew through the air, hit him, and knocked him over.[49]

That event "changed the current of my being," remembered Wardwell. "I began to feel a sympathy for them, and their bleeding faces and hands awoke pity." Leaving his classmates behind, he pushed his way through the crowd to a sergeant who was holding an injured man's rifle as well as his own:

> "Give me the gun, I will carry it for you!" shouted young Wardwell over the din.
>
> "Go away, or I'll run it through you," the sergeant shouted, because he thought Wardwell only wanted to use the gun to attack his men.
>
> "No, no," Wardwell replied, "Give it to me, I'm with you."
>
> "Are you?" the sergeant asked. "Well then, fall in there."[50]

The sergeant pushed Wardwell toward the rear of the men, gave him the rifle, and told a man named Parsons, who was standing next to Wardwell, "to look out for it," meaning the rifle. Wardwell was no longer playing war games with his friends, and "at first I was so confused and frightened at what I had done, that I wished myself away, but before I could think much about it the police had the crowd back a few feet, and the march was resumed." Parsons "was very kind to me," recalled Wardwell. "He pushed me along and told me not to be afraid, that we would soon reach the rest of the Regiment" at the Camden Street station.[51]

Like many of the Massachusetts troops, Wardwell was frozen with fear, as he marched through the screaming mob, trying to avoid being hit by rocks, bricks, and other debris. "I did not fire, in fact I was so terrified that I never knew I had a gun. My brain was in a whirl; I saw dozens of men lying in the street as we ran by and heard the cries and groans of many more."[52]

The march of the Massachusetts men toward the Camden Street station grew bloodier with each new block. Four Massachusetts Volunteers were killed outright or died later of their wounds, and several dozen more were injured so seriously that their comrades had to carry them toward the station. One Massachusetts man, Charles A. Taylor, was struck on the back of the head by a paving stone and fell into the gutter where a crowd surrounded his body and beat him to death.

That brutal act unleashed open gunfire on both sides. The previously untested Massachusetts men started firing at hostile groups or armed onlookers on their own, not as part of a "platoon firing." Their military order was breaking down, and they were continually jostled by the crowd. Sometimes, the troops were pushed as they took aim, and their bullets struck the second floors of nearby buildings, sending pieces of shattered brick to the street and leaving scars in the building's wall. At other times, the soldiers' aim was better. One Massachusetts man spotted a Baltimore man getting ready to shoot at his comrades from the second floor of a nearby building. He fired, and the man tumbled out of the window and onto the sidewalk below.

Several Massachusetts Volunteers later recalled the test that many soldiers must meet: shooting another person for the first time. Edwin T. Spofford, who had been wounded by a member of the mob, described his feelings when he shot and killed an attacker who had fired at one of his comrades: "I felt bad at first when I saw what I had done; but it soon passed off, and as I had done my duty, and was not the aggressor, I was soon able to fire again and again."[53]

While the Sixth Massachusetts was battling its way across Baltimore, the 24 men of their regimental band and the 1,000 unarmed Pennsylvanian Volunteers still waited at the President Street station for orders to move out. Fear mounted as these men heard the screaming mob and gunfire in the distance. The band members had been promised rifles before they left Boston two days earlier but had never received the guns.

Once the mob learned that these Northern troops remained at the President Street station without police protection, some rioters ran back to the station and descended on the band's converted freight car with savage fury, incited by their failure to stop the other Massachusetts troops from reaching the train to Washington. Many in the mob knew what was happening elsewhere because a group of young men on horseback rode from place to place, getting the latest information and sharing it with rioters. At the President Street station, some of the rioters threw stones and scrap iron through the railroad car's shattered windows, while others climbed onto the wooden roof and smashed holes in it with iron bars, screaming that they would kill every man inside. Others began calling for gunpowder to blow the car up.

By now, several band members were badly injured. The men knew that they were trapped and faced a choice: stay and be killed or push their way out, fight their way past the thugs, and run for their lives. Many jumped out of the car under a hail of rocks and started running southward toward the docks, with their would-be killers at their heels. Lost in the maze of streets in an unfamiliar city, the band members' escape seemed hopeless.

Suddenly, a young man who looked more like another thug than a savior shouted: "Follow me!" Running after him, the men went up a narrow street and through an open door. A formidable-looking woman was waiting inside; she grabbed each soldier and urged him up the stairs. The last soldier had been hit on the head by a flying stone and was bleeding, so she slammed the door and carried him to the second floor. "You are perfectly safe here, boys," the woman said reassuringly, while she and several other women started tending to the wounds of the injured men. The woman, 33-year-old Ann Manley, turned out to have quite a collection of clothing, which the uninjured soldiers used as disguises when they returned to the streets to try to learn what had happened to their Massachusetts comrades and the Pennsylvanians Volunteers.

Ann Manley was the keeper of one of Baltimore's best known brothels. "The noble-hearted woman who rescued these men," described a contemporary history, was a "well-known character in Baltimore, and according to all the usages of Christian society, is an outcast and a polluted being." Yet "this degraded woman took them under her protection, dressed their wounds, fed them at her own cost, and sent them back in safety to their homes."[54]

When the men returned to their temporary refuge on Eastern Avenue, they found that their uniforms had been packed up and sent back to the President Street station, where they had arrived several hours earlier. Manley told the men to walk back to the station in their civilian garb. The police had saved the other band members from the mob and prevented any attacks on the Pennsylvania Volunteers in the other cars. They had also ordered a train to carry all the men back to Philadephia.

Meanwhile, Captain Follansbee's now-ragged men arrived at the Camden Street station. Colonel Jones did not want to leave behind their wounded comrades, those who had not been carried to the station, the 24 members of their band, or the 1,000 Pennsylvanians. John W. Garnett, president of the B & O, however, was pleading with him to leave Baltimore before the tracks to Washington were destroyed by the mob. "For God's sake, colonel," he pleaded, "do give the order to start the train, or you will never get out of the city, for they are already tearing up the track."[55]

Colonel Jones faced a tough choice. He could order the regiment to leave Baltimore, fixing the damaged rails along the way—with help from the railroad's workers—and arrive in Washington that afternoon. Doing that, however, meant leaving their band and the Pennsylvania Volunteers to fend for themselves. (He had no way of knowing what was happening back at the President Street station—that his band and the Pennsylvania men would be rescued, and that Baltimoreans would care for his wounded men.) Or he could order his soldiers to remain in Baltimore and try to rescue their band comrades, fighting the mob every step of the way, and hope that they could take a train to Washington—an unlikely event, given that the secessionists would have plenty of time to rip up the tracks headed southward from the station. The Massachusetts men would then have to flee Baltimore on foot, while carrying their wounded, and walk to Washington over unfamiliar countryside with only their weapons and the rations in their packs, harassed and fired on by infuriated secessionists along their line of march. Colonel Jones knew that Washington needed his men now, and ordered the regiment to depart from Baltimore.

The men of the Sixth Massachusetts got onto the train. Among them was a stowaway, the young Wardwell. The soldier named Parsons had helped Wardwell, giving the young man the less obtrusive window seat, letting him wear his overcoat, and giving him his cap so Wardwell could pull down it over his face, while he pretended to sleep. At 12:30 p.m., the train pulled out of the Camden Street station. Secessionists ran ahead of the train, pulling up rails and putting stones, logs, and toppled telegraph poles onto the tracks. The police chased after the mob on foot. Every time something was thrown on the tracks, the police removed it, while the Massachusetts men stood guard.[56]

Still, the mob seemed to be winning. "The train moved a short distance and stopped," recalled regiment chaplain John W. Hanson. "A rail had been removed; it was replaced, and the cars went on, stopped again, the tracks were repaired, and the train went on again, stopped again, and the conductor informed the colonel that it was impossible to proceed, that the regiment must disembark and *march* to Washington."[57] That suggestion brought Jones's wrath down upon the conductor. "We are ticketed through, and are going in these cars," he declared. "If you or the engineer cannot run the train, we have plenty of men who can. If you need protection or assistance, you shall have it; but we go through."[58]

The train started moving again, but the mob would not concede defeat. Following the train for more than a mile out of Baltimore, they continued to toss rocks and logs onto the tracks. And each time the track was cleared by the now exhausted police, the B & O work crews, or the Massachusetts volunteers themselves. Finally, at Jackson Bridge near Chinquapin Hill, the last mob members gave up their pursuit and returned to Baltimore.

Eight miles south of Baltimore, the train was forced to stop at Relay House, where the double track ended and single-track lines headed south to Washington or west to Harper's Ferry and beyond. Because both north- and southbound trains ran along the single-track lines, moving trains in both directions at once required careful coordination by telegraph. When two locomotives approached from opposite directions, the train with less priority was forced to turn onto a siding to let the other train pass by. Bottlenecks often occurred, particularly when a "special" or unscheduled train—like the one carrying the Sixth Massachusetts men—upset the carefully timed schedules. Although the Massachusetts men were traveling under the orders of the secretary of war, the station master forced them to stop and wait two hours for a train that had the right of way.[59] As they waited, sniper fire rang out from the forest, but no one was hit.[60] Around 3 p.m. the train moved forward again toward Washington and, finally, the men hoped, safety.

Shortly before, at 2 p.m., President Lincoln received an urgent telegram from Mayor Brown and Maryland's Governor Hicks, which was followed a half-hour later by the handwritten copy of the original, delivered by a messenger:

Mayor's Office, Baltimore, April 19.
    To His Excellency the President of the United States:

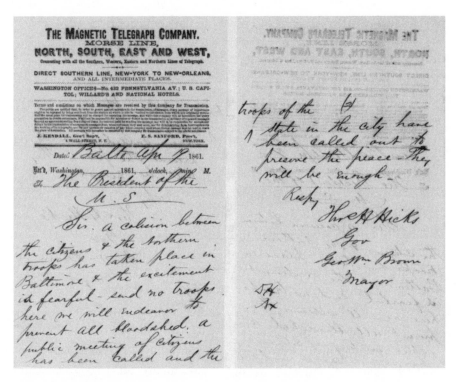

Baltimore Mayor George Brown's April 19 telegram to Lincoln, informing him of an attack on Union troops.

Sir:—A collision between the citizens & the northern troops has taken place in Baltimore, and the excitement is fearful. Send no troops here. We will endeavor to prevent all bloodshed.

A public meeting of citizens has been called, and the troops of the State and the city have been called out to preserve the peace. They will be enough.

Thos. H. Hicks
Gov
George Wm. Brown
Mayor[61]

The meaning of the message was immediately disputed at the White House. "Carefully scrutinized, this dispatch was found to be, like an ancient oracle, capable of a twofold meaning," according to Nicolay and Hay.[62] An edit to the original handwritten telegram text added to the confusion: the word "more" had clearly been blacked from the original line "Send no more troops here," to read "Send no troops here."[63] Lincoln believed that Brown and Hicks remained "loyal to the Constitution" and wished to communicate only that they had sufficient forces in Baltimore and "wanted no Washington troops to preserve order." General Scott and Secretary Seward took another view. "Usually so hopeful," they "thought they could read between the lines that it was desired no more troops should be passed through Baltimore."[64]

Shortly after the messenger arrived at the White House, Lincoln greeted two prominent Baltimore residents—a meeting that had been scheduled several days before. These two men feared that the North would demand retribution for the blood spilled in Baltimore. Lincoln assured them that the North would not seek retaliation, because, as he put it, "Our people are easily influenced by reason." Scott, however, was not conciliatory. He stated firmly that Hicks had no authority to block U.S. soldiers from passing through Baltimore and Maryland. Agreeing with Scott's opinion, Seward repeated: "No right."[65]

When Washingtonians learned late that afternoon of the Sixth Massachusetts Volunteers' impending arrival near 5 p.m., an excited crowd of men and women started gathering at the B & O Railroad station. Their arrival generated rounds of pro-Union men's cheers and women's fluttering of their handkerchiefs, as well as secessionists' boos, hisses, and shouts of pro-Southern slogans. How pro-Union Washingtonians viewed the men as they got off the train varied greatly. "I went to the Depot to see the arrival of the Mass. Regiment," wrote Horatio Taft in his diary that night. "They came at last, after fighting their way through Baltimore loosing [sic] two men killed and firing upon the rioters, killing a number. A splendid looking set of men."[66] To many Washingtonians, however, the newly arrived troops were hardly "splendid looking." Instead, they saw hundreds of exhausted and hungry men in dirty and ripped uniforms, many having suffered wounds from flying rocks or broken glass.

As the Massachusetts men gathered in front of the B & O station, a few men spotted a familiar face in the crowd, Clara Barton. "Miss Barton! Miss Barton!" they shouted; she had been their teacher five years earlier. Barton waved back at her former pupils. Once the Volunteers marched off to the Capitol, the crowd of Washingtonians started breaking up, and Barton and her sister, Sally Vassall, started for home, not failing to be moved by the sight of several dozen badly wounded Massachusetts men borne away on stretchers.[67]

Reports of the attack in Baltimore quickly echoed across the country, first in telegrams, then in newspapers' extra editions. The date of the attack resonated profoundly in the North. April 19, 1861 was the eighty-sixth anniversary of Lexington and Concord, the first battles of the Revolutionary War in 1775. Before the Sixth Massachusetts men left Boston, they had already deemed themselves the "Minute Men of '61," because they were the first regiment to respond to President Lincoln's proclamation for troops. After their baptism by fire at Baltimore, many Northerners adopted the "Minute Men of '61" nickname—which became all the more poignant when Northerners learned that many of the regiment's troops, including two of the dead men, were the grandsons of original Minute Men who had fought in the Revolutionary War. Writing in the notebook in which he summarized the key events of each day, Nicolay solemnly proclaimed: "Friday April 19th 1861 is likely to become historic in the nation's annals."[68] At the White House, Frontier Guard Clifford Arrick made a similar observation in his diary: "The anniversary of the 'Battle of Lexington' and the day of the 'Battle of Baltimore.'"[69]

Meanwhile that day, two Union regiments were staging in New York City for their departure to the capital. At 6:30 a.m. on April 19, the Eighth Massachusetts men arrived in New York at the East Twenty-Seventh Street railroad station. They ate complimentary breakfasts at several of New York's finest hotels, and then assembled for a jubilant parade down Broadway from Union Square to the railroad depot at the foot of Cortlandt Street, where they boarded a ferry across the Hudson River to catch the southbound train in Jersey City. Because these men had barely slept the previous two nights, they simply walked down Broadway rather than marching in formation. Nonetheless, cheering crowds lined the sidewalks, and onlookers ran out into the stream of men to give the volunteers needle-and-thread kits, pocket-size Bibles, food, and sometimes even money.[70]

For most New Yorkers, however, the Eighth Massachusetts's late morning parade down Broadway was only a prelude to the grand spectacle of the day: the dramatic send-off for the city's famed Seventh New York Regiment. Known as the National Guard, the Seventh New York was largely composed of elite young men from families of social prominence or business success. Their ranks included representatives of the city's long-standing Knickerbocker gentry, like the Schuylers and Verplancks, and newly rich families like the Tiffanys and Vanderbilts. Many of New York's better-known young artists and writers were members of the regiment, as well as accomplished professionals like Egbert Viele, chief engineer for the new Central Park in Manhattan and Prospect Park in Brooklyn. Other members of the regiment would soon achieve fame on the battlefield, the most celebrated of whom was Robert Gould Shaw, who later led the all-black Fifty-fourth Massachusetts Infantry.

The regiment was known for its precision drilling, band, and smart-looking gray caps and uniforms with black trim and highly polished white crossbelts. Yet the Seventh New York men were much more than well-born holiday soldiers. Since the regiment's formation in the early nineteenth century, its well-trained members had displayed their military prowess in helping New York authorities to suppress over a dozen dangerous disturbances such as the Astor Place riot of 1849 and the "Dead Rabbits" and municipal police riots of 1857.

At important civic celebrations, the Seventh New York played an important role in the city's welcome for famous visitors, including Presidents Andrew Jackson, John Tyler, and James K. Polk and foreign dignitaries like the Marquis de Lafayette in 1824 and Edward, Prince of Wales, in 1860, who congratulated the men as the "finest regiment I have ever seen in any country."[71] The Seventh New York often participated in other cities' major events. In 1860, the Seventh New York went to Washington, at the invitation of Congress, for the February 22 unveiling of Clark Mills's dramatic bronze equestrian statue of George Washington in the middle of Washington Circle. At the dedication, President Buchanan praised the Seventh New York men for their "military precision" and "stout, hardy, noble, and defiant look" and then concluded that "in the day and hour of battle you would not be mere parade soldiers, but that you would be in its very front."[72]

In 1858, the Seventh New York had won the praise of men who would soon draw arms against the Union. That year, the regiment had accompanied the remains of President James Monroe when they were removed from Manhattan's Marble Cemetery and taken for reburial in the Hollywood Cemetery in Richmond, Virginia, at the request of the Monroe family. After the reinterment, amid solemn pageantry, Governor Henry Wise had delivered a eulogy to Monroe in which he honored the Seventh New York as "the elite of her chivalry." Virginians and New Yorkers were "all *one*," he had said, just as all the states in the Union "are one."[73]

By midmorning on April 19, the streets around the Seventh's armory, on the east side of the Third Avenue between East Sixth and East Seventh streets, were jammed with carriages dropping off the men. While gathering in the armory's drill hall, some members of the regiment recalled the ball held in their honor the previous night, where women would dance with no one but the soldiers. Other men, understandably, talked about wives and families that they were leaving behind, and newspaper reporters recorded some of these conversations. One man had been married for only two days, but his wife had insisted that he must go to Washington with the regiment. Another man had been scheduled to be married two days later, on April 21, but he and his fiance had postponed the ceremony. "I may die a bachelor yet, you know," he told his friends. Two other members of the regiment couldn't wait and were hurriedly married to their fiances before leaving. A young woman had given her soon-to-depart sweetheart a bouquet with the banner "May peace soon bring you back to me."[74]

Shaw, who was living with his family in rural Staten Island at the time, did not have time to say goodbye to his family. "It is very hard for me to go off without bidding you goodbye," he wrote his mother, "and the only thing that upsets me, in the least, is the thought of how you will feel when you find me so unexpectedly gone. But I know, dearest Mother, that you wouldn't have me stay, when it is so clearly my duty to go." Shaw added: "Won't it be grand to meet the men from all the States, East and West, down there, ready to fight for the country, as the old fellows did in the Revolution?"[75]

At 4:30 p.m., the parade commenced as the Seventh New York men marched down East Fourth Street, drums beating and band playing, and turned south on Broadway to the roar of the crowd for the one-and-a-half-mile march through lower Manhattan. The crowd was so enormous that it filled Broadway ahead of the regiment's line of march. As the Seventh headed southward, the crowds pushed themselves back onto the already-jammed sidewalks, waited for the regiment to pass, and then flooded back into the middle of the streets again. Well-connected New York lawyer George Templeton Strong secured an excellent vantage point on the third or fourth floor of a building at Spring Street and Broadway. "After long waiting and watching," he wrote in his diary, "the Seventh Regiment appeared, far up Broadway—a bluish steel-gray light on the blackness of the dense mob that filled the street, like the livid ashiness of the clouds near the horizon just before the thundershower breaks."[76]

Broadway's white marble and brownstone buildings, where the city's most fashionable stores, hotels, and theaters were located, were draped in so much bunting that the men felt that they were walking through a red, white, and blue canyon. At the corner of Duane Street, several blocks north of City Hall, someone had hanged an effigy of Jefferson Davis with a placard that proclaimed: "Jeff. Davis as he will be. Jeff. Davis, Jeff Davis, beware of the day When the Seventh shall meet you in battle array."[77] The scene was a joyous pandemonium of cheering New Yorkers, pealing church bells, and fire engines placed at many street corners, ringing their own bells as well. The regiment's band and drummers were drowned out by the noise.[78]

Some of the soldiers did sense an ominous foreboding. Writer Theodore Winthrop, a member of the Seventh New York who described the parade in his June 1861 *Atlantic Monthly* article "Our March to Washington"—published after his death in battle—felt that the "throng" was "taking the measure of my coffin."[79] Still, Winthrop was moved by the pageantry and display. Women were expected not to cheer in polite society, but they could wave their handkerchiefs to show their enthusiasm: "Handkerchiefs, of course, came floating down upon us from the windows, like a snow," he wrote.[80]

Once the overcrowded ferry carrying the Seventh New York men cast off from Manhattan's waterfront for Jersey City, crowds cheered from the docks on both sides of the Hudson River. The ships in the harbor rang their bells and steam whistles. The regiment's band responded with "The Star Spangled Banner" and "The Girl I Left Behind Me." By now it was early evening, and the sun glanced from the windows of the nearby buildings, with the clouds above aglow.

As the ferry neared the Jersey City waterfront, the chief of police arrived with 40 men to hold back the surging crowds, so that the Seventh New York men could disembark from the boat and board their train, which had 20 passenger cars. Once the train headed southward, it stopped briefly at major stations, and a familiar scene repeated itself; bonfires and fireworks lit the nighttime sky, crowds cheered, and the local bands played military songs. Men and some women rushed forward to hand boxes and baskets of food and drink through the open windows. Fitz-James O'Brien, a young writer and member of the regiment, described the journey: "All along the track through New Jersey, shouting crowds, hoarse and valorous, sent to the troops as they passed, their hopes and wishes." At each torch-lit station stop, "rough hands came in through the windows, as if detached and isolated, until they were grasped by those within; and the subtle magnetic thrill told that there were bold hearts beating at the end."[81]

Baltimore failed to calm down after the Sixth Massachusetts departed town. Violence lasted throughout the day, and parts of town slid toward anarchy. Mobs armed with looted weapons patrolled the city, and a number of streets were barricaded, as the rioters hunted down Union sympathizers and ordered them to leave town.

Nobody was safe from the violence. In the afternoon, social reformer Dorothea Dix of Boston, who was well known for working to improve conditions in the nation's mental hospitals, traveled through Baltimore on her way to Washington to offer her services in setting up a hospital for wounded soldiers. As Dix was driven in a carriage from the President Street station to the Camden Street station to board her Washington-bound train, a paving stone shattered one of the windows and narrowly missed her.[82] Dix, however, would not let a paving stone—or even a bloody riot—stand in the way of her mission. "Yesterday, I followed in the train three hours after the tumult in Baltimore," she wrote her friend Anne Heath the next day from Washington. "It was not easy getting across the city, but I did not choose to turn back."[83] Dix managed to catch the last train allowed out of Baltimore that day and arrived in Washington that evening.[84]

In the wake of the attack on the Sixth Massachusetts Volunteers, Baltimore authorities attempted to regain control of the city, in part by voicing outrage over the passage of Union troops through it. Mayor Brown and Governor Hicks issued a call for a citywide meeting in the wake of the riot, and thousands of residents assembled in Monument Square at 4 p.m. Brown told the crowd that he and Governor Hicks had "telegraphed to Washington and to the North" that they were to allow no more Union soldiers to pass through Maryland, and that he "looked to men of all parties" to "forget all differences and act as brothers."[85] Brown suggested that Maryland would be better off leaving the Union without violence from either party: "If the North cannot live with the South, let us part in peace."[86] Speaking to the crowd after Brown, Governor Hicks declared that he agreed with Brown's remarks and made clear where his allegiance lay. "I am a Marylander; I love my State and I love the Union, but I will suffer my right arm to be torn from my body before I will raise it to strike a sister State."[87]

To diminish the risk of violence in Baltimore, Brown and Hicks had already transferred the command of existing state militias to Baltimore's Board of Police, headed by Kane. The *Baltimore American* explained that the "police were very much exhausted by the severe labors of the last few days, during which the whole force has been on duty almost continuously."[88] At 2 p.m., only an hour and a half after the Sixth Massachusetts men had left for Washington, Major General George H. Steuart, a member of a prominent Baltimore family and the commander of the First Light Division of the Maryland Volunteers, had ordered his unit to "parade forthwith in North Calvert Street, provided with ball cartridge, to suppress the insurrection and riot going on in the streets of this city, and to preserve good order and quiet."[89] At 5 p.m., as the rally wound to a close, these troops gathered in Monument Square, and the city's equilibrium shifted toward calm.

Baltimore's business and civic leaders were frightened about the potential for greater mob violence in coming days. Even the ardent secessionists among the elite who backed attacks on Northern troops knew that an uncontrolled uprising would damage valuable business properties, harm the local economy at a time of high unemployment, and reaffirm Baltimore's unsavory reputation as the "Mob City." Police Chief Kane was no exception. His sympathies were unequivocally for the Confederacy, but he was also a successful grain and grocery merchant who had run for election as chief of police in 1860 as a reformer who would make the department more effective and tame the recurring mob violence. Despite his political beliefs, Kane appears not to have colluded with plotters before the attack on the Sixth Massachusetts Volunteers, and Baltimore newspapers described Kane and his police as maintaining order around the tumultuous secessionist meetings in the days leading up to April 19.[90]

After the day's riots, which had left several dozen Baltimore men dead or wounded, Kane and most of the pro-Southern Baltimore leaders felt they could no longer tolerate Union troops entering their city, even if only in transit to Washington. Equally important, however, was their desire to prevent mobs—who were not under their control—from attacking Northern troops, and they instead chose to mobilize forces to defend the city who would be under their command. That evening, Kane sent a telegram to militia leader Bradley T. Johnson of Frederick, Maryland, in response to Bradley's offer to provide militiamen for Baltimore. Kane wrote: "Bring your men by the first train, and we will arrange with the railroad afterwards. Streets red with Maryland blood. Send expresses over the mountains of Maryland and Virginia for the rifleman to come without delay. Fresh hordes will be down upon us to-morrow. We will fight them and whip them, or die."[91]

Johnson printed the telegram on handbills and distributed them throughout Frederick, asking the militia to join him on a train to Baltimore on April

20 and to bring their own arms. "Double-barreled shotguns and buck shot are efficient."[92]

As Baltimore authorities strengthened the city's defenses, Mayor Brown and Governor Hicks, meanwhile, attempted to prevent any more Northern troops from traveling through Baltimore. That afternoon, they had written to B & O Railroad president Garnett: "We advise that the troops now here be sent back to the borders of Maryland."[93] Agreeing to this request—really an order—Garnett cabled back: "Most cordially approving the advice, I have instructed by telegraph the same to the Philadelphia, Wilmington and Baltimore Railroad Co., and this company will act in accordance therewith."

That evening, Mayor Brown sent a delegation of three prominent citizens to Washington by a special train to see President Lincoln. In the accompanying letter to Lincoln, Brown provided his own report on what had happened that day in Baltimore and offered his advice.

> Sir: This will be presented to you by the Hon. Hugh Lenox Bond, George W. Dobbin and John C. Brune, esqs., who will proceed to Washington by an express train, at my request, in order to explain fully the fearful condition of our affairs in this city. The people are exasperated to the highest degree by the passage of troops, and the citizens are universally decided in the opinion that no more troops should be ordered to come.
>
> The authorities of the city did their best to-day to protect both strangers and citizens, and to prevent a collision, but in vain; and but for their great efforts a fearful slaughter would have occurred.
>
> Under these circumstances, it is my solemn duly to inform you that it is not possible for more soldiers to pass through Baltimore, unless they fight their way at every step.
>
> I therefore hope and trust, and most earnestly request, that no more troops be permitted or ordered by the Government to pass through the city. If they should attempt it, the responsibility for the bloodshed will not rest upon me.[94]

Governor Hicks added his own brief note personal note for President Lincoln to Brown's correspondence: "I have been in Baltimore since Tuesday evening, and co-operated with Mayor Brown in his untiring efforts to allay and prevent the excitement and suppress the fearful outbreak as indicated above, and I fully concur in all that is said by him in the above communication."[95]

Several hours after agreeing to Brown's and Hicks's demand to permit no more troops on their rail line, the officials of the Philadelphia, Wilmington and Baltimore Railroad, backtracked, having realized the "suicidal nature of such refusal," in Nicolay and Hay's description. The railroad officials cabled Secretary Cameron: "We are informed here that the troops sent last night have been stopped at Baltimore, and that it is impracticable to send more through that city. Shall we send them by steamer to Annapolis?"[96]

That evening, Lincoln, Scott, and the rest of the cabinet "fully debated" how to respond to the railroad officials and then directed the War Department to answer "in cipher" to Philadelphia that "Governor Hicks has neither right nor authority to stop troops coming to Washington. Send them on prepared to fight their way through, if necessary."[97]

Meanwhile, secessionists in communities surrounding Washington attempted to block rail access to Washington. The mayor of Charlestown, Virginia, just west of Harper's Ferry, dispatched a messenger on April 19 to the B & O offices in Baltimore, insisting that no Union troops "should be permitted to pass over the main stem" of the railroad headed to the Middle West.[98] If the railroad did not comply, he added, its 1,000-foot-long bridge over the Potomac River at Harper's Ferry would be destroyed, thereby cutting rail connections to Pennsylvania, Ohio, and points west. The *Philadelphia Inquirer* reported that "numerous farmers on the route" of the B & O Railroad had threatened to burn bridges along the line within Maryland "if any troops were allowed to pass over the road."[99]

That night, to secure the rail lines against attack, General Scott issued General Order No. 3, which extended the Military Department of Washington outside of the boundaries of the District of Columbia to include Maryland, Delaware, and Pennsylvania. Scott placed Major-General Robert Patterson, head of the Pennsylvania Militia, in command, with the orders that he would "as fast as they are mustered into service, post the volunteers of Pennsylvania all along the road" from Wilmington to Washington, to "give a reasonable protection to the lines of parallel wires, to the road, its rails, bridges, cars, and stations."[100]

Later that evening, General Scott telegraphed Patterson to see how quickly he could field men to comply with the order.[101] A frustrated Patterson replied that he was "intensely anxious to be with and support you" but that a "very large proportion" of his men were "without muskets, all are without ammunition, service clothing, greatcoats, blankets, knapsacks, haversacks, canteens, &c." Patterson emphasized the painful irony of the situation: "It seems very strange that the people of the South seize the Government property to carry on rebellion, and the men of the North cannot get it to defend the flag of the Union." He concluded that the "law of necessity" required him to wait until his men were properly equipped with "arms, ammunition, clothing, and equipments," paid for if necessary by the state of Pennsylvania. Once that was accomplished, Patterson wrote, "I can have 5,000 men in Washington in five days." In the meantime, the rail lines would remain unguarded by Northern troops and open to sabotage.[102]

Until more men could reach Washington, moreover, the city's security would have to rely on the improvised defenses already in place. Late the night of April 19 and until early the next morning, the *New York Herald's* Washington correspondent patrolled the city, "carbine in hand," with the several dozen members of the Clay Battalion as the men made their rounds of the city.[103] These volunteer troops first visited the Capitol, pausing to be cleared by the sentries. Next to them, "two ladies, escorted by a gentleman, who were understood to be volunteer nurses for the members of the Massachusetts regiment wounded at Baltimore, applied for admittance, though it was then past midnight."[104] The two ladies were Clara Barton and her sister, who had come to visit the soldiers and find out what they needed in terms of food and medical care. The gentleman was a friend who accompanied the two women as a matter of social etiquette and for protection in the dangerous city.

As several members of the Clay Battalion patrol waited to be admitted to the Capitol, they had time to survey the fortifications there, which were "mainly composed of barrels of cement placed endwise, and piled up ten feet high between the immense marble piers and columns that form the various entrances of the building."[105] On entering the building, Clay's men entered the Senate chamber, where they found the "tired and sleeping" men of the Sixth Massachusetts, who were "exhausted by . . . sleepless nights of travel" and "had thrown themselves down to sleep the moment they reached the building." The First Pennsylvania troops, who had arrived the day before, and a company of the U.S. Artillery patrolled the grand hallways: "Alertness and discipline seemed to prevail at every point." Also on alert, the *New York*

Herald's correspondent wryly wrote, were America's elder statesmen, in portraits: "from the walls looked down upon them the counterfeit presentments
[i.e. their painted, not their actual, presences] of the heroes of an earlier age of
the republic, who little dreamed that their countrymen should behold a scene
like this."[106]

On leaving the Capitol, the members of the Clay Battalion returned to
Willard's Hotel, where they "found some hundreds of our comrades under
arms, enjoying, as we arrived, their rations of coffee and biscuit." Earlier
that night at Willard's, 15 piles of fuel had been found strategically placed
throughout the building, with fuses attached and ready to be lit.[107] The
foiling of the plot was a sign that few places in the capital were truly
secure.

Still, for his part, the *Herald* reporter was confident that Washington could
be defended that night with available means: "We maintain our guard till
morning, but all fear of a sudden dash of marauding thieves upon the capital
tonight is dismissed from our minds." He believed that Washington was
"protected in every direction" and that with the arrival of the Massachusetts
soldiers, there were "ample troops now here to protect the city against any
possible attack which can be made upon it by any forces the enemy can
immediately concentrate."[108]

"About midnight," recorded John Hay in his diary, Major David Hunter
and Senator James Lane's Frontier Guard were "quietly asleep on the floor of
the East Room and young careless guards loafed around the furnace fires in
the basement." The scene of the young men clearly moved Hay. "Good looking and energetic young fellows, too good to be food for gunpowder."[109]

At 1 a.m., the three-man Baltimore delegation dispatched by Mayor
Brown and Governor Hicks arrived at the White House with their message for Lincoln. A White House guard awoke Nicolay, who decided to get
up and take the message to the War Department rather than disturb Lincoln's sleep. There, Nicolay found Secretary Cameron, who was sleeping in
his office and "who was not disposed to listen to such a proposition, and
went to sleep again." The chief clerk at the War Department informed him
that no troops would reach Baltimore before 8 a.m. the next day, at which
time, Nicolay told the three men, the president could meet with them.[110]

That night, many Washingtonians again expected an attack on the city.
After the bloody riot against the Sixth Massachusetts Volunteers in Baltimore that day, residents realized that Washington faced danger on two

fronts: from Maryland to the North, as well as from Virginia to the South. In his letter to Therena Bates late that night, Nicolay wrote: "We are expecting more troops here by way of Baltimore, but are also fearful that the Secessionists may . . . cut off all communication" by severing the telegraph and mail conduits into the city. Then, he admitted his fear of a coordinated assault. "We have rumors that 1,500 men are gathered and under arms at Alexandria seven miles below here, supposed to have hostile intentions against this city," he wrote Therena, "and an additional report that a vessel was late this evening seen landing men on the Maryland side of the river." In sum, "all these things indicate that if we are to be attacked at all soon, it will happen tonight."[111]

Lest he alarm his fiancée, Nicolay added, "I do not think any force could be brought against the city to-night, which our men could not easily repel." Washington had "four to five thousand men under arms" and a "very vigilant watch out in the probable directions of approach." More important, Nicolay believed that there would be "enough troops here by to-morrow evening to render the city very safe." Unless, that is, they were "obstructed somewhere on the way."[112]

Saturday, April 20

"Lincoln is in a Trap"

At 8 a.m., General Scott's carriage entered the White House gates and stopped under the main portico. Scott's gout, recalled Nicolay and Hay, made it "painful for him to mount the stairs to the second-floor executive office," so Lincoln planned to meet Scott outside "to save him this exertion."[1] As Lincoln descended the grand staircase, he found the three-man Baltimore delegation Nicolay had turned away from the White House late the previous night. Lincoln quickly read the letter they bore from Baltimore's Mayor Brown and Maryland's Governor Hicks informing him that it was "not possible" for more Union soldiers to pass through Baltimore, unless the president was willing to bear "responsibility for the bloodshed" that would inevitably occur.[2]

Lincoln directed the Baltimoreans outside to Scott's waiting carriage, where "they eloquently portrayed the danger—nay, the impossibility—of bringing soldiers through Baltimore," according to Nicolay and Hay. The previous day, the War Department had telegrammed to Philadelphia, Wilmington & Baltimore Railroad president Samuel Felton in Philadelphia to send troops through Baltimore and "to fight their way through, if necessary."[3] Now Scott took a more pragmatic stance. Looking "solely to the urgency of getting troops to the capital, and perceiving no advantage" to fighting a battle in Baltimore, Scott declared, "March them around."[4]

As Scott's carriage drove away, Lincoln led the Baltimore delegation upstairs to his office, where he composed a response for the men to deliver to Governor Hicks and Mayor Brown.[5] Lincoln wrote, "For the future troops must be brought here, but I make no point of bringing them through Baltimore." In the letter, he repeated Scott's agreement that Union troops would "march around Baltimore, and not through it" and noted that he hoped Brown and Hicks "will consider this practical and proper." In this manner, a "collision of the people of Baltimore with the troops" would be avoided—that is, "unless they go out of their way to seek it."[6] As Lincoln quickly drafted the letter, he quipped to the delegation, standing around him, "If I grant you this concession, that no troops shall pass through the city, you will be back here to-morrow demanding that none shall be marched around it."[7]

Following this meeting, news reached the White House that the critical bridges on the rail lines to the north and west of Baltimore had been destroyed hours before. On April 18, two days before, Scott had warned that if rail communication were broken at Baltimore, in "ten days, Washington would be in a state of starvation and be likely to fall into the hands of the secessionists."[8] Now, Washington's railroad connection to the North was severed.

Mayor Brown, Governor Hicks, and Police Chief Kane had approved the destruction of the rail lines at a meeting late the previous night, ostensibly as a measure to avoid further civil unrest by preventing more Union troops from entering Baltimore.[9] "The point was pressed" by Baltimore authorities that "if troops were suddenly to come to Baltimore with a determination to pass through, a terrible collision and bloodshed would take place, and the consequences to Baltimore would be fearful," Brown asserted two weeks later in a report on the events of April.[10] All the attendees agreed to order the destruction of rail lines and bridges north of the city, including Hicks, who later denied that he had given his assent. Unlike the attack on the Sixth Massachusetts, this decision was officially sanctioned.

In the early morning hours of April 20, armed groups left Baltimore to sever the two rail lines leading north from the city. One was headed by Kane and the other by Colonel Isaac R. Trimble, a ranking Baltimore militiaman. The group led by Kane cut the Northern Central Railroad line to Harrisburg by burning three bridges near Baltimore.[11] Meanwhile, Trimble's destruction of bridges along the Philadelphia, Wilmington & Baltimore line was carried out with precision, involving two fire department companies and 40 men wielding axes. Early in the morning, Trimble and his men hijacked a south-bound passenger train. Holding the engineer at gunpoint, they forced him to reverse the train north to Gunpowder Bridge, 25 miles from Baltimore, where Trimble's men set fire to the 40-foot drawbridge and also scuttled a ferryboat. They then piloted the train back south, burning the drawbridge sections of the Bush River Bridge and Canton Bridge, before arriving back at the President Street station in Baltimore before dawn.[12]

With both the Northern Central Railroad and the Philadelphia, Wilmington & Baltimore Railroad lines severed, Washington lost rail service and mail deliveries to and from points north of Baltimore. Equally momentous, Kane and Trimble's men had cut many northbound telegraph lines that ran along the railroad tracks and pulled the telegraph poles from the ground, so that the lines could not be easily repaired. In Washington, telegraph connections to the North were now sporadic, and important messages were no longer getting through in either direction.

There were ominous signs that secessionist militias planned to attack any Union troops that tried to pass into Maryland. A passenger on a train on the Philadelphia, Wilmington & Baltimore line that was forced to turn around jumped from the train and continued his journey on foot toward Baltimore. At the first downed bridge along the line, he found, according to an account in the *Brooklyn Eagle*, "a party of men with a cannon, with which they said they intended to kill off the New York Regiment."[13]

As news of the Baltimore riot swept Washington on the evening of April 19 and morning of April 20, fear seized many residents, who took flight by the hundreds. Edwin Stanton conveyed the full weight of the shock in a letter to former President James Buchanan: "No description could convey to you the panic that prevailed here for several days after the Baltimore riot." The only response on the part of many residents, he continued, was flight: "Almost every family packed up their effects. Women and children were sent away in great numbers. Provisions advanced to famine prices." Stanton recorded his own reaction to news of the Baltimore riot. "Before long this city is doomed to be the scene of battle and carnage."[14]

An expected secessionist attack was only one reason for the exodus from Washington. Many residents were frightened by the precipitous decline in the federal government's authority, as made plain by the events of recent days. Why had it been unable to prevent the attack on the Sixth Massachusetts and keep Baltimore secessionists from destroying the key rail routes to the city? Other residents were exhausted from the emotional whipsaw of rumors whose import changed hourly, and which became more frightening as the likelihood of an attack appeared to mount. When men started drilling holes at the Treasury to reinforce its entrances, for example, it spawned the rumor that the government was planning to blow up the building if Confederates crossed the Potomac.

On April 20, as Lucius Chittenden recorded, Washington was "again alive with excitement" as it was now "certain this morning that all railroad communication with the north" was "cut off." In sum, he fretted, "Washington seems to be isolated."[15] In his diary, Horatio Taft made similar observations. "Bridges destroyed, track torn up and the Steam Ferry Boat over the Susquehannah scuttled and sunk. Balt in the hands of the mob." He then stated the painfully obvious: "A critical time for Washington."[16]

Depending on their sympathies, Washington residents made their escapes in different directions. Pro-Union families attempted to reach Philadelphia, the first large loyal Union city, and a railroad hub for reaching the North and Midwest. Some men had already sent their families north and stayed in Washington to serve at their jobs, as Secretary Cameron had done the previous day. Others did not want to be separated from their families or, fearing that their names might be on a Confederate arrest list, fled themselves.

By April 20, however, most refugees bound for the North could not get beyond Baltimore since the rail lines to Philadelphia had been severed. To travel beyond, they could take a roundabout route from Relay House on the B & O line west to Wheeling, Virginia, where they could board a train back east through Pennsylvania to Philadelphia, and then on to New York and New England. Or they could try to hire a wagon or carriage to carry them directly north from Baltimore and pay a panic-high price. When one family who had fled Washington could not get to Philadelphia by rail, the father hired a wagon to take them to Chambersburg, Pennsylvania, 85 miles northwest of Baltimore. The cost was $60. (By comparison, a large fashionable house in Washington rented for $100 a month.)[17]

On April 20, the preferred route south from Washington—a 35-mile steamer journey from the Sixth Street Wharf down the Potomac to Aquia Creek and the terminus of the Richmond and Potomac Railroad—was also cut off, but in this case by Union hands.[18] The previous day, the U.S. government had begun seizing all Potomac steamers, even the tour boats for Mount Vernon. Southerners instead would have to take a circuitous 113-mile rail route to Richmond. From Alexandria, they boarded the Orange and Alexandria Railroad, which traveled southwest to Gordonsville, Virginia, where they would then travel on the Virginia Central Railroad southeast to Richmond and beyond. These two railroads, with only a single set of tracks to serve both directions, were ill-equipped to handle the surge of passengers on April 20 and for the next few days. The crush became so intense that the railroad all but broke down. Former U.S. Army quartermaster general Joseph E. Johnston and his wife, Lydia, left Alexandria for Richmond on April 23 but did not arrive until a full two days later.[19]

The impulse for flight sometimes outweighed reason. On April 21, Lucius Chittenden was walking up Pennsylvania Avenue when he was nearly pushed into the roadway by a man "with his head bowed down, [who] was rushing madly forwards, apparently desirous of avoiding observation." Chittenden recognized the man as James Wynne, a Virginia-born author who had been living in New York. "He would not recognize me at first," Chittenden recalled, "but on my insisting, he assumed a position of entreaty and exclaimed, 'Hush! Hush! I must not be known. For God's sake, tell me how I can get across the river.' . . . I thought that he had gone crazy, but he proved to be only excited," continued Chittenden. "I invited him, and, after much persuasion, induced him, to go to my rooms. But he insisted that he was pursued—that his life was in danger, and he should not be safe until he could reach Virginia." Chittenden secured a pass for Wynne across the heavily guarded Long Bridge.[20]

Even as panic mounted, Washington was in fact better protected than it had been in recent days because of the arrival of the Sixth Massachusetts Volunteers early the evening before. Shortly after dawn, the men—and the young Baltimorean Ernest Wardwell—were awakened by the fife-and-drum reveille in the Senate chamber. Minutes later, the men assembled for roll call, but, as Wardwell later recalled, he "remained sitting on the folded blanket [on the floor], and watched with keen interest how the men as each one had his named called answered 'here' and came from the position of 'support' to one of 'order' arms."[21] Breakfast was a repeat of dinner: hard bread, cold beef, and a cup of coffee. Enviously, Wardwell "noticed that many of the men had chicken, cake and other delicacies which I was informed was not part of the army rations, but food that the men had brought with them from home."[22]

Nearly all the Massachusetts men were eager to explore Washington during their periodic leave times to visit landmarks that they had only seen as engravings. At mid-afternoon that day, "Private Parsons had two hours [leave of] absence," according to Wardwell, "and we made the most of it by visiting many places of interest." Wardwell did not record what they saw, but as nearly every out-of-town visitor invariably did, they would have traveled to the White House to see the constant flow of visitors. Next to the White House, they would have admired the Treasury, the most impressive building in Washington after the Capitol. If they were fortunate, they were allowed to step inside the sandbagged entrance to see its marble hallways and decorative frescoes.

Heading back toward the Capitol, Parsons and Wardwell—like so many visitors—would have walked along the north side of Pennsylvania Avenue, which was lined by Washington's finest hotels, restaurants, and shops. The street was the city's only real promenade, though the roadway was poorly paved, dusty in dry weather, and muddy after rains. Most residents and visitors avoided the avenue's south side, whose ramshackle buildings housed cheap boardinghouses, saloons, inexpensive restaurants, brothels, the essential Center Market, and the Murder Bay slum, one block behind the Avenue between Thirteenth and Fifteenth streets.[23]

At Eighth Street, Parsons and Wardwell could have turned left and walked three blocks north from Pennsylvania Avenue to the Patent Office building. The favorite destination of most visitors was the third-floor galleries, where models of recent inventions were displayed in glass cases, including mundane but essential items like fire escapes, water closets, and "vermin and rat traps."[24] Many people, however, overlooked the greatest treasure on display: the original Declaration of Independence, which was framed and hung on one wall, where years of sunlight had bleached the document into its now nearly unreadable condition. Surprisingly, some nineteenth-century observers mocked this national icon. *United States* magazine described it as "that old looking paper with the fading ink,"[25] while guidebooks dismissed it as "old and yellow."[26]

Before reaching the Capitol, Parsons and Wardwell might have stopped at a small, inexpensive restaurant near B Street, today's Constitution Avenue but in 1861 the foul-smelling City Canal, filled with garbage and the carcasses of horses, pigs, and cows. At this modest establishment, little more than a shack, which became a favorite of soldiers bored with army rations, a plump and gregarious German woman known only as Julia served fried oysters, soup, pies, beef, and gin drinks.[27]

After an early dinner at the Capitol that night, Parsons told Wardwell that they would locate the regiment's Company F to "see if we can find out anything about your folks," for Parsons had learned that Wardwell's

Massachusetts-born father had grown up in the same town as many of the Sixth Massachusetts Volunteers. On reaching Company F in a corner of the Senate chamber, Parsons found Corporal Jim Troy and introduced Wardwell as the "little rebel." When Corporal Troy asked his fellow Company F members if anybody knew Wardwell's family, half the company answered in the affirmative. A small crowd gathered around Wardwell.

"Is Willard your father?" asked a Private Frank Sanborn. When Wardwell said that he was, Sanborn replied, "Parsons, I want this lad. I will look out for him and take him to his folks—they are all friends of mine."[28] Captain Melvin Beal, who commanded Company F, "greeted me with a hearty welcome," according to Wardwell, and ordered the men to find him a uniform. "I was rigged out complete, and wore on my shirtfront a big gold '6'—of which I was a[s] proud as though it were a 'Victoria Cross.'" He recalled that the "men made much of me, and took turns in teaching me the drill," noting that he marched "quite creditably as a new recruit."[29] Wardwell had found his calling and soon enlisted in the U.S. Army; he left the service as a captain in 1865.[30]

Colonel Robert E. Lee submitted his formal resignation to the U.S. Army on April 20. His letter to Secretary Cameron read in its entirety: "Sir, I have the honor to tender the resignation of my commission as Colonel of the 1st Regt. of Cavalry."[31] Lee's resignation, scarcely noted in the Northern press, gained immediate attention across the Confederacy because of Lee's prominence in the U.S. Army. Many had been expected Lee to become commander in chief of the U.S. Army after General Scott's retirement; now, in a stunning military coup for the South, Lee instead had decided to leave Washington to lead the Virginia military that many thought was ready to march on the capital. In New York on April 20, Major Robert Anderson ate dinner with George Templeton Strong and his wife, Ellen, at her father's mansion on Union Square. "Anderson tells Ellie we must not underrate the rebel army," Strong wrote in his diary later that evening. Then, Strong—who had no knowledge of Lee's resignation earlier that day—made a prophetic statement: "Should Providence send them a great general, woe to the North!"[32]

In his haste to leave Washington for Richmond, Lee left an unpaid balance of 37 cents for repair of his saddle bags at the Lutz leather goods shop at 392 Pennsylvania Avenue NW. For years after the war, Lutz would tell customers that Robert E. Lee had not paid his bills and could show them his ledger to prove it.[33] Lee's family, however, was dogged in attempting to secure his full army pay right up to his last day of service. "The officers of the army and navy, who resigned to take service with the Confederacy," recalled Lucius Chittenden, "secured an arrangement with their departments by which they were paid, to the date of their resignations, by treasury-warrants."[34] It was "General [Francis E.] Spinner, the treasurer," continued Chittenden, "who suggested that, as these gentlemen were going South, we should pay them by drafts on the stolen assistant-treasuries in the seceded states."

On April 20, the last day of the six-day workweek for some at the Treasury, one of Chittenden's colleagues brought him a warrant made out to a member of Lee's family for signature. "I marked it, 'Pay by draft on Richmond,' as there was more government money there than in the treasury at Washington," Chittenden recalled. "My innocent note made trouble." Several of Lee's friends called on Chittenden to complain that he was doing Lee and his family "great injustice; that they were all loyal; that he resigned because he could not fight his native state—but he would never fight against the Union."[35] Chittenden soon became annoyed by the repeated requests on Lee's behalf. The amount due to Lee—the unpaid portion of his salary of $194 a month— was a trivial sum for a man who lived in one of northern Virginia's grandest homes and owned dozens of slaves, some of whom he leased to other plantations. "I was inflexible," Chittenden remembered. "I would not change the order except upon the written pledge of the offer [Lee] not to enter the Confederate service."[36]

That day another resignation did *not* take place—General Scott's. Shortly after Scott received Lee's personal letter detailing the reasons for his resignation, he was surprised to see his longtime friend Judge John Robertson of Virginia walk into his War Department office, accompanied by several other men. This delegation, appointed by the Virginia Secession Convention, offered the Virginia-born Scott both money and command of the Virginia militia. This purpose of this offer was less to gain Scott's services and more to remove him from his command of Washington's defense, as well as to deliver the Confederacy the propaganda coup of engineering the defection of the U.S. Army's longest-serving general.[37]

Before Robertson could make the full offer, Scott raised his hand. "Friend Robertson, go no farther," he said. "It is best that we part here before you compel me to resent a mortal insult." Once the delegation was out on the street, Judge Robertson spotted longtime acquaintance Senator Stephen A.

Douglas of Illinois and told him that while Scott had been polite, he had expressed his decision quite forcefully, saying, "I have served my country under the flag of the Union for more than fifty years, and as long as God permits me to live, I will defend that flag with my sword, even if my own native State assails it."[38]

Even before Scott was offered the command, Virginians in Washington had spread the rumor that he would return to his home state and serve the Confederacy. The day before the Virginia delegation came to Scott's office, a telegram sent to New Orleans announced Scott's resignation from the Union army. "The intelligence being fully credited occasioned general rejoicing," according to later newspaper reports, "and in compliance with an order of Gov Moore, a 'royal salute' of twenty-one guns was fired in compliment to the old hero."[39] When Scott learned about this, he sent telegrams to prominent friends. To Senator John J. Crittenden, who worked to keep Kentucky in the Union, Scott wrote, "I have not changed, I have not thought of changing. Always a Union man."[40]

By now, Scott was holed up in his office at the Army headquarters in the Winder Building almost every hour of the day and night. A newspaper correspondent visited Scott in his office at midnight and found the elderly general sitting up in a plain bed in a plain room. Two candles sat on a nearby table, and two aides were taking down his orders "as dispatches constantly arrived by messenger."[41]

Scott maintained long hours that would have tired a younger officer, and still performed his duties with an obvious sense of satisfaction and his customary precision amid the turmoil. Visiting General Scott at his office that week, Secretary of State Seward found him "placid as a summer morning, and renewing the military activity of his youth in the bustle of giving orders and receiving reports."[42] Scott's success, of course, depended on officers who were dedicated to both him and the Union, including his chief of staff, Edward Townsend, and aides-de-camp including Henry Van Rensselaer, E. D. Keyes, and H. G. Wright.

In his April 20 dispatch to Lincoln, written earlier that day, before the reporter's visit, Scott had complained about the lack of funds to secure Washington. "Several smart & trusty men offer to visit the principal towns in Virginia & Maryland to collect & report on matters important to the defense of this Capital," he wrote, but he could not employ them for such intelligence work—useful as it would have been—for he was "without funds applicable to this use."[43] Money was so tight that Secretary Cameron did not want to accept volunteer regiments unless they were fully clothed, armed, and provisioned. Of course, the War Department recognized that Washington badly needed volunteers, outfitted or not, so a stopgap policy was put into practice. If a state sent unequipped volunteers, the War Department would send a bill for any needed arms and uniforms that it provided. The lack of appropriations nevertheless forced some offers of aid to be rejected.

The Twelfth New York Volunteers—who were ready and equipped to depart for Washington—almost did not receive approval to set off for the capital because of another endemic problem at the cabinet departments: the crowds of men without appointments still crowding government offices, who prevented officials from focusing on their work and hampering those with legitimate business from reaching the necessary authorities. "[E]xcited crowds thronged the streets and buzzed in the Departments," recalled Frederick Seward, assistant secretary of state.[44] "My room at the State Department was filled with visitors, officials on business, members of Congress with their protégés, who wanted offices, consulates, clerkships, claims or commissions, reporters who came to get news, or to bring it, and loungers and rumour-mongers who appear at such times like birds of ill-omen."

This morning, Seward spotted Daniel Butterfield, a classmate from Union College and now a successful New York businessman, in the throng at his office. "Why Dan, where did you come from?" Seward asked his friend. "And what are you doing here?"[45] As colonel of the Twelfth New York Volunteers, Butterfield had gone to the War Department to gain permission to bring his regiment to Washington, "to defend the capital," he told Seward. "I supposed troops were wanted." Now, however, Butterfield was heading home. He had waited at the War Department all day, but been unable to "get a hearing" for his offer of 1,000 men. "The halls and rooms are crowded," he informed Seward. "The doorkeepers say they are not allowed to take any more names, or cards, to the Secretary of War."

Seward was just the man to get Butterfield an immediate appointment with Secretary Cameron, and they hurried over to the nearby War Department. Within minutes, they entered Cameron's office, where they found him "surrounded by an eager crowd, the foremost of whom seemed to be haranguing him on the merits of something he wanted to sell to the

Government."[46] In response to Butterfield's offer, Cameron wanted to know if the regiment was "armed or equipped or clothed." When Butterfield said that it was, Cameron replied, "Well, Colonel, your regiment will be very welcome. You will have your orders at once." Later that day, the War Department sent the necessary orders to General Charles Sandford in New York, and the Twelfth New York Volunteers set out for Washington the following morning.

That afternoon, two members of the Maryland congressional delegation, Senator Anthony Kennedy and Representative J. Morrison Harris, both Unionists, arrived at the White House to discuss the passage of Union troops through Maryland. They telegraphed to Baltimore's Mayor Brown that they had seen Lincoln, members of the cabinet, and General Scott and that these men had authorized the "transmission of orders that will stop the passage of troops through or around the city."[47] Separately, from Annapolis, Governor Hicks wrote Cameron that given the outburst of violence in Baltimore it was "prudent to decline (for the present)" Cameron's requisition for Maryland to furnish four regiments from the state for the defense of Washington.[48] Hicks's letter, along with the "scattering of sensational telegrams received" convinced Lincoln that it was necessary to invite Hicks and Brown to a conference at the White House "relative to the preserving of peace of Maryland."[49] He asked that they come to Washington immediately.

Later that day, a response from Mayor Brown to Lincoln's morning letter reached the White House. Brown again asked Lincoln to offer him reassurance that no more troops would be brought through the city, with the new stipulation that none also pass "so immediately into its neighbourhood as to provoke the uncontrollable feeling of its people."[50] With those assurances, Brown stated, "City authorities" would use "all lawful means" to "prevent their fellow citizens" from attacking "Northern Militia who may pass at a distance from their jurisdiction." However, he also wrote he had "no authority to speak for the people of Maryland, and no means of keeping any promise they might make." In other words, Brown's communication meant that Union volunteers would not be attacked only where Lincoln had pledged *not* to send them, and that, regardless, if any Maryland secessionists attacked federal troops, the violence would not be the responsibility of Baltimore authorities.

To circumvent Baltimore, the defense of Washington now depended on the Union reinforcements traveling to the capital via Annapolis. Once these men landed there, they would take a little-used B & O feeder line from Annapolis to Annapolis Junction, 15 miles south of Baltimore, and then catch trains dispatched by the War Department from Washington, 25 miles to the south.

Scott dispatched a quartermaster to Annapolis to prepare to receive troops arriving by boat there and transport them to Washington, by rail or, failing that, horse-drawn wagons. Scott expected that the Eighth Massachusetts and the Seventh New York could reach Annapolis as early as the night of April 20, or at least by the next day, and get to Washington soon afterward. Even without them, Scott assured Lincoln—perhaps overoptimistically—that "we are in advance of all preparations for an attack upon us" in Washington.[51]

Late in the night on April 19, immediately after arriving in Philadelphia, General Benjamin Butler, commander of the Eighth Massachusetts Volunteers, had immediately telegraphed Massachusetts' Governor Andrew that he and his men planned to leave for Washington shortly. But when Butler learned

General Benjamin F. Butler of the Eighth Massachusetts (left) and Colonel Marshall Lefferts of the Seventh New York.

of the deadly attack on the Sixth Massachusetts men earlier that day in Baltimore, he sent a follow-up note an hour later, now early in the morning of April 20: "I will telegraph again, but shall not be able to get ready as soon as I had hoped."[52]

At 2 a.m., soon after Butler sent that telegram, the Seventh New York Regiment arrived in Philadelphia. At the station, a messenger asked Colonel Marshall Lefferts, their commander, to come to the office of Samuel Felton, the railroad's president, where Lefferts learned that his men would not be continuing by train onto Washington later that morning. Felton told Lefferts that Governor Hicks and Mayor Brown had asked that no more trains be sent to Baltimore. His own intelligence reports indicated the destruction of the rails and bridges north of Baltimore. Lefferts prepared a telegram for Cameron, which Felton sent from his office, after the text was put into the cipher code that he had adopted for his own messages:[53]

> Philadelphia, 5 o'clock A.M., April 20, 1861.
> Hon. S. Cameron, Secretary of War, Washington.
> Sir,—Having arrived at Philadelphia, we are informed by the President of the Philadelphia and Baltimore Railroad that Governor Hicks states that no more troops can pass. In fact, the Baltimore and Ohio Road refuses to transport. We will wait instructions.
> Marshall Lefferts[54]

When Lefferts did not receive a timely response, Felton's office sent the telegram a second time. Lefferts still received no reply and decided that the telegraph lines must have been severed. That left him with two possible ways to reach Washington: via Annapolis or up the Potomac River.

While both Butler and Lefferts were resourceful and dedicated Union men, their personalities clashed in working together, slowing their respective regiments' progress to Washington and greatly imperiling its safety. Both men were self-made, but they could not have been more different in almost every other respect. Butler was overweight and balding, with his remaining hair flowing in scraggly locks over his ears. His acute strabismus kept his left eye in a perpetual off-angle squint. Butler was often argumentative, condescending, and loud. The Republican politician Carl Schurz described Butler after he met him in Annapolis on April 25: "I found him clothed in a gorgeous militia uniform adorned with rich gold embroidery.... His rotund form, his squinting eye, and the peculiar puff of his cheek made him look a little grotesque."[55]

Born in 1818 in Deerfield, New Hampshire, Butler had been a sickly child, but early on showed intellectual promise, reading the New Testament and *Robinson Crusoe* at a precocious age. He never knew his father, who died in 1819, four months after his birth, but learned that he had been a privateer in the Caribbean. Schoolmates taunting Butler called his father a dangerous pirate "who had been hung in irons from the yard-arm of a vessel at Cadiz for piracy and murder on the high seas."[56]

His widowed mother kept a boardinghouse in Lowell, Massachusetts, and scarcely could afford to rear him. In the early 1830s, he attended Philips Exeter Academy and then the Edson School. In 1834, still somewhat frail and skinny, he tried to gain an appointment to West Point, where education was free. Lacking political connections, he could not secure an appointment. During his entire military career, he held a grudge against officers who had attended West Point.[57]

Butler enrolled instead at Waterville College (now Colby College), and by his junior year was determined to become an attorney. Four years later, as a precocious 20-year-old, he was admitted to the Massachusetts bar. He made a fortune by investing in Lowell textile companies, and he served in the Massachusetts House of Representatives and Senate. While Butler enjoyed his wealth and success, he did not forget his origins, and he sometimes assisted working men and women in their struggles against the more powerful. On one occasion, for example, he represented a young factory employee who had been fired without being paid her final wages. He met with a company representative, who still refused to pay. Only when he prepared to file a lawsuit did the young woman get her money.[58]

On April 15, when Butler had received orders from Governor Andrew to muster his troops at Boston Common, he was serving as counsel at a trial in Boston. He requested a postponement and strode out of the courthouse, where an enthusiastic crowd greeted him.[59] He was determined to move quickly to achieve a lifelong ambition: to become commanding general of the Massachusetts Militia. That prize required getting Governor Andrew to pass over several more senior officers with far greater military experience. However, Butler also knew that while Andrew wanted to respond to the patriotic fervor sweeping his state, the state treasury had no funds to send volunteers to Washington. Only the legislature could appropriate the money, and it had adjourned the day before. Early on the morning of April 16, Butler met with James G. Carey, president of the Bank of Mutual Redemption of Boston, who knew Butler from his service in the state legislature and his investments in Lowell. Butler asked Carney for a $50,000 loan to the state so that it could dispatch its militia to Washington that very day. The legislature would pay back the bank when it reconvened. Carney assented, but made the loan subject to one condition: Butler must command the brigade.[60]

Now Butler had only one final thing to do. He strode toward the State House as Bostonians and militiamen were gathering in the Common for a rally to save the Union and asked Governor Andrew to appoint him commander of the troops. Surprised by Butler's boldness, Andrew pointed out that several men had more experience and longer service than he did. At that very moment, Henry K. Oliver, treasurer of the Commonwealth, as if on cue, reportedly interrupted the meeting to tell Andrew that the state did not have any the money to transport the men.[61] "Governor," Butler told the shaken Andrew, "I am aware of this condition of things, and I can remedy it." He handed Andrew a letter from Carney with the offer of the loan. The governor had no choice but to name Butler commanding general of the Massachusetts Militia in the field.

Officers with more military experience questioned Andrew's unexpected choice. When Butler heard that a U.S. Army lieutenant had complained that he had not graduated from West Point, Butler responded: "He forgot that putting an animal into a stable does not make him a horse."[62] Butler did not care what people thought of him. In subsequent weeks, he openly told people that his appointment had been a condition for the emergency loans.[63]

In contrast to Butler's sometimes disheveled appearance, Lefferts cut a dashing figure. He was a slender man with handsome chiseled features, a full head of slightly graying hair, and an erect military posture. His oversize moustache—a favorite look for military men at the time—punctuated his impeccable grooming. While Lefferts proudly carried a prominent Dutch surname, he attended tuition-free "common schools" (as public schools were called) and got his first job as a counting-house clerk. Lefferts became a civil engineer in rapidly growing Brooklyn, then a separate city from Manhattan. Turning to business several years later, he went to work for Morewood & Co. importers and was quickly named a partner in the firm. By the mid-1840s, he had become fascinated with telegraph technology and, while running More-wood's day-to-day operations, became an expert in electrical engineering. By 1850, he was president of the New York, New England & New York State Telegraph Company and had left Morewood to focus on the rapidly ad-vancing—and profitable—telegraph. Not only did he run that company; he also received patents for several inventions, which were purchased by the American Telegraph Company.

Lefferts joined the Seventh New York Regiment as a private in 1851. A year later, he was elected the regiment's lieutenant colonel, and in 1859 he became its colonel. He and his family lived on East Fourth Street, west of Second Avenue, a once-fashionable, now-fading address. Lefferts could have easily purchased a new brownstone on Murray Hill, where by 1861 many of the Seventh New York men lived, but he stayed on East Fourth Street because it was only a few minutes' walk from the regiment's newly opened armory, built of cast iron, on the east side of Third Avenue between East Sixth and East Seventh streets. With James Bogardus, a pioneer in New York's cast-iron buildings, Lefferts had even designed the innovative building, which housed the public Tompkins Market on the ground floor and the regiment's quarters and drill hall on the top two floors.[64]

From the moment they met in Philadelphia on the morning of April 20, Butler and Lefferts took an immediate dislike to each other. Butler repeatedly pulled rank on Lefferts, though he had virtually no military experience and indeed no authority over another state's militia. In Butler's eyes, Lefferts was only a colonel and commander of a single regiment of so-called holiday soldiers. Lefferts, however, was commander of the nation's best trained and best-known state militia and he matched Butler in stubbornness and tenacity. The two men argued over the fastest way to get their men to Washington. When disagreement turned into outright hostility, each man went his own way. At 3 p.m., Butler's men left Philadelphia by rail for Perryville on the Susquehanna River, where they caught the steamship *Maryland* to Annapo-lis, where he planned to use the secondary rail line to reach Washington. But-ler had considered taking a ship directly to Washington but feared that the Confederates would shell any Union boat sailing up the Potomac River, a course Lefferts chose to undertake. At 5 p.m., Lefferts's men boarded the steamship *Boston* to sail directly to Washington. Unwilling to bend to Butler's will or delay his own departure for the capital, Lefferts had rented the ship with his company's money. Lefferts and Butler now expected to greet each other in Washington, though they did not wager whose regiment would arrive first.

Late that afternoon in Washington, the Sixth Massachusetts men, to raise morale in a Washington sullen from the failure of more volunteer regiments to arrive, staged a march down Pennsylvania Avenue that included a street-firing drill. To make their regiment look larger than it really was, the men marched in a slightly more dispersed formation known as "open order."[65] Horatio Taft, who was hoping that more troops might arrive in the city, recorded his thoughts on this march in his diary that evening: "went to the depot and to the Capitol again tonight. . . . The Mass. Regt marched out and through Pa Ave to 15 st making a fine appearance and being cheered frequently by the people."[66] Not all onlookers, however, were so enthusiastic. Sergeant John A. Lovell later wrote that a few white-haired gentlemen drove past in their buggies and called out, "Sorry for you boys. You'll all get killed."[67]

The mood at the White House was not far off from that assessment. The Lincoln administration had experienced the last few days as a "startling succession of disasters to the Union cause," Nicolay remembered, cataloguing the series of apparent calamities compressed into that short span of time: "Virginia's secession on the 17th; Harper's Ferry lost on the 18th; Baltimore in arms, and the North effectually cut off on the 19th; the Gosport Navy Yard sacrificed on the 20th."[68] The Navy Yard at Norfolk was attacked that night and would be evacuated by the next morning. Though the Southerners failed to gain all the ships there because the defenders scuttled them in the harbor, it was a massive loss of war materiel and government property and a humiliating blow for the Navy and the national government. When, the administration officials asked themselves, would this "tide of misfortune stop?" For now, Nicolay recalled, history seemed to be on the side of the Confederacy and against Washington's survival as capital of the United States: "Wavering Unionists found no great difficulty in forecasting the final success of rebellion; sanguine secessionists already in their visions saw the stars and stripes banished to the north of Mason and Dixon's line."[69]

The feeling of isolation was now acute in Washington. For the third consecutive night, Hay recorded in his diary, there were "feverish rumours about the meditated assault upon this town."[70] On the previous two nights, April 18 and 19, the fear of attack had been tempered by the arrival of troops from Pennsylvania and Massachusetts, however ill-equipped or battered-looking.

Tonight, everyone knew that no new reinforcements had come, and with the rails line to the North severed, it was now uncertain when any more new defenders would reach the city. The gravity of Washington's plight was underscored by the knowledge that the first casualties of the war had been soldiers on their way to defend the capital, and by the likelihood that more Union volunteers might be killed on their way to protect the city.

At the White House, Clifford Arrick of the Frontier Guards recorded the mood of his fellow defenders in his diary: "A universal gloom and anxiety sits upon every countenance." Again, it appeared that Confederates might reach Washington before more Union volunteers arrived. "When will re-inforcements come?" Arrick wondered. "Will it be too late?"[71]

Southerners recognized Washington's precarious position and saw the opportunity for the Confederacy to translate months of "On to Washington!" calls into something more than rhetoric. "Lincoln is in a trap," wrote H. D. Bird, the superintendent of Virginia's South Side Railroad, to Confederate Secretary of War Leroy Walker: "He has not more than twelve hundred regulars in Washington and not more than three thousand volunteers. An hour now is worth years of common fighting. One dash and Lincoln is taken, the country saved, and the leader who does it will be immortalized."[72]

Bird's letter stressed the necessity of immediate action—"one dash and Lincoln is taken"—because the window of time in which a successful attack on Washington could be launched was narrow, no more than several days, and would close once the Union troops stalled north of Baltimore made their way to Washington. In a separate communication to Walker written the same day, Bird proposed that confiscated James River steamboats be used to carry troops by water directly to Baltimore. Bird claimed that 7,000 men could be transported in that manner in 24 hours, and that his railroad could move that number of men from points south to Petersburg in the same amount of time.[73] All that the seizure of Washington and checkmate of Lincoln required was the coordination—and the will—to move on the city swiftly.

The city, observed Lucius Chittenden in his diary, now wore the "aspects of a besieged town."[74] With railroad and mail routes cut off, the capital's only link to the North was the telegraph, which could be severed in moments by a simple pair of wire cutters. By April 20, the *New York Herald* reported that Washington was now at risk in all directions from new dangers that had flared in the past 24 hours, noting the "destruction of railway bridges in Maryland,

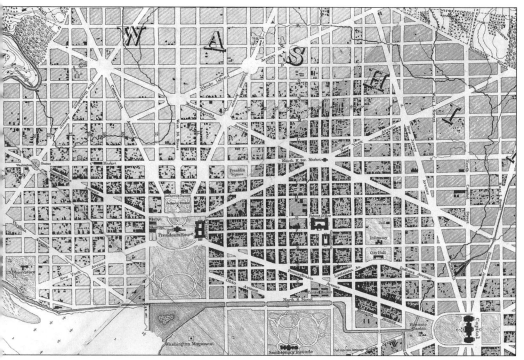

Washington in 1861. Within hundreds of yards from the Capitol and White House, the blocks laid out in Pierre L'Enfant's 1791 plan remained largely empty.

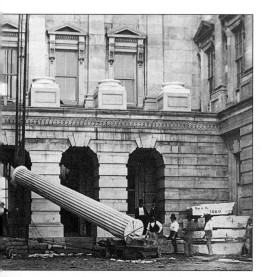

The "Lincoln monolith"—the first column of the Capitol's new Senate wing—was raised on the day of Lincoln's election, November 6, 1860 (left). Five months later, on March 4, 1861, Lincoln was sworn in as president on the Capitol's East Front amid rumors of secessionist conspiracy to seize Washington (right).

Pennsylvania Avenue looking westward from the Capitol rooftop, 1861.

A handful of monumental buildings, like the Greek revival-style Patent Office building pictured here, ros over a city otherwise composed of modest brick and wooden structures.

General Winfield Scott, general-in-chief of the U.S. Army in April 1861, photographed in the 1850s.

Nicholas Biddle, a former slave who served as an orderly for the First Pennsylvania Volunteers, shed the Civil War's "first blood" as the first casualty at enemy hands, his comrades maintained, when he was severely wounded in Baltimore on April 18.

The newly expanded Capitol served as quarters for the First Pennsylvania Volunteers and Sixth Massachusetts men.

The earliest extant photograph (c.1860–61) of the recently completed House of Representatives chamber, much as it looked when the volunteer regiments arrived at the Capitol.

Oliver Bosbyshell (seated) and Curtis C. Pollock (standing, left) were members of the First Pennsylvania Volunteers, here photographed with another Pennsylvania comrade, Henry Clay Jackson in 1862. Of the three, only Bosbyshell survived the war, and he carried with him the memory of watching Lincoln greet the just-arrived Pennsylvania men at the Capitol on April 18—"towering over all in the room was the great central figure of the war."

Harper's Ferry Armory and Arsenal, located at the confluence of the Potomac and Shenandoah Rivers 65 miles northwest of Washington.

David Hunter Strother, a journalist and prominent illustrator, arrived at Harper's Ferry early in the morning of April 19 shortly after Union defenders had destroyed the arsenal and fled to Pennsylvania. He sketched the fires for *Harper's Weekly*.

The April 19 attack on the Sixth Massachusetts Regiment in Baltimore.

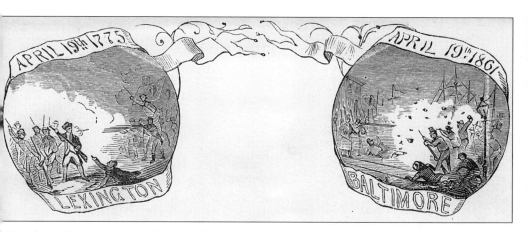

When they left Boston for Washington, the Massachusetts troops were dubbed the "Minutemen of '61." Their passage through Baltimore on April 19 fell on the eighty-sixth anniversary of the 1775 Battles of Lexington and Concord, a historical resonance deeply felt in the North.

LUTHER C. LADD, of Alexandria, N. H., was shot in the Baltimore riot, April 19th, 1861, and bled to death on the same day. He was only 17 years of age. — Just before he expired, he exclaimed — "ALL HAIL TO THE STARS AND STRIPES."

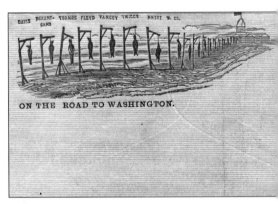

ON THE ROAD TO WASHINGTON.

Patriotic stationery flooded Northern mails after the fall of Fort Sumter. One envelope honored Luther Ladd, a 17-year-old member of the Sixth Massachusetts Volunteers, who was killed in the April 19 riot in Baltimore. Many of the envelopes imagined gruesome fates for secessionists, as this one, where a line of gallows toward the Capitol mark the path of Confederate leaders like Davis and Beauregard.

ABOUT THIS TIME YOU WILL HEAR THUNDER

THE GREAT "COMET" OF 1861.

General Scott was a favorite protagonist in patriotic cartoons and envelopes while the South threatened Washington. Scott was depicted as "The Great 'Comet' of 1861"—a reference to the Thatcher Comet discovered in early April—and as a fierce-looking bulldog daring the mutt Jeff Davis to take the prize meat of Washington.

The Seventh New York Regiment, popularly known as the "National Guard," was famous for its impressive military drills, band, and chorus, as well as its rousing parades at civic events. Pictured here, members of the Seventh gather near their armory at the Bowery and Fifth Street in Manhattan, one block south of their armory, preparing to set off for Washington on April 19.

The departure of the Seventh New York brought out several hundred thousand cheering New Yorkers along the shown parade route, as shown here looking south on Broadway from walker street. "Was there ever such an ovation?" wrote playwright Fitz-James O'Brien, a private in the Seventh New York. The Seventh included many members of New York's social elite, such as Lyman Tiffany (right), photographed here in full uniform.

The U.S. Treasury building (left), located next to the White House, was designated as the site of a last sta
against Confederate troops. Barrels of food were stored in the basement, and the monumental south porti
pictured here, was sandbagged to hold off an assault. Both the Chain Bridge (pictured right), located upri
from Georgetown, and the Long Bridge, which crossed the Potomac directly into the heart of the city, w
closely guarded day and night.

The Ringgold Artillery of the First Pennsylvania Volunteers were photographed on April 21 at the Washingt
Navy Yard, three days after they arrived in the capital.

The sabotage of rail lines north of Baltimore forced Northern volunteer regiments to take circuitous routes to Washington. The Seventh New York originally planned to reach the capital by ship, as depicted in this drawing by Thomas Nast.

On April 24, the Seventh New York and members of the Eighth Massachusetts set out from Annapolis to Annapolis Junction 25 miles from Washington, where they hoped to meet a train that would take them to the capital, as drawn by Thomas Nast.

The Eighth Massachusetts helped repair damaged rail lines on the way to Washington. Here, one soldier dives into a stream to recover a railroad tie.

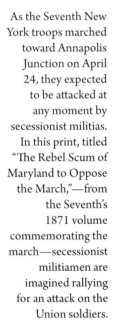

As the Seventh New York troops marched toward Annapolis Junction on April 24, they expected to be attacked at any moment by secessionist militias. In this print, titled "The Rebel Scum of Maryland to Oppose the March,"—from the Seventh's 1871 volume commemorating the march—secessionist militiamen are imagined rallying for an attack on the Union soldiers.

The Seventh New York and Eighth Massachusetts ended their grueling, day-long march at 4 a.m. on April 25 just outside Annapolis Junction, where they camped, hungry and exhausted, as depicted in this romanticized drawing of their wooded campsite.

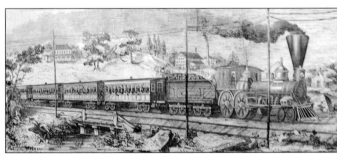

The Seventh New York boarded a train to Washington at Annapolis Junction on the morning of April 25. Andrew Carnegie (pictured c. 1878), then a 26-year-old assistant in the military telegraph and railroads division of the War Department, was on board.

On April 26, one day after they arrived in Washington, breaking the siege, the Seventh New York staged a formal parade along Pennsylvania Avenue and past the White House. In this drawing, Lincoln is visible standing beneath the awning, while General Scott is seated to his right.

The House of Representatives became the temporary barracks for the Seventh New York.

Most of the Seventh New Yorkers slept on the carpeted floor or benches in the galleries of the House of Representatives. Many officers, meanwhile, were given offices and lounges.

Eighth Massachusetts received the last available accommodations at the Capitol: the open rotunda ...eath the uncompleted dome.

This photograph of President Lincoln and Senator James H. Lane's Frontier Guard was taken on the Wh[ite] House's South Lawn on April 27, the day they were disbanded. With thousands of U.S. troops now stream[ing] into Washington, the Frontier Guard and the similar Clay Battalion, both hastily organized a week bef[ore] were no longer needed to defend the capital.

The Treasury Guard, comprised of the department's clerks, were formed during the siege of Washing[ton]. Unlike other temporary defenders raised in April 1861, they remained on duty throughout the war, as [this] April 1865 photograph attests. That month, two Treasury Guard flags screened the presidential box at Fo[rd's] Theatre the night of Lincoln's assassination.

the general arming of Baltimore, the detention of our Seventh regiment at Philadelphia, the prevailing fear of the descent of an overwhelming secession mob upon Washington," and the rumor of the "planting of secession batteries along the Virginia side of the Potomac." Despite these new dangers, the *Herald* also maintained that the city could be held against any attackers.[75]

Others took a more pessimistic view of Washington's prospects. In New York, George Templeton Strong wrote in his diary that night of the capital: "People talk darkly of its being attacked before our reinforcements come to the rescue, and everyone said we must not be surprised by news that Lincoln and Seward and all the Administration are prisoners."[76]

Sunday, April 21

"A Real State of Siege"

On Sunday morning, the city "seemed very quiet," wrote Lucius Chittenden in his diary. A week had passed since news of the fall of Fort Sumter had reached Washington, but looking out from the window of his boarding house at Fourteenth and K streets, two blocks from the Treasury, Chittenden observed, "I can hardly appreciate that we are in the midst of all the din and bustle of preparation for war."[1]

The calm of the early morning, however, belied the anxiety that was felt in every neighborhood and continued to prey on the apprehensions of the city's residents. Rumors of attack, commonplace for several days, had now been magnified by the city's nearly complete isolation from the North. Sporadic telegraph service was its only tenuous connection to the rest of the Union. "Dangers were thickening around the Federal city in all directions," recalled Frederick Seward. "It was realized that Washington was isolated, and beleaguered by its enemies."[2]

The loss of mail service the day before meant that residents could not send letters to family and friends, nor of course receive their replies. Many administration officials had already been separated from their families, because they had come to Washington alone, given the risk of war and the city's unhealthy living conditions. For Frances "Fanny" Seward, wife of Secretary Seward (and mother of Frederick), "These were terrible days of suspense." She had remained in Elmira, New York, where their other son, William H. Seward, Jr., regularly visited the telegraph office in case one of his father's telegraphs arrived. No messages got through that week.[3]

From Boston, Edward Everett, the storied Massachusetts politician and orator, fretted over the safety of his daughter and her family in Washington.

In a letter to his son Willy dated April 21, Everett wrote, "If the city becomes the theatre of war while they are there, the situation will be too fearful to be described. We must leave them in the hands of a merciful Providence. I would fly to them if I saw any means of being useful to them."[4]

With Washington cut off, "the wildest rumors gained credence," Frederick Seward recalled.[5] "A mob was reported to be coming over from Baltimore to burn the public buildings and sack the town. Rebel vessels were declared to be coming up from Norfolk to bombard it. Rebel troops were asserted to be marching up from Richmond and down from Harper's Ferry to take possession." Residents congregated at street corners to share the latest news or rumors, according to Seward, "exchanging in low tones their forebodings of disaster or their hopes for relief."[6]

Under such trying circumstances, residents—from ordinary citizens to cabinet members and President Lincoln himself—suffered through what John Nicolay described as "a dreary and anxious Sunday."[7] The government unwittingly contributed to this apprehension when it closed public amusements such as theaters that day. While this decision was meant to reduce the potential for riots growing out of large crowds, it denied the public one way to forget the troubling events for a few hours.[8]

Everyone in the city was so edgy that the sound of a deep rumble from the vicinity of the White House and then Pennsylvania Avenue that afternoon created fears that the city was finally under attack. Had it come from Southern gunboats shelling the city from the Potomac? Or had the Confederates put cannon on Arlington Heights and begun to bombard the city into submission? The rumbling sound, it turned out, came from U.S. Army wagons hauling flour from a Georgetown warehouse to secure storage at the Capitol.[9]

At 10 a.m., Baltimore's Mayor Brown and a delegation of civic and business leaders arrived in Washington by a special train to meet with Lincoln, Scott, and the cabinet. Governor Hicks, whom Lincoln had also asked to come to Washington, had chosen to remain in Annapolis. The Baltimoreans, described as a "penitent and suppliant crowd of conditional Secessionists" by Hay in his diary, presented the view that all Marylanders, not just Baltimoreans, were "up in arms and were resolved to the sacrifice of their lives to permit no more troops to come through their State."[10] According to Brown's account of the meeting, given in an interview that night with the Washington

National Intelligencer, Lincoln assured them that the transport of troops through Maryland was solely for the "protection of Washington," not aggression. The situation was stark, Lincoln said. "Being now unable to bring them up the Potomac in security, the Government must either bring them though Maryland or abandon the capital."[11]

Scott explained to the meeting that troops "could only come in one of three ways": the first through Baltimore; the second by boat from Perryville to Annapolis and then by rail to Washington; the third from Harrisburg on the Northern Central railroad, marching from the severed line around to the Relay House and then by rail to Washington.[12] If the troops were attacked on the second and third more circuitous routes, they would be forced to "select their own best route, and, if need be, fight their way through Baltimore," although Scott hoped such an outcome would not be necessary. Lincoln, Scott, and Secretary Cameron then agreed that no more troops would be ordered directly through Baltimore, a pledge already made the previous day. The meeting concluded with the "distinct assurance" from Lincoln that "no more troops would be sent through Baltimore unless obstructed in their transit in other directions" and that Baltimore authorities "should do their best to restrain their own people."[13]

Mayor Brown and the delegation departed the White House for Washington's B & O Railroad station, apparently satisfied with the administration's assurances. Just as Brown's train was under steam to depart, however, an urgent telegram from B & O Railroad president John W. Garrett reached Brown. Garrett asked for the result of Brown's meeting with Lincoln, as there had been a startling development in Baltimore: "Three thousand Northern troops are reported to be at Cockeysville. Intense excitement prevails. Churches have been dismissed and the people are arming in mass. To prevent terrific bloodshed, the result of your interview and arrangement is awaited."[14]

Cockeysville, whose quarries provided the marble for the Capitol enlargement and the uncompleted stump of the Washington Monument, was only 15 miles north of Baltimore. A new unit of Pennsylvania Volunteers there had moved south from York to await the arrival of "trains loaded with lumber to rebuild" the burned bridges on the Northern Central Railway that blocked them from moving further, and then to proceed through Baltimore, apparently unaware of Lincoln's command of the previous day to march no more troops through the city.[15]

At 1:25 p.m., Brown telegraphed back to Garrett, "Be calm, and do nothing till you hear from me again. I return to see the President, Cabinet and General Scott."[16] Bearing Garrett's telegram in hand, Brown hurriedly returned to the White House shortly after 2 p.m., much to Lincoln's "astonishment." He had considered the Baltimore matter to be settled and was even more astonished when he read in the telegram that Northern troops were at Cockeysville.[17] The Baltimore delegation suggested that "advantage had been taken of their presence in Washington to bring these forces within striking distance of Baltimore."[18] In response, Lincoln hastily gathered Cameron, Scott, and the rest of the cabinet back together. "The President, at once, in the most decided way urged the recall of the troops," Brown recounted.[19] Before the assembled group, Lincoln stressed that "he had no idea" that the Pennsylvania Volunteers at Cockeysville "would be there to-day; lest there should be the slightest suspicion of bad faith on his part in summoning the mayor to Washington, and allowing troops to march on the city during his absence."[20] Lincoln ordered the troops sent back to York or Harrisburg immediately.

At 3:15 p.m., Brown telegraphed to Garrett in Baltimore the results of the meeting: "the troops are ordered to return forthwith to Harrisburg." Brown informed Garrett that Major James Belger would return to Baltimore with him so that he could deliver the new orders to the Pennsylvania Volunteers in person, given that no telegram from Washington could reach there over downed lines. The orders commanded the troops to return to Pennsylvania, guard the Northern Central Railroad's lines against sabotage, and come to Washington via Annapolis.[21]

According to Brown's account of the meeting, General Scott was enthusiastic about the decision, and even said, "Mr. President, I thank you for this, God will bless you for it."[22] Some cabinet members were not so charitable. That afternoon, at the cabinet meeting, Secretary Welles was so disgusted that he abruptly got up from the table, swinging "his hat under his arm and hastily walked out, telling them if that was their policy *he* would have no responsibility in the matter." Indeed, the North's response to Lincoln's decision would be equally savage, although the news would not be known for several days. On April 26, the *New York Tribune* published an editorial condemning what it believed to be appeasement: "We are not allowed to defend our Capital. . . . So we will placidly bare our bosoms to the shot from the Slavery camp. Let us die like men, but do not let us hurt the noble feelings of Baltimore plug-uglyism."[23]

Secretary Cameron went further. He was determined to circumvent Lincoln's and Scott's decision and order the Pennsylvania Volunteers through Baltimore without their approval. Once Mayor Brown and the three Baltimoreans had left the White House for the B & O station by carriage for a second time, Cameron jumped into another carriage and drove to the station. His intention was to intercept Major Belger, who was headed for Baltimore carrying written orders. At the station, Cameron verbally commanded Belger to order Major Fitz-John Porter to "bring on the troops at all hazards" through Baltimore.[24] Belger, however, disregarded Cameron's shocking interference and refused to deliver Cameron's order to the Pennsylvanians.[25]

As Mayor Brown and his delegation conducted their meetings in Washington, Baltimore's residents frantically prepared for battle with the Pennsylvanians should they try to march through the city. Brown later described the events of April 21 as a "fearful day in Baltimore. Women and children, and men, too, were wild with excitement. A certainty of a fight in the streets if Northern troops should enter was the pressing danger."[26] He neglected to mention the active role the city's authorities and military leadership had played in planning to attack Northern troops if they entered Baltimore. Since the afternoon of April 19, recruiting for the Maryland militia had proceeded rapidly under the command of Major General Steuart of the First Light Division, the official militia in Baltimore.[27] A special unit within the group was also formed under the name "Guerilla Corps," the *Baltimore American* reported, to serve in the First Light Division "so long as the exigency of the times shall continue."[28] On April 20, the Board of Police had ordered citizens to hand over firearms to authorities, which served the dual purpose of disarming the mob and transferring weapons into the hands of the militia. Within a few days, the police also obtained "every available arm that was for sale in the city," with 3,000 stand of arms acquired in this manner.[29] Still, the militia volunteers received revolvers, not rifles, because Baltimore was still far short of military arms necessary to supply the militia recruits.[30]

Brown and Kane later countered accusations of treason by claiming that the militia was raised purely for self-defense, to shield Baltimore against Union aggression. However, the militia troops at their direction were ready, if ordered, to intercept the Union volunteers even if they did not directly enter Baltimore, as they were prepared to do after learning that Pennsylvania troops were nearing the city on the morning of April 21. "Squads of volunteers [i.e. members of the Maryland militia], armed with muskets and weapons of every description," started out on roads north to Cockeysville "on horseback and in vehicles, for the purpose of waging a guerilla warfare on the troops, as they passed down, outside the city limits," the *Baltimore Sun* reported.[31] After "ascertaining the reliability of the information," they "gave orders for the assembling and arming of the infantry, as well as all other military corps," all under the command of Steuart.[32] *The South*, a new Baltimore pro-Confederate newspaper, reported in its first issue that in the commercial streets near the harbor, "preparations were made for a conflict, and large quantities or grape and canister shot, besides heavy balls, were provided," including "a heavy thirty-two pounder pivot gun," which could be placed on a street and rotated to fire to decimate the ranks of Union volunteers.[33] With these preparations under way, Steuart dispatched some of his cavalry to Cockeysville to ascertain the seriousness of the threat. Once the men realized that the Pennsylvanians could not proceed any further south by rail because of the destroyed bridges, Baltimore's military leadership decided not to attack them.[34] Though the Maryland militia was prepared to engage the Northern troops if they moved into Baltimore (or around the city)—again, in "self-defense"—attacking the Union soldiers at Cockeysville would have been a brazen act of aggression, running completely counter to Hicks's and Brown's claims that Maryland had no quarrel with the Union if it did not molest Marylanders.

Baltimore's leaders, however, had not yet regained control over all the city's citizens. A rogue group, formed to attack the troops at Cockeysville and numbering, according to the *Baltimore Sun*, "not less than five hundred men . . . left Baltimore for this purpose, armed with shot guns and rifles." Later, after news of Lincoln's order to pull back the Northern troops to Pennsylvania was heard, "earnest fears prevailed that these hot and eager men would begin an attack upon the Northern troops, and so lead to a most unnecessary and melancholy waste of human life."[35]

Secessionists in Baltimore believed that Virginia was ready to act decisively against Washington and in support of Maryland. That afternoon, these secessionists were "informed by a gentleman from Washington that the presence of Col. Lee with Virginia troops on Arlington Heights, which command Washington" had been sighted—a rumor that *The South* reported was "*a fact*."[36] Later that evening, Baltimoreans learned that "3,000 Virginia troops had crossed the line into Maryland en route to Baltimore, to resist the passage of troops."[37]

With these rumors—neither of which was true—in circulation, it appeared that secessionists had the upper hand in determining Washington's fate. The defense of the capital, wrote Edward Mansfield in his biography of General Scott in 1862, was "really a question of superior enterprise; for if the Northern volunteers had arrived slowly, and the Southern army had moved quickly, the result might have been different." If Maryland could block reinforcements, it would give valuable time to troops in Virginia ready to attack Washington: "beyond doubt, it was their object to obstruct the advance of one army and hasten the approach of the other."[38]

Shortly after Mayor Brown left the White House for the second time, Lincoln, Scott, and the cabinet convened at the Navy Department, to avoid public notice. There, Lincoln posed the question whether he should let the government collapse if he only used the means which Congress had appropriated before adjourning or look to the "spirit of the Constitution" and use any available measures against the rebellion?[39] The cabinet unanimously approved the latter strategy. The cabinet also supported Lincoln's plans to extend extraordinary authority to two groups of leading New York figures, members of the newly founded Union Defense League, to act on the government's official behalf, given that Washington was now cut off from the North. Several men, including New York's Governor Morgan, were empowered to purchase or charter steamboats to send volunteer regiments and supplies to Washington. Several leading businessmen were given authority to spend money on behalf of the Treasury for such actions, and Lincoln secretly ordered the transfer of $2 million to the Union Defense League to fund these actions. The city's Board of Aldermen borrowed $1.5 million to raise additional volunteer regiments, send them to Washington, and assist their families financially during their 90 days of unpaid service.

The reason for such bold actions went beyond Washington's isolation from the North. "The several departments of the Government at that time contained so large a number of disloyal persons," declared Lincoln a year later, "that it would have been impossible to provide safely, through official agents only, for the performance of the duties."[40] Messengers who worked for private companies carried secret messages from Washington to New York via a roundabout route through Pennsylvania. "I believe, that by these and similar measures taken in that crisis," said Lincoln, "some of which were without any authority of law, the Government was saved from overthrow."[41]

The double blow of Washington's isolation and the government's apparent powerlessness were now visibly starting to affect Lincoln's demeanor, revealing what his aides saw as genuine apprehension. Indeed, it was hard to underestimate the danger posed to Washington and federal government: "The events of Friday, Saturday, and Sunday," April 19–21, judged Nicolay and Hay, "exhibited a degree of real peril such as had not menaced the capital since the British invasion in 1814. Virginia was in arms on one side, Maryland on the other; the railroad was broken; the Potomac was probably blockaded; a touch would sever the telegraph."[42] Lincoln had to display leadership and self-confidence beyond the substance of his decisions at this time of crisis. "Mr. Lincoln was never liable to sudden excitement or sudden activity," judged Nicolay and Hay. "Through all his life, and through all the unexpected and stirring events of the rebellion, his personal manner was one of steadiness of word and act."[43]

In private, however, Lincoln was growing shorter in temper, particularly in his exasperation about the failure of expected Northern regiments to arrive. "Now go away!" he shouted at a visitor who clung to him, repeating a request over and over again. "Go away!" Lincoln shouted, "I cannot attend to all these details. I could as easily bail out the Potomac with a teaspoon."[44] On the evening of April 21, Lincoln's friend the Illinois representative Philip B. Fouke found the cabinet and Lincoln "all hourly expecting an attack from the Virginia side, but determined to hold their ground to the last." According to Fouke, Lincoln "appeared to be especially exercised at the critical condition of the Federal capital."[45] Lincoln's apprehension was more than reasonable, as Southerners had repeatedly called for his imprisonment or hanging if they seized Washington. He was concerned about the safety of his family, too. More than once, Lincoln and General Scott urged Mary Lincoln to flee back to Springfield with her sons, just as Simon Cameron's wife, Margaret, had left for Philadelphia two days earlier. Mary Lincoln's stock response was: "I am as safe as Mr. Lincoln, and I shall not leave him."[46]

At the depth of Washington's isolation, Lincoln still managed to find moments of escape, such as the late afternoon carriage rides with Mary or his two sons in good weather. He read to Tad and Willie, and to their best friends, Bud and Holly Taft, sons of Horatio Taft, who were constant visitors at the White House and the same ages, respectively, as his own sons. Their older sister, 16-year-old Julia, accompanied her younger brothers, and she was a favorite of both Lincolns, the daughter they never had. More than once, Mary Lincoln told Julia, "I wish I had a little girl like you."[47]

Julia Taft recorded aspects of life in the White House that few ever saw. After bringing her brothers to the White House one day, she heard a "terrible racket" coming from a nearby room. She opened the door, expecting to find the Lincoln boys and her brothers roughhousing. Instead, she "beheld the President lying on the floor, with the four boys trying to hold him down." Lincoln was grinning as Willie Lincoln and her brother Bud tried to pin his arms and Tad and her other brother, Holly, lay across his legs. "As soon as the boys saw my face at the door," Julia recalled, "Tad called, 'Julie, come quick and sit on his stomach.' But this struck me too much like laying profane hands on the Lord's anointed, and I closed the door and went out."[48]

Tad and Willie Lincoln did their part to defend Washington by building a fort on the White House roof. "Let 'em come," Tad told his friend Julia Taft at Sunday school at the New York Avenue Presbyterian Church. "Willie and I are ready for 'em." A day or two later, Julia Taft visited the fort at Tad Lincoln's invitation with her young brothers. "It did not present a very formidable appearance, with a small log to represent a cannon and a few old condemned rifles," Taft later recalled, "but the boys took a great deal of pride in it and laid private plans for the defense of the White House in case the city was attacked."[49]

At night, Lincoln, like many other Washington residents, searched the sky for the Thatcher Comet, a comet that had been discovered on April 4 and many viewed as a portent of the war. Julia Taft later recounted a startling prophecy from an elderly slave woman named Oola, owned by William R. Woodward, whose children were Julia's friends. Several days before the surrender of Fort Sumter, Oola—who as a slave had no last name—spotted the comet in the dark skies of a new moon. She described the comet to Julia as a "great fire sword," and she told her that a "great war is coming . . . and the North is going to take that sword and cut the South's heart out." But as for President Lincoln, she solemnly foretold, "if he takes the sword, he's going to perish by it." Julia told the Lincoln brothers about the prophecy, she later recalled, "carefully omitting, however, the dire prediction regarding their father." She thought Lincoln would put no credence in such an omen, though later she caught him gazing at the heavens in contemplation. (The comet was not visible to the naked eye until summer, so Taft's story was perhaps a con-flation of events.)

Many of Washington's Southern residents, briefly muted by a surge of Union sentiment, now cheered the apparent ease with which the city could be cap-tured by Confederate forces. "When it began to look as if the latter [Wash-ington] were cut off from all Northern help, and would soon be captured by troops advancing from the South," recalled Frederick Seward, "the exultation of secession sympathizers was neither concealed nor repressed."[50] That day, a group of secessionists stood before a small crowd at the entrance of a hotel on Pennsylvania Avenue, cheering for Jefferson Davis, then for the Confed-eracy, followed by "three groans" for the U.S. government. That was too much for one Unionist onlooker, 37-year-old Colonel J. H. Hobart Ward, who slugged a man and planned to hit another man until he ran away.[51]

An extended glimpse into the secessionist mindset in Washington comes from a letter written that day, one of the rare surviving accounts from a supporter of the Confederacy from inside the capital during its isolation. William B. Gulick, a government clerk in the Department of the Interior, wrote to North Carolina's Governor Ellis with the hope that his letter would arrive in North Carolina despite "very uncertain" mail communica-tion. Gulick informed Ellis that he planned to resign his government post in a day or two, out of loyalty to North Carolina, and offered his services in Washington or in his home state, though he preferred to stay in the capital, since he was "desirous of seeing the end of this affair, on this spot." Gulick first described the number of defenders in the city, a key item of intelli-gence for those countenancing an attack. There were "about 3,000 troops," both volunteers and U.S. Army regulars, as well as "2000 men, volunteers of the District of Columbia, under arms, doing quasi police duty." Though Washington was not formally under martial law, it was effectively in that state. The federal government had "seized this terminus of the telegraph lines, and nothing is allowed to pass over the line, except such information as the government does not object." At the same time, Gulick stressed, Washington was increasingly isolated. Rail travel into the city was "entirely cut off," and "[e]very avenue into the City is in the hands of the military, and scouts and sentinels are kept on them all the time—night and day."

Gulick informed Ellis that Washington had been successfully hemmed in on all sides by hostile forces, by both land and water routes. To the north, the "collision" of the April 19 attack on the Sixth Massachusetts and the subsequent burning of bridges had blocked the path of reinforcement through Maryland except on foot, while the Virginia militia at Harper's Ferry would "prevent the ingress of troops" from Pennsylvania and the Middle West along the B & O line. The river path up the Potomac, Gulick reported, was rumored to have been mined with "numerous canal boats" that had been "sunk at proper points in the channel to prevent the approach of vessels." Another rumor, this one more likely to be true, he wrote, was that "Alexandrians were sending down a steamer to Acquia [*sic*] Creek," the railroad terminus of the Richmond and Potomac Railroad line, when it was fired on from Fort Washington, forcing it to turn back. A Washington secessionist of his acquaintance, Gulick continued, had been at "Alexandria during the day. He says that there is undoubtedly a large depot of soldiers a short distance from Alexandria, ready for some enterprise, and that doubtless it must be designed for Washington."

On the Washington side of the Potomac, Gulick wrote, the secessionist militia group the National Volunteers was "said to be a thousand strong" and "ready to cooperate with any Southern troops who may attack the City." He also believed the District Militia had been "entrapped by the assurance that they were only required to defend the City from attack," but since many of them were Marylanders and Virginians, "their sympathies" were "pretty certain to control their actions when the issue" was brought to a head by a Confederate attack. Gulick hoped that an attack on Washington from Virginia would spur secessionists in Baltimore to reinforce the offensive parry. "If a demonstration be made against the Capital by Virginia, I have no doubt large bodies of Baltimore soldiers will co-operate."

Washington, in sum, was ripe to fall. "Some night a single soldier may discharge his gun, when a panic will ensue," wrote Gulick. "The City is, now just sufficiently excited to be disturbed by the merest trifle." Indeed, he told Ellis, the "Republicans here are frightened to death, and scarcely know what to expect. They anticipate an attack every night from an unseen force." Gulick— surely hoping to provide ample suggestion to forces assembling in the South—speculated on how such an attack might be launched: "I believe a column of determined men, 3 or 4 thousand strong, making a dash at the White house, would drive Old Abe out of the City as disgracefully as he came into it. If once out, I have no doubt, quiet would prevail at once. Still many believe, if the Republicans are driven out, that they will destroy all the public buildings before they depart. I should not be surprised, for they know that, in such case, they would never return, and they are vindictive enough to commit any destruction with their power."[52]

That day, Colonel Stone and General Scott prepared the details, building by building, of how Washington would be defended if overrun by Confederate attackers. Stone recounted this meeting at length in his postwar account "A Dinner with General Scott in 1861," presenting large parts of the encounter as a dialogue between Scott and himself. Scott summoned Stone to the meeting that morning, when he arrived at Scott's office at 9 a.m. to give his regular report on the previous night's events and to receive his orders for the coming day. He found Scott busy writing at his desk. "As I approached and saluted," Stone later recalled, "the general looked up over his spectacles, and on seeing who had entered, said, a little sharply: 'Colonel Stone, you will please come and dine with me this afternoon at half-post four o'clock. Good morning, sir!' and immediately resumed his writing."

At exactly 4:30 p.m., Stone arrived at Scott's residence near the White House. The general welcomed Stone "with a preoccupied air," and the two men finished the first course, soup, in silence. Next, Scott's valet served a roasted chicken, which Scott asked Stone to carve. The two men ate in silence, interrupted only when an orderly knocked on the door to deliver a telegram. After Scott wrote out his response and handed it off, the two men finished eating, still without conversation. Then, at Scott's request, Stone poured two glasses of sherry from the bottle that had sat on the table untouched during the meal. Scott raised his glass, and staring into it, catalogued the events of the past few days that had, one by one, further isolated Washington. He concluded: "They are closing their coils around us, sir!"

With that, Stone remembered, "he drained his glass, while I bowed and followed his example." Next, Scott asked, "how long can we hold out here?" Stone replied: "Ten days, General, and within that time the North will come down to us."

"How will they come?" asked Scott. "The route through Baltimore is cut off."

Replied Stone, "They will come by all routes. They will come between the Capes of Virginia, up through Chesapeake Bay, and by the Potomac. They will come, if necessary, from Pennsylvania through Maryland directly to us; and they will come through Baltimore and Annapolis."

Referring to Northern troops in Washington, Scott asked, "Well, sir, how many men have you?"

"In all, General, there are four thousand nine hundred," replied Stone. "But that number includes the battery of artillery near your headquarters, and the Ordnance men at the Arsenal, not under my command, and who will have enough to do to guard the Arsenal."

"How many miles of picket line between your outposts?" asked Scott.

"About eighteen miles, General."

"Eighteen miles of picket line and less than five thousand men!" Scott exclaimed. "Then you must, in case of attack, fight [with] your pickets!"

"Yes, General," replied Stone, who then explained his strategy. Stone believed that the Southerners did not have enough forces to attack more than one outlying location. If those pickets were overpowered at their posts, they could fall back while shooting at the enemy. What Stone called "the moving fire" would alert other troops about the attack's location, and forces could be "withdrawn from unthreatened points and marched to strengthen the real resisting force." Stone concluded, "This is all we can do, and what we can do must be done."

At this point, Scott switched the conversation to the most defensible locations within Washington, which Stone had selected shortly after Scott had appointed him inspector general of the District of Columbia Militia on January 1. Scott asked, "Where are your centers?"

"There are three, General," answered Stone. "First, the Capitol, where have been stored some two thousand barrels of flour, and where Major McDowell remains every night with two hundred to three hundred of my volunteers. Second, the City Hall hill, a commanding point [several blocks north of Pennsylvania Avenue between Fourth and Fifth streets], with broad avenues and wide streets connecting it with most important points, having in its vicinity the Patent-Office and the General Post-Office, in each of which I place a force every night. . . . Third, the Executive Square, including the President's house, the War, Navy, State, and Treasury Departments, in each of which, and in Winder's building, I place a force every night after dusk.

"The citadel of this center is the Treasury building," he continued. "The basement has been barricaded very strongly by Captain Franklin of the

Engineers, who remains there at night and takes charge of the force. The front of the Treasury building is well flanked by the State Department building, and fifty riflemen are nightly on duty there." Overall 2,000 barrels of flour had been stored in the Treasury, and a spring at the building provided water if the defenders were trapped inside.

Finally, Stone pointed out that Washington was "so admirably laid out in broad avenues and wide streets centering on the three positions chosen, that concentration for defense at any one of the three is made easy. The field battery can move rapidly toward any outpost where heavy firing shall indicate that the attack is there serious." Leaving the worst-case scenario for the end of his presentation, Stone informed Scott: "In the case a sharp resistance outside the city may fail to prevent an advance of the enemy, we can occupy the centers until the North shall have time to come to our relief."

"The general listened attentively," Stone recalled, "and looked over the map of the city which I had drawn from my pocket and placed before him while indicating the positions." Then, he said: "Your plan is good. . . . But you have too many centers. You cannot hold three. You will need all your force concentrated to hold one position against an energetic force equal to or superior in numbers to all you have. The first center to be abandoned must be the Capitol." The building was too large and had too many entrances to be defended by a limited number of troops. "The second center to be abandoned will be the City Hall hill," said Scott. Commenting on that decision, Stone said that the location had two advantages: "so commanding a position" because of the elevation and "such admirable avenues of communications"— that is, several major diagonal streets like New York and Massachusetts Avenues. "It is a pity to abandon so commanding a position, as you say, my young friend," replied Scott. "But we must act according to the number of troops we have with which to act."[53]

In the event of Washington being overrun with Southern troops, "all else must be abandoned, if necessary, to occupy, strongly and effectively, the Executive Square," ordered Scott, "with the idea of finally holding only the Treasury building, and, perhaps, the State Department building, properly connected." Stopping briefly, Scott followed a line of thought: "The seals of the several departments of the government must, this night, be deposited in the vaults of the Treasury. They must not be captured and used to deceive and create uncertainty among public servants distant from the capital."

Finally, he exclaimed: "Should it come to the defense of the Treasury building as a citadel, then the President and all the members of his cabinet must take up their quarters with us in that building! They shall not be permitted to desert the capital!"

By the end of the day on April 21, hostiles forces in Maryland had successfully cut off Washington's supply and communication lines, stopping nearly all government messengers, military supplies, and food from reaching the city. All train travel from the North through Baltimore was now impossible, though the B & O's main line from Wheeling and through Harper's Ferry to the Relay House remained open. These trains, however, were scrupulously inspected for any suspect passengers and cargo before they headed for Relay House. "On reaching the bridge at Harper's Ferry, the train was stopped by Virginia soldiers with a loaded cannon planted in front of the cars," wrote one passenger. Once the conductor assured them that "no United States agents, soldiers, or reporters were on the train, they were allowed to cross the bridge" over the Potomac, the border between Virginia and Maryland. On the Maryland side, the train was again stopped and a "loaded cannon pointed obliquely at the cars so that they could demolish the whole train, with men standing at the touch holes ready to fire." Just after midnight one evening, the inspection team discovered and detained General William S. Harney, who was wearing civilian clothes but reporting for duty in Washington.[54]

"There are many scouting parties of Baltimoreans in the outskirts of the city, prowling about in various directions," observed the *Philadelphia Inquirer*.[55] The Maryland militia posted sentries on major roads, such as the Baltimore-Washington Turnpike, and its cavalry patrolled back roads. Just north of Washington, militiamen of Montgomery and Prince George's counties caught a number of travelers just before they crossed over the District of Columbia line. Some messengers adopted disguises to get past the militiamen and vigilantes patrolling the roads to Washington. Pennsylvania politician Morrow Lowry, who carried important messages for Lincoln, dressed as a Methodist preacher. On his way to Washington by horseback, Lowry was stopped by men with rifles who wanted to know he was. "A Methodist preacher," he replied. "Go to hell," shouted one vigilante. Lowry answered, "Brethren, I can pray for you, but I cannot go there." They released him.[56]

Only those civilians blessed with wits, determination, and sheer luck could reach Washington. Henry Villard of the *New York Herald* faced daunting challenges when he attempted to return from New York to deliver the message he was carrying to President Lincoln from *Herald* publisher Bennett in support of the Union. While Villard's journey from Washington to New York on April 17 had been routine, his return journey on April 19, which should have been an overnight train trip, turned into a two-day test of his stamina and ingenuity.

On April 19, Villard boarded the night train in New York, expecting to arrive in Washington the next morning. At Perryville, Maryland, however, his journey came to an unexpected halt. There, passengers always left their train to take a ferryboat across the wide Susquehanna River to Havre de Grace, where they boarded another train to Baltimore. When Villard's train reached Perryville at 3 a.m. on April 20, its passengers disembarked and boarded the ferry. The boat, however, did not depart. "One weary hour after another passed without any light as to the cause of the delay," Villard wrote in his autobiography. "There was not even a chance to sit down on the boat, except on the deck."

At dawn, an exasperated Villard walked to the Perryville telegraph station, where the operator finally showed up at 7 a.m. During the night, he explained to Villard, the railroad had shut down all trains between Havre de Grace and Baltimore because bridges and trestles had been burned between the two cities. "Here was a predicament for me," remembered Villard, who immediately surmised that the damage was sabotage by secessionists. "On the one hand, the very interruption of communication with Washington made it the more desirable and necessary for me to be there, in order to supply news" to the *New York Herald*. "On the other, there was the embarrassing question how to get through, the broken railroad being the only line of land communication between the north and the capital." Villard decided that he was willing to take any step—literally—to get to Washington. Before setting off on foot, however, "the first thing I did was to beg for a breakfast at one of the few houses in the hamlet of Perryville—there being no hotel—and I got one of bacon, 'hoe cakes' [small fried or baked cakes of cornmeal], and indescribable coffee."

Next, Villard had to find a way to get across the Susquehanna River to Havre de Grace so that he could travel on to Baltimore, 38 miles away. Seeing several small boats moored at the riverbank in Perryville, he found a man who rowed him across the river for $1. Once in Havre de Grace, Villard discovered his next hurdle. No livery stable existed in the village, and no carriage owner would take him to Baltimore. "I determined to start on foot just as I was—my valise being checked to Washington—and take my chances of finding means of transportation on the way."

After walking six miles, he passed a farmer's home. "My request for a meal was readily acceded to," recalled Villard. "To my great relief, he consented, in response to my offer to pay twenty-five dollars for the accommodation, to send me in a buggy with one of his slaves to Baltimore." While rumors told of all roads "'swarming with rebel cavalry,' we met no armed men, nor any sort of adventure, and arrived at our destination a little before dark." Once checked into the Eutaw House, Villard read various newspapers' accounts of the "fearful occurrences the day before." To his dismay, he also read the "alarming announcement" that all rail travel between Baltimore and Washington had ended. He was too tired to consider a solution, so he had dinner and "sought my bed without delay."

The next morning, April 21, Villard tried to rent a carriage at one of the Baltimore livery stables, but the proprietors refused. He decided to rent a saddle horse, and one stable agreed on condition that he leave $100 with the Eutaw House's manager as security. By 9 a.m., he was riding in "leisurely fashion . . . like a pleasure-rider to the suburbs" on back roads, which were less likely to be patrolled by Maryland militiamen and vigilantes than the main highway to Washington. "I arrived at seven o'clock without having met any one but harmless country folk en route."[57] Villard checked into Willard's Hotel, had dinner, and, exhausted from his exploits, went to sleep.

By the evening of April 21, Washington had lost all telegraph service to the north. The city had already "been quite unable to get anything of much consequence over the telegraph wires" since April 19, reported the Washington correspondent of the *New York Times*, although there still had been "lucid intervals" of communication.[58] During the Baltimore riot, the lines had been severed at the main office, but the telegraph operators had quickly restored service. By the early morning hours of April 20, service was sporadic, because those who had burned the railroad bridges north of Baltimore had also cut telegraph lines running alongside the tracks. Even when telegrams to or from the North were successfully transmitted, they were scrutinized by telegraph operators with Southern sympathies unless sent in cipher.

On the evening of April 21, a group of secessionists seized Baltimore's main telegraph station, which lacked any police protection. Before the office was shuttered, one of the telegraph operators tapped out his last message to Washington. "The authorities have possession of office." The Washington operator wired back: "Of course this stops all."[59]

At the White House that night, Clifford Arrick of the Frontier Guards wrote in his diary that the severing of all communications meant that Washington had no means of knowing when expected reinforcements would arrive: "no reliable word can be had as to the whereabouts of the N.Y. 7th and other forces known to be moving hither."[60] As a result, he concluded, "unabated anxiety prevails." Worse, though the lines north were cut, reported the New York Times, the lines from Alexandria to the South were still operational, "notifying the rebels of our exposed condition" and "inviting them consequently to the attack before the Government should be able to bring hither the troops necessary to defend the Capital."[61]

Late that night, Horatio Taft also wondered about the fate of the Northern volunteer regiments in his diary. "We seem to be surrounded [by enemies] in our midst. No troop [sic] have yet arrived since the Mass. Regt. How anxiously have we looked for the 7th Regt of NY today." Once again, he expected the capital to be the scene of battle at any moment. "We may be in the midst of bloodshed any hour, and I am looking for an outbreak or attack all the time." As he finished that day's entry, his thoughts took on a new note of desperation. "Famine stares us in the face unless the routes are kept open. Where are the expected troops?"[62]

When Lincoln recalled the events of April 1861 one year later, he described the city's isolation: "mails in every direction were stopped," while telegraph lines were "cut off by the insurgents" and "all the roads and avenues to this city were obstructed." At the same time, the "military and naval forces . . . called out by the Government for the defence of Washington . . . were prevented from reaching the city by organized and combined treasonable resistance." In short, Lincoln wrote, the "capital was put into the condition of a siege."[63] From inside the city on April 21, William Gulick described Washington's plight the same way: "A real state of siege exists."[64]

Monday, April 22

"Enveloped by the Traitors"

Walking down Pennsylvania Avenue on Monday morning, Henry Villard noted that an "extraordinary change had, indeed, taken place at the capital" since his departure from Washington five days before.[1] Villard, who had returned to Washington the previous night, recalled, "I could almost count the people in sight on my fingers. A great many private houses and a number of stores were also shut up. The whole city had a deserted look." It seemed "as though the government of a great nation had been suddenly removed to an island in mid-ocean in a state of entire isolation."[2]

Outside Washington, millions of Northerners and Southerners were transfixed by the capital's plight. Frederick Douglass described the anxiety of many Northerners that week in terms of collective experience. We "opened our papers, new and damp from the press, tremblingly, lest the first line of the lightning should tell us that our National Capital has fallen."[3] The April 22 edition of the *Philadelphia Public Ledger and Daily Transcript* reported, "Every eye is now turned to Washington City, in anxious expectation of the events which seem to be impending in that quarter."[4] The *New York Tribune* warned that Washington was "temporarily enveloped by the traitors . . . with the Secessionists in force on every side." It was "imperative that communications to the capital be "opened by strong moving columns from the North."[5]

Southerners, of course, viewed Washington's position quite differently, and a few newspapers and politicians blamed Lincoln's determination in holding Washington as a casus belli for the war, especially since Washington would be entirely surrounded by Confederate states if Maryland seceded, as expected. The "great present obstacle to a peaceful solution" of the crisis between North and South, the *Baltimore Sun* argued in its Monday edition, was the "occupancy of the city of Washington."[6] Viewing the secession of

Maryland as a foregone conclusion, the newspaper called for the North to abandon and evacuate its old capital. The less circumspect and ardently secessionist Baltimore newspaper *The South*, on only its second day in print, was giddy about Washington's probable capture. On the basis of the Baltimore delegations' White House visits, this newspaper claimed that Lincoln was "thoroughly frightened" and was now concerned "much more about his own personal safety" than "subjugating the South." Lincoln, the paper gloated, was "effectively caged—caught, to use his own expression, 'like a rat in a trap.'"[7]

That morning, for the third successive day, Lincoln met with a delegation from Baltimore, this time a 30-person group of Baltimore YMCA members. It was led by South Carolina–born slaveholder Reverend Richard Fuller, a pastor at Baltimore's influential Seventh Baptist Church and the president of the Southern Baptist Convention.[8] Their intention was to stress religious principles to make their arguments for peace. Nicolay called the men the "Committee of 'Christians,'" sarcastically adding scare quotes around the word in the list he kept of important events. Hay was more direct, calling the men "whining traitors" in his diary entry for that day.[9]

By April 22, Lincoln suspected that the goal of the Baltimore delegations was not to negotiate peace and prevent the "effusion of blood"—as the YMCA Committee presented its mission—but to act as instruments of obstruction.[10] In their "lamb-like bleatings for peace," recalled Frederick Seward, the Baltimore delegations wanted to delay or prevent the arrival of Northern reinforcements in Washington and assure its surrender to the South.[11] The YMCA delegation went far beyond the previous two delegations, requesting that Lincoln recognize the Confederacy, prevent the upcoming "unnatural conflict" by dismissing all military forces in the capital, and refuse to transport any more troops through Maryland to Washington. On hearing this catalogue of demands, Lincoln's temper, which had been fraying, finally snapped. "You, gentlemen, come here to me and ask for peace on any terms, and yet have no word of condemnation for those who are making war on us," he exclaimed. "You express great horror of bloodshed, and yet would not lay a straw in the way of those who are organizing in Virginia and elsewhere to capture this city."[12] Lincoln continued: "I have no desire to invade the south, but I must have troops to defend the capital. Geographically it lies surrounded by the soil of Maryland, and mathematically the necessity exists that they shall come here over her territory. Our men are not moles, and can't dig in the earth; they are not birds, and can't fly through the air. There is no way but march across, and that they must do."[13] In another published version of the remarks, Lincoln also pointed out to Fuller the irony of his request, since Confederate forces were also crossing through neighboring states on their way to Washington: "Those North Carolinians are now crossing Virginia to come here to hang me, and what can I do?"[14]

Lincoln's stance aligned with growing calls for retribution against Baltimore, which had echoed in Washington and across the North since the deadly April 19 attack on the Sixth Massachusetts Volunteers. On April 20, Horatio Taft described Baltimore as a "doomed city."[15] In the *New York Tribune*, Albert D. Richardson, one of its Washington correspondents and later a Union spy, proclaimed, in an italicized typeface for emphasis, *"That city has stood long enough."* Baltimore, he wrote, "should be razed to the earth, and not one stone left upon another."[16] On April 22, Orville Browning, a Lincoln confidant in Illinois, wrote the president (his letter could not reach Washington for days due to the blockage of mail): "The fall of Washington would be most disasterous [*sic*]. Communication ought to, and must be kept open to Washington." Browning suggested that Baltimore be punished if it did not allow Union troops to pass; it "should be seized and garrisoned, or, if necessary to the success of our glorious cause, laid to ruin."[17]

In speaking to the YMCA delegation that day, Lincoln was forceful enough to make sure that his words were not interpreted as a bluff. After telling the Marylanders that the volunteer regiments now landing at Annapolis had to travel to Washington without any interference, he sharply warned them: "If you won't hit me, I won't hit you!" Should the Union troops be harmed in any way, he warned ominously, "I will lay Baltimore in ashes."[18]

Though the federal government still lacked enough soldiers to adequately safeguard Washington, much less undertake such a mission against Baltimore, Lincoln's threat was real. The previous day, reports had circulated in Washington, later reported in the *New York Times*, that the governors of Massachusetts, New York, Pennsylvania, and Ohio had sent telegrams to Governor Hicks and Mayor Brown, informing them that if they obstructed these states' volunteer regiment's progress on their way to Washington, the Union volunteers would level Baltimore.[19] The War Department, moreover, could direct Northern states to send thousands more volunteers straight through Baltimore, and before they arrived, cannon of Fort McHenry and

U.S. Navy gunships ordered to the harbor could bombard the city. Or Northern troops could simply isolate Baltimore and blockade it into starvation.

Indeed, on the morning of April 22, some Baltimore residents believed that the city would imminently be attacked by the Pennsylvania Volunteers who had come within 15 miles of the city the previous day. Many people assumed that Lincoln's much-publicized order to send those troops back to Pennsylvania was no more than a ruse. "Instead of returning to Harrisburg," declared the *Baltimore Sun*, "they would, having been reinforced, unexpectedly make their appearance" in the streets of Baltimore and at "all hazards force their way through and reach Washington."[20] To repel any forces, the "regular military"—that is, the Maryland militia—remained "unusually active," the *Sun* wrote, and three heavy cannons had even been left in the street overnight for immediate use against any Union soldiers who reached the downtown.

By now the Baltimore militia formed under the direction of the Board of Police and led by Kane and General Steuart numbered 15,000 men. The scarcity of arms, however, meant that many soldiers lacked weapons, and even those who had guns could not obtain enough ammunition. The city's foundry shops were working to cast "cannon balls and grape in large quantities at the order of the city," the *Sun* reported.[21] The most active factory belonged to Ross Winans, one of Baltimore's wealthiest citizens, who had led calls to oppose Northern troops before the April 19 riot and now had 700 workers forging pikes day and night to use for hand-to-hand combat in the streets. Winans had pledged $500,000 of his own money to Baltimore for its defense, and allegedly promised another $500,000 to the Confederate government in Montgomery. The city purchased one of Winans's newest and deadliest armaments, the "centrifugal steam gun," which could reportedly fire three hundred rounds of ammunition per minute. "It is the intention of the authorities to place the gun at the head of the street up which the invading troops attempt to march," wrote *The South*, "sweep the ranks" of any Union volunteers unlucky enough to caught in its fire.[22]

Meanwhile, General Steuart was strengthening his contacts with Virginia and with the Confederate government in preparation for joint action against Union troops and the federal capital. On April 22, John Scott, a Virginian, telegrammed Confederate Secretary of State Robert Toombs that reports had just been received from an "agent of [Virginia] Governor Letcher" indicating "that dispatches have just been received from General Steuart, in command of troops at Baltimore, stating that 3,000 are in camp ten miles from Baltimore, waiting re-inforcements before proceeding to Washington."[23] The lack of military weapons and ammunition in Maryland was acute, and Scott reported that secessionists there were beseeching Virginia leaders for aid: "Baltimore is almost bare of arms and asks of loan of them from Virginia." Steuart's militia was ranging well outside Baltimore, to strike Washington if Virginia provided support, it appeared. His sizable force was not alone; the "light cavalry of Prince George"—the Maryland county bordering Washington—was reported to be "swarming to the very edge of the District" on April 21.[24]

When Jefferson Davis learned of Steuart's request, he cabled Letcher: "Sustain Baltimore, if practicable. We re-enforce you."[25] Thirteen regiments, Davis wrote, would head north for Virginia from the South, in addition to the two regiments Davis had directed to Norfolk from South Carolina.[26] On April 21, Davis had ordered South Carolina's Governor Pickens to redirect those troops to Richmond, given that the Norfolk Navy Yard would fall without additional soldiers. When the South Carolina troops arrived at the Virginia capital, they would report to Letcher—all troops within the state were nominally under the Virginia governor's command—until a formal military alliance between the Confederacy and the Old Dominion could be secured. Vice President Stephens had left Montgomery to negotiate this alliance, and he arrived in Richmond by train on April 22.

Letcher appeared to have no intention of launching a direct attack on Washington with Virginia forces. The Virginia troops who had seized Harper's Ferry the night of April 18 had halted there, apart from making forays across the Potomac to scour the Maryland countryside for arms. In Richmond, the most belligerent voice to push "On to Washington!" former governor Henry Wise, had departed to his plantation near Norfolk, reportedly in ill health, after organizing the successful raids on the Navy Yard there and at Harper's Ferry. On April 22, a full week after Lincoln's proclamation, Letcher finally authorized the formation of a Virginia volunteer force to augment existing county militias across the state. His order "authorized and required to call into the service of the State as many volunteers as may be necessary to repel invasion and protect the citizens of the State in the present emergency."[27] These volunteers, like their Union counterparts, were officially to be enrolled purely for defensive means, and Letcher showed no inclination to order them forward until Robert E. Lee arrived in Richmond to assume command.

Many Southerners, however, believed that the volunteer regiments heading to Richmond from other states would immediately join Virginia troops to attack Washington—and under Jefferson Davis's personal command. An 1828 graduate of West Point who had served as a colonel in the Mexican-American War, Davis seemed the likely leader for an assault the federal capital. On April 21, Edmund Ruffin had written in his diary: "One regiment of [South Carolina] volunteers is to go on tonight to Va. to be soon followed by another. Other southern states it is understood will also furnish troops, to be concentrated in Va, & to attack Washington City, under immediate command of Pres. Davis."[28] According to the *Charleston Mercury*'s Richmond correspondent, a rumor circulated in the Virginia capital on the evening of the April 22 claimed that Davis would arrive the next day with 3,000 South Carolinians, "every man of whom was burning to be first in the great battle at Washington."[29]

Leading Confederate officials in Montgomery, however, knew that Davis did not intend to lead an attack on Washington. Nonetheless, they hoped that he could soon arrive in the former federal capital in triumph. On April 21, former Virginia Senator James Mason, one of the plotters of the raid on Harper's Ferry, had written to Davis that he believed Washington's seizure was likely, adding, "I trust in god that Lincoln's Congress called for the 4th. July, (Should it venture thitherward,) will find the capitol under your guns."[30]

Vice President Stephens's train trip from Montgomery to Richmond to secure the military union with Virginia strengthened Southerners' expectations—and Northerners' fears—of an impending attack on Washington. A man from Massachusetts, who had been living in North Carolina and had decided to flee the South to avoid being forced to serve in the Confederate military, rode on the same train as Stephens through North Carolina to Norfolk. According to his account, Stephens shouted "On to Washington!" to large crowds at nearly every station: "The capture of Washington was the grand idea which he enforced, and [he] exhorted the people to join in the enterprise.... 'It must be done!' was his constant exclamation."[31]

Stephens arrived in Richmond on the morning of April 22 and was greeted with enthusiasm. He immediately cabled an update to Davis on military operations, reporting that "4,000 arms" had been saved at Harper's Ferry—an unrealistic figure, in fact only hundreds—and that Letcher had ordered a thousand of them to be sent to General Steuart in Baltimore.[32] Stephens also reported Letcher's proclamation "ordering 5,000 infantry and rifles to rendezvous immediately" by railroad. In short, Stephens wrote, "Plenty awaiting a commander-in-chief" to direct their actions. He added that Robert E. Lee, who was expected to arrive that day, was "looked to as the commander."

Lee's arrival was anxiously expected in Richmond. And to Maryland secessionists who hoped to coordinate military action with Virginia, it was critical to establish communication with the new commander of the Virginia forces. Steuart had attempted to reach Lee while he was still in northern Virginia on April 21. Steuart had dispatched his letter by two high-level messengers, Baltimore merchants L. P. Bayne and J. J. Chancellor, who reached Washington by train early in the morning on April 22. On crossing the Potomac River to Alexandria, the two men learned that Lee had already departed for Richmond, and they wrote their own dispatch, enclosing Steuart's original letter. Their most urgent news was that Steuart had "declared Washington road to be under military rule," meaning the 30 miles of the B & O Railroad from Relay House to Washington. Bayne and Chancellor added that if Lee or Letcher desired to communicate with Steuart, the Virginians' letters "would be forwarded by horse express" over vedette lines to Baltimore, as "General Steuart will be most anxious to hear from you immediately."[33]

On the evening of April 22, Lee arrived in Richmond by train from Alexandria. He first secured a room at the Spotswood Hotel and then met with Governor Letcher, who formally offered him command of Virginia's army and navy. The nomination was submitted to the Virginia Convention and was approved unanimously. Lee returned to the hotel for the night; his military preparations would begin the next day.[34]

The morning after Lee's arrival, the city's most belligerent newspaper, the *Richmond Examiner*, proclaimed that the Confederacy still had time to seize Washington. "The capture of Washington City is perfectly within the power of Virginia and Maryland, if Virginia will only make the proper effort by her constituted authorities." The paper was exasperated that there had been any delay in moving on the federal capital; Virginia and Maryland had not "a single moment to lose" if they were to "take Washington and drive from it every Black Republican who is a dweller there." The paper's declaration then turned apocalyptic: "From the mountain-tops and valleys to the shores of the sea there is one wild shout of fierce resolve to capture Washington City at all and every human hazard. The filthy cage of unclean birds must and will assuredly be purified by fire."[35]

Shortly after midnight on April 22, the steamship *Boston*, overcrowded with the 1,000 men of the Seventh New York, neared the mouth of the Severn River on Chesapeake Bay. There, the ship halted until dawn, more than a day and a half after it had left Philadelphia at 5 p.m. on April 20. At dawn, with the fog lifting, the Seventh New York men spotted the USS *Constitution*, "Old Ironsides," and let loose "hearty cheers" when they glimpsed the Stars and Stripes flying from the famed ship's mast. Half a mile ahead and closer to their destination—Annapolis—they spotted the steamship *Maryland*, which had transported the Eighth Massachusetts Volunteers under the command of General Butler. The sighting of the *Maryland* was no surprise for the Seventh New York men, for it had left Perryville, Maryland, in midafternoon on April 20, three hours before their own departure from Philadelphia on the *Boston*. The trip from Perryville down the northern end of Chesapeake Bay to Annapolis should have taken no more than half a day, and the New Yorkers assumed that the ship had anchored after having discharged the Massachusetts on shore. But as the *Boston* drew closer to the *Maryland*, the Seventh New York spotted bayonets gleaming in the early morning sun, and the outlines of soldiers crowding the deck. The Eighth Massachusetts men were still on board.

For their part, the Seventh New York had expected to be docked in Washington by that morning, not sailing into the Annapolis harbor. But Colonel Lefferts, their commander, had been forced to order his ship back from the mouth of the Potomac River late in the day on April 21 because he had found no government vessel waiting to give the all-clear signal for the trip up the river to Washington. (His earlier telegram requesting such assurance had never reached the War Department.) Without protection, Lefferts did not dare sail the *Boston*, overcrowded and unarmed, up the Potomac, where enemy guns might shell them from the Virginia shore. He had also worried that ships captured by the Virginians after they seized the Norfolk Navy Yard—news he had learned from passing boats as they sailed down the Chesapeake Bay—might be lying in wait upriver. So he had ordered the *Boston* to turn around and set a course for Annapolis. There, he planned to follow the same route as Butler and the Eighth Massachusetts, which, to his chagrin, he expected to be a full day ahead of his own regiment in reaching Washington.

The mood aboard the *Boston* during the trip to the mouth of the Potomac was anything but glum. The men passed the time by telling jokes and singing popular songs, including one written right on board by their comrade-in-arms Fitz-James O'Brien, a poet, journalist, and Bohemian around town. Set to accompaniment of the mandolin and sung to the tune of a popular Irish melody, O'Brien's song started:

> *Och! we're the boys*
> *That hearts desthroys* [sic]
> *Wid making love and fighting,*
> *We take a fort,*
> *The girls we court*
> *But most the last delight is*
> *To fire a gun*
> *Or raise some fun*
> *To us is no endeavor*
> *So let us hear*
> *One hearty cheer,*
> *The Seventh's lads for ever.*

Some of the lyrics pointed to the well-to-do Seventh New York men's love of fine food and wine.

> *Like Jove above,*
> *We're fond of love,*
> *But fonder still of victuals,*
> *Wid turtle steaks*
> *An' codfish cakes*
> *We always fills our kittles.*
> *To dhrown sich dish,*
> *We dhrinks like fish.*
> *And Mumm's the word we utter,*
> *An' thin we swill*
> *Our Leoville,*
> *That oils our throats like butter.*[36]

"Mumm's" was of course the fashionable French champagne, while "Leoville" referred to one of the priciest clarets (red Bordeaux wine) of the nineteenth century.

At sunset on April 21, the men with the best voices in the regiment had sung religious hymns. "As the softened flood of harmony floated out upon the solemn stillness of the air," wrote William Swinton, another journalist and member of New York's Bohemian circle, "the scene, the measureless sea, and the hour,—that of parting day,—added effect to the chant."[37] As the nearly full moon rose in the sky, "the rugged mate of the steamer, glancing toward it, saw three distinct and beautiful circles surrounding it,—red, white, and blue! 'There!' he cried, 'is our flag in the sky! God never will let it be struck down under foot!' A thrill ran through the men as all, looking into the heavens, recognized the phenomenon, clear and unmistakable. Cheers and songs greeted the felicitous omen."

As soon as the Seventh New York pulled into Annapolis harbor early on the morning of April 22 and unexpectedly spotted the Massachusetts troops clustered on the deck of the *Maryland*, Colonel Lefferts ordered his ship to pull alongside the ship. Even before he and several of his officers boarded the *Maryland*, the Eighth Massachusetts men shouted that they had arrived in Annapolis the day before but had been marooned on a mud bank for nearly a day. "The sorry plight in which the Seventh found their gallant friends removed all disposition to banter them," recalled Swinton, and both regiments were reminded of the many challenges ahead.[38]

Once on board, Colonel Lefferts learned the full story behind the plight of the Massachusetts regiment. The *Maryland* had reached Annapolis at midnight the night before.[39] General Butler had hoped to sail into the harbor in the fog without attracting attention and then wait until early morning to disembark his men from the overcrowded vessel at the pier near the Naval Academy. Suddenly, however, a burst of signal rockets had unexpectedly lit up the foggy night sky. Their ship had been spotted. "As we got fairly in sight," recalled Butler in his autobiography, "the 'assembly' was beaten, men were forming, the lights were glancing, the academy was all lighted up, and it was quite evident that we were expected."[40]

Before leaving Philadelphia, Butler had heard reports that his men might be attacked on disembarking at Annapolis, and did not take any chances. At 1 a.m., the *Maryland* had dropped anchor two miles from shore. Butler had sent Captain Peter Haggerty to learn the latest news in town. Shortly thereafter, as Butler stood on the gangway, he had heard the sound of muffled oars coming closer, and a boat pulled alongside the *Maryland*, carrying a lieutenant from the Naval Academy, who had delivered a letter from Captain George S. Blake, the superintendent. A loyal Union man, Blake was apprehensive that the secessionists might try to seize the *Constitution*, which was being used as a training ship and dormitory space for midshipmen. The ship could not easily be moved, because it was stuck in a mud bank. Blake had already stationed a sailor at the ship's magazine, which held considerable gunpowder, ready to blow up the vessel if he gave the order. Blake expressed his hope that the *Maryland* could save the revered old ship.[41]

Just after dawn, Captain Blake had arrived at the *Maryland* to plead his case to Butler in person. He found a receptive audience. Butler considered the ship a national icon known for, as he termed it, "deeds of daring, successful contests, and glorious victories," and responded to Blake's entreaty.[42] To forestall the theft or destruction of the *Constitution*, he had agreed to pull her further out into the harbor. When Butler had asked who among his Massachusetts troops knew how to handle sailing ships, no fewer than 54 men had stepped forward—including the grandson of one man who had helped build the *Constitution* in Boston Harbor, where she had been launched in 1797.[43]

As Butler was preparing to leave the *Maryland* to breakfast with Captain Blake at the Naval Academy, Captain Haggerty had returned from his news-gathering visit to Annapolis and handed Butler a note from Governor Hicks. "Sir, I would most earnestly advise that you do not land your men at Annapolis," Hicks cautioned. "The excitement here is very great, and I think that you should take your men elsewhere."[44]

After his meal with Blake, Butler had met with Governor Hicks himself. "He was accompanied by the mayor of Annapolis," John R. Magruder, recalled Butler in his autobiography, "and both of them exhorted me not to think of landing."[45] Hicks had given Butler many reasons. "All of Maryland was ready to rush to arms," he had said. "The railroad towards Washington had been torn up and was fully guarded." Hicks had even told Butler that he "could not buy an ounce of provisions in Annapolis." Magruder seconded this caution, assuring that "no patriot would sell to Yankee troops provisions with which to march to Washington." At this, Butler admitted in his autobiography, he had become "a little aroused." He replied, "I suppose there are sufficient provisions in this capital of Maryland to feed a thousand men, and if the people will not sell those provisions, a thousand hungry, armed men have other means of getting what they want to eat besides buying it." That had been the end of the meeting.

Meanwhile, Butler's men had labored to free the *Constitution*. To lighten its weight, they moved its heavy cannons and gun carriages to the *Maryland*.

They pulled up the anchors, which were buried several feet deep in the mud. Finally, the *Maryland* had dislodged the *Constitution* and pulled her further out from shore.

The *Maryland*, however, had run "hard and fast aground" while sailing back toward Annapolis to land at the pier near the Naval Academy, "and that closed the day Sunday," according to Butler. In his later recollections, though, he left out one important fact: because he had set off so quickly for Annapolis, his men did have adequate provisions onboard the *Maryland*. The ship now lay aground in the harbor, exactly where the Seventh New York found the famished Massachusetts men crowding the vessel on the morning of April 22.

Colonel Lefferts told the Eighth Massachusetts that he would try to pull the *Maryland* out of the mud at the high tide in several hours. In the meantime, "the persevering Massachusetts lads had for hours been resorting to all sorts of devices . . . to get clear, and had put forth herculean efforts," wrote Swinton; "they threw over the baggage-trucks, coal, crates, shifted themselves forward and aft, and ran suddenly from side to side, but all in vain." At high tide, the *Boston* tried to pull the *Maryland* out of the mud bank for several hours, "all, too, in vain."[46]

When these efforts proved fruitless, as the tide went out the Seventh New York men aboard the *Boston* sailed into Annapolis harbor at 4 p.m. to take quarters at the Naval Academy. They planned to dispatch a more powerful steamer to pull the *Maryland* off the mud bank. By 5 p.m., the New York men were disembarking at the wharf, and they marched up a grassy slope to the Naval Academy, where a number of rooms were available because many Southern midshipmen had returned home. A more powerful steamboat was not available immediately, so the *Boston* returned to the still-stuck *Maryland and* by mid-evening had brought all her thirsty, hungry, and coal-soot-covered men to shore.

"Tired soldiers, just from the cramped discomforts and foul smells of a three-days' sea-voyage in an overcrowded boat, could never have had a more welcome sight or one of greater beauty," *Harper's Weekly* described the scene.[47] The men were left to rest in the unexpected idyll of the Academy grounds, and soon "stretched them-selves on the bright green grass, or tumbled in the new hay, in a perfect glory of delicious luxury," Nevertheless, military preparations continued apace: "under some trees, where every gentle breeze covered them with the pink fragrant peach blossoms, the howitzers were drawn up, loaded to the muzzle with canister shot."[48]

Shortly after they arrived, many Seventh New York men wrote home about their journey to Annapolis, and expectations of fighting in the next few days. "I stand it much better than some of the poor devils around me, who faint from privation and fatigue," wrote one New Yorker that evening about his comrades and the just-arrived Massachusetts men.[49] "Rumors fly thick that we are surrounded by enemies on every side, and will have a bloody march of it. We went at the call of duty to do service for our country, and not only am I prepared to suffer fatigue, but to spill my blood in her cause."

Meanwhile, Colonel Lefferts met with several Annapolis residents, including Mayor Magruder. The conversation did not go well. Magruder complained about the Seventh New York's "assault on Maryland soil." Lefferts replied that he was headed to Washington at the command of the Secretary of War. Magruder urged Lefferts to move the Seventh New York out of Annapolis, because it "was a great outrage" and "would lead to trouble." "That rests with yourselves," Lefferts replied. "If left alone, we shall disturb nobody but you must keep hands off."[50]

That evening, the Seventh New York and later the Eighth Massachusetts dined at the Naval Academy. For the New Yorkers, who had eaten adequate provisions on board the *Boston* and were accustomed to Manhattan fare, the meal was a letdown: hardtack and salt pork from barrels stamped "1848." Without a fire for cooking the men were forced to eat the pork "raw or not at all."[51] The drink was plain water and a little coffee. For the Eighth Massachusetts, on the other hand, the minimal rations were a relief—starving aboard the *Maryland*, several men had even drunk seawater and become delirious.

That night, most of the Seventh New York occupied the vacant rooms at the Naval Academy, and the academy's midshipmen in residence invited the overflow to share their own rooms. The Eighth Massachusetts arrived later and slept on the Academy grounds, wrapping themselves in their blankets and using their knapsacks as pillows. The guards posted to protect the troops, wrote Theodore Winthrop, now, for the first time, "paced their beats in a hostile country."[52]

Butler and Lefferts met that evening to determine how to reach Washington, now only 35 miles away. Once again, the two regiments' commanders clashed, threatening to delay their critical mission. Butler narrated the dispute—with his obvious slant in his own favor—in his autobiography.

According to his account, Lefferts told Butler that he had consulted his men about the best time to set off from Annapolis for Washington, and that they had decided to wait until more Union reinforcements arrived in the Maryland capital until they departed for Washington.[53]

That response set off Butler's temper. "Colonel Lefferts," he said, "war is not carried on in this way. A commander doesn't consult his regiment as to the propriety of obeying his orders; he must judge of what those orders should be." Butler was not finished. "Now, by the Articles of War," he informed Lefferts, "I am in command, as brigadier-general of the United States militia, called into service, and actually in service. I take the responsibility of giving you an order to march, and shall expect it to be followed," Butler recounted.[54]

Butler was not only infuriated that Lefferts—whom he somewhat inexplicably called "butcher boy" behind his back—had refused his order; he was further aggravated by the presence of Congressman Samuel R. Curtis of Iowa, one of Butler's loathed West Point graduates.[55]

In response to Butler's demand that the Seventh New York Regiment follow his orders, Congressman Curtis replied, "General Butler, you don't appear to be aware that a general of the United States militia has no right to command New York State troops."

"No, sir" said Butler. "I am not aware of that, and it is not the law. Have you got a copy of the Articles of War in your pocket?"

"No, sir," replied Curtis.

"Have you examined them?" asked Butler.

"No, sir; but I was educated at West Point," said Curtis, providing the necessary spark to set off Butler.

Looking at Lefferts, Butler asked: "What rank does this man hold in your command?"

"None at all," said Lefferts.

"Well, then, I have nothing to do with him," replied Butler, who again asked Lefferts, "Will you march [to Washington]?" He sternly concluded: "I hope you won't refuse to obey my order." Butler had already threatened to arrest Lefferts for insubordination.

Curtis again stepped into the fray. "Well, what will you do if the colonel refuses to march?"

"If he refuses to march," responded Butler, "I certainly have this remedy: I will denounce him and his regiment as fit only to march down Broadway in gala dress to be grinned at by milliners' apprentices."

Unwilling to take this insult, Curtis baited Butler. "Such language as that, General, requires reparation among officers and gentlemen."

"Oh well, as far as Colonel Lefferts is concerned, I shall be entirely satisfied with him if he shows a disposition to fight anybody anywhere; let him begin on me," replied Butler. "But as for you, if you interrupt this conversation again, and if you do not leave the room instantly, I will direct my orderly to take you out. Good afternoon, Colonel Lefferts."

Thus ended the meeting. It was the last time Butler and Lefferts ever spoke to each other in person.

In Washington, the constant rumors of a Southern assault, followed by the failure of any such attack to materialize, had rendered many officials and residents deeply skeptical. Lucius Chittenden recorded in his diary that "no troops"—that is, hostile ones—had "arrived from any quarter, either by land or sea," showing the "untruthfulness of rumors of last night."[56] Indeed, some in the North believed that Washington would quickly be made safe because it was now a matter of hours until sufficient reinforcements arrived. The *New York World* predicted that if Washington was "not attacked by the rebels before tomorrow [April 23], it will probably be out of danger, and the country, relieved by the agony of suspense, will breathe more freely."[57]

Washington residents found other reasons for optimism, even as they waited for the Seventh New York and Eighth Massachusetts to arrive from Annapolis. That afternoon, the delayed steamer *Anacostia*, which had been dispatched two days earlier from the Washington Navy Yard with a small company of Marines to survey the Potomac for obstructions, returned to the city, and her men reported that the river was clear. That same day, the steamship *Pocahontas*, which had sailed up the Potomac from its mouth on the Chesapeake Bay, reported "no batteries at the White House Point," a narrows on the Potomac four miles south of Mount Vernon, and "no record of any hostile demonstrations from the banks of Alexandria."[58] Noting this, Hay concluded: "The very fact of the *Pocahontas* coming so quietly in, is a good one."

Also on that day, Timothy Webster, a detective who worked for Allan Pinkerton in Chicago, managed to reach Washington bearing an offer of assistance. Pinkerton, who had helped uncover a plot to assassinate Lincoln in Baltimore on the way to his inauguration, wrote the president, "When I saw you last I said that if the time should ever come that I could be of service to you I was ready," he wrote. "If that time has come, I am at hand."[59]

Pinkerton declared himself "at your command" for "obtaining information of the movements of Traitors, or Safely conveying your letters or dispatches." Stressing the necessity that all communications be *"strictly private,"*
Pinkerton had provided a copy of his extensive cipher codes, in case Lincoln
wanted to send him a telegram. Pinkerton's code specified "nuts" for *President* and "prunes" for *Vice President*. "Copper Rivets" and "Large Rivets"
meant *Congress* and *Senate*, respectively, while "Small Rivets," "Brass Rivets,"
and "Iron Rivets" ominously meant *destroy*, *hide*, and *dangers*.[60] After reading
this letter, Lincoln decided that Pinkerton should come to Washington at
once, and at Webster's request wrote his response on a piece of onionskin
paper. According to Pinkerton's account, Webster rolled up the paper into a
ball, hid it in the knob of his walking stick, and departed immediately for
Chicago.

Meanwhile, after receiving numerous death threats, General Scott vacated
his quarters at Mrs. Duvall's fashionable boarding house on the south side of
Pennsylvania Avenue between Seventeenth and Eighteenth Street. There,
Colonel Edward Townsend, Scott's chief of staff, had slept on a sofa outside
the door to his room, armed with a pistol and knife. Scott now moved full-
time to the greater security of the Winder Building, where he would be safer
and better able to respond to any emergency.[61]

In his private dispatch to Lincoln that day, Scott again alerted the president
to reports that Confederate forces posed a threat to Washington. Scott
believed that a force of 1,500–2,000 men was likely preparing to attack Fort
Washington "on the two sides of the river"—that is, from both the Maryland
and Virginia banks of the Potomac. More worrisome to Scott were reports
that "extra cars went up, yesterday," along the B & O Railroad line to "bring
down from Harpers Ferry, about 2,000 other troops to join in a general attack
on this Capital, that is, on many of its fronts at once." Scott was again convinced that the city could be defended successfully. "I feel confident that with
our present forces, we can defend the Capitol, the Arsenal & all the executive
buildings—seven, against ten thousand troops not better than our District
Volunteers."[62]

Still, the most promising news of the day was the arrival of the Seventh
New York and Eighth Massachusetts regiments at Annapolis one day earlier.
Although War Department messengers dispatched from Washington had
failed to reach these troops, a "telegram intercepted on its way to Baltimore"
reported their landing—"our Yankees and New Yorkers," as Hay described

them.[63] Though Scott reported to Lincoln that many rails on the feeder line from Annapolis to Annapolis Junction, where the men could catch the train to Washington, had been "taken up," he believed that the regiments would have "no difficulty in reaching Washington on foot."[64]

Scott, in a letter dispatched by horse express to General Patterson in Pennsylvania that day, wrote that he believed that Massachusetts and New Yorkers had already "commenced their march upon" Washington after reaching Annapolis the previous day. Still, he could not be sure: "Up to this moment we do not know that the march has commenced." Scott described further possible routes around Baltimore by which to send additional volunteers to Washington, as "we greatly need ten or twelve additional regiments for this place, now partially besieged, threatened, and in danger of being attacked on all sides in a day or two or three."[65]

Though Scott still predicted an imminent assault, others in the administration took the news of the regiments' landing as a sign that the capital's isolation would soon be over. That night, the mood among the members of Clay Battalion at their "armory"—Willard's Hotel—was still mirthful and relaxed, as Hay described the scene in his diary. "Raw patriots lounge elegantly on the benches—drink coffee in the anteroom—change the boots of unconscious sleepers in the hall—scribble busily in editorial notebooks."[66] Hay expected to see the soldiers in Washington the next day: "Weary and foot-sore, but very welcome, they will probably greet us tomorrow."[67]

Tuesday, April 23

"Fight, Sir, Fight!"

Early in the morning, two messengers from General Scott arrived separately in Annapolis. The day before, after learning of the arrival of the volunteer regiments at the Maryland capital, Scott had dispatched eight men from Washington. Six had failed to reach Annapolis, having either been captured or forced to turn back. The two messengers who arrived safely carried the urgent message that the capital was still in Union hands, and Lefferts and Butler were to speed the arrival of the troops by train.

The news of the landing of the Union troops at Annapolis had spread throughout Washington since the previous day, and many residents expected the troops to reach the city by Tuesday morning. "A large and disappointed throng gathered at the depot this morning hoping to get deliverance," recorded Hay later in the day. "But the hope was futile."[1] That disappointment was compounded by frightening rumors that General Beauregard had been "reconnoitering in the neighborhood of Washington" the night before, according to the Washington correspondent of the *New York Times.*[2] That report was quite plausible, given that more than ample time had passed since the surrender of Fort Sumter for Beauregard to have reached Washington from Charleston, as it was no more than three days by train to Richmond, and from there no more than another day to Alexandria. An even more frightening rumor also gained credence, reported in the *Philadelphia Inquirer*: that Beauregard had recently sent a note to President Lincoln, recommending the removal of women and children from Washington, if Lincoln "wished to avoid the effusion of blood."[3]

A new wave of panic ensued. The main roads out of Washington were once again jammed with people trying to leave in carriages, wagons, and on foot, described by the *Times* correspondent as a "great caravan of flight."[4] The

Relay House on the B & O line had become "a much-desired 'Mecca' for the wives and families of officials at Washington," reported the *Baltimore Sun*, "and the residents of the city, all of whom, imperiled by a sense of either real or fancied insecurity, are 'fleeing from the wrath to come.'"[5] Because the Relay House was only 30 miles north of Washington, some younger men and women walked there. Families and older people paid "exorbitant sums" to hire wagons or carriages for the trip from Washington, the *Sun* described, "but any demand is willingly paid, so anxious are persons to get away."[6]

As the mood in Washington oscillated between hope and fear, the Lincoln administration still maintained a united public front against the specter of Confederate attack and the failure of reinforcements to arrive in the city. In private, however, tempers were fraying. Many cabinet members were becoming angry about policies undertaken in the wake of the humbling series of defeats in the past week. "All these failures," Treasury Secretary Chase told Lincoln, "are for want of a strong young head," an obvious jab at Scott. "Everything goes in confused disorder. Gen. Scott gives an order, Mr. Cameron gives another. Half of both are executed, neutralizing each other."[7] Members of the administration were aware that they would be arrested if Confederate troops overran Washington—or hanged. That day, the *Richmond Examiner* called for the "cleansing and purification" of the "festering sink of iniquity, that wallow of Lincoln and Scott—the desecrated City of Washington." That work could be accomplished by only capturing "Scott, the arch-traitor," and Lincoln, the "Illinois Ape." And they would not be alone, the paper warned: "many indeed will be the carcasses of dogs and caitiffs that will blacken the air upon the gallows."[8]

Administration officials directed their fury toward Baltimore. "They think and in fact find it perfectly safe to defy the Government," wrote Attorney General Edward Bates in his diary on April 23. "And why? Because we hurt nobody; we frighten nobody; and do our utmost to offend nobody. *They* cut off *our* mails; *we* furnish theirs gratis. *They* block our communications, *We* are careful to preserve theirs—*They* assail and obstruct our troops in their lawful and honest march to the defense of this Capitol [*sic*] while *we* as yet have done nothing to resist or retort the outrage."[9] On the same day, Secretary Seward fumed that the treason of Governor Hicks would not surprise him and, more severely, that "Baltimore *delenda est*," an echo of Cato the Elder's call in the second century B.C. that Carthage, Rome's longtime rival, "must be destroyed."[10]

While the administration might have seemed impotent that day, it was nevertheless undertaking decisive military actions well outside Washington to ensure the safety of the capital. Scott ordered District Militia commander Colonel Stone to secure the B & O railroad as far out of Washington as could be done—to Annapolis Junction if possible—by stationing guards at strategic intervals along the track, particularly at vital locations, such as bridges. Secessionist Maryland militias had patrolled the route for the past several days, and it was critical to assert Union control over the route to bring reinforcements from the Junction to the capital. The scouting mission would also attempt to confirm the location of the volunteers who had landed at Annapolis and find out whether there was enough spare railroad material along the Washington branch of the B & O to repair the Annapolis line if necessary.

First, however, Secretary Cameron had ordered Stone to secure the B & O depot within the city.[11] Although Cameron had delegated the takeover of the station to Stone, he wanted to witness the actual seizure firsthand. "On the morning of April 23, as I happened to come out of the office opposite the War Department, Secretary Cameron drove to the door in a buggy," recalled Edward Thompson, his chief of staff. "Seeing me, he turned his driver out, and invited me to take his place."[12]

Thompson inquired, "Where shall I drive, sir?"

"I wish to go to the railroad depot as fast as possible," Cameron answered.

There, they found the District Militia under the direction of Stone, who had been "collecting all the extra rails and material he could find," Thompson recalled. Cameron had directed Stone to seize all railroad cars and keep them under military control. But Stone found only a broken-down engine used as a water pump and two or three cars that were useless.

Cameron had also ordered Stone to seize any trains that arrived at the station, because the army needed working engines and cars to transport Northern volunteers from Annapolis Junction to Washington. "Soon there rang out a loud whistle, and a powerful locomotive drawing only two passenger cars and one baggage car rushed into the station," recalled Stone.[13] The train's three passengers walked quickly through the station to the street, and the baggage car crew "rapidly threw onto the platform what luggage and freight the baggage car contained, after which they called out, 'All right' and got back to their places."[14] The crew was getting ready to take the train back to Baltimore.

Colonel Stone went straight to the engineer and told him that train would stay put, no matter what his schedule or his orders were. The engineer "looked astonished and informed me that he had received orders to go directly back to Baltimore, and go he must," remembered Stone. "Looking to the rear as if with the intention to rush his train out of the station, he saw the track covered with armed soldiers, and sullenly he obeyed my orders."[15]

Next, Stone learned from the conductor that a freight train would arrive shortly, and that its engineer had also been told to deliver the freight and return to Baltimore immediately. After that train pulled into the station, Stone informed its engineer that he was seizing the engine and cars. The engineer rebuffed Stone's order and reversed the locomotive toward Baltimore. He then caught a glimpse of Stone's armed troops, who had been out of sight when the train arrived, standing on the tracks with raised rifles pointed in his direction. Without words, he, too, surrendered his train.

Next Colonel Stone executed Scott's order to post guards along the B & O line. The men would be fully provisioned and would conceal themselves in the woods near the tracks, so they could surprise and shoot at anyone who began ripping them out. This stretch of the B & O Railroad between Washington and Annapolis Junction was undamaged, and Scott needed it to remain intact so that the Northern regiments who had landed at Annapolis could immediately be taken by train to Washington.

Colonel Stone's men assembled the most functional four-car train they could from the two engines and cars that his men had just seized at the B & O station. He now faced three challenges. The train was ready to go, but both of the engineers had disappeared. The engineer of the first train lived in Washington, so Stone sent his troops to the man's home and forced him back to the station, along with the train's fireman. Stone informed both men that they were going to run a train for the Union side, and that he would brook no trouble. "Do you see those two riflemen on the front platform?" Stone told the two men, according to his account. "It is only fair to you that I should inform you what orders they have received. From his moment until the train shall return here, should either of you attempt to leave your places, one of those soldiers will shoot the attempted deserter."[16]

To Stone's surprise and annoyance, his second challenge was fixing the two engines. In the brief period between both trains' arrival at the station and their preparation for departure, the locomotives had been sabotaged. Thinking quickly, Stone remembered that some of the Sixth Massachusetts men were train mechanics. He dispatched a rider to the Capitol—right up the hill from the station—and told him to find several men who had brought their tools to Washington, and bring them back to the B & O station as soon as possible. "In a few minutes," he recalled, "half a dozen delighted mechanics (in Massachusetts uniforms) came running into the station, one waving a monkey-wrench, another a hammer, and chisel, another files, etc, etc., all calling out 'Where is she? Let us get at her!'"[17]

A final obstacle remained: Stone's troops were Washington volunteers, and their enlistment provisions specified that they could only serve in the District of Columbia. Yet Stone needed several hundred of these men to guard the railroad north of Washington in Maryland, a potentially dangerous duty. He assembled his first company. "Soldiers," he announced, "you have been mustered into the service for duty in the District of Columbia only. I do not claim the right to send you out of the District without your consent, and will not do so. But now, I want 200 men to board that train yonder, to go wherever I say, to do whatever there may be to do, under the command of any officer I may designate. This service is important for the government, and it may be dangerous. All in this company, who wish to go under these conditions, step one pace to the front!" The entire company stepped to the front except the bugle boy. When the next company assembled in front of Colonel Stone, he gave them the same speech. Every single man stepped forward.

Soon after, one of the men, Captain John Franklin, piloted a train all the way to Annapolis Junction, returning to several hours later. He reported that he had not seen any Union volunteers there, but the "rails toward Annapolis had been torn up and carried away as far as he could see."[18] Stone immediately dispatched another train to the Junction to meet any Northern troops arriving from Annapolis, a scouting mission that would be repeated until, he hoped, the Union troops appeared.

At the Capitol the previous day, Colonel Edward Jones, the commander of the Sixth Massachusetts, had ordered his men to gather in a square formation outside the East Front. There, General Irvin McDowell, who supervised the defense of the Capitol, administered an oath of allegiance to the Union, as specified by Lincoln's April 15 proclamation. The Sixth Massachusetts men formally became U.S. Army soldiers for the next 90 days, a step all volunteer regiments arriving at Washington would take.

The daily routine for the soldiers had been established soon after their arrival several days before. Shortly after dawn, each company, one after another, sounded its reveille, which echoed down the marble hallways. The Capitol, silent only minutes before, was transformed by "a most vociferous uproar" as men dressed and folded up the greatcoats under which they slept, as Theodore Winthrop described in his account titled "Washington as a Camp" published in the July 1861 *Atlantic Monthly*.[19]

Next, the men ate breakfast, which was prepared in the Capitol kitchens. The Sixth Massachusetts men received only two meals per day: a breakfast, served between 8 and 9 a.m., and a dinner, served from 8 p.m. to midnight. The kitchen staff did not give the soldiers' food the same care that they reserved for senators and congressmen. It was cooked in giant kettles, and whatever one company did not eat was tossed back into the kettles and formed part of the next company's meal.[20]

Later in the morning, the Sixth Massachusetts troops held dress parades near the East Front or marched down Pennsylvania Avenue, where they staged street-firing drills in public to buoy local morale. "The Massachusetts men drilled tonight on the Avenue," recorded Hay after witnessing one of the parades. "They step together well and look as they meant business."[21]

The soldiers were often bored when off duty; they passed their free time by walking down the west side of Capitol Hill to Tiber Creek (which had been dammed for bathing), playing cards, or telling stories about their fathers and uncles in the Mexican War or their grandfathers in the Revolutionary War. Few men in the Sixth Massachusetts could surpass Private Muhlenberg's true story about one of his relatives, the Reverend Peter Muhlenberg of Woodstock, Virginia. The Revolutionary War had just begun, and one Sunday the minister told his congregation that there was a time for peace and a time for war, and that the time for war had arrived. He then doffed his Lutheran clergyman's robes and stood in front of his stunned congregation wearing the uniform of a colonel in the Continental Army.[22]

Inside the Capitol, the men, many of them in their teens, made spirited stump speeches and staged mock debates in the House and Senate chambers, with two or three often going on at the same time. They kept "calling each other to order, with an occasional 'you lie, sir!' in imitation of the usual occupants of the House," reported one newspaper. If somebody's speech went on too long or didn't include enough jokes, his fellow "members" started coughing loudly, shouted him down, or threw "paper missiles" from the gallery.[23] Soldiers lounged at the vacated desks of leading secessionist senators, like Louis T. Wigfall of Texas, who had sent confidential reports about Washington's defenses to the Confederates in early 1861 before resigning from the U.S. Senate in late March. The *New York Times* reporter observed that it "was a kind of poetic justice that filled Wigfall's abandoned seat with a stalwart man fresh from his forge" and that the Virginia senators who had recently departed southward were now "succeeded by operatives from the factories of Lowell."[24]

Colonel Jones had to improvise a space where he could perform his duties as commander of the Sixth Massachusetts. Deciding that his rank gave him a select choice of accommodation, Jones took the vice president's chair, which sat on a white marble rostrum; here he worked during the day and slept at night. The adjutant and his assistants took over the clerks' desks on the floor below, from which they prepared messages for Massachusetts's Governor Andrew and other officials, prepared muster rolls, and made requisitions.[25]

While the commanders of the regiment completed their official correspondence, the men wrote letters home on the engraved official House or Senate stationery.[26] The Massachusetts men in particular lined up to pen their notes at the desk of Senator Charles Sumner. Several congressmen who had stayed in town readily signed—or franked—the envelopes to save the men the 3 cents postage.

One letter written inside the Senate records the experiences of George A. Reed, an 18-year-old a farm laborer from Acton, Massachusetts. He wrote to his uncle, whom he addressed as "Dear Unkle," on April 20, the day after he arrived in Washington. The purpose of the letter was to "Let you know that i still Live"— his family would surely have greeted the news of the attack on the Sixth Massachusetts in Baltimore with concern—and that he was writing the letter from the "Gallery over the Senate Chamber." He wrote that the three other Reeds in the unit had arrived safely, though they were a bit worn down: "we are all Pretty well After So Long a Journey we arrived here Last Night 15 of 6 tired and hungry." He described the attack in Baltimore as "quite a Little Brush . . . we lost 3 of our men. They Lost 8 of the Rebels. they throwed Stones into the Cars and tore up the Track But as soon as we fired they Scattered." In conclusion, Reed wrote that the regiment was awaiting orders, but whatever they might be, he hoped "i Shall Live to come Back to Massachusett and see you all."[27]

George A. Reed of the Sixth Massachusetts and his April 20 letter home, written from inside the Senate Chamber of the Capitol.

Many of the younger men, who had never traveled more than a few miles from where they had born, were terribly homesick. Clara Barton, who nursed the wounded and brought food and supplies to the men at the Capitol, was instantly popular among the soldiers whom she had taught as young children at a one-room schoolhouse in North Oxford, Massachusetts. The men could not receive letters while Washington was cut off, and longed to hear news from home, even if it was out of date, as Barton discovered when she found a recent copy of the *Worcester Spy*. In a letter to a friend, Barton described how the men were "all were so anxious to know the contents that they begged me to read it aloud to them." She read the paper from the vice president's seat. "You would have smiled to see *me* and my *audience* in the Senate Chamber of the United States."[28]

At night, some of the men were assigned guard duty at major landmarks around Washington. The Capitol was especially difficult to protect, both because of its size and its numerous ground-floor entrances and windows. Stone placed dozens of men in full view at the entrances and stationed dozens more in the many dark arches and alcoves on the building's ground floor. Guards were also positioned throughout the Capitol's cavernous crypts and basements, and sentries patrolled the perimeter beyond. A howitzer was placed at the steps on the East Front.[29] To enter the Capitol, visitors needed to give both a password and a countersign to a sentry, who, on the day that a *New York Times* reporter visited, had a "bronzed face that betokens service and the resolution which grows out of service, backed by a fixed bayonet on a musket."[30] The men knew that they might be ready to face Confederate attackers at any moment. "We have constantly all sort of rumors here and are ready for any alarm at a moment's notice," a Sixth Massachusetts man, known only by the initials J.W.D., wrote his mother, and "we wear our equipments at all times, day and night."[31]

The unfinished Capitol posed a multitude of problems in its improvised role quartering the volunteer regiments. The marble hallways, not surprisingly, were soon covered in mud from dirty boots, ashes carelessly shaken off cigars, and chewing tobacco spittle that had not landed in the spittoons. The most pressing problem, however, was adequate sanitation for the 2,000 men. No one had found a solution for the shortage of toilets inside the overcrowded structure. "The smell is awful," wrote Thomas U. Walter to his wife, Amanda, who had left Washington with their children for Germantown, Pennsylvania, at his insistence. "The building is like one grand water closet—every hole and corner is defiled—one of the Capitol police says there are cart loads of — [*sic*] lined through in the dark corners."[32]

Walter's dismay was understandable, given that he was the architect in charge of the enlargement of the Capitol—the design commission of a lifetime. This work, which had begun in the 1850s, included the construction of the grand cast-iron dome and large wings for the new House and Senate chambers. These new wings displayed the era's classically inspired Italianate style at its most opulent. No building in the United States, not even in New York, came close to the Capitol in grandeur in its size, huge rooms and corridors, and in its lavish use of fine materials and custom furniture. Walter was soon squeezed out of his own quarters. "My office is at this moment . . . filled with soldiers," he complained to his son. He lamented that his masterpiece had been defiled: "The Capitol itself is turned into a barracks."[33]

Military drills were marring the costly hallway floors. "Upon the rich encaustic tiling falls with a dull, heavy sound the iron-shod butts of musket and rifle," reported the *New York Times*, describing the "echoes and re-echoes" of the "ringing clatter of the ramrod" off the "arched and frescoed ceiling" as the volunteers perfected the manual loading of their rifles.[34] Everything possible was done to make the troops as "comfortable as the circumstances permitted," wrote one of the Capitol doorkeepers. "But it almost broke my heart to see the soldiers bring armfuls of bacon and hams, and throw them down upon the floor of the marble room. Almost with tears in my eyes, I begged them not to grease up the walls and the furniture."[35]

Some observers were less dismayed at the presence of so many men, believing that the building's design veered toward vulgarity. The *Times* correspondent visiting the Sixth Massachusetts described how the marble statues had been boxed up and the paintings "faced over with heavy planking" to secure them from harm. "I almost regret that some of them have been the object of such precaution," he noted wryly. "A brief campaign might be atoned for, if a few of the exaggerations in marble, some of the burlesques on canvas, and a goodly portion of the Capitol extension could be subjected to the rude shock of contending armies." Theodore Winthrop shared that disdain. "The pictures (now, by the way, carefully covered) would most of them be the better, if the figures were bayoneted and the backgrounds sabred out."[36]

Some of the paintings were objectionable for their subjects rather than their artistic merit. The portraits of several presidents viewed as pro-Southern were taken down from the walls, lest the troops or visitors intentionally damage them. The portrait of President John Tyler, who had just presided over Virginia's momentous Secession Convention, was hidden in a storeroom, "the object of so much vituperation" that it was deemed endangered. The portrait of President James Buchanan, whose indecisive policies had enabled the South to gain a head start on the war, was moved to the superintendent's office "to protect it from threatened indignity."[37]

The main chambers were so showy that Winthrop thought they lent the Capitol a "slight flavor of the Southwestern steamboat saloon."[38] "Southwestern"—then a term referring to the lower Mississippi states—was an oblique swipe at Jefferson Davis, who had overseen the expansion of the Capitol while serving as secretary of war in the Pierce administration. In fact, Davis had taken such a keen interest in the Capitol expansion that he had guided the design of the architecture and interior down to the details, including the red leather-upholstered armchairs Walter designed for the House of Representatives.[39]

Davis's former desk, not surprisingly, was cursed at and spat on by the Sixth Massachusetts men, most of whom knew nothing about his participation in the Capitol's design but were well aware of his role in the current conflict. One day, Isaac Bassett, the Senate's assistant doorkeeper, walked into the chamber and heard cheering and the sound of wood being split apart. One of the Massachusetts men was thrusting his bayonet into Davis's desk. Horrified, Bassett asked them what they were doing. "We are cutting that damned traitor's desk to pieces!" was the reply. Bassett explained that Davis did not own the desk; it was government property. He scolded them: "You were sent here to *protect*, not destroy!"[40]

In Annapolis, early in the morning of April 23, General Butler and Colonel Lefferts were still wrangling, via proxies, over the best way to get their troops to Washington. Butler wanted to follow the rail line from Annapolis along the feeder line to Annapolis Junction, although secessionists had ripped up some of the tracks and no working locomotives were available in Annapolis. Lefferts preferred a march to Washington via the direct wagon road, but his quartermaster could not find enough horses and wagons for their supplies, ammunition, and baggage.[41] Once again, Butler and Lefferts were planning to take their regiments on separate routes, this time into the Maryland countryside, filled with armed men whom both Butler and Lefferts expected to attack them. Together, the Seventh New York and the Eighth Massachusetts would have a better chance to fight a secessionist force—rumored to number as many as 15,000 men—but the two commanders' enmity appeared to foreclose that possibility for the moment.

When General Scott's messengers reached Annapolis that morning with his plea to hurry to Washington, however, it finally spurred Butler and Lefferts into action.[42] Lefferts ordered his men to be ready for an early morning departure the following day. Before the arrival of Scott's order, Butler had already decided that his men would march along the feeder line to Annapolis Junction and fix the torn-up tracks as they went, so that the additional volunteer regiments—the Fifth Massachusetts and the First Rhode Island—that would soon land in Annapolis could reach the B & O line to Washington more easily. Early that morning, he mounted his horse and led two of his companies to seize the railroad station at Annapolis. The station keeper offered no resistance, Butler recalled in his memoirs, until "I asked him what this particular one [building] contained." "Nothing," was the reply. Butler therefore asked for the key, which the station keeper said he did not have. "Where is it?" Butler responded. The keeper did not know.

Butler ordered his men to force open the door, and they found what But-ler termed a "small, rusty, dismantled locomotive, portions of which had been removed in order to disable her."[43] He asked his men whether anyone knew anything about engines. One of his men, Private Charles Homans, examined the damaged locomotive and told his commander, "That engine was made in our shop; I guess I can fit her up and run her."[44] With that fairly stunning coincidence established, they found the parts that had been removed. The locomotive was soon repaired and ready to depart for Annapo-lis Junction.

Next Butler asked how many of his men knew how to lay—in this case, fix—railroad track. Twenty men stepped forward. By mid-afternoon, two advance companies of the Eighth Massachusetts Volunteers had started down the feeder line, making repairs as they went along, guarded by two other companies against the expected attack. At dusk, they camped two miles from Annapolis. The repaired locomotive was kept running back and forth along the repaired track during the night to keep the passage clear.

Meanwhile, members of the Seventh New York and the Eighth Massachusetts bought food to eat once they had left Annapolis the next morning. The townspeople, whom some officers had reported to be standoffish or hostile, became quite agreeable once they discovered they could sell their wares at higher-than-normal prices. The soldiers had been ordered to be polite and pay for their purchases. "The solders were buying freely of the inhabitants, and striking bargains for poultry and spring chicken, and pay whatever price was asked," reported the *New York World*.[45]

Other troops foraged for food at small farms outside the town. Several men found a farmhouse where a woman, who was alone, feared that they would steal all her food, and then prepared their breakfasts after assurances they would pay her. She "lost all her fears when the young men stood for a moment around the table, heads bared, and said grace," and then she broke into tears, one member of the Seventh New York later told Washington's *Daily National Intelligencer*. She "emptied the men's canteens of the muddy water inside, and filled them up with fresh hot coffee. She was still surprised, however, when they actually did pay her for the food consumed."[46]

No matter how gentlemanly the Northern troops' behavior, most Annapolis residents still deeply resented their presence. "Not a Union flag is to be seen, nor did I hear one loyal sentiment uttered in the city," described one soldier several days later; indeed, the locals expressed "intense hatred toward the troops."[47] On the evening of April 23, while they waited for their order to leave for Washington, the Seventh New York's well-known band and chorus staged a concert at the Naval Academy. The favor was not returned in kind: afterward, the men found that the regiment's two howitzers had been spiked.[48]

The Seventh New York men fully expected enemy guns to be turned on them the next day once they left Annapolis, and some expected to find Washington occupied by Confederate troops. A letter from one New Yorker, written on April 22 while still aboard the *Boston* and published unsigned on the front page of the *New York Times* on April 25, said, "The secession men have everything on the Potomac, and it is reported to us that Washington is in their hands." Though Scott's message of the morning of April 23 showed the Seventh New York that the rumor was false, the sentiment the soldier expressed in the next lines of his letter still rang true regardless of those facts:

"We are going there [to Washington], at all events, or we will be heard of no more. Tell the Union boys to come along in strength; there is work to do, and it must be done at once."[49] Robert Gould Shaw worried in his April 23 letter to his parents that a "small force as ours could do no good" if the "enemy . . . have possession of Washington." Still, he concluded on a bright note: "Hope to see 'Old Abe' soon!"[50]

Even before the Seventh New York had landed at Annapolis, reports that the men had been slaughtered on their way to Washington had reached Confederate leaders. On April 22, Vice President Stephens telegraphed Jefferson Davis from Richmond that the Seventh New York had been reported "cut to pieces" near Marlboro, Maryland, east of the capital.[51] The source of the rumor was former U.S. Navy lieutenant Charles Carroll Simms, a secessionist who had just resigned his commission at the Washington Navy Yard. The next day, however, Stephens cabled Davis that the rumor was "not confirmed" and "without foundation."[52]

The news of an attack on Union volunteers heading to Washington would have been welcome news in Richmond, where there was "No organization yet," as Stephens reported to Davis on April 23, about military preparations in the Virginia capital.[53] That day, Stephens met with representatives of the Virginia Secession Convention to negotiate a formal military alliance between Virginia and the Confederacy. In his long remarks before the convention, Stephens talked of the critical nature of Confederate support for Virginia's military, because the state was likely to be the scene of battle, though he said that Virginia's "distinguished commander-in-chief," Robert E. Lee, could give better information about battles plans than "any conjecture of mine."[54] The majority of Stephens's remarks were a reprisal of his "cornerstone" speech, first given in Georgia in March 1861, in defense of the legitimacy of secession and slavery, now reworked to underline Virginia's special role. "The great truth, I repeat, upon which our system rests, is the inferiority of the African," Stephens told the Virginia Secession Convention.[55] "But for the South, what would have become of the principles of Jefferson, Madison, and Washington, as embodied in the old constitution long ago?"[56]

Talks between Stephens and the Virginia government would take several days. These political steps, however necessary, were consuming valuable time in readying a viable military force at Richmond. That day, for example, the convention's advisory council had recommended to Governor Letcher that he ask Davis to delay the transport of 13 regiments of the troops pledged for Virginia until Lee personally approved the transfer of troops from other states, which meant waiting until Lee formally took command of Virginia's military later that day.[57]

The chance of swift movement against Washington that Henry Wise had envisioned was fading with each passing hour. Wise's plot to take Harper's Ferry, planned on April 16 and carried out the night of April 18, might have led to Washington's fall had Union troops not destroyed the supply of weapons needed to arm an attacking army. The raid against the Navy Yard at Norfolk, which Wise had also set under way without the Virginia government's official approval, had resulted in a huge windfall of weaponry and ships for the Confederacy when it had fallen on the night of April 21. By April 23, however, the window of time to seize Washington was rapidly closing, now that Northern volunteers had landed in Annapolis—unless they were intercepted en route to the capital.

Some leading Virginians feared that hesitation was letting Virginia's chance to seize Washington slip away. They pleaded with Davis to speed reinforcements to the state. On April 23, Richmond journalist John Beauchamp Jones wrote in his diary: "Several prominent citizens telegraphed President Davis to-day to hasten to Virginia with as many troops as he can catch up, assuring him that his army will grow like a snow-ball as it progresses." Jones believed that such a force could set out from Richmond and march on the capital immediately and without provisions, because Virginians would gladly feed and assist the soldiers along the way, and the force would quickly swell to "50,000 before reaching Washington." In the same diary entry, however, Jones expressed a note of resignation. He believed that Davis "could drive the Abolitionists out of Washington even yet, if he would make a bold dash," but he was not responding to their entreaties. The other border slave states had yet to secede, so their troops would be delayed, and Jones judged that Virginia had been "too late moving." The prize of Washington was slipping from their grasp.[58]

Sentiments that the South had not taken decisive steps quickly enough were not confined to Richmond. In Baltimore, secessionists were anxious for the Confederacy to aid them directly. Baltimorean G. D. Harrison composed a breathless letter, dated April 23 and addressed to both Davis and Stephens, calling for them quickly to bring troops north. "As you have no use for only part of your forces now—Send to Virg. & this noble state all you can spare," Harrison wrote; Maryland was "virtually out of the Union & in a complete state of revolt & the noble state is in a perfect blaze."[59]

In Baltimore, Harrison claimed, 15,000 men were under arms and an additional force in the countryside was ready "to carry on a guerilla war against the Myrmidons of the North." The main purpose of the guerilla force was to attack the Union volunteers who landed at Annapolis, "for they will not be permitted to pass this City to Washington." Harrison begged Davis to attack the federal capital now, an assault Maryland troops would join and support. "Washington has now 6000 to 7000 troops & it can be taken in 24 hours." Time was critical. "We can proclaim the Southern Empire at Washington if he will hurry on."[60]

A high-ranking Davis informant in Washington echoed that viewpoint the same day, though in more subdued terms. Justice John Campbell, from Alabama, who still remained at the Supreme Court, wrote to Davis on April 23 that Maryland was the "object of chief anxiety with the north & the administration." He believed that the "pride" and "fanaticism" of the North would be "sadly depressed" if the Lincoln administration failed to "command the Chesapeake & retain this capital." The military position of Maryland was "weak," he wrote, advising Davis to "Think of the condition of Baltimore & provide for it."[61]

The day before, Davis had urged Virginia's Governor Letcher to support Maryland, and Letcher had approved the shipment of arms from Harper's Ferry to Baltimore. Many secessionists in Baltimore believed that the transfer of arms was the prelude to reinforcement of their city by a larger force from Virginia. Reports spread that 3,000 troops were massing as part of the "expected aid from Virginia for the defence of Baltimore," wrote the *Baltimore American*.[62] It was rumored that the Virginia troops were to be "concentrated at a point within striking distance from Baltimore, and that upon the first intimation of a wish for their presence they would pour into the city, with the delay of but a few hours at most," the newspaper asserted. These Virginia troops were expected to reinforce Baltimore simultaneously to a "rumored movement of the Confederate forces upon Washington," although the report did not name their expected route.[63]

The leader of the Maryland First Light Division, General Steuart, was working to secure the entry of Virginia forces and weapons directly into

Maryland. On April 22, he had written to Major General Kenton Harper, the commanding Virginia officer at Harper's Ferry, asking him to transfer 1,000 of his troops along the B & O Railroad line to the Relay House junction during the next day.[64]

The arrival of the Union volunteers at Annapolis, however, caused Steuart to change his plans. At 5:30 a.m. that morning, he wrote Harper that "new and unexpected movements and operations of the troops landed at Annapolis have altered the plans I was preparing to carry out" and cancelled his request for the Virginia troops to be sent to the Relay House.[65] "Our eyes are now turned to another point," Steuart wrote, referring to Seventh New York and Eighth Massachusetts regiments at Annapolis, where Harper's "co-operation could not easily be availed of." Steuart wrote that he might still ask for Harper's "valuable assistance" if it was possible to give sufficient notice for troops to be sent from Harper's Ferry to points in Maryland in time. Meanwhile, he and other "military chiefs" in Baltimore turned their attention to the "arrangement and maturing of plans for the repulse of Northern troops from Maryland," reported the *Baltimore American*.[66]

By April 23, secessionist forces were spread across the Maryland countryside outside Annapolis and Baltimore, lying in wait for the Seventh New York and Eighth Massachusetts men to begin their passage to Washington. Steuart had stationed a force at Millersville, halfway between Annapolis and Annapolis Junction and just north of the rail line between those two points, while other forces were positioned at other locations where the Union volunteers might pass.[67] Early in the morning on April 23, some "125 men with a 12 pounder" gun were also on hand at "Harrison's Tavern, seventeen miles out on the Baltimore and Washington turnpike . . . awaiting the Seventh Regiment," reported the *Baltimore American*.[68] The newspaper also said that a "considerable force" was "stationed at the Junction of the Annapolis and Washington [rail]roads, at which point, we understand, the passage of the Northern troops . . . will be disputed."[69] For the moment, "All was quiet along the roads" to Washington, reported the *Baltimore Sun*, but the calm was merely the prelude to an attack: "armed men were stationed everywhere, determined to give the Northern troops a fight in their march to the capital."[70]

Among those planning to intercept the Union volunteers was Steuart's son, Captain George H. Steuart, Jr., who had resigned his U.S. Army commission on April 22.[71] Less than two months before, the younger Steuart had commanded a U.S. Army cavalry company that had escorted Lincoln at his inauguration. Now he planned to lead a cavalry force directly against Union volunteers trying to save the capital, as he described in an April 22 letter to Charles Howard, the president of the Baltimore Board of Police. "If the Massachusetts troops are on the march" from Annapolis to Washington, he wrote, "I shall be in motion very early tomorrow morning to pay my respects to them."[72]

In Washington, reports circulated of secessionist plans to attack the Union volunteers as they tried to reach the city from Annapolis. Secretary Seward heard "rumors of batteries and ambush parties lying in wait for them," and the absence of news from either regiment on April 23 compounded fears that they might have already suffered horrible losses.[73] As Lucius Chittenden remembered, secessionists regarded the volunteer regiments with special contempt as "counter-jumpers" and "kid-gloved darlings," whose destruction would simply be "pleasant pastime."[74] The same sentiment was also felt on the Union side. William Stoddard recalled that everyone had "serious doubts" about the Seventh New York's "ability to cut its way through the barrier of foes which now isolated Washington."[75] Union General Edward Townsend described General Scott's exchange with a visitor who had asked what the Seventh New York were going to do after arriving at Annapolis, given the well-known threats. "March to Washington," Scott replied. "March!" the visitor remarked, "why, general, its tracks will be marked with blood; it will have to fight its way through hordes of rebels!" Scott, nonplussed, answered: "Fight, sir, fight! That is what the regiment came for!"[76]

Scott's reaction revealed the temper of the moment, now eight days since Lincoln had issued his emergency proclamation. First bullish about Washington's defense, then despairing that it could be accomplished with the available troops, Scott sensed that the moment of truth had arrived—and for the Confederates had perhaps even passed, since they had as yet failed to attack. Washington could escape a Southern assault if enough volunteers reached Annapolis Junction—even if they had to fight their way through— and then took the protected railroad route to Washington. The challenge was to endure the wait, a feat that was as much psychological as it was practical. In those eight days, Washington residents had been beset and whipsawed by ever-changing rumors, had watched the arrival of the bloodied Pennsylvania and Massachusetts volunteers who had fought their way through Baltimore, and had endured boredom, isolation, and abject fear about their own safety.

A few scattered moments of brightness were visible through the dread and panic that day. "We got some three-days-old New York papers," wrote John Hay in his diary that evening, "and it seemed like a glimpse of a better world to contrast the warm open enthusiasm of the Empire city with the cold distrust and grim earnest that mark the countenance of the dwellers in Washington."[77] The newspaper articles, Nicolay and Hay both later recalled, "contained breezy premonitions of the Northern storm," the most cheering of which was the news of a "monster meeting in Union Square" in New York, where a reported crowd of 500,000 had gathered on April 20. It was one among many reports from around the North of the "wild, jubilant uprising of the whole immense population of the free States."[78]

Several events in Washington that day also brought cheer amid the isolation and seemed to confirm that Union forces could stand firm against the threats surrounding them. Lane's Frontier Guards made an expedition across the Potomac to Virginia and returned with a souvenir, a "Secession flag," which Frontier Guard Clifford Arrick described in his diary as "piratical-looking rag."[79] The steamers *Pawnee* and *Keystone State* from Norfolk landed that afternoon with a company of 250 Marines, a small but welcome addition to Washington's defenders.[80] The government's control of the rail line from Washington to Annapolis Junction also eased fears that Virginia or Maryland troops might use the B & O Railroad to run soldiers directly into the center of town, as Arrick recorded in his diary: "The Rail Road having passed into the hands of the Government, a better feeling prevails to-day—a rapid movement from toward [*sic*] Baltimore being thereby prevented."[81]

The greatest reason for optimism, however, was the proximity of the volunteer regiments at Annapolis—even though they as yet had failed to arrive—with an additional dozen regiments close behind. Arrick recorded that it was "confidently asserted" that the Seventh New York was "nearby & will be in to-night."[82] That evening, the State Department received what was thought to be "reliable news" that both the Seventh New York and Eighth Massachusetts would set out from Annapolis later that evening to march to Annapolis Junction under the full moon. Hay was almost jaunty as he imagined their march in his diary. "The hostile peasantry can harass them fearfully on the way from fence corners and hillsides if they are ready and brave."[83]

Still, hope was not the prevailing mood. Many felt frustration and anger, not the least because Washington still had so few defenders more than a week after Lincoln had called for 75,000 troops. Two days earlier, Lucius Chittenden had recorded his exasperation in his diary: "Our position here at this moment is a disgrace to the nation. The idea that the capital is to be cut off from communications with the North is enough to render one indignant. Such a state of things would never exist in a Northern city."[84]

Indeed, the optimism that more troops would soon arrive was mixed with the fear that they might not arrive at all. With the failure of the Northern regiments to appear that day, the "most intense anxiety to hear from the Seventh prevailed at Washington," reported the *New York Times*. Questions echoed: "'Has the Seventh come?' 'Where is the Seventh?' 'When will the Seventh be here?'" were the "queries most frequently heard during several days past."[85]

By April 23, Lincoln was visibly worn down and weary. He was carrying the impossible burden of the responsibility both of defending the national capital, which he had little means to effect except by waiting, and of planning the course of the war as leader of the Union, from which he was entirely cut off. "In the eyes of his countrymen and of the world he was holding the scales of national destiny," recalled Nicolay and Hay, yet Lincoln "alone knew that for the moment the forces which made the beam vibrate with such uncertainty were beyond his control."[86]

Still, Lincoln held such thoughts to himself, betraying none of these "inner emotions" to others, they remembered. However, on April 23, with the "business of the day being over, the Executive office deserted, after walking the floor alone in silent thought for nearly half an hour, he stopped and gazed long and wistfully out of the window down the Potomac in the direction of the expected ships," recalled Hay, who had quietly witnessed the scene. Lincoln, "unconscious of other presence in the room, at length broke out with irrepressible anguish in the repeated exclamation, 'Why don't they come! Why don't they come!'"[87]

Wednesday, April 24

"The Destiny of the Capitol . . . Suspended by a Hair"

Washington was a city in "entire ignorance of the outside world," observed Edmund Stedman of the *New York World* on April 24.[1] That day's *Washington Star* headline stated the capital's plight succinctly: "NO TRAINS—NO TELEGRAPH—NO ANYTHING."[2] Mary Henry recorded her feelings in her diary with a mixture of stoicism and resignation: "We are now untimely cut off from all intercourse with the North. . . . We cannot now leave the city & must face the danger whatever it may be."[3]

Many of the city's residents were numb from a seemingly endless cycle of alarm: "Another night of feverish public unrest, another day of anxiety . . . no attack on the city; but, on the other hand, no arrival of troops to place its security beyond doubt," recalled Nicolay and Hay.[4] Even the possibility of imminent attack—a recurring rumor for a week—was no longer enough to spark panic: a "de[s]cent may be made on us anytime," recorded Horatio Taft in his diary that day, "but we are get[t]ing used to strange things now."[5]

The glimmers of hope that many had felt the previous day had faded when they realized that Washington's situation was unchanged. Trepidation and fear remained the dominant emotions; that morning, the city's residents remained "very much afrighted," observed Stedman.[6] "Night and day," they were "anxiously and prayerfully looking out for troops," either the Confederate forces that might attack the city or the Union volunteers that would rescue it.[7] According to Stedman, Virginia forces were some 2,000 strong and gathering just out of view beyond Alexandria. In Maryland, militias patrolled the countryside, monitoring traffic in and out of Washington. Many residents expected them to sweep southward on the city in a coordinated assault with the Virginia forces. For nervous residents, the boom of distant cannon fire from Fort Washington was especially ominous. Union troops had recently reinforced the fort and were firing warning shots at boats that failed to stop for inspection. Many residents feared the start of an attack until they realized that the muffled rumbles were made by friendly forces. Or so they hoped.

The worst was that no news had reached the city from the Seventh New York and Eighth Massachusetts volunteers, whose landing at Annapolis two days before should have given them more than ample time to have reached Washington. "All are disappointed at the non-arrival of the N.Y. 7th," recorded Clifford Arrick in his diary on April 24. The "worst apprehension prevails," he wrote, and the "anxiety of all is greater than any [day] which has passed."[8] Anger continued to mount against the Lincoln administration for its failure to bring the Union troops by the most direct route—through Baltimore. Critics in Washington continued to view Lincoln's acquiescence to Baltimore's leader's demands to allow no Union troops to pass through the city as a "shuffling, diplomatic delay," recorded Stedman.[9] More galling, the soldiers might have been attacked in Maryland even though they had been routed around Baltimore—which would explain their failure to appear. Arrick noted the growing skepticism that more troops would ever arrive in the capital: "Why do the re-inforcements delay? No one it seems can tell. Yet it is asserted that they are in striking distance. The most of people doubt it."[10]

For some, Washington's fate was a bellwether of the grim course of the war to come. Dorothea Dix, who arrived in Washington on April 20, was morose over the events of April. She immediately offered her service as a volunteer nurse at military hospitals, and on April 23 Secretary Cameron appointed her superintendent of women nurses to care for the expected wounded. Several days after she arrived, Dix visited Joseph Henry and his family at their Smith-sonian Castle home. "Miss Dix was with us yesterday," Mary Henry wrote in her diary, noting the despondency Dix felt about the breakup of the Union. Dix was "very sad indeed about the state of affairs. Said the South was deter-mined to fight. Said she had never shed so many tears in one year before." With clarity shining through a typical note of sentimentality, Henry wrote that Dix's "earliest lessons of her childhood" and "her progress to God" had instilled in her a "love of her country," which she now "feared was soon to be desolated by a war too fearful to imagine."[11]

By April 24, Henry Villard remembered, the "impatience, gloom, and depression were hourly increasing.[12] No one felt it more than the President." Until today, Lincoln had kept his melancholy hidden, but his face now betrayed his true feelings. After the long and fretful days spent waiting for reinforcements to arrive, Lincoln's "countenance wore that peculiar expression, I think the saddest ever shown upon the face of man," recalled Lucius Chittenden.[13]

That morning, Lincoln met with members of the Sixth Massachusetts who had been wounded at Baltimore at the White House. Some of the men were shy, but he "quickly won their trust," according to Nicolay and Hay, with "his words of sincere thanks for their patriotism and their suffering."[14] Lincoln contrasted the importance of "their prompt arrival with the unexplained delay which seemed to have befallen the regiments supposed to be somewhere on their way from the various States." Then, Lincoln confided his doubts openly. "I don't believe there is any North. The Seventh Regiment is a myth. . . . You are the only Northern realities."[15]

An eerie "holiday quiet" presided over the city, recalled Nicolay and Hay. Washington was largely silent except for the "occasional clatter of a squad of cavalry from point to point."[16] So many people had fled that the grand Pennsylvania Avenue hotels stood empty. Willard's Hotel, which a week before had been swarming with crowds, was "now deserted as if smitten by a plague, with only furtive servants to wake echoes along the vacant corridors."[17] The previous day, only 16 people had shown up for the 2 p.m. meal at the National Hotel and nine at Brown's Hotel.[18]

Most of the stores were locked up, from the fashionable retailers on Pennsylvania Avenue to small neighborhood shops, because so many of their customers had left and the proprietors could not restock merchandise. The near-ubiquitous street vendors who sold snacks, flowers, or children's toys from pushcarts on almost every downtown block had largely disappeared. On residential streets, countless houses were shuttered because their owners had fled. For residents who believed that Washington would not fall, it was an ideal time to purchase or rent a house. After work on April 22, Lucius Chittenden "went on a house hunt" with one of his colleagues, Edward Jordan, the solicitor of the Treasury. The house Jordan decided to rent, at the corner of Twelve and I streets, was being vacated by a North Carolina-born auditor at the Treasury who was resigning his position and wanted to quickly dispose of all his furnishings before departing from Washington.[19]

Food shortages were now being felt citywide. Groceries were increasingly scarce and expensive—up more than 50 percent in price over the past few days. On April 22, noted Mary Henry, the price of flour had more than doubled, from $6 a barrel to $15.[20] If households had not stockpiled easy-to-store foods a fortnight before, they faced the looming prospect of hunger, or being forced to pay much higher prices for groceries. "Every effort has been made by the rebels to starve us out," observed Stedman in the *New York World*, because supply lines from Baltimore and Alexandria were severed, and even market wagons were blocked on their routes from farms to the city.[21] A few of Washington's neighborhood grocers still had foodstuffs, which they sold exclusively to their best customers and in modest quantities. At the normally bustling Center Market, a rambling collection of shabby, one-story, canopied buildings on the south side of Pennsylvania Avenue between Seventh and Ninth streets (now site of the National Archives), most of the food stalls were empty, and only a few hopeful customers bothered to show up, far outnumbered by the rats and flies that plagued the food stalls and slaughter pens.[22]

Not surprisingly, speculators turned up in Washington and offered to sell scarce supplies at three or four times the usual price. One man from Bladensburg, Maryland, loaded up two large wagons with cornmeal, which he had purchased at 60 cents a bushel, and covered them with a tarpaulin. He bribed his way past the Maryland militia who were guarding the Bladensburg Pike outside northeast Washington and made his way into the city. Once there, he stopped his wagons, put up a sign, and sold out the cornmeal for $1.50 a bushel, a quick 250 percent profit.[23] The government intervened to save some Washington residents from immediate hunger by selling flour that it had seized from warehouses in Georgetown to the city's working classes at a much reduced rate.[24] Still, supplies would only hold out for so long, as many in the North realized. Scott's 10-day window for Washington's food supply to be exhausted would fall on May 1, the same day Confederate Secretary of War Leroy Walker had predicted the capital would be in Southern hands.

By April 24, shortages extended well beyond food. The simplest items, such as cloth, patent medicines, and candles, were unavailable at stores, because residents were hoarding these items and stores could not obtain new stock. Even the city's newspapers were impacted. Two days earlier, the *National Republican* contained an odd request to its readership: "We would respectfully thank as many of our friends as can accommodate us with last Friday's issue." The newspaper wanted to recycle newsprint from old editions, because the paper shortage had forced it to reduce its length from the customary four pages to two.[25] That request did not fix the problem. By April

24, most Washington newspapers had become one-page half-sheets, printed front and back.[26]

Hard currency was another scarce commodity. A report on April 24 that one of Washington's banks was collapsing immediately put all the city's banks under suspicion. Panicky depositors lined up to withdraw funds in gold or silver. Most banks did not have the specie to give their customers. "The interruption between New York and Washington," reported the *New York Times*, had "seriously embarrassed some of the Washington banks, which, having paid out all their specie for Northern checks and drafts have no means of making exchange and replenishing their coffers."[27] Frightened depositors did not want the paper money issued by individual banks (the U.S. did not release its own paper money until 1862) because such currency rapidly depreciated in value and would be worthless if the institution went bankrupt. Others feared that the local banks' paper money would lose all value if Southern troops occupied Washington. People also feared Confederates would seize the banks—and their savings accounts—just as they had done with the New Orleans mint and federal deposits in the banks of various Southern cities.

The banking panic affected the few stores that were still open. To encourage business, some shop owners advertised that they would accept any "good bank notes with no discount," that is, no reduction in face value. Other merchants were more cautious. "NOTICE TO OUR CUSTOMERS," Riley and Brothers' classified advertisement read. "In consideration of the state of the country, our sales hereafter will be made exclusively for cash," that is, silver or gold coinage, not paper money.[28] Another merchant, J. W. Cooley was pessimistic about the future. "In consequence of the unsettled state of the country and general suspension of business," their classified advertisement read, "we desire to close all accounts on our books, and will thank all indebted to come forward and settle as soon and possible."[29]

One of Washington's richest residents, banker William W. Corcoran, faced a far different money problem. In a city threatened by attack, he had too much gold—$500,000 worth. Corcoran had made his fortune by cofounding Corcoran & Riggs Bank, which had become the sole Federal depository in Washington in 1844 and later the Riggs Bank, the largest in the city for decades. Today, Corcoran is best known for constructing a showy red-brick Second Empire–style gallery (now the Smithsonian Institution's Renwick Gallery) to accommodate his art collection at Pennsylvania Avenue and

Seventeenth Street, diagonally across the street from the White House. That Wednesday, April 24, Corcoran met with the U.S. treasurer, Frances E. Spinner, and made a proposal. He graciously offered to loan his gold to the Treasury, and rather than ask for any interest he would accept in exchange a "draft" drawn on the federal government's account in New York.[30]

Although Skinner had been treasurer for only six weeks, he recognized the reason behind Corcoran's seemingly patriotic offer. If the city fell to Confederate troops, Corcoran's gold—whether held in his vault or the U.S. Treasury—would probably be confiscated, whereas the $500,000 check in Corcoran's name would still be good at the federal account in New York. Spinner told Corcoran that "if he had any gold, he must arrange for its protection. The Government would not do it for him." Spinner knew the banker was a Confederate sympathizer, so he told several newspaper correspondents about the "offer" of a loan, turning Corcoran into the object of derision across the North days later.[31]

That one of Washington's financial pillars was wagering that the capital would fall reflected the mood in the city that day. "This has been a day of gloom and doubt," recorded John Hay in his diary. "Everybody seems filled with a vague distrust and recklessness."[32] Few openly displayed their secessionist leanings, but to some observers this was merely an indication that they were waiting for the opportune moment to strike from within. "We all know that if the cowards who are stimulating the rebellion had a leader, and had the nerve," recorded Clifford Arrick, "this city would fall a prey to its own traitors."[33]

Sabotage was discovered that day at the Washington Navy Yard: some recently manufactured shells had been found filled with sand and sawdust instead of gunpowder, and a battery of cannon to protect the installation had also been spiked.[34] The commander of the Navy Yard, Lieutenant John Dahlgren, ate and slept in the room opposite his office because "the attention demanded by various matters is incessant; there is no respite." He wished to be "ready for a Confederate attack at a moment's notice."[35]

Dahlgren, a 52-year-old U.S. Navy officer, was prepared to give his life in defense of Washington. In January, when the first solid reports of a secessionist plot to interrupt Lincoln's inauguration and take the capital had been circulating, Dahlgren had asked a friend to transfer his savings to a bank in Philadelphia. He wrote that the sum had "to be *perfectly secure*, as it is to provide bread for the family."[36] After 35 years of service to the U.S. Navy, including celebrated ordnance improvements, Dahlgren had only $600 to send. Shortly before he died in 1870, he revealed to his wife that he had been determined, if Washington had been attacked, to blow up the Navy Yard's shell house and "perish in it, if need be, rather than deliver up the Yard to the rebels."[37]

Lincoln expressed a similar defiance that day in a letter to Maryland politician Reverdy Johnson, who was staying in Washington and two days earlier had written to ask whether the troops destined for Washington were meant only for defensive purposes and not to invade the surrounding states. On April 24, Johnson pressed Lincoln for a response to this letter. Lincoln wrote that he did not intend to "*invade* Virginia" since the "sole purpose of bringing troops here is to defend this capital." He offered a hypothetical case, however, one that could have proven true even as he penned the letter: "But suppose Virginia sends her troops, or admits others through her borders, to assail this Capital, am I not to repel them, even to the crossing of the Potomac if I can?" Lincoln concluded: "I have no objection to declare a thousand times that I have no purpose to *invade* Virginia or any other State; but I do not mean to let them invade us without striking back."[38]

Clara Barton echoed that sentiment, believing the city was certain to be attacked. If the assault on Washington was to happen, she wrote in a letter, "let it come; and when there is no longer a soldier's arm to raise the Star and Stripes above the Capitol, may God give strength to mine."[39]

Since losing telegraph service on April 21, operators in Washington had nevertheless kept listening to the lines and the "ticking of their instruments," at the direction of the Army, occasionally catching "fugitive dispatches passing between Maryland secessionists," recalled Nicolay and Hay.[40] On April 24, Washington operators intercepted a telegram from Frank A. Bond, the captain of the United Rifles militia in Anne Arundel County, Maryland, to Baltimore's Police Chief Kane. The telegram indicated that Kane was plotting with rural Maryland militias to intercept Union troops, but that Baltimore authorities had backed off from sending soldiers to reinforce the local militia. Bond complained, "I have acted on your advice but am disappointed about the troops from Balto. who were to come here."[41] Bond also wrote that he had been "informed by a messenger from Prince George [County]" that 5,000 Virginians were near Bladensburg, just northeast of Washington and only a mile from the District of Columbia border, but that he did not believe the report true. Officers in Washington who read the intercepted telegram certainly hoped the rumor to be false.

The telegraph lines remained silent, however, on the fate of the troops who had landed at Annapolis. From the government messengers who had returned to Washington after reaching Annapolis, however, General Scott had confirmation beyond doubt that the Seventh New York and the Eighth Massachusetts had landed there and were preparing to depart for Washington. "There is reason to hope that the volunteers which arrived Sunday last at Annapolis are now advancing, in detachments, by means of 4 small cars, over the partially broken road, to the Junction-house," Scott wrote in his April 24 dispatch to Lincoln. From Annapolis Junction, the trip to Washington would be far easier, since the Union was, "as yet, masters of the road & the cars" on the B & O railroad from the Junction to the capital. On that route, Scott wrote, "pioneer trains, of a few cars" were continuing to advance "to gain information & to give comfort to the volunteers, & assistance."[42]

Scott's speculation that troops were moving out of Annapolis was correct, though he could not confirm it from Washington. Lefferts had decided to march alongside the railroad to Annapolis Junction, rather than use the more direct wagon route he had preferred earlier, since he had obtained "secret information" to "suppose that we were waited for on the latter route," according to Seventh New Yorker Fitz-James O'Brien.[43] During the night, a steamships carrying four other Northern regiments, totaling some 7,000 soldiers, had arrived in the Annapolis Harbor. If the Seventh New York and Eighth Massachusetts volunteers could repair and guard the twenty-mile rail line to Annapolis Junction, thousands of Union troops could be rushed from Annapolis to Washington in the next day or two, without exposing them to attack from the rear. The reinforcements arriving by ship would be "enough to hold Annapolis against a square league of Plug Uglies," wrote Theodore Winthrop in his account of the march.[44]

Two companies of the Seventh New York, numbering some 250 men, left Annapolis at 4 a.m. that morning to serve as an "advanced guard" for the rest of the of the regiment, who were to set out several hours later, as Robert Gould Shaw, who was in one of the advance companies, described in a letter to his mother about the march.[45] Under Lefferts's orders, they were to reach a point six miles outside Annapolis, where they were to wait for the rest of the New York men to arrive. Shaw wrote that the two companies considered their duty as advance guard a "great honor," and the men stepped off through

Annapolis in the pre-dawn hours in "good spirits, waking up all the people as we went."[46]

At the depot, the advance companies found the Massachusetts soldiers who had worked to repair the locomotive discovered the day before, led by Private Homans. The Massachusetts men eagerly "got up the steam," Shaw described, as the Seventh "packed our knapsacks in one car and started off in the other." The train consisted of "two platform-cars, in front of the engine, upon which were mounted the howitzer and its caisson," followed by two passengers cars after the locomotive, in which the men rode, as Captain Emmons Clark—who led one of the advance companies—described in the Seventh New York's 1864 official history.[47]

A mile out from Annapolis, the advance guard encountered the detachment of Eighth Massachusetts men who were stationed as pickets. The Eighth men told the New York men that they had not eaten since leaving Annapolis 24 hours before; they had been "constantly on duty" and were now in a pitiable condition, wrote Clark.[48] Without hesitation, the New Yorkers shared their food with the famished Massachusetts men, and then both groups pressed forward into the hostile countryside. The Eighth Massachusetts men had repaired the rail line from Annapolis to this point, and the work continued as the regiment pushed forward. The repair work had been made difficult by well-planned sabotage along the line. Stretches of the track had been ripped up and their rails and wooden ties had been tossed off to the side, or worse, carried into the pine woods or thrown into a stream, making them virtually impossible to retrieve. To replace the missing materials, the Massachusetts repair crew ripped up rail material from the side switches, which were used to allow trains to pass each other on the single-track lines, and then relaid the track. Lacking enough hammers, some of the men had to use stones to pound the spikes back into place.[49]

"We had scouts and skirmishers all around and about us," Shaw wrote, "for we had been positively assured that we should be attacked by a large body of cavalry." However, no enemy soldiers were seen, only "women and negroes," according to Shaw, which "made the reports of the body of men being assembled somewhere on the road seem true." Regardless, the advance party "trudged forward . . . with muskets loaded and cartridge-boxes full, ready for a brush at any moment."[50]

Meanwhile, at dawn, the Seventh New York's drummers sounded the reveille at the Naval Academy. The men awoke and donned their heavy complement of gear, which included their rifles and side arms, rounds of lead ammunition, and a knapsack filled with 60 pounds of equipment, in addition to their rolled overcoats and haversacks.[51] They also packed three days of rations—pork, beef, and hardtack—though they hoped to be dining in Washington before they exhausted their supply. At 7:30 a.m., the main contingent of the Seventh New York left the Naval Academy grounds and soon reached the Annapolis railroad depot. Once they left the outskirts of town, the volunteers knew they were in hostile territory. Most local farmers, who barely made a living from the thin, sandy soil, had disappeared into the woods, fearing the passage of the Yankee soldiers. Periodically, the New York men sighted one or two horsemen in the distance, who quickly vanished. Ahead, their advance "skirmishers" periodically spotted men ripping up the railroad and chased after them, but those men, too, vanished into the surrounding woods. As Shaw described, the "Annapolis men were perfectly certain we should be cut to pieces"—yet this placid spring morning hardly seemed the stage for the predicted ambush.[52] "The country about us" was "open and newly plowed," observed Winthrop. The fruit trees were in bloom, and most trees were covered with the small and delicate leaves of early spring.[53]

The men's thoughts drifted from immediate threats of attack to their ultimate destination: Washington. Had the city been attacked since Scott had sent his urgent note on April 22? Beyond that terse message, they had not received any hard news since they departed Philadelphia on the afternoon of April 20. Winthrop recalled their thoughts as they moved forward: "Nobody knew whether Washington was taken. Nobody knew whether Jeff. Davis was now spitting in the Presidential spittoon, and scribbling his distiches with the nib of the Presidential goose-quill."[54]

Although it was still late morning, the heat of unseasonably warm weather—in contrast to April 23's "halcyon" spring day—was beginning to bear down on them.[55] The weather on April 24 was "sultry," wrote Winthrop, "one of those breezeless baking days which brew thunder-gusts."[56] The first section of railroad out of Annapolis ran in a deep cut, made to provide a level passage for the trains, which became a heat trap for the marching men; it was a place "where no breeze ruffled the stifling atmosphere," according to William Swinton in another regimental history.[57] Once the men had gotten through the cut, the heat was nearly as oppressive because the tracks were now out in the open under the blazing sun, which Fitz-James O'Brien remembered as pouring over the men's heads "like hot lava."[58] Clark wrote that the "march of six miles in the extreme heat was not without its effect upon the young and inexperienced soldiers." Some men collapsed from heat stroke or exhaustion. Still, they pressed forward.[59]

At 9 a.m., the advance regiment halted at six miles out, as ordered by Lefferts. While waiting for the rest of the regiment, a reconnaissance party reported only "mounted citizens flying from the path" of the approaching Union soldiers.[60] A party led by Captain Thomas B. Bunting went off to survey an uninhabited farmhouse on the hill above where they had temporarily camped. Inside, they raided the cupboard, sucking down raw eggs found in a basket. As they left, the farm's owner—he and his frightened family had hidden in the nearby woods once they heard the troops' approach—returned to the house. The Seventh New York men informed him of what they had taken and then asked him to name a price. The farmer said "we were heartily welcome,—we knew he lied," recounted Bunting, a broker by profession in Manhattan. The farmer said they were worth $3. "We gave him $10, and he was the happiest man in the State."[61]

At 10 a.m., the advance party spotted the main body of the Seventh New York catching up to them, moving up the line on foot. Despite those men's evident fatigue, their unit still appeared "imposing and formidable," with their "bright bayonets glistening in the sunlight," Clark wrote.[62] Private Homans announced that he was heading back to Annapolis with the two passenger cars to fetch the main body of the Eighth Massachusetts, and he disconnected the two platform cars from the train. The Seventh New York would have to pull them forward manually with ropes. The men continued forward together, with the better-rested advance party pulling the flatcar with the howitzer and the rest of the regiment following behind. Forced periodically to stop and repair the rail line, they averaged "only about one mile per hour," according to Clark, and reached the water station at Millersville, halfway between Annapolis and Annapolis Junction, at 2 p.m.[63]

There the wooden railroad bridge over the ravine had been destroyed, forcing the men to halt. One of the Seventh New York men, an engineer, said that they could fix the bridge and rail line if they reused existing timbers and fabricated several missing pieces by felling and shaping nearby trees. Before the men started work, however, a thunderstorm that had threatened since midday finally broke. "So, we had not battle there, but a battle of the elements," noted Winthrop. The storm was a relief from the heat, but the men were left "thoroughly drenched," and could not dry themselves off in the late afternoon sun.[64]

As repair work on the bridge proceeded, Homans's train returned from Annapolis with the Eighth Massachusetts, and the New Yorkers shared their rations with them in an impromptu meal by the ravine as they waited for the bridge to be repaired. It was a gathering of men who would not likely have crossed paths in civilian life. Winthrop shared his meal with Stephen Morris of Marblehead, as he had the previous morning. "I make shoes in winter and fish in summer," Morris told Winthrop.[65] Winthrop was a New England aristocrat descended from John Winthrop, the first governor of Massachusetts, and the prominent theologian Jonathan Edwards. He was also an 1848 Yale graduate who had given up the law to become a writer and joined New York's best bohemian circles. Shaw, another privileged, well-educated member of the Seventh New York, described the admiration the Massachusetts men had gained in his heart. Writing to his mother on April 26, he observed: "They are rough fellows, but of the best kind. The feeling of affection that has spring up between us is really beautiful!"[66] The mutual appreciation was well-earned, Shaw wrote, since "Neither they nor we could have got through without each other's assistance."[67]

By twilight the railroad bridge had been repaired, and the Seventh New York men continued their march toward Annapolis Junction under the nearly full moon, while the Eighth Massachusetts troops stayed behind to guard the rail line and prevent further sabotage. The fatigued and sunburned New Yorkers continued to drag the platform cars behind them, while those who could walk no further because of heatstroke, blistered feet, or sheer exhaustion lay down on the flatcars as their tired but determined comrades pressed forward with the ropes in hand. Nevertheless, under the moonlight, "the night [was] inexpressibly sweet and serene," according to Winthrop. "The air was cool and vivified by the gust and shower of the evening."[68] The line of the marching men was half a mile long. Winthrop recorded that it was "beautiful to stand on the bank above a cutting, and watch the files strike from the shadow of a wood into a broad flame of moonlight, every rifle sparkling up alert as it came forward."[69]

O'Brien described the scene differently, one marked by fatigue and trepidation: "I have dim recollections of deep cuts through which we passed, gloomy and treacherous looking," he wrote, "while the banks were wrapped in shade, and each moment expecting to see the flash and hear the crack of the Southern guerillas." The rhythm of the evening was kept by the "bass commands" of "Halt!" and "Forward, march!"[70]

"As the night wore on the monotony of the march became oppressive," wrote O'Brien. The men's still-wet clothes clung to them. The moon, whose light enabled them to keep marching, slipped behind clouds. Fixing the rails became increasingly difficult as the men became more and more hungry, thirsty, and exhausted, especially since the men had run "out of stimulants, and almost out of water." At one embankment over a stream, they could not find one of the missing rails and jerry-rigged a plank in its place.

By midnight, the men were six miles from Annapolis Junction.[71] There the regiment halted, again forced to repair another section of track. Reaching for a box of supplies, one of the repair crew accidentally discharged his musket. The advance scouts, who had traveled ahead of the unit on foot a half a mile ahead, heard the noise, and "discharged several muskets and pistols as a signal that they were not far distant." The main body of the Seventh men misinterpreted the shots, having "naturally inferred that the skirmishers had met the enemy and were in danger of being overpowered." The two parties sped toward each other, and almost fired upon each other, before a "familiar voice was recognized," Clark recorded, causing them to realize their mistake and avoiding a "serious loss of life."[72]

The thunderstorm had dispatched the heat of the day, and the evening had become "extremely cold," with the "damp and chilly air almost unendurable," Clark remembered. "Wet, hungry, tired, and sleepy, the men only needed this change in the weather to complete their misery."[73] Still, they resolutely pressed on. "Most of us had not slept for four nights, and as the night advanced our march was almost a stagger," remembered O'Brien. When the regiment was forced to stop to repair the railroad, some men would fall asleep, and could only be roused again with great effort.[74] "When on the march," Clark wrote, "they trudged along, half conscious, half dreaming."[75] Shaw described these final hours of the march as ideal for the enemy to fall upon the weary men. "We went through all sorts of defiles," he wrote, "where the Marylanders might have pounced upon us with great advantage."[76]

Finally, around 4 a.m., near dawn, they came within a mile of Annapolis Junction. They halted to obtain news from their advance scouts, as they still expected a large concentration of hostile Maryland forces to be gathered there to greet them. Shaw described the scene: the soldiers were "perfectly overcome with sleep, shivering with cold, and a good many of us grumbling in quite a mutinous way." They built fires and contemplated the "gloomy prospect" before them. "Provisions all gone,—a good chance of having to march to Washington, twenty miles farther," with no report of a train, and the possibility that they would have to stand their ground against Maryland secessionists without rest. "Our officers told us we should have to fight then, if ever."[77]

However, the advance scouts, led by Lieutenant Noah L. Farnham, returned from Annapolis Junction to report that they had found no such threat. From the "sleeping inhabitants" of the "little village," they learned that Maryland troops had been present at the Junction during the previous days but the "extravagant reports" about the number of Northern troops arriving from Annapolis had frightened them away.[78] The soldiers also learned that a train had been sent from Washington to the Junction that day to meet them and that it was expected to return in the morning, when it could carry them to the capital.

With that welcome news borne back to the main body of the Seventh, Colonel Lefferts allowed the men to rest where they had halted. Many were already asleep on the ground in their damp and filthy uniforms.

Back in Washington, the streets were silent. Nonetheless, the city was poised to resist attack, whether it came from Maryland, Virginia, or both. Troops were stationed at all major roads into the city, such as Bladensburg Pike or the Seventh Street Road. Others guarded the bridges over the Potomac and Anacostia rivers. Down the Potomac, the guns of Fort Washington stood ready to prevent any hostile naval approach on the city.

As on previous nights, guards were stationed at the Capitol, the Patent Office, and B & O station. The greatest concentration of troops, of course, safeguarded the White House and the Treasury, where any last stand would be made against Southern troops. Sentries guarded the White House grounds, and armed men were concealed in the shrubbery. Inside the White House, troops were stationed in the basement and hallways. Lane's Frontier Guard were still camped out in the East Room, in case the long-expected emergency came.

Before falling asleep on the East Room's carpet, Frontier Guard Clifford Arrick recorded in his diary the city's precarious position and its residents' long-dashed expectations for rescue. "So the destiny of the Capitol is really suspended by a hair," he wrote. "Wellington never wished for Blucher more than we do for Lefferts."[79]

Thursday, April 25

"The Seventh Have Come!"

The day dawned with Washington on the lookout for any sign of the Seventh New York or Eight Massachusetts regiments. That morning, Lincoln spotted a ship on the Potomac River. "At the request of the Tycoon"—as Hay called Lincoln—"who imagined he had seen something significant steaming up the river," Hay wrote in his diary that day. He hurried off to the Navy Yard to see if the ship carried the reinforcements.[1] The boat turned out only to be the *Mt. Vernon*, a steamship that had taken tourists to George Washington's home and now patrolled the Potomac.

Across town, an early morning train left the B & O Railroad station for Annapolis Junction, along the tracks that had been under Union control since April 23. The train was under the command of Major John R. Smead of the National Rifles of the District Militia, and it carried food and medical supplies for the sentries protecting the undamaged tracks north of Washington, as well as supplies for the Union volunteers, who—all of Washington hoped—would be waiting at the Junction, ready to make the short trip back to the capital. Because both U.S. Army and local militia troops were in such short supply in Washington, Smead had been allocated only 70 of the National Riflemen for the journey, including William Stoddard, who had taken a brief leave of absence from his White House duties to serve in the unit. According to Stoddard, many still feared that the train would be attacked by Maryland militias, despite the fact that such trips had been safely made for the past two days. "Washington people said goodbye to us as if we were a forlorn hope, going to destruction," he wrote.[2]

Meanwhile, the Seventh New York remained camped outside the Annapolis Junction station, where they had stopped to rest after dawn. Earlier that morning, the men from the Second Company, who had slept briefly on the railroad platform at the Junction itself, searched the station and discovered a handcar that could be propelled down the tracks manually by two men. Without hesitating, a group of them hopped on and started piloting the car toward Washington, hoping to meet a train moving north or, barring that, to reach the capital and bring a train forward to the Junction. Six miles south of the Junction, they spotted the northbound train commanded by Major Smead coming up the tracks ahead.

Fifteen minutes later, the train pulled into Annapolis Junction. They notified Colonel Lefferts of their arrival, and he in turn ordered as many of the Seventh New York men as he could summon to convene at the railroad platform. The troops were elated. While they had learned from Junction residents that the Union still held Washington, hearing the good news directly from Major Smead and his men dispelled lingering fears that they might arrive in an occupied and subjugated capital.

Suddenly, some of Smead's men shouted that the "Rebs" were coming, and they grabbed their guns as a line of soldiers came into view from the forest toward the east. "Nonsense!" corrected Smead to his men. "Don't you see the flag?"[3] The approaching men, who were also from the Seventh New York, had not yet learned that Washington was safe. Once they met their comrades, Theodore Winthrop recorded in his account, they learned that "Our Uncle Sam was still a resident of the capital."[4]

The National Riflemen readied the train for its immediate return to Washington carrying the Seventh New York. As some of the National Riflemen hurried off to secure Annapolis Junction from attack and set up checkpoints, other men unloaded the provisions from the train and distributed the food to the hungry New Yorkers. "How they did eat!" exclaimed Stoddard.[5] Two Annapolis Junction taverns also did a "thriving business, while the liquor lasted, the soldiers imbibing freely," according to the *Baltimore Sun*. The New York men were eager for news—any news—because they had been so isolated during their stay in Annapolis, and "with avidity" read several copies of the previous afternoon's *Baltimore Sun* extra, which they found at the station.[6] If this afternoon edition had carried the same articles as the *Sun*'s April 24 morning edition, they would have read an article about plans to attack their very unit. The *Sun*'s morning front page had reported that "armed men were stationed everywhere" and intended to "give the Northern troops a fight in their march to the capital." The two companies of Maryland troops at Annapolis Junction and the other militia at Millersville mentioned in the newspaper, of course, had failed to appear the day before.[7]

At 9 a.m., the troops of the Seventh New York boarded the train for the long-delayed final leg of their trip. The ride took longer than the usual 45 to 50 minutes, because a team of telegraph men who were aboard stopped to make repairs to the lines along the way. Their leader was a 26-year-old Scottish immigrant named Andrew Carnegie, who had just been appointed an assistant in the military telegraph and railroads division of the War Department. "I took my place on the first engine which started for the Capital, and proceeded very cautiously," Carnegie recalled in his *Autobiography*, published in 1920, a year after his death. Some distance from Washington, he spotted downed telegraph wires, had the locomotive stopped, and ran over to release them. He failed to notice that the wires were staked to the ground under pressure, possibly as a booby trap. "When released, in their spring upwards, they struck me in the face, knocked me over, and cut a gash in my cheek which bled profusely." For his entire life Carnegie was proud of the scar the wires had left. "I gloried in being useful to the land that had done so much for me."[8]

Around noon, loud cheers rang out on Capitol Hill from the Sixth Massachusetts men. From their vantage point, they had spotted the train, with the soldiers of the Seventh New York waving from the open windows of the passenger cars. At the B & O station, an excited crowd had already gathered in anticipation of the troops' arrival. The locomotive whistle shrieked, and the train rounded a bend, came into sight, and pulled up to the platform. For the men and women assembled, the suffocating fear and anxiety of the previous ten days was transformed into joyous exultation at the sight of the smiling and waving troops. They knew that their city was saved. "And now a thousand voices," described the *New York World*, "shouted with one acclaim: 'It's the Seventh Regiment! It's the Seventh! Hurrah for the gallant Seventh! Three cheers for the New Yorkers!'"[9]

The roar of the crowd at the station spread across the city, swiftly followed by a cacophony of bells from church steeples and firehouses. Major General Lorenzo Thomas, the adjutant general of the army, remembered, "In every direction you could hear, 'The Seventh Have Come!'"[10] Washington residents swarmed out of homes and offices to meet their saviors. "At once the city, before so dull, was alive and running toward the station," observed the *New York Tribune*.[11] In addition, men and women in carriages, hack drivers who had been waiting at hotels, and delivery men with their wagons all hurried to the station, creating a traffic jam of shouting and whinnying that was "one of the wildest scenes of excitement ever witnessed here," according to the New York World. "One would have thought the invasion was of a foe, and that a panic had seized the population. . . . People seemed to dance for joy when the train entered the depot and the soldiers commenced to alight from the cars."[12] New York newspaper correspondents, who had lived through days of isolation and mounting uncertainty, were hyperbolic in their own exhilaration and relief. "I never saw such a scene of enthusiasm," wrote the World's correspondent. "The fears, the hopes, the false alarms, the doubts, and the prayers of all for the past week were satisfied in an instant."[13]

The thunder of jubilation soon reached the White House. Hay raced to the B & O station, pushed his way through the mob to meet Colonel Lefferts, who "communicated the intelligence of their peaceful passage," and then rushed back to the White House with the news "with which I straightaway gladdened the heart of the Ancient," another nickname for Lincoln.[14] For the first time in days, Lincoln "seemed to be in a pleasant, hopeful mood," recorded Hay in his diary that night. Lincoln could now safely turn his mind to his basic military strategies for the war, including the complete safeguarding of Washington, the reinforcement of Fort Monroe, and the blockading of Southern ports. In the joy of the moment, recorded Hay, Lincoln wryly told him that he would "go down to Charleston and pay her the little debt we are owing her" for the attack on Fort Sumter.[15]

At 12:30 p.m., the Seventh New York men—unshaven, sunburned, and still wearing their filthy uniforms—assembled in ranks, left the B & O station, and started marching down Pennsylvania Avenue toward the White House. Robert Gould Shaw described the scene: "we all turned out for a parade just as we were, covered with dust, and with our blankets slung over our shoulders."[16] As they headed west down the avenue, the sidewalk crowds swelled, and their cheering grew louder with the passing blocks. "When in place of drums and fifes the full band struck up, the whole city danced with delight," observed the New York Tribune.[17] Both men and women—"in their overwrought emotion"—ran out to the marching troops to grasp their hands. A few men slipped cigars and whiskey into their knapsacks.[18] Women wore Union badges or rosettes in their bonnets, while men put the same patriotic emblems in their buttonholes.[19]

The Seventh New York volunteers "seemed to sweep all thought of danger and all taint of treason out of that great national thoroughfare and out of every human heart in the Federal city," recalled Nicolay and Hay. "The presence of this single regiment seemed to turn the scales of fate. Cheer upon cheer greeted them, windows were thrown up, houses opened, the population came forth upon the streets as for a holiday."[20] Crowds gathered at the entrances and balconies at hotels, while still more watched the parade from the rooftops, the women waving their handkerchiefs and the men waving the Stars and Stripes.[21]

Once the parade reached the Treasury, the New Yorkers turned right onto Fifteenth Street, which was much narrower than Pennsylvania Avenue. As the crowd cheered, the band played, and the sound of brass and drums resonated off the stone walls of the Treasury and the buildings facing it. "Thank God for this hour!" exclaimed Lucius Chittenden, who watched the parade from the Treasury. "As I am writing this, I can hear the glorious music of its band and the loud cheers of thousands of happy men. How they came, we know not, nor do we care. It is enough to know that they are here and the Capitol of the Nation is safe!"[22]

Like many, Chittenden was overwhelmed with joy and relief. "There were many wet faces as this noble regiment marched up Pennsylvania Avenue and I do not deny that mine was one," he wrote in his journal later that day. "It is not to be disguised that we have been in a state of intense anxiety here. There was no fear about it, but a settled, careworn look was upon every face that did not sympathize with treason."

After marching a brief distance up Fifteenth Street, the parade turned left at the unfinished north front of the Treasury and back onto Pennsylvania Avenue. The soldiers saw cheering crowds lining the sidewalks on both sides of the street, and then hundreds more cheering onlookers in Lafayette Park on the right. As people ran out of the crowd to shake their hands, the Seventh New York volunteers marched past the White House and then swung around in the middle of the street and entered the West Gate. There they gave a marching salute to President Lincoln, who was standing with Secretary Cameron, Secretary Welles, and several U.S. Army officers under the portico. They then passed out through the East Gate onto Pennsylvania Avenue, where more overjoyed onlookers cheered and grabbed their hands.[23]

The outburst of emotion transformed the despairing Lincoln: he was now the "happiest-looking man in town as the regiment was marching by him," recorded the *New York Tribune*. The president "smiled all over, and he certainly gave in his countenance clear expression to the feeling of relief born in all by this wished-for arrival."[24] Once the men had marched past the White House, they raised nine cheers for Mr. Lincoln and three cheers for Mrs. Lincoln.[25]

And with that, the spontaneous parade was over. The crowds drifted away. Colonel Lefferts entered the White House to meet with Lincoln. The Seventh New York men were dismissed. About a third of them—300 men— went to Willard's, another third to Brown's, and the remaining ones to the National Hotel. The regiment's commissary had already made arrangements for the men to bathe, shave, and change into clean clothes, since they had not taken off their uniforms since leaving New York six days earlier. Some found time to write letters to their families or take a nap on a real bed. Dinner that night would be the first complete meal they had enjoyed in almost a week.[26]

At 7 p.m., they gathered in the square in front of the National Hotel at the northeast corner of Sixth and Pennsylvania. "The colors were then advanced to the centre," reported the *New York Times*, "and the band struck up the 'Star Spangled Banner,' the Regiment saluted the Stars and Stripes, and the crowd again cheered themselves hoarse." Then the men marched to the Capitol, where they were to be quartered in the House. Some Washington residents offered the officers comfortable accommodations in their own homes; the offers were politely refused. As several soldiers replied, "they preferred accepting the quarters provided by the Government, and, as they expressed it, 'roughing it from the start.'"[27]

The Seventh New York began to mythologize its march from Annapolis to Annapolis Junction soon after its arrival in Washington, and the result would receive a welcome response from a Northern public keen for heroes after the week of setbacks following Fort Sumter. Fitz-James O'Brien penned a song, "The Midnight March," which described the end of their journey under moonlight:

> All along the weary miles,
> Down through the dark defiles,
> Through the woods of pine and larch,
> Under midnight's solemn arch,
> Came the heavy sounding march
> Of the Seventh!

Plod! plod! plod! plod!
Over gravel, over sod,
Over uptorn railroad-tracks,
With their bending belted backs,
Waiting—hoping vain attacks,
Marched the Seventh!

In one stanza, the song alluded to the Maryland attackers who had failed to materialize:

Though the dark night was serene,
Never foeman's form was seen;
Though like flies they buzzed around,
Haunting every shady ground,
Fleeing at the slightest sound
From the Seventh![28]

And, indeed, why had the men not been attacked by Maryland secessionists? As the song suggested, many believed that their numbers and military hardware had frightened off the Maryland men. Sullivan H. Weston, the regiment's chaplain, recalled that a colonel of the enemy's cavalry had been "sent in disguise to Annapolis, to watch our movements." He wrote that this colonel was "there on the eve of our march, and the saw the rapid formation of the troops in order of battle." The scout, claimed Weston, based on telegrams that he had reportedly had seen in Washington at the War Department in late April, returned to Baltimore and "reported it was inexpedient to attack."[29]

No corroboration exists for Weston's story, though a surviving piece of correspondence from General Steuart in Baltimore suggests that Steuart may have received faulty intelligence reporting that the Seventh New York had already reached Washington when they were in fact only halfway between Annapolis and the Junction, and still exposed to attack from Maryland forces. On the afternoon of April 24, Steuart wrote that "[a]t least 3 or 4000" men had traveled from Annapolis to Washington "yesterday and today"—among them the Seventh New York, whose name he underlined—"and they now have at the Federal Capitol not less than 8000 men."[30] Still, by the evening of April 24, Steuart, who had sent out cavalry scouts into the Maryland countryside, must have received more accurate intelligence about the numbers of the New York and Massachusetts regiments, their condition after the long march that sweltering day, and where they had camped. Maryland troops could still easily have launched an attack against the weary troops on the evening of April 24 or early on the morning of April 25.

In the same letter, however, Steuart expressed the worry that Baltimore wass "threatened with invasion from the four quarters," indicating the prevailing fear that Baltimore was surrounded by Union forces on all sides.[31] To the north, some 2,500 Union volunteers were camped at Perryville, Maryland, on their way to Annapolis, and thousands more were waiting behind them in Pennsylvania, both in Philadelphia and Harrisburg.[32] On the eastern side of Baltimore's inner harbor, Fort McHenry had turned its cannon around against the city, and Union gunboats could be dispatched up Chesapeake Bay to bombard the city. To the south, danger came from the thousands of Union volunteers of the Northern regiments landing at Annapolis. To the west, Baltimore's lifeline to the Confederacy through Virginia would be threatened if the Relay House were taken by Union forces and the lifeline of the B & O Railroad should be cut off.

The Union's successful April 23 seizure of the Washington branch of the B & O Railroad as far north as Annapolis Junction had forced the Baltimore militia to focus on defensive measures, most critically the reinforcement of the Relay House, nine miles south of Baltimore. At midnight on April 23, for example, 2,000 Maryland men with four cannon had been transported to the Relay House, far more than the number dispatched to Annapolis Junction or Millersville, where the Seventh New York and subsequent Union volunteers would pass.[33] By the evening of April 25, Steuart's main military objective had become entirely defensive, as he wrote Virginia Governor Letcher that day in a letter thanking him for the transfer of Virginia weapons to Maryland. Steuart was "very anxious" to hold a "strong position at or near the Relay House, so as to guard and keep open" railroad communication "from Baltimore to the West, and at the same time cutting it off from Washington."[34]

In planning their strategies, the Baltimore leadership had an even greater fear: that a brazen attack on the Seventh New York and Eighth Massachusetts would precipitate the realization of Lincoln's threat to "lay their city to ashes" if any Northern troops were harmed on their way to Washington. Hundreds of similar calls were resounding across the North, and many usually moderate political leaders and newspapers had called for Baltimore's immediate bombardment as retribution for the deadly riot against the Sixth Massachusetts on April 19. Unlike the assaults on the Union volunteers of April 18 and 19, which could be blamed on the mob, or the plans to attack Pennsylvania volunteers should they enter Baltimore on April 21—plans that secessionists argued were measures of self-defense—any decision to send troops against the Seventh New York and Eighth Massachusetts would be a naked challenge to the credibility of the Lincoln administration and the United States government.

The unequivocal and repeated calls for retaliation against Baltimore, both from Washington and elsewhere in the North, had clearly made city leaders there wary of any action that would trigger the fury of the Union. Even without a devastating reprisal, Baltimore already faced economic ruin, and many residents, like those in Washington, perceived that their city was under siege. Mail had not been delivered for several days, and the number of food deliveries had dropped dramatically since the riot. Northern merchants refused to sell or ship anything to Baltimore, and the railroads from the north and west into Baltimore had been torn up. Also since the riot, the city's businesses and shops, like those in Washington, had been silent. By April 24, some Baltimore banks were teetering on collapse after runs by panicked depositors.[35]

William G. Pratt, a former Maryland governor and U.S. Senator, was a forceful voice in advising against an attack on the Union volunteers. Pratt was decidedly sympathetic to the Confederacy and a defender of slavery, and his counsel was apparently decisive, as recorded in the diary of Williams Watkins Glenn, a prominent Baltimore lawyer. In his April 23 entry, Glenn wrote that many "young men were mounted, armed, and organized" to attack the Union volunteers. He was "satisfied they would have been attacked, had it not been for the counsel of Govr. Pratt who advised them to keep quiet."[36]

On the evening of April 24, Pratt expressed his fear that Union forces were massing to exact retribution, reporting from Annapolis that a "joint movement of the forces from Annapolis and Pennsylvania" was "contemplated upon Baltimore, against which city the Northerners swear vengeance." Maryland, he argued, was in dire need of military support from the Confederacy to protect itself from an assault. "Prompt and immediate action of the Southern forces for the relief of Maryland is absolutely necessary to prevent the military occupation of the State by the Federal forces." That day, another Marylander, E. W. Bell, wrote to Steuart arguing that the moment had come for their southern neighbor to take the offensive against the Union: "It is no time for Virginia to stand on etiquette."[37] Steuart forwarded both Pratt's and

Bell's letters by horseback to Virginia forces in Alexandria, where these pleas for aid arrived on the afternoon of April 25. From there, the letters were forwarded to Robert E. Lee in Richmond, whom Marylanders hoped would answer their call for help.[38]

What they did not know as they pleaded for military support—nor did the Lincoln administration know at the hour of its greatest despair, when it appeared that no reinforcements would arrive—was that Robert E. Lee had already issued an order that Virginia would not carry out any attack on Washington. Once Lee had assumed command of the Virginia military on April 23, military commanders across the state, including Brigadier General Philip St. George Cocke, the commander at Alexandria, had written him for orders. In a letter to Lee on April 24 describing his position facing Washington, Cocke lamented the paucity of men and materiel at his command and simultaneously overestimated the number of defenders in the capital before the arrival of the Seventh New York. "I stand here to-day in sight of the enemy's position, an army now numbering from ten to twelve thousand men, under arms, and rapidly increasing by re-enforcements from the North, while I have to-day but three hundred men fit for duty."[39]

Still, while Cocke lacked enough trained men to take Washington—given how many forces he incorrectly thought had already arrived in the city—he recognized that swift action was critical in this early stage of the war. Many leaders in Virginia and throughout the South echoed his belief each moment in April 1861 registered with profound impact upon the future course of the Civil War: "Time, therefore, gained on the one side will enable us to organize and strengthen; but, unless every possible nerve is strengthened on our side, and every moment reckoned as a month, our enemy will press us in this race."[40]

That day, April 24, however, Lee was unequivocal in his reply to Cocke. Though he affirmed that the "invasion of our soil will be considered an act of war," he wrote: "Let it be known that you intend no attack."[41] Lee succinctly repeated his policy when he wrote to General Daniel Ruggles at Fredericksburg, Virginia, the same day: "You will act on the defensive."[42]

"Three hours ago we were the dullest, most tired people in the world. Now every man is on the alert," the *New York Tribune*'s correspondent wrote of Washington's citizens, including himself. The Seventh New York's arrival—or, as he called it, "infusion"—was "like a cordial, and even the most sluggish are now enthusiastic."[43] The presence of the Seventh marked not only the immediate salvation of Washington but an open route for the floods of Northern regiments to follow, ensuring that the city would remain secure regardless of how many troops the Confederates could raise in the coming days. Clifford Arrick recorded the sentiment of relieved Washingtonians that day in his diary: "the way is open, and soon others are to follow—All is safe now—everybody thinks so. Everybody says so. Everybody feels so."[44]

For the city's residents, the day's other great event was the resumption of mail service. That afternoon, one train from Annapolis delivered bags upon bags. By evening, the Post Office had delivered letters to hundreds of homes, a fitting end to a joyous day.[45] "This evening we get mail from the North, the first for six days, and it brings us the most gorgeous of all tidings, good news from home," wrote Lucius Chittenden after dinner. "I get a long and patriotic letter from my dear wife, not asking me to desert my post but proposing to come here and share the danger with me." He concluded, "I do not go to rest until I have written a long answer to her thrice welcome letter. . . . For the first time in many days I go to my bed happy."[46]

With the Seventh New York's arrival, "all the gloom, and doubt, and feeling of danger to the capital, vanished," remembered Nicolay in his history of the early days of the war, *The Outbreak of the Rebellion*.[47] From the perspective of a quarter century later, as Nicolay and Hay composed their joint biography of Lincoln, the intervening four years of the Civil War did nothing to dim the significance of April 25, 1861. "It was an epoch in American history," they wrote. "For the first time, the combined spirit and power of Liberty entered the nation's capital."[48]

On the afternoon and evening of April 25, however, the thoughts of Washington's men and women, who had just lived through tense, dread-filled days of siege, were not on long historical judgment but simply on their own feelings of relief. At Willard's Hotel, Senator Jim Lane and Cassius Clay feted the Seventh New York volunteers.[49] Lane's Frontier Guard and Clay's Battalion, who had protected the White House for a week, reveled in the success of their mission, and the fiery and theatrical Lane made a triumphant speech to the crowd gathered there. "The point of danger is past," Lane proclaimed to cheers. "Secession may howl but the Union is safe."[50]

With a defiant flourish, Lane declared: "Twenty-four hours ago they might have seized the Capitol. Now all Hell can't take it!"[51]

Epilogue

"Jeff Davis Shan't Get It Without Trouble"

By April 26, the siege was lifted, and defenders were flooding into Washington. "The whole North is on the move," was how Lucius Chittenden described the scene.[1] The threat of Southern attack had ebbed, and would subside further as each new regiment disembarked at Annapolis, rode the repaired feeder line to Annapolis Junction, and caught the train from there to the capital. The Eighth Massachusetts arrived by that route that day, and the off-duty Seventh New Yorkers "rushed out and cheered them" as their train pulled into the B & O Depot.[2]

Washington was a city transformed. In his April 26 diary entry, Clifford Arrick recorded that "numerous arrivals from the North of brave and true men, have given a Union spirit to Washington City unfelt by it for years." Residents again began to "regard ourselves more as the citizens of a great nation."[3]

Now one of the government's most pressing problems was housing and feeding the thousands of new troops who threatened to overwhelm the city's limited resources. The Eighth Massachusetts camped out in the Capitol rotunda, which was still open to the sky. The First Rhode Island stayed in the Patent Office, where some men slept in triple bunks between the glass display cases. The Fifth Massachusetts, who arrived in Washington at 8 a.m. on April 27, camped out in an open courtyard at the Treasury, where the smell of their cooking drifted into Lucius Chittenden's office. "They are noble fellows," he wrote that day. "I have given up my office furniture to them, and have been all day furnishing them with stationery."[4]

On April 26, Secretary Seward wrote to his wife, Fanny, "Eight thousand troops have actually arrived; we are safe from surprise."[5] The next day, he told her that "ten thousand of our troops are arrived here, and the city is considered safe." It was now almost two weeks after Lincoln's emergency proclamation, when General Scott had grimly informed the cabinet that he had only 1,500 troops at his command, some of whose loyalty he could not guarantee.

While administration officials and military leaders had, for the most part, maintained a confident public front, they knew how perilous Washington's condition had been. That summer, when Seward met with William Russell, correspondent from the *Times* of London, he confided: "we had a few hundred regulars and some hastily-levied militia to defend the national capital," which had been, he could now admit, "surrounded by treason."[6] On April 26, Nicolay also could admit to his fiancée, Therena Bates, how "demoralized" the city had been "with secession fever," to the degree that "no one could *know* whom of the residents to trust." Were Washington attacked, "we would have to look down the muzzles of our own guns." In the capital, one was not only surrounded by the enemy, but also in "the midst of traitors."[7]

Despite the widespread feeling of relief, some members of the Lincoln administration warned that the reinforcement of Washington had not reversed the series of losses the Union had suffered in the first two weeks of the war. "Let me beg you," wrote Secretary Chase to Lincoln on April 25, "to remember that the disunionists have anticipated us in everything, and that as yet we have accomplished nothing but destruction of our property."[8] General Scott, in particular, was concerned that both troops and civilians believed that the greatest danger had passed. On April 26, he issued a general order to all troops, starting with the reminder that "hostile bodies of troops" were near the city and "that an attack upon it may be expected at any moment." "In such an event," he continued, "to meet and overwhelm the enemy, it is necessary that some plan of harmonious operation be adopted on the part of all the forces, regular and volunteer."[9] The remainder of the general order specified his thorough defensive strategies, which were essentially a formalization of the steps Colonel Charles Stone and he had laid out for the defense of Washington. The same day, James H. Blake, commissioner of public buildings, sent a note to Secretary Cameron requesting six "additional Colt's pistols, Navy size, for police at [the] Executive Mansion. Six now on hand are deemed insufficient under existing circumstances."[10]

Still, on April 26, the mood in Washington remained festive. The Seventh New York held a formal military review up Pennsylvania Avenue, a reprisal of the spontaneous parade of the day before, this time with more pomp. General Scott sat in a White House armchair, while Lincoln stood to receive the men's cheers and salutes, under a striped tent whose roof was a huge American flag. The three tailors in the regiment had worked all night fixing the men's gray uniforms. Theodore Winthrop later wrote, "Every fellow had whitened his belts, burnished his arms, curled his moustache, and was scowling his manliest for Uncle Sam's approval."[11] Robert Gould Shaw described the scene in a letter to his mother: "'Old Abe' stood out in front of us, looking as pleasant and kind as possible, and when we presented arms, took off his hat in the most awkward way, putting it on again with his hand on the back part of the rim, country fashion."[12]

The following evening, the band of the Seventh New York gave a concert on the White House's South Lawn, while handsomely dressed guests strolled the pathways. The same day, April 27, Mary Lincoln wrote to Mrs. Samuel H. Melvin, a friend in Springfield, "Thousands of soldiers are guarding us, and if there is safety in numbers, we have every reason to feel secure."[13]

The first residents to return were those who had fled only in the previous few days and had, for example, encamped with their families at such places as Perryville and Relay House, or stayed in roadside country inns that had overcharged guests in the exodus from the capital. "Nobody is leaving the city at present from fear of trouble," reported the *New York World*, "but those who had left are returning."[14] Within days of the city's rescue, some military officers who had resigned asked their superiors to be reinstated to their former positions. A humbled Franklin Buchanan, former commander of the Washington Navy Yard, wrote to Secretary Welles to inquire whether his resignation could be rescinded. Welles brusquely replied that Buchanan's name had been removed from the Navy list.[15]

Some of the happiest arrivals in Washington were wives and children who had been separated from their husbands and fathers during the crisis. In this category were the daughters of Secretary Chase: 19-year-old Kate and her 13-year-old sister Janette ("Nettie"), who had been visiting New York when the Baltimore riots had prevented their return. They had initially insisted on going to Washington to be with their father. Only after learning that even armed troops could not reach the capital had they agreed to stay in New York until they could depart safely.[16]

On April 30, Kate and Nettie departed for Washington with Major Robert Anderson, formerly commander at Fort Sumter, who had been exuberantly feted in New York and was going to meet with Lincoln. Because the railroad north of Baltimore was still impassable, they took the same route as the

Union volunteers: by train to Perryville, then by steamer to Annapolis. Out in Chesapeake Bay, a vessel started following their ship's wake. "I believe she is a privateer," the captain informed his passengers. The Confederate government had authorized the issuing of letters of marque licensing privateers to harass Northern shipping. A "shot came booming through the air and then another to bring us to," recalled Nettie Chase. "Our captain, however, crowded on the steam, and we moved forward at a rapid rate." Despite their "intense wish to see it all," the two young women were sent below for safety. "Tidings were brought to us that we were gaining ground, and when our adversary—adversary she really was—saw that pursuit was hopeless, she ran up a black flag, changed her course, and was soon out of sight."[17]

Anderson and the Chase daughters next landed safely at Annapolis, where they met General Butler, promptly boarded a train to Annapolis Junction, and from there caught another train to Washington. On their arrival, Major Anderson went to the White House, and Kate and Nettie were reunited with their father at their townhouse at Sixth and E streets. They carried a special gift for him: bars of gold that had been hidden in their luggage, destined for the U.S. Treasury.

Now that Washington was filling with volunteers, Lane's and Clay's emergency guards were no longer necessary. On the morning of April 27, Lane wrote to Secretary Cameron: "in consequence of the arrival of large numbers of troops in this city, I am satisfied the emergency has ceased that called our company into service." In reply, Cameron approved the dissolution of the company and thanked Lane for the "very prompt and patriotic manner in which your company was organized for the defence of the Capital."[18]

The same day, Lane's Frontier Guard assembled at the White House at a ceremony in their honor. Lincoln thanked the men for their service to the nation, and then he placed their actions in the wider context of the national conflict, which he said he hoped might still end with a peaceful resolution. "I will not say that all hope has yet gone," he said. However, he continued, "if the alternative is presented whether the Union is to be broken in fragments and the liberties of the people lost, or blood be shed, you will probably make the choice with which I shall not be dissatisfied."[19]

Lincoln had already weighed such decisions himself. On April 25, Lincoln had written to General Scott that it would soon be necessary to decide between the bombardment of cities such as Baltimore, which had raised arms against the Union, and the suspension of habeas corpus to suppress insurrection. The latter course was chosen, and on April 27, Lincoln suspended the writ of habeas corpus along the railroad line between Philadelphia and Washington, effectively placing it under martial law. At the same time, the administration prepared to put Baltimore under a strict military occupation, which General Butler would shortly command.

Meanwhile, Washington's once vocal secessionists had now "wilted away," the *New York Tribune* noted. Chittenden expressed pleasure that the menacing Plug Uglies had disappeared from their usual haunt near the National Hotel at Sixth Street and Pennsylvania Avenue shortly after the arrival of the Seventh New York. "Treason finds it dangerous to show itself in the presence of such men as compose these New York and New England regiments, men who can fight and build railroads at the same time."[20] The few secessionists left in Washington, the *New York Tribune* reported, were now "anxiously looking toward Virginia."[21]

Clifford Arrick echoed that observation in his diary, noting that the pro-Union Virginians who had fled from Virginia into the capital had now switched positions with the secessionist Virginians who thought Washington would soon be under Confederate control. "The poor Virginia exile to-day," wrote Arrick of the pro-Union Virginians, "who with weeping eyes exclaimed, 'Alas! Alas! I, have no country' may take courage." As for the "traitors" in Virginia who wanted to seize the capital, they could only utter the sad refrain: "Mine was the land of Washington, and they have robbed me of it."[22]

With the onset of war, runaway slaves in nearby counties headed for Washington, as many assumed that the Fugitive Slave Act of 1850 would no longer be enforced. On April 22, the *Baltimore Sun* had printed a classified advertisement offering a reward for a runaway slave, "Lewis, who calls himself Lewis Willet," who had fled from a Maryland farm. "He has relatives living in Washington City, D.C." the ad read, offering $100 for "his apprehension if taken out of the State or in the District of Columbia," though only half that if he was captured in slave Maryland.[23]

On April 28, Frederick Douglass—who himself had fled from slavery in Maryland for freedom in the North in 1838—delivered an address in Rochester, New York, titled "Hope and Despair in These Cowardly Times." In the speech, Douglass celebrated Washington's escape from Confederate plots as he placed the securing of the Union capital in the wider meaning of the war. "We all know what the rebels and traitors mean," said Douglass. "They mean the perpetuity, and supremacy of slavery." By controlling the seat of government power, Washington, they would be free to extend slave power over the rest of the nation—an outcome that had been averted for the moment but remained the "purpose" animating "all their movements," he said. "Once in possession of the machinery of the Federal Government," the Confederacy "would place their iron yoke upon the necks of freemen, and make the system of Slavery the great and all commanding interest of the whole country."[24]

Why had the Confederacy failed to attack Washington after the fall of Fort Sumter? The specter of Pierre G. T. Beauregard, in particular, had hung over those who lived through the siege of Washington. Administration officials and military men wondered why this commander, the hero of Fort Sumter, had not sent the South Carolina militia northward by rail. In his autobiography, published three decades later, General Butler envisioned a scenario in which Beauregard could have seized Fort Sumter and then been sent by Jefferson Davis to Washington immediately afterward:

> Leaving five hundred men to watch Anderson's seventy-five and work their batteries against the fort [Sumter], why did not Davis cut the telegraph wires connecting with Washington, put say four thousand of his troops in the cars, and in thirty-six hours at farthest,—passing through the State of North Carolina, whose governor had refused to furnish any troops at the call of Lincoln, and through Virginia, which then had a convention called to pass an ordinance of secession, which they did on the 17th of April—march his rebel column across Long Bridge, where there were no forces to oppose him, and capture Washington?[25]

The simple answer is that Beauregard had no plans to seize Washington at that moment, nor did Davis. The rumors that Beauregard was gathering troops on the Virginia banks of the Potomac River—so rife in Washington in the panic after the loss of Fort Sumter, Harper's Ferry, and the Norfolk Navy Yard—were false, bred by fright. Beauregard himself had believed that "the North in its madness" might try to recapture Fort Sumter—as he had told *Times* of London correspondent William Russell on April 18 in Charleston, for a news article that no one in Washington saw for some time—and that his priority was necessarily strengthening the defenses of the Confederacy.[26]

The questions about Beauregard's inaction extended to the Confederacy's wider war aims: why had the South not attacked Washington in the days of its isolation, before the arrival of the Seventh New York and the Eighth Massachusetts? General John A. Logan expressed bafflement in his 1886 book *The Great Conspiracy*: "Informed, as the Rebels must have been, by their swarming spies, of the weakness of the Federal metropolis . . . [i]t seems absolutely marvelous that instant advantage was not taken of it."[27] General Butler believed that the capital had been open for the taking before the Seventh New York and his own Eighth Massachusetts men had finally reinforced the city: "The prize to be won was gloriously magnificent. The capital of the nation, with its archives, its records and its treasure, and all of its executive organization, was there."[28] Henry Villard, writing from the distance of a half-century, believed that the taking of Washington might have ended the war in April 1861.[29]

On April 25, the *Philadelphia Inquirer* speculated whether there were "any conclusive indications that an attack upon Washington is any part of the strategy of the Confederate Government?"[30] The newspaper hazarded a guess, a surprisingly accurate one in hindsight, given that its writers had no access to the internal deliberations of the Confederate government. According to the newspaper's account, the Confederate leaders were as yet "too wary to stake its existence, at this early day, upon a contest of such grand dimensions." As of April 25, the *Inquirer* concluded, any "demonstration against Washington, therefore, appears to be a revolutionary dash by the hot-head traitors in eastern Virginia. The Cabinet at Montgomery does not seem to be conducting it."[31]

The *Inquirer*, however, could not know of the Confederate leadership's closer and cagier involvement in plots to seize Washington shortly after Fort Sumter. On April 16, South Carolina's Governor Pickens had written to Davis that he hoped Virginia and Maryland would attack Washington rather than "to involve our Confederate Govt," but advised Davis to support an attack if one was made.[32] Davis's subsequent actions—especially his urging Virginia to "sustain Baltimore" in rebellion, while the Confederacy would in turn reinforce Virginia—seemed to indicate that this covert strategy was, in fact, deliberate.[33] It would have allowed the Confederacy to hold and reinforce Washington if secessionists moved on it first but to deny involvement if the plot failed. The existence of such a strategy was also surmised by Gates his 1884 *War of the Rebellion*: if the attack by secessionists on Washington "proved successful," he wrote, "the Confederate government was to advance its troops and occupy the captured town." However, "if the Federals developed unlooked-for strength and the assailants were repulsed, the Confederate government would stand in a position to shirk all responsibility, and treat the affair as the exploit of unauthorized partisans."[34]

One of those "unauthorized partisans," Henry Wise, still advocated an immediate attack on the federal capital on the day Lee had ordered Virginia troops to be put on the defensive, April 24. Wise, who had helped engineer Virginia's secession and the attacks on Harper's Ferry and the Norfolk Navy Yard, begged for immediate action. "For God's sake, urge 'em at Richmond to press forward" on "Harper's Ferry, to cut off the West, to form camp for Baltimore and point of attack on Washington from the west," and on the "Potomac River from every point where heavy guns can be put to resist reenforcements river to Washington.[35] His desperate cries went unheeded.

Indeed, the logistics of successfully seizing—and, equally critical, holding—Washington overpowered the cries of "On to Washington!" The Confederacy had fired on the inadequately armed and provisioned Sumter and forced its surrender, and Virginia militias had quickly seized and occupied Harper's Ferry and the Norfolk Navy Yard when they were virtually undefended. Like the North, however, the Confederacy was ill-prepared to carry out major military actions in April 1861. It did not have enough arms and materiel or, certainly, transport and provisions, for the large number of troops needed for such an ambitious target as Washington.

Most of the South's weapons were still held in those states that had already seceded, captured from U.S. installations during the previous months. Military arms were scarce in Virginia and in Maryland, and the burning of the Harper's Ferry armory on the night of April 18 destroyed the greatest cache of weapons near Washington. And despite the rumors of a large, well-disciplined force of Virginia troops—estimated by the *New York Tribune's* Washington correspondent on April 22 at 6,000 men—lying in wait just across the Potomac, in reality there were only several hundred, and ill-trained at that.[36]

Many of the troops under the direct command of the Confederate government were stationed deep in the South, and sending those men north would have forced the Confederacy to leave key Southern positions underdefended.

As the *Philadelphia Inquirer* surmised, again correctly, the Confederacy had "not troops enough to spare, and scarcely enough under arms to make a deliberate movement upon Washington, the defence of which would be sustained" by the entire North.[37] If Virginia or Maryland had attacked Washington, more troops would have been rushed there from points south, of course, but the failure of both states' governments and secessionist parties to strike the first blow against the capital meant that Confederate leaders were never forced to test the logistics of quickly sending reinforcements to hold Washington.

Still, like many in the North, a number of Confederate leaders in states that had seceded before Lincoln's inauguration could not understand why the Confederacy had failed to march on Washington immediately after the Union surrendered Fort Sumter. On April 24, former U.S. Senator John Slidell of Louisiana wrote to Jefferson Davis arguing that he should order an attack on Washington and spread word of the attack among Confederate recruits at once: "In a contest like this the boldest course is the safest, we can I think take & hold Washington & if we do so, can soon dictate our own conditions of peace," he wrote. "Would it not be well to let it be known at once that the troops you have called are destined to Washington?"[38]

Even after Lee had decisively scuttled any remaining chance of an attack on Washington with his April 24 order for Virginia's military to remain on the defensive, many Southerners still believed that the Confederacy was poised to take the Union capital. In North Carolina, where Governor Ellis on April 17 had urged Davis to act quickly, many assumed that the hastily formed militia units were heading north with Washington as their ultimate destination, not Richmond. On April 24, the *Goldsboro Tribune* reported that one of the local militias had received a "special order" the previous day directly from Governor Ellis to "march to the city of Washington." Next to that article, the newspaper also reported news of Maryland's secession from the Union. Both articles were fanciful rather than factual: "To have gained Maryland is to have gained a host," it boasted. "It insures Washington city, and the ignominious expulsion of Lincoln and his bodyguard of Kansas cut-throats from the White House." The newspaper concluded that the prophecy of April 12—that the Confederate flag would fly over the Capitol by May 1— would prove true: "It makes good the words of Secretary Walker at Montgomery in regard to the Federal Metropolis."[39]

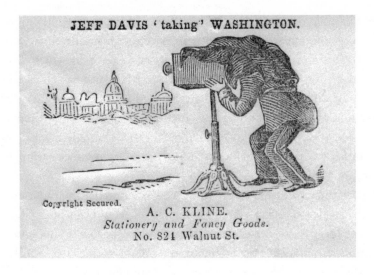

These grandiose dreams were now little more than wishful thinking: the Stars and Stripes would fly over the Capitol on May 1, the same date on which Varina Davis had invited Southerners to a soirée at the White House. Robert Gould Shaw, writing to his mother on April 27, described the Capitol, where the Seventh New York had lodged the previous night, as a "magnificent building"—and held that "Jeff Davis shan't get it without trouble."[40] That understated remark was echoed in a popular envelope featuring a cartoon titled "Jeff Davis taking Washington." It showed the Capitol in the distance and Davis standing under a black camera hood ready to "take" the city—with the camera.

The rescue of Washington inspired a grander affirmation of national destiny. Just as the Baltimore attack on the Sixth Massachusetts "Minute Men" echoed across generations from April 19, 1775, to April 19, 1861, the rescue of Washington fulfilled the vision of the man whose name it bore. As John Nicolay wrote in his *Outbreak of the Rebellion*, published in 1881, the reinforcement of the city against Confederate threats proved it was "the will of the people that the capital of the Union should remain where George Washington planted it."[41]

Two weeks after Lincoln had issued his proclamation calling for volunteers, Washington had unmistakably been transformed into the capital of a nation at war. Thousands of soldiers crowded the sidewalks, and they slept in the grand improvised barracks of the Capitol and Patent Office, as well as in tents hastily pitched in public squares. Gun carriages and supply wagons rumbled through the streets at all hours. Troops conducted their drills wherever they could, and newly arrived regiments repeated the parade route by marching up Pennsylvania Avenue to show President Lincoln that they, too, were ready to defend the nation's capital. Observed William Seward: Washington "begins to be a camp." And so it would remain for the next four years.[42]

On April 26, Nicolay completed his first letter to his fiancée, Therena Bates, since the lifting of the siege. The arrival of the Seventh New York Regiment the previous day had brought Washington back to its normal life—as least to casual observers—as "men went to talking, laughing, trading and working as before." Yet it was impossible not to see the shadow of the conflict whose course the capital would command. Wrote Nicolay: "Since yesterday morning at ten o'clock you could not discover from anything but the every-where-ness of uniforms and muskets that we are in the midst of revolution and civil war."[43]

ACKNOWLEDGMENTS

This book could not have been written without the unflagging assistance of Patrick Ciccone. His research uncovered critical (and sometimes forgotten) historical material, especially on secessionist plots against Washington, which he formed into a logical story. He was also invaluable in structuring and editing the manuscript at all stages, and his deft touch marks both turns of phrase and the wider canvas of the book's narrative. Patrick has a long writing career ahead of him, and we look forward to reading his first book.

Tim Bent, our editor at Oxford University Press, deserves our special appreciation for believing that this book would offer a new perspective in a market crowded with 150 years of works on the Civil War. Tim is the rare editor whose hand marks every page of the book, and his care, patience, and knowledge of American history have immeasurably enriched this story. At Oxford, we also want to thank our production editor, Marc Schneider; Tim Bent's assistant, Mally Anderson; our marketing coordinators, Josh Landon and Megan Kennedy; and our publicists, Tara Kennedy and Sarah Russo.

Alexander C. Hoyt, our literary agent, worked his magic and found the right publisher for our book.

Several librarians assisted our research above and beyond the call of duty: Norman Chase, a librarian in the Newspapers and Periodicals Reading Room of the Library of Congress; Patricia Feeley, Reference Librarian in the Social Sciences Department at the Boston Public Library; Doris Grier, Reference Librarian in the Washingtonian a Room at the Martin Luther King, Jr., Memorial Library in Washington, D.C.; Marcia Rich, Director, Acton Memorial Library in Acton, Massachusetts; Josh Larkin Rowley, Research Services Assistant at the Book, Manuscript, and Special Collections Library at Duke University in Durham, North Carolina; and William V. Jones, Assistant Manager of the Maryland Department at the Enoch Pratt Free Library in Baltimore.

John: I extend my thanks to Wayne G. Braxton and Rebecca Karcher, Supervisory Park Rangers on the National Mall, Washington, D.C. I also thank Dave Owens, Pastor, Christ Church on Embassy Row. My special appreciation goes to Timothy Smithson.

Charles: First, I want to remember three people who played important roles in my life and career: Sylvia Gerber, my Latin teacher at Woodrow Wilson High School in Washington, D.C., who taught me both mental exercise and the delights of Latin; Professor Donald D. Egbert of Princeton University, my faculty advisor, who encouraged me to write a thesis that could be turned into a book; and Robert A. Sincerbeaux, president of the Eva Gebhard-Gourgaud Foundation, whose support enabled me to transform that thesis into my first book, *Bricks and Brownstone,* a history of the New York townhouse.

For their invaluable help in the preparation of this book, I would like to thank Lucia Aparicio, Douglas Brenner, J. Chun, Ernie Davis, Susanna Hecht, Lori and Jeffrey Hyland, Peter V. Persic, Carol and Bill Schreiber, and Carol and John Young.

I extend my deepest gratitude to Dr. Youram Nassir and Dr. Richard Sokolov for their advanced medical expertise and commitment to my health. I also extend the same profound appreciation to Dr. Nicholas N. Nissen and Dr. Payman Khorrami. I also want to thank Maureen Baum and Isaac Malitz, longtime friends with whom I have shared so many good times. Over the past year, they showed me the meaning of the true friendship. Thank you, Maureen and Isaac.

Finally, I could not have written this book without the at-home support and encouragement of my husband, Carlos Boyd. My thanks, too, go to Jane, Annabelle, and Cordelia.

We both want to thank Dr. Edward M. Dean, Daniel W. Polachek, and Marianne G. Zurn in Northampton, Massachusetts. In particular, we remember the late Richard Garvey, associate publisher of the *Springfield (Massachusetts) Union-News,* who was our stepfather. A lifelong journalist and historian, "Garv" would talk with us for hours, and he encouraged our research and writing. He was a devoted husband, too. We will always cherish his memory.

We have dedicated this book to our mother, Allison Lockwood, who often read to us as children, wrote her own books, encouraged our writing, and shared her lifelong love of history with us.

NOTES

Preface

1. Edward Deering Mansfield, *The Life and Services of Lieut. Gen. General Scott* (New York: N. C. Miller, 1862), 532.
2. Alexander Kelly McClure, *Abraham Lincoln and Men of War-Times: Some Personal Recollections of War and Politics during the Lincoln Administration* (New York: The Times Publishing Company, 1892), 69.
3. Abraham Lincoln, Message to Congress, May 27, 1862, in *Rebellion Record*, ed. Frank Moore, vol. 5 (New York: G. P. Putnam, 1863), 145.
4. Theodore B. Gates, *The War of the Rebellion* (New York: P. F. McBreen, 1884), 16.
5. Benjamin Franklin Butler, *Butler's Book, Autobiography and Personal Reminiscences of Major-General Benj. F. Butler* (Boston: A. M. Thayer, 1892), 219.
6. Henry Villard, *Memoirs of Henry Villard, Journalist and Financier, 1835–1900*, vol. 1 (Boston: Houghton, Mifflin, 1904), 167.
7. Lucius Chittenden, *Recollections of President Lincoln and His Administration* (1904).

Prologue

1. Evert A. Duyckinck, *National History of the War for the Union, Civil, Military and Naval*, vol. 1 (New York: Johnson, Fry and Company, 1861), 118. The speech is rendered with slight variations in many early Civil War works of 1861–1862. The speech's next line was "Let them try Southern chivalry and test the extent of Southern resources, and it may float eventually over Faneuil Hall itself."
2. Ibid., 129.
3. U.S. House of Representatives, Reports of the Select Committee of Five, sec. 2, *Alleged Hostile Organization against the Government within the District of Columbia* (Washington, D.C.: Government Printing Office, 1861), 166.
4. William Holdredge to W. H. Seward, April 17, 1861, Seward Papers, University of Rochester Library Special Collections.

5. Republished in *Charleston Mercury*, April 23, 1861, 1.
6. John William Draper, *National History of the American Civil War* (New York: Harper & Brothers, 1868), 71.
7. Benjamin Franklin Butler, *Butler's Book, Autobiography and Personal Reminiscences of Major-General Benj. F. Butler* (Boston: A. M. Thayer, 1892), 220.
8. John Slidell to Davis, April 24, 1861, in Lynda L. Crist and Mary S. Dix, eds. *Papers of Jefferson Davis*, vol. 7 (Baton Rouge: Louisiana State University Press, 1992), 122.
9. *Richmond Enquirer*, December 25, 1860, quoted in James Ford Rhodes, *History of the United States from the Compromise of 1850*, vol. 3 (New York: Macmillan, 1907), 300.
10. U.S. House of Representatives, Reports of the Select Committee of Five, sec. 2, *Alleged Hostile Organization against the Government within the District of Columbia.* (Washington: U.S. Government Printing Office, 1861), 2.
11. Jacob D. Cox, "War Preparations in the North," in *Battles and Leaders of the Civil War*, vol. 1 (New York: Century Company, 1887), 89.
12. Theodore B. Gates, *The War of the Rebellion* (New York: P. F. McBreen, 1884), 13.
13. Martha Colson, *A Signal Success* (Philadelphia: J. B. Lippincott Co., 1886), 89.
14. *National Republican* (Washington, D.C.), April 15, 1861, 3.
15. William Tecumseh Sherman, *Memoirs of Gen. William T. Sherman*, 2nd ed., vol. 1 (New York: D. Appleton Co., 1889), 194–195.
16. Ibid., 195.
17. Ibid.
18. Charles P. Stone, "Washington in March and April, 1861," *Magazine of American History* 14:1 (July 1885): 2.
19. Gates, *War of the Rebellion*, 12.
20. Quoted in "A Page of Political Correspondence: Unpublished Letters of Mr. Stanton to Mr. Buchanan," *North American Review* vol. 129 (November 1879): 476.
21. Mary Ashton Livermore, *My Story of the War* (Hartford: A. D. Worthington & Co., 1890), 86.
22. *Douglass Monthly*, May 1861, 1.
23. Henry Ward Beecher, *Patriotic Addresses in America and England, from 1850 to 1855*, ed. John R. Howard (New York: Fords, Howard & Hulbert: 1891), 273.
24. Cox, "War Preparations in the North," 86.
25. "The Lincoln Log: A Daily Chronology of the Life of Abraham Lincoln," April 14, 1861, www.thelincolnlog.org/. National Center for Supercomputing Applications at the University of Illinois at Urbana-Champaign.
26. Frederick W. Seward, *Reminiscences of a War-time Statesman and Diplomat, 1830–1915* (New York: Putnam's, 1916), 152.
27. Gideon Welles, *Diary of Gideon Welles*, vol. 1 (Boston: Houghton Mifflin, 1911), 47.
28. Seward, *Reminiscences of a War-time Statesman and Diplomat*, 152.
29. Ibid.

30. Quoted in John S. Wise, *The End of an Era* (Boston: Houghton, Mifflin, 1901), 103.
31. Ibid., 103–104.
32. Frederick W. Seward, *Seward at Washington as Senator and Secretary of State: A Memoir of His Life, with Selections from His Letters, 1846–1861* (New York: Derby & Miller, 1891), 560.
33. George Ticknor Curtis, *Life of James Buchanan, Fifteenth President of the United States*, vol. 2 (New York: Harper & Brothers, 1883), 548.
34. Charles P. Stone, "Washington on the Eve of War," *Century Illustrated* 26:3 (July 1883): 458–459.
35. Charles Stone, "A Dinner with General Scott in 1861," *Magazine of American History* 9:6 (June 1884): 528–532.
36. Burrows and Wallace, *Gotham*, 865.
37. Quoted in Edwin Burrows and Mike Wallace, *Gotham: A History of New York City to 1898* (New York: Oxford University Press, 1999), 867.
38. www.usgovernmentrevenue.com/yearrev1865_0.html#usgs302. Government Revenue in the United States of America.
39. William Howard Russell, *My Diary North and South* (Boston: T. O. H. P. Burnham, 1863), 56.
40. Seward, *Seward at Washington*, 545.
41. Helen Nicolay, *Lincoln's Secretary: A Biography of John G. Nicolay* (New York: Longmans, Green, 1949), 84.
42. John G. Nicolay, *With Lincoln in the White House: Letters, Memoranda, and Other Writings of John G. Nicolay, 1860–1865*, ed. Michael Burlingame (Carbondale: Southern Illinois University Press, 2006), xviii.
43. John G. Nicolay and John Hay, *Abraham Lincoln: A History*, 10 vols. (New York: Century Co., 1890).
44. Merrill Peterson, *Lincoln in American Memory* (New York: Oxford University Press, 1994), 116–127.
45. Daniel Mark Epstein, *Lincoln's Men: The President and His Private Secretaries* (New York: HarperCollins, 2010), 5.
46. Ibid., 11.
47. Ibid., 7.
48. Ibid., 4.
49. Nicolay, *Lincoln's Secretary*, 76.
50. Quoted in Doris Kearns Goodwin, *Team of Rivals: The Political Genius of Abraham Lincoln* (New York: Simon & Schuster, 2006), 334.
51. John Nicolay to Therena Bates, April 15, 1861, in *With Lincoln in the White House*, 34.

Monday, April 15

1. Abraham Lincoln, Proclamation on State Militia, April 15, 1861, Abraham Lincoln Papers, Library of Congress (LOC).

2. Abraham Lincoln, notes prepared for speeches after the *Dred Scott* decision, August 21, 1858, in *The Collected Works of Abraham Lincoln*, ed. Roy P. Basler, vol. 2 (New Brunswick, N.J.: Rutgers University Press, 1955), 553.

3. *New York Herald*, April 15, 1861, 1.

4. Thomas Griess, *The American Civil War* (Garden City: Square One, 2002), 20.

5. Frederick W. Seward, *Reminiscences of a War-time Statesman and Diplomat, 1830–1915* (New York: G. P. Putman's Son, 1916), 152.

6. Quoted in John A. Logan. *The Great Conspiracy: Its Origin and History* (New York: A. R. Hart & Co., 1886), 218.

7. Margaret Leech, *Reveille in Washington: 1860–1865* (New York: Harper, 1941), 55.

8. Wilhelmus Bogart Bryan, *A History of the National Capital from Its Foundation through the Period of the Adoption of the Organic Act*, vol. 2 (Washington, D.C: Macmillan, 1916), 460.

9. Quoted in Bryan, *History*, 460.

10. *New York Times*, April 16, 1861, 1.

11. *New York Times*, April 16, 1861, 1.

12. Long and Long, *Civil War Day by Day*, 59.

13. *New York Times*, April 15, 1861, 1.

14. The exchange is recounted in Alexander Kelly McClure, *Abraham Lincoln and Men of War-Times: Some Personal Recollections of War and Politics during the Lincoln Administration* (New York: Times Publishing Company, 1892), 59–61.

15. Ibid., 61.

16. Simon Cameron, requisition request, April 15, 1861, in *War of the Rebellion: A Compilation of the Official Records of the Union and Confederate Armies*, (Washington, D.C.: U.S. Government Printing Office, 1880–1901) OR, vol. 23, pt. 1, 68–69.

17. Indiana Governor O. P. Morton to Abraham Lincoln, April 15, 1861, OR, vol. 23, pt. 1, 70.

18. Israel Washburn, Jr., to Simon Cameron, April 15, 1861, OR, vol. 23, pt. 1, 71.

19. Ida Tarbell, *Life of Abraham Lincoln*, vol. 2 (New York: Doubleday & McClure, 1900), 34–35.

20. Benson Lossing, *Pictorial Field Book of the Civil War: Journeys through the Battlefield in the Wake of Conflict*, vol. 1 (New York: T. Belknap, 1868–69), 203.

21. Abraham Lincoln to Andrew Curtin, April 8, 1861, in Lincoln, *Collected Works*, 4:324.

22. *The Press* (Philadelphia), April 10, 1861, 2.

23. Diary entry, April 1861 (no exact date, apparently shortly after Fort Sumter), in *Louisa May Alcott: Her Life, Letters, and Journals*, ed. Ednah Cheney, (Boston: Little, Brown, 1914), 127.

24. G. H. to Governor Andrew, quoted in Phineas Camp Headley, *Massachusetts in the Rebellion: A Record of the Historical Position of the Commonwealth, and the Services of the Leading Statesmen, the Military, the Colleges, and the People, in the Civil War of 1861–65* (Boston: Walker, Fuller and Co., 1866), 104.

25. *National Republican* (Washington, D.C.), May 2, 1861, 2.
26. John G. Nicolay and John Hay, *Abraham Lincoln: A History*, 10 vols., vol. 4 (New York: Century Co., 1890), 80.
27. Ibid., 83.
28. Ibid., 84.
29. John W. Ellis to Simon Cameron, April 15, 1861, in *The Papers of John W. Ellis*, ed. Noble J. Tolbert, vol. 2 (Raleigh, N.C.: State Department of Archives and History, 1964), 612.
30. John Letcher to Simon Cameron, April 16, 1861, OR, ser. 3, 1:76.
31. *Charleston Mercury*, n.d., quoted in *Rebellion Record*, ed. Frank Moore, vol. 1 (New York: G. P. Putnam, 1861), 26.
32. *Mobile Advertiser*, April 16, 1861, quoted in ibid., 42.
33. *Richmond Enquirer*, April 13, 1861, quoted in "The Attack on Washington," in Moore, *Rebellion Record*, 1:188.
34. Edward C. Anderson to Jefferson Davis, April 15, 1861, OR, ser. 1, vol. 51, pt. 2, 11.
35. "Pritchard" to D. G. Duncan, April 15, 1861, OR, ser. 1, vol. LI, pt. 2, 11.
36. Reprinted in *New York Tribune*, April 16, 1861, 7.
37. Ibid.
38. Anthony Trollope, *North America* (New York: Harper & Brothers. 1862), 302.
39. G.W. Busby [unsigned], "Washington City," The Atlantic Monthly 7:39 (January 1861): 1
40. William Howard Russell, *My Diary North and South* (Boston: T. O. H. P. Burnham, 1863), 32.
41. Ibid, 32–33.
42. Ibid., 33.
43. Ibid.
44. Nathaniel Hawthorne, "Chiefly About War Matters, by a Peaceable Man," Atlantic Monthly 10: 57 (July 1862): 62.
45. Julia Taft Bayne, *Tad Lincoln's Father* (Lincoln: University of Nebraska Press, 2001), 10.
46. Constance McCaughlin Green, *Washington Village and Capital, 1800–1878* (Princeton: Princeton University Press, 1962), photo insert between 236 and 237.
47. William O. Stoddard, *Lincoln's Third Secretary: The Memoirs of William O. Stoddard*, (New York: Exposition Press, 1955) 99.
48. Ibid.
49. Tarbell, *Life of Lincoln*, 2:47.
50. Helen Nicolay, *Lincoln's Secretary: A Biography of John G. Nicolay* (New York: Longmans, Green, 1949), 80.
51. "Daily Schedule and Routines Section of the Mr. Lincoln's White House," Gilder Lehrman Institute of American History, www.mrlincolnswhitehouse.org/inside.asp?ID=518&;subjectID=5.

52. Abraham Lincoln to Winfield Scott, April 1, 1861, Abraham Lincoln Papers, LOC.
53. Nicolay to Therena Bates, April 15, 1861, in John G. Nicolay, *With Lincoln in the White House: Letters, Memoranda, and Other Writings of John G. Nicolay, 1860–1865*, ed. Michael Burlingame (Carbondale: Southern Illinois University Press, 2006), 34.
54. *Lincoln's Men*, 22.
55. Quoted in Wendell Garrett, *Our Changing White House* (Boston: Northeastern, 1995), 116.
56. Tarbell, *Life of Abraham Lincoln*, 46.
57. *Philadelphia Inquirer*, April 20, 1861, 1.
58. Quoted in John Stevens Cabot Abbott, *The History of the Civil War in America*, vol. 1 (New York: Henry Bell, 1863), 92.
59. William H. Hallahan, *Misfire: The History of How America's Small Arms Have Failed Our Military* (New York: Scribner's, 1994), 112.
60. *Springfield Daily Republican* (Massachusetts), April 15, 1861, 4.
61. John A. Andrew to Adjt. Gen. Lorenzo Thomas, OR, vol. 23, pt. 1, 71.
62. Quoted in J. W. Hanson, *Historical Sketch of the Old Sixth Regiment of Massachusetts Volunteers* (Boston: Lee and Shepard, 1866), 14.
63. Ibid., 17.
64. *Farmer's Cabinet* (Amherst, N.H.), May 3, 1861, 2.
65. Lord Richard Lyons to Earl Russell, April 15, 1861, in *American Civil War through British Eyes: November 1860 to April 1862*, comp. James J. Barnes & Patience Barnes (Ohio: Kent State University Press, 2003), 49–50 (emphasis in original).

Tuesday, April 16

1. *New York Times*, April 17, 1861, 4.
2. Frederick W. Seward, *Reminiscences of a War-time Statesman and Diplomat, 1830–1915* (New York: G. P. Putman's Son, 1916), 152.
3. *Boston Transcript*, June 19, 1861, reprinted in *Rebellion Record*, ed. Frank Moore, vol. 1 (New York: G. P. Putnam, 1861), 121 (excerpt).
4. "Abraham's Daughter," Civil War Songsheets, Library of Congress (LOC).
5. *New-York Courier and Enquirer*, reprinted in *New York Tribune*, April 16, 1861, 7.
6. *Philadelphia Inquirer*, April 16, 1861, 2.
7. Reprinted in *New York Tribune*, April 16, 1861, 7.
8. *New York Tribune*, April 16, 1861, 7.
9. In Moore, *Rebellion Record*, 1:34.
10. *Worcester Spy*, April 22, 1861, 2.
11. *Richmond Whig*, April 22, 1861, quoted in James Grant Wilson, *The Memorial History of New York*, vol. 3 (New York: New-York History Company, 1893) 497.

12. Arthur Orrmont, *Master Detective: Allan Pinkerton* (New York: Julian Messner, 1965), 83.
13. *Daily Evening Traveller* (Boston), April 16, 1861, 1.
14. Wise, *The End of an Era* (Boston: Houghton, Mifflin, 1901), 165–166.
15. *New York Tribune*, April 16, 1861, 6.
16. *Daily National Intelligencer* (Washington, D.C.), April 17, 1861, 3.
17. Quoted in Wilder Dwight and Elizabeth Amelia Dwight, eds., *Life and Letters of Wilder Dwight* (Boston: Ticknor and Fields, 1868), 39.
18. David Homer Bates, *Lincoln in the Telegraph Office: Recollections of the United States Military Telegraph Corps during the Civil War* (Lincoln: University of Nebraska Press, 1995) 35–36. Congress appropriated the money to reimburse the American Telegraph Company for the salaries, telegraph poles, wires, and other "instruments" at the end of 1861.
19. William Rattle Plum, *The Military Telegraph during the Civil War in the United States* (New York: Arno Press, 1974), 68–69.
20. John A. Dahlgren, *Memoir of John A. Dahlgren, Rear-Admiral United States*, ed. Madeleine Vinton Dahlgren (Boston: J. R. Osgood, 1882), 332.
21. "On This Day in Virginia Legislative History," February 13, 1861, Virginia Historical Society, www.vahistorical.org/onthisday/21361.htm.
22. *New York Times*, April 17, 1861, 4.
23. Scott Daily Dispatch No. 14, April 16, 1861, Abraham Lincoln Papers, LOC.
24. Roger Jones, testimony before U.S. Senate, November 26, 1861, in *The Reports of Committees of the Senate of the United States for Second Session of the Thirty-Seventh Congress 1861–1862* (Washington, D.C.: U.S. Government Printing Office, 1862), 243.
25. Ibid.
26. Scott Daily Dispatch No. 14, April 16, 1861.
27. John G. Nicolay and John Hay, *Abraham Lincoln: A History*, 10 vols., vol. 4 (New York: Century Co., 1890), 88.
28. "Sixth Massachusetts Volunteer Regiment," Mass Moments, Massachusetts Foundatoin for the Humanities, http://massmoments.org/moment.cfm?mid=26.
29. Ibid.
30. Ibid.
31. *Daily Louisville Democrat* (Kentucky), April 23, 1861), 1.
32. Theodore B. Gates, *The War of the Rebellion* (New York: P. F. McBreen, 1884), 17.
33. *New York Herald*, January 1, 1861, reprinted in Wilhelmus Bogart Bryan, *A History of the National Capital from Its Foundation through the Period of the Adoption of the Organic Act*, vol. 2 (Washington, D.C: Macmillan, 1916), 460.
34. *New York Times*, March 11, 1861, 1
35. Helen Nicolay, *Lincoln's Secretary: A Biography of John G. Nicolay* (New York: Longmans, Green, 1949), 75.
36. Katherine Helm, *The True Story of Mary, Wife of Lincoln* (New York: Harper, 1928), 189.

37. *New York Times*, April 15, 1861, 1.

38. *Evening Star*, April 19, 1861, 3.

39. *National Republican* (Washington, D.C.), April 26, 1861, 2.

40. Diary of Mary Henry, Joseph Henry Papers, Smithsonian Archives.

41. *Douglass Monthly*, May 1861, 1.

42. Stanley Preston Kimmel, *Mr. Lincoln's Washington* (New York: Coward-McCann, 1957), 33.

43. Julia Taft Bayne, *Tad Lincoln's Father* (Lincoln: University of Nebraska Press, 2001), 6.

44. Jennifer Fleischner Mrs. Lincoln and Mrs. Keckly, (New York: Broadway, 2004), 192.

45. Ibid., 183.

46. Handbill, "Railroad Rules for Blacks," 1858. New York Public Library Digital Collection, ID 1206623.

47. John W. Cromwell, "The First Negro Churches in the District of Columbia" *The Journal of Negro History* (January 1922): 64–69.

48. Constance McLaughlin Green, *The Secret City: History of Race Relations in the Nation's Capital* (Princeton: Princeton University Press, 1969), 52.

49. Ibid, 50.

50. Anthony Trollope, *North America* vol. 2 (Philadelphia: Lippincott, 1862), 14.

51. Lynda Jones, *Mrs. Lincoln's Dressmaker: The Unlikely Friendship of Elizabeth Keckley and Mary Todd* Lincoln (Washington, D.C.: National Geographic Books, 2009), 34–35.

52. Ibid., 43–45.

53. Ernest Ferguson, *Freedom Rising*, 7.

54. Charles L. Blockson, *The Underground Railroad* (New York: Prentice Hall, 1987), 152–153.

55. Richard McGowan Lee, *Mr. Lincoln's City: An Illustrated Guide to the Civil War Sites of Washington*, (n.p.: EPM Publications, 1981), 58.

56. Edmund Ruffin, *Anticipations of the Future: To Serve as Lessons for the Present Time.* (Richmond: J.W. Randolph, 1860).

57. Ibid., 298–299.

58. Ibid., 300.

59. James Henderson to Abraham Lincoln, April 16, 1861, Abraham Lincoln Papers, LOC.

60. Scott Daily Dispatch No. 14, April 16, 1861, Abraham Lincoln Papers, LOC.

Wednesday, April 17

1. *The Press* (Philadelphia), April 18, 1861, 2; "mulberry livery . . ." *Brooklyn Daily Eagle*, April 12, 1861, 2.

2. *New York Times*, April 18, 1861, 1.

3. Ibid.

4. *New York Daily Tribune*, April 18, 1861, 5.

5. Frederick W. Seward, *Seward at Washington as Senator and Secretary of State: A Memoir of His Life, with Selections from His Letters, 1846–1861* (New York: Derby & Miller, 1891), 563.

6. Ibid.

7. Vera's Victorian Variety. www.shasta.com/suesgoodco/victorianvera/stationery/unionset.jpg.

8. *New York Times,* April 28, 1861.

9. Horatio Nelson Taft, diary entry, April 17, 1861, Taft Diary, Manuscript Division, Library of Congress (LOC).

10. *New York Tribune,* April 19, 1861, 1.

11. Train schedule, *National Republican* (Washington, D.C.), April 17, 1861, 3.

12. *New York Tribune,* April 18, 1861, 5.

13. Ibid.

14. *New York Tribune,* April 18, 1861, 5.

15. *Weekly Anglo-African* (New York), May 4, 1861, 1.

16. Winfield Scott to Abraham Lincoln, Dispatch No. 15, April 17, 1861, Abraham Lincoln Papers, LOC.

17. Heber S. Thompson, *The First Defenders* (n.p.: First Defenders Association, 1910), 14.

18. Ibid., 14.

19. Ibid., 15.

20. Samuel P. Bates, *History of the Pennsylvania Volunteers, 1861–1865* (Harrisburg: B. Singerly, 1869), 4.

21. J. W. Hanson, *Historical Sketch of the Old Sixth Regiment of Massachusetts Volunteers* (Boston: Lee and Shepard, 1866), 17–18.

22. Livermore, *My Story of the War,* 95.

23. Hanson, *Historical Sketch of the Old Sixth Regiment of Massachusetts Volunteers,* 16.

24. *New York Tribune,* April 18, 1861, 5.

25. Taft, diary entries, April 14, April 15, 1861, Taft Diary.

26. Quoted in Ernest B. Furgurson, *Freedom Rising: Washington in the Civil War* (New York: Random House, 2005), 20.

27. Taft, diary entry, April 4, 1861, Taft Diary.

28. *Evening Star* (Washington, D.C.), April 3, 1861, 3.

29. Lucius Chittenden, *Recollections of President Lincoln and His Administration* (New York: Harper & Brothers, 1891), 127.

30. Taft, diary entry, April 20, 1861, Taft Diary.

31. Ida Tarbell, *Life of Abraham Lincoln,* vol. 2 (New York: Doubleday & McClure, 1900), 44–45.

32. Elizabeth Brown Pryor, *Clara Barton: Professional Angel* (Philadelphia: University of Pennsylvania Press, 1987), 56.

33. Ibid., 57.

34. Ibid., 60–61.

35. Stephen B. Oates, *A Woman of Valor: Clara Barton and the Civil War* (New York: Macmillan International, 1994), 11.

36. Pryor, *Clara Barton*, 60–62.

37. In *The Collected Works of Abraham Lincoln*, ed. Roy P. Basler, vol. 4 (New Brunswick, N.J.: Rutgers University Press, 1955), 335.

38. William O. Stoddard, *Inside the White House in War Times* (New York: C. L. Webster & Co., 1890), xi.

39. John G. Nicolay and John Hay, *Abraham Lincoln: A History*, 10 vols., vol. 4 (New York: Century Co., 1890), 68.

40. Brayton Harris, *Blue and Gray in Black and White* (Washington: Brassey's, 1999), 9.

41. *New York Herald*, December 29, 1860, quoted in Wilhelmus Bogart Bryan, *A History of the National Capital from Its Foundation through the Period of the Adoption of the Organic Act*, vol. 2 (Washington, D.C: Macmillan, 1916), 461.

42. Emmet Crozier, *Yankee Reporters, 1861–65* (New York: Oxford University Press, 1956), 46.

43. Henry Villard, *Memoirs of Henry Villard, Journalist and Financier, 1835–1900*, vol. 1 (Boston: New York, Houghton, Mifflin, 1904), 161.

44. Ibid., 162.

45. Lucius Chittenden, diary entry, April 17, 1861, in Lucius Chittenden, *Invisible Siege: The Journal of Lucius E. Chittenden, April 15, 1861–July 14, 1861* (San Diego: Americana Exchange Press, 1969), 2.

46. *New York Times*, April 18, 1861, 1.

47. Craig M. Simpson, *A Good Southerner: The Life of Henry A. Wise of Virginia* (Chapel Hill: University of North Carolina Press, 1985), 239.

48. Ibid., 248.

49. John Beauchamp Jones, *Rebel Clerk's War Diary at the Confederate State's Capital* (Philadelphia: Lippincott, 1866), 17.

50. Ibid., 20.

51. John Imboden, "Jackson at Harper's Ferry in 1861," in *Battles and Leaders of the Civil War*, vol. 1 (New York: Century Co., 1888), 111.

52. Barton Haxwell Wise, *Life of Henry Wise* (New York: Macmillan, 1899), 276.

53. Ibid., 277. Imboden's account, less detailed that the one offered in Wise, *Life of Henry Wise*, states that Letcher agreed to the plan shortly after midnight, and does not mention the oath to Wise.

54. Imboden, "Jackson at Harper's Ferry in 1861," 114.

55. *New York Times*, April 19 1861, 5.

56 . John Marshall Hagans, *Brief Sketch of the Erection and Formation of the State of West Virginia* (Charleston, W.V.: Butler Printing Company, 1891), 28.

57. Jones, *Rebel Clerk's War Diary*, 22.

58. Ibid., 23.

59. Ibid., 23–24.

60. J. M. Mason to Jefferson Davis, April 27, 1861, OR, vol. 51, pt. 2, 14.

61. Davis, endorsing letter from J. W. Woltz, April 17, 1861, in *Papers of Jefferson Davis*, ed. Lynda L. Crist and Mary S. Dix, vol. 7 (Baton Rouge: Louisiana State University Press, 1992), 108.

62. Francis W. Pickens to Jefferson Davis, confidential communication, April 16, 1861, in *Papers of Jefferson Davis*, 7:105.

63. Ibid.

64. *New York Tribune*, April 17, 1861, 4.

65. Ibid., April 18, 1861, 5.

66. Alexander H. Stephens, diary entry, April 17, 1861, in Richard Malcolm Johnston and William Hand Brown, *Life of Alexander H. Stephens* (Philadelphia: J. B. Lippincott, 1878), 396–397.

67. Ibid., 397.

68. John Ellis to Jefferson Davis, April 17, 1861, in *Papers of John W. Ellis*, 2:623.

Thursday, April 18

1. *New York Tribune*, April 19, 1861, 1.

2. *New York Tribune*, April 19, 1861, 1; *Washington National Intelligencer*, April 18, 1861, 2.

3. *Washington National Intelligencer*, April 19, 1861, 3.

4. Lucius Chittenden, diary entry, April 18, 1861, in Chittenden, *Invisible Siege: The Journal of Lucius E. Chittenden, April 15, 1861–July 14, 1861* (San Diego: Americana Exchange Press, 1969), 3.

5. *New York Times*, April 15, 1861, 1.

6. *New York Tribune*, April 19, 1861, 1.

7. Winfield Scott to John B. Floyd, May 8, 1857, quoted in Armistead Lindsay Long and Marcus Joseph Wright, *Memoirs of Robert E. Lee* (New York: J. M. Stoddart & Company, 1886), 481.

8. Frederick W. Seward, *Seward at Washington as Senator and Secretary of State: A Memoir of His Life, with Selections from His Letters, 1846–1861* (New York: Derby & Miller, 1891), 560. The date is given as "One day, soon after the first call for troops," thus around the same time as the offer to Lee.

9. John G. Nicolay and John Hay, *Abraham Lincoln: A History*, 10 vols., vol. 4 (New York: Century Co., 1890), 104–105.

10. John A. Dahlgren, diary entry, April 18, 1861, *Memoir of John A. Dahlgren*, ed. Madeleine Vinton Dahlgren (Boston: J. R. Osgood, 1882), 330.

11. Alexander H. Stephens, diary entry, April 18, 1861, in Richard Malcolm Johnston and William Hand Brown, *Life of Alexander H. Stephens* (Philadelphia: J. B. Lippincott, 1878), 397.

12. Winfield Scott, OR, ser. 1, vol. 2: 578.

13. Ibid.

14. Scott Dispatch to Lincoln, No. 16, April 18, 1861, Abraham Lincoln Papers, Library of Congress (LOC).

15. *New York Tribune*, April 23, 1861, 4.

16. Ibid., 5.
17. Ibid.
18. *New York Tribune*, April 17, 1861, 7.
19. Felton to Cameron, OR, ser. 1, 2:577.
20. Cameron to Hicks, OR, ser. 1, 2:564.
21. Unknown to Abraham Lincoln, April 11, 1861, Abraham Lincoln Papers, LOC.
22. Craig L. Symonds, *Confederate Admiral: The Life and Wars of Franklin Buchanan* (Annapolis: Naval Institute Press, 1999), 137.
23. Quoted in Charles W. Mitchell, *Maryland Voices of the Civil War* (Baltimore: Johns Hopkins University Press, 2007), 43.
24. John W. Forney. *Anecdotes of Famous Men*, vol. 1 (New York: Harper & Brothers, 1873), 158.
25. *Baltimore Sun*, April 19, 1861, 4.
26. *New York Herald*, April 19, 1861, 3.
27. Granville Fernald, *Story of the First Defenders* (Washington, D.C.: Clarence E. Davis, 1892), 19.
28. Ibid., 19–20.
29. Ibid., 20.
30. *Baltimore Sun*, April 19, 1861, 4.
31. Fernald, *Story of the First Defenders*, 20.
32. Quoted in John David Hoptak, *First in Defense of the Union: The Civil War History of the First Defenders* (Bloomington, Ind.: AuthorHouse, 2004), 22.
33. Quoted in ibid., 22.
34. Quoted in ibid., 24.
35. Fernald, *Story of the First Defenders*, 21.
36. Heber S. Thompson, *The First Defenders* (n.p.: First Defenders Association, 1910), 147.
37. Benson Lossing, *Pictorial Field Book of the Civil War: Journeys through the Battlefield in the Wake of Conflict*, vol. 1 (New York: T. Belknap, 1868–69), 406.
38. Lucius Chittenden, *Invisible Siege*), 3.
39. *New York Times*, April 18, 1861, 1.
40. J. M. Holloway, *History of Kansas* (Lafayette, Ind.: James, Emmons, & Co., 1868), 378.
41. John Speer, *Life of Gen. James H. Lane* (Garden City, Kans.: John Speer, 1896), 284, 255.
42. H. Edward Richardson, *Cassius Marcellus Clay: Firebrand of Freedom* (Louisville: University Press of Kentucky, 1974), 83.
43. *Daily Picayune* (New Orleans), April 26, 1861, 1.
44. *Alexandria Gazette*, April 27, 1861, 2.
45. Paul Jennings, *A Colored Man's Reminiscences of James Madison* (Brooklyn: G. C. Beadle, 1865), 15.
46. Jacob Dodson to Simon Cameron, April 23, 1861, OR, ser. 3, 1:106.

47. John Aaron Wright, *Discovering African American St. Louis: A Guide to Historic Sites* (St. Louis: Missouri History Museum, 2002), 6–7.
48. Simon Cameron to Jacob Dodson, April 29, 1861. OR, ser. 3, 1:133.
49. Gideon Welles, "Mr. Welles in Answer to Mr. Weed: The Facts of the Abandonment of Gosport Navy-Yard," *Galaxy* 10 (November 1870): 111.
50. Ibid.
51. Ibid.
52. Roger Jones, testimony before U.S. Senate, November 26, 1861, in *The Reports of Committees of the Senate of the United States for Second Session of the Thirty-Seventh Congress 1861–1862* (Washington, D.C.: U.S Government Printing Office, 1862), 239.
53. Forney, *Anecdotes of Public Men*, 158.
54. Quoted in Charles M. Sumner, *Works of Charles Sumner* vol. 5 (Boston: Lee & Shepard, 1872), 492.
55. Forney, *Anecdotes of Public Men*, 138–139.
56. *Springfield Daily Republican* (Massachusetts), April 24, 1861, 4.
57. Lossing, *Pictorial Field Book of the Civil War*, 409.
58. See George William Brown, *Baltimore and the Nineteenth of April, 1861: A Study of War* (Baltimore: N. Murray, Johns Hopkins University Press, 1887), 38.
59. Thomas J. Scharf, *History of Baltimore City and County, from the Earliest Period to the Present Day*, vol. 3 (Philadelphia: Louis H. Evarts, 1881), 401.
60. Lossing, *Pictorial Field Book of the Civil War*, 410.
61. Papers of Elizabeth Cady Stanton, reel 1 of 5 (general correspondence), containers 1–2, shelf no. 17, 781.s, Manuscript Division, LOC.
62. Quoted in Hoptak, *First Defenders*, 31.
63. Quoted in Hoptak, *First Defenders*, 31.
64. Gay to Benson Lossing, n.d., in Lossing, *Pictoral Field Book of the Civil War*, 406.
65. Oliver C. Bosbyshell, "When and Where I Saw Lincoln," in Abraham Lincoln (Philadelphia: Military Order of the Loyal Legion of the United States Commandary of the State of Pennsylvania, 1907), 18.
66. Ibid., 17.
67. Ibid.
68. Quoted in *Abraham Lincoln: The Observations of John G. Nicolay and John Hay*, ed. Michael Burlingame (Carbondale: Southern Illinois University Press, 2007), 49.
69. Oliver C. Bosbyshell, "When and Where I Saw Lincoln," 17.
70. John Hay, April 18, 1861, diary entry, *Inside Lincoln's White House: The Complete Civil War Diary of John Hay*, eds. Michael Burlingame and John R. T. Ettlinger (Carbondale: Southern Illinois University Press, 1999), 1.
71. Clifford Arrick, diary entry, April 18, 1861, Clifford Arrick Diary, Frontier Guard Records, LOC.
72. John Hay, April 18, 1861, diary entry, *The Complete Civil War Diary of John Hay*, 2.
73. Nicolay and Hay, *Abraham Lincoln*, 4:107.
74. *Evening Star* (Washington, D.C.), April 19, 1861, 3.

75. John Hay, April 18, 1861, diary entry, *The Complete Civil War Diary of John Hay*, 1.
76. Ibid.
77. Clifford Arrick, April 18, 1861, diary entry, Clifford Arrick Diary.
78. Jones testimony, testimony before U.S. Senate November 26, 1861 in *The Reports of Committees of the Senate of the United States for Second Session of the Thirty-Seventh Congress 1861–1862* (Washington, D.C.: U.S Government Printing Office), 1862, 240.
79. Scott Dispatch No. 15, April 17, 1861, Abraham Lincoln Papers, LOC.
80. Jones testimony, testimony before U.S. Senate November 26, 1861 in *The Reports of Committees of the Senate of the United States for Second Session of the Thirty-Seventh Congress 1861–1862*, 240.
81. John Hay, April 18, 1861, diary entry, *The Complete Civil War Diary of John Hay*, 2.
82. Ibid.
83. John A. Dahlgren, diary entry, April 18, 1861, *Memoir of John A. Dahlgren*, 330.
84. John A. Dahlgren, April 18, 1861 diary entry, *Memoir of John A. Dahlgren*, 330.

Friday, April 19

1. Samuel P. Bates, *History of the Pennsylvania Volunteers, 1861–1865* (Harrisburg: B. Singerly, 1869), 7.
2. Lucius Chittenden, *Recollections of President Lincoln and His Administration* (New York: Harper & Brothers, 1891), 115.
3. John Hay, diary entry, April 19, 1861, in *The Letters of John Hay, Inside Lincoln's White House: The Complete Civil War Diary of John Hay*, eds. Michael Burlingame and John R. T. Ettlinger (Carbondale: Southern Illinois University Press, 1999), 3.
4. Lieutenant Roger Jones to Winfield Scott, April 19, 1861, OR ser. 1, vol. 2: 4.
5. Ibid.
6. *New York Herald*, April 22, 1861, 1.
7. See Craig M. Simpson, *Good Southerner: The Life of Henry A. Wise of Virginia* (Chapel Hill: University of North Carolina Press, 1985), 381 n. 105.
8. Ibid., 249.
9. Barton Haxwell Wise, *Life of Henry Wise* (New York: Macmillan, 1899), 276.
10. John Imboden, "Jackson at Harper's Ferry in 1861," in *Battles and Leaders of the Civil War*, vol. 1 (New York: Century Co., 1888), 111–125.
11. Ibid., 112.
12. U.S. House of Representatives, *Reports of the Select Committee of Five, sec. 2, Alleged Hostile Organization against the Government within the District of Columbia* (Washington, D.C.: Government Printing Office, 1861), 13, 92, 128.
13. Imboden, "Jackson at Harper's Ferry in 1861," 112.
14. "Harper's Ferry Armory and History," in *Rebellion Record*, vol. 10, ed. Frank Moore (New York: D. Van Nostrand, 1867), 322. Though the article is unsigned and written in the third person, it appears to have penned by Kingsbury

himself. Preference is given to Kingsbury's Senate testimony in November 1861 as a source rather than the account in Moore, *Rebellion Record*, since it was conducted months afterward. A letter written that night confirms Kingsbury's brief capture. At 2 a.m. on April 19, while fires were still burning at the arsenal, George Mauzy—who had created the Minié bullet while serving as the Harper's Ferry master armorer in the 1850s, and maintained a residence there—wrote a letter to his son-in-law James Burton, the superintendent of the Richmond armory. "After these buildings were set on fire," Mauzy wrote, "Lieut. Jones & his men walked across the Bridge" toward Pennsylvania, while Captain Kingsbury remained there, "under guard." George Mauzy to James. Burton, 2 a.m., April 20, 1861, John Brown/Boyd B. Stutler Collection Database, West Virginia Division of Culture and History, www.wvculture.org/history/wvmemory/imlsintro.html.

15. Charles P. Kingsbury, testimony before U.S. Senate, November 26, 1861, in *The Reports of Committees of the Senate of the United States for Second Session of the Thirty-Seventh Congress 1861–1862* (Washington, D.C.: U.S Government Printing Office, 1862), 247.

16. Ibid.

17. *New York Herald*, April 22, 1861, 1.

18. "Harper's Ferry Armory and History," 322. Both Jones and Kingsbury mentioned the small kegs of gunpowder in their congressional testimony, but only Kingsbury asserted that they were remnants of the Brown raid.

19. Cameron to Roger Jones, April 22, 1861, in *Appletons' Annual Cyclopaedia and Register of Important Events*, vol. 1 (New York: D. Appleton, 1861), 363.

20. *New York Herald*, April 19, 1861, 1.

21. Ibid.

22. *Boston Daily Globe*. May 27, 1906, 52.

23. J. W. Hanson, *Historical Sketch of the Old Sixth Regiment of Massachusetts Volunteers* (Boston: Lee and Shepard, 1866), 21.

24. Ibid., 22.

25. Ibid., 21.

26. *Washington Post*, April 22, 1891, 2.

27. Charles P. Dare, *Philadelphia, Wilmington & Baltimore Railroad Guide*, (Philadelphia: Fitzgibbon & Van Ness, 1856), 120–121.

28. *Boston Journal*, April 16, 1911, 7.

29. *Philadelphia Inquirer*, April 20, 1861, 4.

30. *Philadelphia Inquirer*, April 20, 1861, 4.

31. George W. Nason, *History and Complete Roster of the Massachusetts Regiments. Minute Men of '61* (Boston: Smith & Nance, 1910.), 194.

32. Hanson, *Historical Sketch of the Old Sixth Massachusetts*, 24.

33. Phineas Camp Headley, *Massachusetts in the Rebellion: A Record of the Historical Position of the Commonwealth, and the Services of the Leading Statesmen, the Military, the Colleges, and the People, in the Civil War of 1861–65* (Boston: Walker, Fuller and Co., 1866), 113.

34. Ibid.

35. *Boston Daily Journal,* April 20, 1861, 2.
36. *Baltimore Sun,* April 19, 1861, 4.
37. John David Hoptak, *First in Defense of the Union : the Civil War history of the First Defenders* (Bloomington, Indiana: AuthorHouse, 2004), 24.
38. Ernest Wardwell, "Military Waif," *Maryland Historical Magazine,* 39:4 (winter 1994): 429.
39. Nason, *History and Complete Roster of the Massachusetts Regiments,* 194.
40. Benson Lossing, *Pictorial Field Book of the Civil War: Journeys through the Battlefield in the Wake of Conflict,* vol. 1 (New York: T. Belknap, 1868–69), 411.
41. J. Thomas Scharf, *Chronicles of Baltimore* (Baltimore: Turnbull Bros., 1874), 589.
42. *Baltimore American,* April 20, 1861, 1.
43. Scharf, *Chronicles of Baltimore,* 589.
44. Ibid.
45. Nason, *History and Complete Roster of the Massachusetts Regiments,* 195.
46. Scharf, *Chronicles of Baltimore,* 405.
47. Wardwell, "Military Waif," 430.
48. Ibid., 429.
49. Ibid., 430; *Pittsfield Sun* (Massachusetts), May 23, 1861, 4.
50. Ibid., 430–431.
51. Ibid., 434.
52. Ibid.
53. *Frank Leslie's Illustrated Newspaper,* May 18, 1861, 3.
54. *Anecdotes, Poetry, and Incidents of the War: North and South: 1860–1865,* ed. Frank Moore (New York: Printed for the subscribers, 1866), 36.
55. Hanson, *Historical Sketch of the Old Sixth Massachusetts,* 31.
56. Ibid., 30–31.
57. Ibid., 31–32.
58. Ibid. 32.
59. Nason, *History and Complete Roster of the Massachusetts Regiments,* 197.
60. *Richmond Daily Dispatch,* April 22, 1861. 2.
61. Brown to Lincoln, April 19, 1861, Abraham Lincoln Papers, Library of Congress (LOC). The telegram carries the correct date; the handwritten original of the same message that arrived has the erroneous date of April 18, 1861, as do other documents from the Baltimore mayor's office delivered that day.
62. John G. Nicolay and John Hay, *Abraham Lincoln: A History,* 10 vols., vol. 4 (New York: Century Co., 1890), 123.
63. As noted above, the original handwritten text has the erroneous date of April 18.
64. Nicolay and Hay, *Abraham Lincoln,* 4:123.
65. John Hay, diary entry, April 19, 1861, in John Hay, *Inside Lincoln's White House: The Complete Civil War Diary of John Hay,* ed. Michael Burlingame and John R. T. Ettlinger (Carbondale: Southern Illinois University Press, 1999), 3.
66. Horatio Nelson Taft, diary entry, April 19, 1861, Taft Diary, Manuscript Division, LOC.

67. Elizabeth Brown Pryor, *Clara Barton: Professional Angel* (Philadelphia: University of Pennsylvania Press, 1987), 78.
68. John Nicolay, memorandum, April 19, 1861, in John G. Nicolay, *With Lincoln in the White House: Letters, Memoranda, and Other Writings of John G. Nicolay, 1860–1865*, ed. Michael Burlingame (Carbondale: Southern Illinois University Press, 2006), 34.
69. Clifford Arrick, diary entry, April 19, 1861, Frontier Guard Records, LOC.
70. *The Press* (Philadelphia), April 20, 1861, 3.
71. William Swinton, *History of the Seventh Regiment, National Guard, State of New York, during the War of the Rebellion* (New York, Boston, Fields, Osgood & Co., 1870), 18–19.
72. Ibid., 19.
73. Udolpho Wolfe and Hudson G. Wolfe New York, *Grand Civic and Military Demonstration in Honor of the Removal of the Remains of James Monroe, Fifth President of the United States, from New-York to Virginia* (New York: U. Wolfe, 1858), 148.
74. *New York Morning Express*. April 22, 1861, 2; *New York Times*. April 30, 1861, 1.
75. Robert Gould Shaw to Sarah Blake Sturgis Shaw, April 18, 1861, in *Blue-Eyed Child of Fortune: The Civil War Letters of Colonel Robert Gould Shaw*, ed. Russell Duncan (Athens: University of Georgia Press, 1992), 73.
76. George Templeton Strong, April 19, 1861 diary entry, in *The Diary of George Templeton Strong*, vol. 3: *The Civil War, 1860–1865*, eds. Allan Nevins and Milton Halsey Thomas (New York: Macmillan, 1952), 126.
77. *Cincinnati Daily Commercial*, April 23, 1861, 2.
78. *New York Herald*, April 20, 1861, 2.
79. Theodore Winthrop, "New York Seventh Regiment: Our March to Washington," *Atlantic Monthly* (June 1861): 744.
80. Ibid., 745.
81. Quoted in John Stevens Cabot Abbott, *The History of the Civil War in America*, vol. 1 (New York: Henry Bell, 1863), 101.
82. Francis Tiffany, *Life of Dorothea Lynde Dix* (Boston: Houghton Mifflin, 1890), 335.
83. Charles M. Snyder, ed., *The Lady and the President: The Letters of Dorothea Dix Millard Fillmore* (Lexington: University Press of Kentucky, 1975), 350.
84. Tiffany, *Life of Dorothea Lynde Dix*, 335.
85. *Baltimore Sun*, April 20, 1861, 1.
86. Ibid.
87. See George William Brown, *Baltimore and the Nineteenth of April, 1861: A Study of War* (Baltimore: N. Murray, Johns Hopkins University Press, 1887), 56.
88. *Baltimore American*, April 20, 1861, 1.
89. *Baltimore Sun*, April 20, 1861, 1.
90. *Baltimore Sun*, April 19, 1861, 1; *Baltimore American*, April 19, 1861, 1.
91. *Congressional Globe* (Washington, D.C.), July 18, 1861, 201.

92. "The Indictment of George Kane involved in the Baltimore 'Riot' of 1861," April 19, 1861, newspaper clipping, George P. Kane indictment, National Archives Archival Research Collection, NARA ARC Identifier 278860.
93. "The Baltimore Riot," documents in Moore, *Rebellion Record*, 1:79.
94. George Brown to Abraham Lincoln, April 19, 1861, Abraham Lincoln Papers, LOC (again, the note carries the incorrect date of April 18, 1861).
95. Thomas Hicks, addendum to ibid.
96. John Nicolay and Johny Hay, "Abraham Lincoln—The National Uprising," *Century* 25 (1888): 912 ("suicidal nature"). The *Century* article contains a handful of details not included in the *Abraham Lincoln: A History*; telegram in "The Baltimore Riot," in Moore, *Rebellion Record*, 1:79.
97. Nicolay and Hay, "Abraham Lincoln—The National Uprising," 912.
98. *Philadelphia Inquirer*, April 20, 1861, 1.
99. Ibid.
100. Winfield Scott to Robert Patterson, April 19, 1861, OR, ser. 1, 2:579.
101. Winfield Scott to Robert Patterson, 7:30 p.m., April 19, 1861, OR, ser. 1, 2:579.
102. Robert Patterson to Winfield Scott, April 19, 1861, OR, ser. 1, 2:579.
103. *New York Herald*, April 22, 1861, 1.
104. Ibid.
105. *New York Herald*, April 22, 1861, 1.
106. Ibid.
107. *Easton Gazette* (Easton, Md.), April 27, 1861, 2.
108. *New York Herald*, April 22, 1861, 1.
109. John Hay, diary entry, April 19, 1861, in *Inside Lincoln's White House*, 3.
110. John Nicolay, Memorandum, April 19, 1861, in Nicolay, *With Lincoln in the White House*, 34.
111. John Nicolay to Therena Bates, April 19, 1861, in Nicolay, *With Lincoln in the White House*, 34–35.
112. Ibid.

Saturday, April 20

1. John G. Nicolay and John Hay, *Abraham Lincoln: A History*, 10 vols., vol. 4 (New York: Century Co., 1890), 126.
2. George Brown to Abraham Lincoln, April 19, 1861, Abraham Lincoln Papers, Library of Congress (LOC).
3. Adjutant-General L. Thomas to Samuel Felton, April 19, 1861, OR, ser. 1, 2:578.
4. Nicolay and Hay, *Abraham Lincoln*, 4:126.
5. Ibid.
6. Nicolay and Hay, *Abraham Lincoln*, 4:340.
7. Ibid., 127.
8. Fitz-John Porter to Lorenzo Thomas, May 1, 1861, OR, ser. 1, vol. 51, pt. 1, 1897, 345.

9. Report of Office of the Board of Police Commissioners (Baltimore), OR, ser. 1, 2:10.

10. Report of Mayor George Brown, May 9, 1861, OR, ser. 1, 2:13.

11. Nicolay and Hay, *Abraham Lincoln*, 4:120–121.

12. *New York Herald*, April 24, 1861, 3; *The Press* (Philadelphia), April 22, 1861, 2.

13. *Brooklyn Daily Eagle*, April 27, 1861, 1.

14. Edwin M. Stanton to James Buchanan, May 16, 1861, in George Ticknor Curtis, *Life of James Buchanan, Fifteenth President of the United States*, vol. 2 (New York: Harper & Brothers, 1883), 547. Stanton's earlier letters had been lost in the mail during Washington's isolation, and in writing to Buchanan again attempted to recreating his thoughts from the earlier letters.

15. Lucius Chittenden, diary entry, April 20, 1861, in Lucius Chittenden, *Invisible Siege: The Journal of Lucius E. Chittenden, April 15, 1861–July 14, 1861* (San Diego: Americana Exchange Press, 1969), 5–6.

16. Horatio Nelson Taft, diary entry, April 20, 1861, Manuscript Division, LOC.

17. John Niven, *Salmon P. Chase: A Biography* (New York: Oxford University Press, 1995), 255.

18. Stanley Preston Kimmel, *Mr. Lincoln's Washington* (New York: Coward-McCann, 1957), 59.

19. Craig L. Symonds, *Joseph E. Johnston* (New York: Norton, 1992), 97.

20. Lucius Chittenden, *Recollection of President Lincoln and His Administration* (New York: Harper & Brothers, 1891), 118–119.

21. Ernest Wardwell, "Military Waif," *Maryland Historical Magazine* 39:4 (winter 1994): 436.

22. Ibid.

23. Richard M. Lee, *Mr. Lincoln's City*, (McLean, Va.: EPM Publications, 1981), 91.

24. John B. Ellis, *Sights and Secrets of the Nation's Capital* (Chicago: Jones, Junkin, Co., 1869), 342.

25. Ibid.

26. Ellis, *Sights and Secrets*, 348.

27. *Washington Post*, April 22, 1891, 2.

28. Wardwell, "Military Waif," 438.

29. Ibid., 438.

30. Ibid., 428.

31. John Williams Jones, ed., *The Life and Letters of Robert E. Lee* (New York: Neale, 1906), 133.

32. George Templeton Strong, diary entry, April 20, 1861, in George Templeton Strong, *The Diary of George Templeton Strong*, vol. 3: *The Civil War, 1860–1865*, eds. Allan Nevins and Milton Halsey Thomas (New York : Macmillan, 1952) 127.

33. *Washington Post*, March 8, 1925, 83.

34. Chittenden, *Recollections of President Lincoln and His Administration*, 99.

35. Ibid.

36. Ibid.

37. Nicolay and Hay, *Abraham Lincoln*, 4:103–104.
38. Ibid., 103.
39. *Baltimore Sun*, April 27, 1861, 1.
40. Nicolay and Hay, *Abraham Lincoln*, 4:103.
41. *Atlas & Argus* (Albany, N.Y.), May 1, 1861, 2.
42. Frederick W. Seward, *Seward at Washington as Senator and Secretary of State: A Memoir of His Life, with Selections from His Letters, 1846–1861* (New York: Derby & Miller, 1891), 552.
43. Scott Dispatch to Lincoln, April 20, 1861, Abraham Lincoln Papers, LOC.
44. Frederick W. Seward, *Reminiscences of a War-time Statesman and Diplomat, 1830–1915* (New York: Putman's, 1916), 162.
45. Ibid., 162.
46. Ibid., 163.
47. See George William Brown, *Baltimore and the Nineteenth of April, 1861: A Study of War* (Baltimore: N. Murray, Johns Hopkins University Press, 1887), 63.
48. Hicks to Cameron, April 20, 1861, in *The Lincoln Papers: The Story of the Collection, with Selections to July 4, 1861*. vol. 2, ed. David Chambers Mearns (Garden City, N. Y.: Doubleday, 1948), 574.
49. Nicolay and Hay, *Abraham Lincoln*, 4:127.
50. Brown to Lincoln, April 20, 1861, in *The Lincoln Papers*, 574.
51. Scott Dispatch to Lincoln No. 17, April 20, 1861, Abraham Lincoln Papers, LOC.
52. William Swinton, *History of the Seventh Regiment, National Guard, State of New York, during the War of the Rebellion* (New York: Fields, Osgood & Co., 1870), 56.
53. Ibid., 52.
54. Ibid., 56.
55. Carl Schurz, *The Reminiscences of Carl Schurz* (New York: McClure, 1907), 225.
56. Robert S. Holzman, *Stormy Ben Butler* (New York: Macmillan, 1954), 3.
57. *Boston Daily Evening Transcript*, May 24, 1861, 2.
58. Ibid.
59. Hans L. Trefousse, *Ben Butler: The South Called Him Beast!* (New York: Twayne, 1957), 63.
60. Holzman, *Stormy Ben Butler*, 27.
61. Ibid., 27.
62. Ibid., 28.
63. Ibid.
64. Margot Gayle and Carol Gayle, *The Significance of Cast-iron Architecture in America* (New York: Norton, 1998), 188.
65. *Washington Post*, April 22, 1891, 2.
66. Horatio Nelson Taft, diary entry, April 21, 1861, Taft Diary, LOC.
67. *Washington Post*, April 22, 1891, 2.
68. John Nicolay, *The Outbreak of the Rebellion* (New York: Scribner's, 1882) 98.

69. Ibid.
70. John Hay, diary entry, April 20, 1861, in John Hay, *Inside Lincoln's White House: The Complete Civil War Diary of John Hay*, ed. Michael Burlingame and John R. T. Ettlinger (Carbondale: Southern Illinois University Press, 1999), 4.
71. Arrick, diary entry, April 20, 1861, Clifford Arrick Diary, Frontier Guard Records, LOC.
72. H. D. Bird to Leroy Walker, April 20, 1861, OR, ser. 1, 2:771.
73. H. D. Bird to Leroy Walker, April 20, 1861, OR, ser. 1, 2:771 (Separate telegram from above).
74. Lucius Chittenden, diary entry, April 20, 1861, in *Invisible Siege*, 6.
75. *New York Herald*, April 21, 1861, 1
76. George Templeton Strong, diary entry, April 20, 1861, *The Diary of George Templeton Strong*, vol. 3:127.

Sunday, April 21

1. Lucius Chittenden, April 20, 1861 diary entry, in Lucius Chittenden, *Invisible Siege: The Journal of Lucius E. Chittenden, April 15, 1861–July 14, 1861* (San Diego: Americana Exchange Press, 1969), 6–7.
2. Frederick W. Seward, *Seward at Washington as Senator and Secretary of State: A Memoir of His Life, with Selections from His Letters, 1846–1861* (New York: Derby & Miller, 1891), 550.
3. Doris Kearns Goodwin, *Team of Rivals* (New York: Simon & Schuster, 2005), 354; Frances Seward, diary entry, May 19, 1861, Frances Seward Diary, William H. Seward Papers, University of Rochester Rare Books & Special Collections.
4. Edward Everett to Willy Everett, April 22, 1861, Edward Everett Papers, microform edition, reel 32, Letter Books 1.
5. Seward, *Seward at Washington*, 550.
6. Ibid., 551.
7. Quoted in Helen Nicolay, *Lincoln's Secretary: A Biography of John G. Nicolay* (New York: Longmans, Green, 1949), 92.
8. *Washington Star*, April 20, 1861, 3.
9. Charles P. Stone, "Washington in March and April, 1861," *Magazine of American History* 14:1 (July 1885): 10–11.
10. John Nicolay, Memorandum of Events, April 21, 1861, in John G. Nicolay, *With Lincoln in the White House: Letters, Memoranda, and Other Writings of John G. Nicolay, 1860–1865*, ed. Michael Burlingame (Carbondale: Southern Illinois University Press, 2006), 37.
11. *National Intelligencer* (Washington), April 23, 1861, 3.
12. John G. Nicolay and John Hay, *Abraham Lincoln: A History*, 10 vols., vol. 4 (New York: Century Co., 1890), 131.
13. Ibid., 131.

14. John W. Garrett to George W. Brown, April 21, 1861, quoted in George W. Brown, *Baltimore and the 19th of April, 1861* (Baltimore, N. Murray, 1887), 74; time from *The South* (Baltimore), April 22, 1861, 3.

15. Fitz-John Porter, "Curtin's Early War Trials," in *Life and Times of Andrew Curtin*, ed. William Henry Egle (Philadelphia: Thompson Pub. Co., 1896), 339.

16. *The South*, April 22, 1861, 3.

17. Nicolay and Hay, *Abraham Lincoln: A History*, 4:131.

18. Ibid., 132.

19. Interview with Brown (April 21, 7:30 p.m.), *National Intelligencer*, April 23, 1861, 3.

20. Ibid., 3.

21. *The South*, April 22, 1861, 3.

22. Brown, *Baltimore and the 19th of April, 1861*, 75.

23. *New York Tribune*, April 26, 1861, 6.

24. William Bender Wilson, *A Few Acts and Actors in the Tragedy of the Civil War* (Philadelphia: William Bender Wilson, 1892), 50.

25. Cameron's postwar explanation to Porter reads: "On the way to the depot, I met with him [Major Belger] with this order, and after reflecting upon the importance of getting the troops immediately to Washington I wrote in pencil upon it that the order had been changed, and directed him to say to you [Porter] to bring on the troops at all hazards. I learned long ago from himself that he never did convey this order. I suppose I ought to have put in writing but could not do so sitting the carriage in the depot. Had I done so, I am sure you would have executed it, and dared much trouble and bloodshed, caused afterwards by the riots in Baltimore." Simon Cameron to Fitz-John Porter, September 3, 1881, Fitz-John Porter Papers, Manuscript Division, Library of Congress (LOC).

26 Brown, *Baltimore and the 19th of April, 1861*, 75.

27. *The South*, April 22, 1861, 3.

28. *Baltimore American*, April 23, 1861, 1.

29. *Baltimore Sun*, April 23, 1861 1.

30. *Baltimore American*, April 22, 1861, 1.

31. *Baltimore Sun*, April 22, 1861, 1.

32. *Baltimore American*, April 21, 1861, 1.

33. *The South*, April 22, 1861, 3.

34. *Baltimore American*, April 22, 1861, 1.

35. Ibid.

36. *The South*, April 22, 1861, 2.

37. Ibid.

38. Edward D. Mansfield, *The Life and Military Services of Lieut.-General Winfield Scott* (New York: N. C. Miller, 1862), 532.

39. Seward, *Seward at Washington*, 551.

40. Abraham Lincoln, message to Congress, May 27, 1862, in *Rebellion Record*, ed. Frank Moore, vol. 5 (New York: G. P. Putnam, 1863), 146.

41. Ibid.
42. Nicolay and Hay, *Abraham Lincoln: A History*, 4:137.
43. Ibid., 70.
44. Nicolay, *Lincoln's Secretary*, 85.
45. *New York Tribune*, April 24, 1861, 4.
46. Ida Tarbell, *Life of Abraham Lincoln*, vol. 2 (New York: Doubleday & McClure, 1900), 37.
47. Julia Taft Bayne, *Tad Lincoln's Father* (Lincoln: University of Nebraska Press, 2001), 35.
48. Ibid., 48.
49. Ibid.
50. Seward, *Seward at Washington*, 550.
51. *New York Times*, April 24, 1861, 1.
52. William B. Gulick, Washington, D.C., to John W. Ellis, in *The Papers of John W. Ellis*, ed. Noble J. Tolbert, vol. 2 (Raleigh, N.C.: State Department of Archives and History, 1964), 647–652.
53. Charles Stone, "A Dinner with General Scott in 1861," *Magazine of American History* 9:6 (June 1884): 528–532.
54. *New York Times*, April 28, 1861, 1.
55. *Philadelphia Inquirer*, April 22, 1861, 1.
56. Ibid.
57. Henry Villard, *Memoirs of Henry Villard, Journalist and Financier, 1835–1900*, vol. 1 (Boston: Houghton, Mifflin, 1904), 163.
58. *New York Times*, April 24, 1861, 5.
59. *Boston Daily Globe*, April 25, 1911, 12.
60. Clifford Arrick, diary entry, April 21, 1861, Clifford Arrick Diary, Frontier Guard Records, LOC.
61. *New York Times*, April 24, 1861, 5.
62. William Horatio Taft, diary entry, April 21, 1861, Taft Diary, Manuscript Division, LOC.
63. Abraham Lincoln, Message to Congress, May 27, 1862, in *Rebellion Record*, ed. Frank Moore, vol. 5 (New York: G. P. Putnam, 1863), 145.
64. William B. Gulick, Washington D.C., to John W. Ellis, April 21, 1861, in *Papers of John W. Ellis*, vol. 2:648.

Monday, April 22

1. Henry Villard, *Memoirs of Henry Villard, Journalist and Financier, 1835–1900*, vol. 1 (Boston: Houghton, Mifflin, 1904), 166.
2. Ibid., 167.
3. Frederick Douglass, "Hope and Despair in Cowardly Times," in *The Frederick Douglass Papers*, ser. 1, *Speeches, Debates and Interviews*, ed. John W. Blassingame, vol. 3 (New Haven: Yale University Press, 1985), 101.
4. Quoted in David Detzer, *Dissonance: The Turbulent Days between Fort Sumter and Bull Run* (New York: Harcourt, 2006), 199.

5. *New York Tribune*, April 22, 1861, 4.
6. *Baltimore Sun*, April 22, 1861, 2.
7. *The South* (Baltimore), April 22, 1861, 2.
8. In Charles W. Mitchell, *Maryland Voices of the Civil War* (Baltimore: Johns Hopkins University Press, 2007), 490 n. 63.
9. Helen Nicolay, *Lincoln's Secretary: A Biography of John G. Nicolay* (New York: Longmans, Green, 1949), 92; John Hay, diary entry, April 22, 1861, *Inside Lincoln's White House: The Complete Civil War Diary of John Hay*, eds. Michael Burlingame and John R. T. Ettlinger (Carbondale: Southern Illinois University Press, 1999), 7.
10. Frederick W. Seward, *Seward at Washington as Senator and Secretary of State: A Memoir of His Life, with Selections from His Letters, 1846–1861* (New York: Derby & Miller, 1891), 554.
11. Ibid., 554. Some of the text in this account appears to have been plagiarized from John William Draper, *National History of the American Civil War* (New York: Harper & Brothers, 1868), 75.
12. Quoted in Michael Burlingame, *Abraham Lincoln: The Observations of John G. Nicolay and John Hay* (Carbondale: Southern Illinois University Press, 2007), 55.
13. Ibid.
14. Evert A. Duyckinck, *National History of the War for the Union, Civil, Military and Naval*, vol. 1 (New York: Johnson, Fry and Company, 1861), 173.
15. Diary Horatio Nelson Taft, diary entry, April 20, 1861, Taft Diary, Manuscript Division, Library of Congress (LOC).
16. Quoted in Burlingame, *Abraham Lincoln: The Observations of Nicolay and Hay*, 56.
17. Orville H. Brown to Abraham Lincoln, April 22, 1861, quoted in Mitchell, *Maryland Voices*, 63.
18. Quoted in Burlingame, *Abraham Lincoln: The Observations of Nicolay and Hay*, 55.
19. *New York Times*, April 24, 1861, 5.
20. *Baltimore Sun*, April 23, 1861, 1.
21. *Baltimore Sun*, April 23, 1861, 3.
22. *The South*, April 23, 1861, 4.
23. John Scott to R. Toombs, April 22, 1861, vol. 51, pt. 2, supp. to ser. 1, vols. 1 and 2, 1897, 24.
24. *The South*, April 23, 1861, 2.
25. Jefferson Davis to John Letcher, April 22, 1861 in OR, ser. 1, vol. 2:773.
26. See various cables between Davis, Confederate leadership, and states governors in *Papers of Jefferson Davis*, ed. Lynda L. Crist and Mary S. Dix, vol. 7 (Baton Rouge: Louisiana State University Press, 1992), 109.
27. Printed in its entirety in *Richmond Enquirer*, April 23, 1861, 1.
28. *The Diary of Edmund Ruffin: Toward Independence, October 1856–April 1861* (Baton Rouge: Louisiana State University Press, 1972), 609.

29. *Charleston Mercury*, April 26, 1861, 1.

30. J. M. Mason to Jefferson Davis, April 21, 1861, in *Papers of Jefferson Davis*, 7:113.

31. *New York Tribune*, April 25, 1861, 5. The same account is cited in a footnote as *New York Commercial Advertiser*, April 25, 1861, in Benson Lossing, *Pictorial Field Book of the Civil War: Journeys through the Battlefield in the Wake of Conflict*, vol. 1 (New York: T. Belknap, 1868–69), 379. In his 1868 *A Constitutional View of the Late War between the States* (Philadelphia, Pa.: National Publishing Company, 1868–70), Stephens disputed Lossing's claim that he made the call "On to Washington!" during his trip north: "No such sentiments were ever uttered by me as given in these reported speeches." (24). However, Stephens did not address the veracity of the original *Tribune* article or its subsequent republications in other newspapers.

32. Alexander Stephens to Jefferson Davis, April 22, 1861, in OR, vol. 51, pt. 2, Supp. to ser. 1, vols. 1 and 2, 1897, 24.

33. L. P. Bayne, J. J. Chancellor to Col. R. E. Lee, April 22, 1861, in OR, ser. 1, 2:774.

34. Emory M. Thomas, *Robert E. Lee: A Biography* (New York : Norton, 1995), 188–189.

35. *Richmond Examiner*, April 23, 1861, quoted in Frank Moore, ed., *Rebellion Record*, vol. 1 (New York: G. P. Putnam, 1861), 189.

36. *New York Times*, May 2, 1861, 2; *Pittsfield, Massachusetts Sun*, May 16, 1861, 1.

37. William Swinton, *History of the Seventh Regiment, National Guard, State of New York, during the War of the Rebellion* (New York: Fields, Osgood & Co., 1870), 65.

38. Ibid., 67.

39. *Boston Daily Journal*, April 27, 1861, 2.

40. Benjamin F. Butler, *Butler's Book: Autobiography and Personal Reminiscences of Major-General Benj. F. Butler* (Boston, A.M. Thayer, 1892), 191.

41. George W. Nason, *History and Complete Roster of the Massachusetts Regiments. Minute Men of '61* (Boston: Smith and McCance, 1910), 232.

42. Butler, *Butler's Book*, 198.

43. *New York Times*, April 27, 1861, 1.

44. Hicks to "Commander of the Volunteers Troops on board the steamer," April 21, 1861, OR, 2, 586–587.

45. Butler, *Butler's Book*, 195.

46. Swinton, *History of the Seventh Regiment*, 70; *Boston Evening Transcript*, April 26, 1861, 1.

47. *Harper's Weekly*, May 11, 1861, 294.

48. Ibid.

49. Swinton, *History of the Seventh Regiment*, 75.

50. Ibid., 72–73.

51. George W. Nason, *History and Complete Roster of the Massachusetts Regiments. Minute Men of '61* (Boston: Smith & Nance, 1910.), 233.

52. Swinton, *History of the Seventh Regiment*, 74.

53. Swinton, *History of the Seventh Regiment*, 73.
54. Butler, *Butler's Book*, 199.
55. Ibid., 200.
56. Chittenden, diary entry, April 22, 1861, in Lucius Chittenden, *Invisible Siege: The Journal of Lucius E. Chittenden, April 15, 1861–July 14, 1861* (San Diego: Americana Exchange Press, 1969), 9.
57. *New York World*, April 22, 1861, 3.
58. John Hay, diary entry, April 22, 1861, in *Letters of John Hay*, 8.
59. James A. Mackay, *Allan Pinkerton: The First Private Eye*, (New York : Wiley & Sons, 1997), 107.
60. Pinkerton to Lincoln, April 21, 1861, in *Lincoln Papers*, in *The Lincoln Papers: The Story of the Collection, with Selections to July 4, 1861*. vol. 2, ed. David Chambers Mearns (Garden City, N. Y.: Doubleday, 1948), 577.
61. Edward D. Townsend, *Anecdotes of the Civil War* (New York: D. Appleton, 1884), 22–27.
62. Winfield Scott to Abraham Lincoln, April 22, 1861, Abraham Lincoln Papers, LOC.
63. John Hay, April 22, 1861 diary entry, in *Letters of John Hay*, 6.
64. Winfield Scott to Abraham Lincoln, April 22, 1861, Abraham Lincoln Papers, LOC.
65. Scott to Patterson, April 22, 1861, OR ser. 1, vol. 2: 587.
66. John Hay, diary entry, April 22, 1861, in *Letters of John Hay*, 8.
67. John Hay, April 22, 1861 diary entry, in the *Letters of John Hay*, 6.

Tuesday, April 23

1. John Hay, April 23, 1861, diary entry, in *Inside Lincoln's White House: The Complete Civil War Diary of John Hay*, eds. Michael Burlingame and John R. T. Ettlinger (Carbondale: Southern Illinois University Press, 1999), *The Letters of John Hay*, 10.
2. *New York Times*, April 25, 1861, 1.
3. *Philadelphia Inquirer*, April 25, 1861, 4.
4. *New York Times*, April 28, 1861, 1.
5. *Baltimore Sun*, April 27, 1861, 1.
6. Ibid.
7. John Hay, diary entry, April 22, 1861, in *Letters of John Hay*, 7. In all likelihood Chase was unaware that Cameron had countermanded Lincoln and Scott on April 21.
8. *Richmond Examiner*, April 23, 1861, 1.
9. Edward Bates, diary entry, April 23, 1861, in *Diary of Edward Bates, 1859–1866*, ed. Howard K. Beale and Mary Parker Ragatz (Washington, D. C.: U.S. Government Printing Office, 1933), 185.
10. John Hay, diary entry, April 23, 1861, in *Letters of John Hay*, 9.
11. Stanley Preston Kimmel, *Mr. Lincoln's Washington* (New York: Coward-McCann, 1957), 38–39.

12. Edward D. Townsend, *Anecdotes of the Civil War* (New York: D. Appleton, 1884), 21.
13. Charles P. Stone, "Washington in March and April, 1861," *Magazine of American History* 14:1 (July 1885): 17.
14. Ibid., 18.
15. Ibid., 18.
16. Ibid., 19–20.
17. Ibid., 19.
18. Ibid., 20.
19. Winthrop, "Washington as a Camp," *Atlantic Monthly*, July 1861, 107.
20. *Boston Daily Journal*, April 30, 1861, 4.
21. John Hay, diary entry, April 20, 1861, in *Letters of John Hay*, 5.
22. *The Press* (Philadelphia), April 20, 1861, 2.
23. *Newark Daily Advertiser*, May 2, 1861, 2.
24. *New York Times*, April 24, 1861, 1.
25. Ibid.
26. Ibid.
27. George A. Reed to Nathan Reed, April 20, 1861, Civil War Collections Acton Memorial Library, Acton, Massachusetts.
28. Barton to B.W. Childs, April 25, 1861 in William E. Barton, *The Life of Clara Barton, Founder of the American Red Cross*, vol. 1 (Boston and New York: Houghton Mifflin, 1922), 110.
29. Winthrop, "Washington as a Camp," 262; William Swinton, *History of the Seventh Regiment, National Guard, State of New York, during the War of the Rebellion* (New York: Fields, Osgood & Co., 1870), 127–128.
30. *New York Times*, April 20, 1861, 1.
31. *Worcester Daily Spy*, April 25, 1861; the letter is dated April 21.
32. William C. Allen, *History of the United States Capitol: A Chronicle of Design, Construction, and Politics* (Washington, D.C.: U.S. Government Printing Office, 2001), 314.
33. Ibid.
34. *New York Times*, April 24, 1861, 1.
35. Richard A. Baker, *Two Hundred Notable Days: Senate stories, 1787 to 2002*, (Washington, DC : U.S. Government Printing Office, 2006), 66.
36. Winthrop, "Washington as a Camp," 108.
37. William S. Wood to George P. A. Healy, July 20, 1861, quoted in Allen, *History of the United States Capitol*, 316.
38. Winthrop, Washington as a Camp," 108.
39. Allen, *History of the United States Capitol*, 266.
40. The repair from the attack can still be seen in the desk in two inlaid pieces of wood. Office of Senate Curator. http://www.senate.gov/vtour/jddesk.htm
41. Swinton, *History of the Seventh Regiment*, 77.
42. Hans L. Trefousse, *Ben Butler: They Called Him Beast*, (New York: Twayne Publishers, 1957), 70.

43. Benjamin F. Butler, *Butler's Book: Autobiography and Personal Reminiscences of Major-General Benj. F. Butler* (Boston, A.M. Thayer, 1892), 201.

44. Ibid., 202.

45. *New York World*, April 27, 1861, 4.

46. *Daily National Intelligencer* (Washington), May 9, 1861, 3.

47. *New York Times*, April 27, 1861, 1.

48. *Newark Daily Advertiser*, April 26, 1861, 2.

49. "Letter from Another Member," *New York Times*, April 25, 1861, 1.

50. Shaw to "Father and Mother," April 23, 1861 in *Blue-Eyed Child of Fortune: The Civil War Letters of Robert Gould Shaw*, ed Russell Duncan (Athens and London: The University of Georgia Press, 1992), 76.

51. Alexander H. Stephens to Jefferson Davis, April 22, 1861, in *Papers of Jefferson Davis*, ed. Lynda L. Crist and Mary S. Dix, vol. 7 (Baton Rouge: Louisiana State University Press, 1992), 116.

52. Stephens to Davis, April 23, 1861, in *Papers of Jefferson Davis*, 7:121.

53. Stephens to Davis, OR vol. 51, pt. 2, :26.

54. *Proceedings of the Virginia State Convention of 1861, February 13–May 1*, ed. George Reese (Richmond: Virginia State Library, Historical Publications Division, 1965), 378.

55. Ibid., 386.

56. Ibid., 383.

57. OR, vol. 51, pt. 2, : 28. Lee formally took command of the Virginia army and navy under General Orders No. 1 on April 23, after the Virginia Secession Convention approved his nomination unanimously.

58. John Beauchamp Jones, *Rebel Clerk's War Diary at the Confederate State's Capital* (Philadelphia: Lippincott, 1866), 27.

59. G. D. Harrison to Alexander Stephens and Jefferson Davis, April 23, 1861, Alexander H. Stephens Papers, Manuscript Division, Library of Congress (LOC).

60. Ibid. The letter was addressed first to Stephens and only second to Davis, which may account for the somewhat odd references to Davis in the third person.

61. John A. Campbellto Jefferson Davis, April 23, 1861, in *Papers of Jefferson Davis*, 7:117.

62. *Baltimore American*, April 24, 1861, 1.

63. Ibid.

64. Steuart describes the plan to send 1,000 troops to the Relay House in a letter to his son, Gen. George H. Steuart to William James Steuart, April 24, 1861, George H. Steuart Papers, Duke University Archives, Durham, North Carolina.

65. Gen. Steuart to Harper, 5:30 a.m., April 23, 1861, OR, vol. 51, pt. 2, :35.

66. *Baltimore American*, April 24, 1861, 1.

67. *Baltimore Sun*, April 25, 1861, 1.

68. *Baltimore American*, April 24, 1861, 1.

69. Ibid.
70. *Baltimore Sun*, April 24, 1861, 1.
71. *Annual Reunion: United States Military Academy. Association of Graduates* (Baltimore: Press of Isaac Friedenwald, 1904), 2.
72. George H. Steuart, Jr., to Charles Howard, April 22, 1861, quoted in Edward McPherson, *The Political History of the United States during the Great Rebellion* (Washington, D.C.: Philp & Solomons, 1865), 393.
73. *Seward at Washington as Senator and Secretary of State: A Memoir of His Life, with Selections from His Letters, 1846–1861* (New York: Derby & Miller, 1891), 537.
74. Lucius Chittenden, *Recollections of President Lincoln and His Administration* (New York: Harper & Brothers, 1891), 127.
75. Stoddard, *Lincoln's White House Secretary*, 226.
76. E. D. Townsend, *Anecdotes of the Civil War*, (New York : D. Appleton, 1884), 20–21. Scott's interlocutor, who is not identified, in all likelihood was Townsend himself.
77. John Hay, diary entry, April 23, 1861, in *Letters of John Hay*, 10.
78. John G. Nicolay and John Hay, *Abraham Lincoln: A History*, 10 vols., vol. 4 (New York: Century Co., 1890), 150.
79. Clifford Arrick, diary entry, April 23, 1861, Clifford Arrick Diary, Frontier Guards Records, LOC.
80. *National Republican* (Washington, D.C.), April 24, 1861, 3.
81. Clifford Arrick, diary entry, April 23, 1861, Clifford Arrick Diary.
82. Ibid.
83. John Hay, diary entry, April 23, 1861, in *Letters of John Hay*, 9
84. Lucius Chittenden, diary entry, April 21, 1861, in Lucius Chittenden, *Invisible Siege: The Journal of Lucius E. Chittenden, April 15, 1861–July 14, 1861* (San Diego: Americana Exchange Press, 1969), 9.
85. *New York Times*, April 25, 1861, 1.
86. Nicolay and Hay, *Abraham Lincoln: A History*, 152.
87. Ibid.

Wednesday, April 24

1. *New York World*, April 26, 1861, 4.
2. *Washington Star*, April 24, 1861, 1
3. Mary Henry, diary entry, n.d, Mary Henry Diary, Joseph Henry Papers, Smithsonian Archives.
4. John G. Nicolay and John Hay, *Abraham Lincoln: A History*, 10 vols., vol. 4 (New York: Century Co., 1890), 149.
5. Horatio Nelson Taft, diary entry, April 24, 1861, Taft Diary, Manuscript Division, Library of Congress (LOC).
6. *New York World*, April 26, 1861, 4.
7. Ibid.

8. Clifford Arrick, diary entry, April 24, 1861, Clifford Arrick Diary, Frontier Guard Records, LOC.

9. *New York World*, April 26, 1861, 4.

10. Clifford Arrick, diary entry, April 24, 1861, Clifford Arrick Diary.

11. Mary Henry, diary entry, n.d., Mary Henry Diary.

12. Henry Villard, *Memoirs of Henry Villard, Journalist and Financier, 1835–1900*, vol. 1 (Boston: Houghton, Mifflin, 1904), 169.

13. Lucius Chittenden, *Recollections of President Lincoln and His Administration* (New York: Harper & Brothers, 1891), 130.

14. Nicolay and Hay, *Abraham Lincoln: A History*, 4:153.

15. John Hay, diary entry, April 24, 1861, in *Inside Lincoln's White House: The Complete Civil War Diary of John Hay*, ed. Michael Burlingame and John R. T. Ettlinger (Carbondale: Southern Illinois University Press, 1999), 11. The dialogue is slightly altered in their presentation in *Abraham Lincoln: A History*, 4:153. Villard was present at the scene and confirms the statement in his *Memoirs*, 1:170.

16. Nicolay and Hay, *Abraham Lincoln: A History*, 4:149.

17. Ibid.

18. *New York Times*, April 25, 1861, 1.

19. Lucius Chittenden, diary entry, April 22, 1861, in Lucius Chittenden, *Invisible Siege: The Journal of Lucius E. Chittenden, April 15, 1861–July 14, 1861* (San Diego: Americana Exchange Press, 1969), 10–11.

20. Mary Henry, diary entry, n.d., Mary Henry Diary.

21. *New York World*, April 26, 1861, 4.

22. Richard M. Lee, *Mr. Lincoln's City*, (McLean, Va.: EPM Publications, 1981), 63; *Washington Evening Star*, April 25, 1861, 2.

23. *Washington Evening Star*, April 25, 1861, 2.

24. *New York Times*, April 25, 1861, 8.

25. *National Republican* (Washington, D.C.), April 22, 1861, 2.

26. *National Republican*, April 25, 1861, 1.

27. *Philadelphia Inquirer*, April 27, 1861, 1; *New York Times* April 25, 1861, 8.

28. *Evening Star*, April 25, 1861, 2.

29. *Evening Star*, April 25, 1861, 1.

30. *New York Times*, April 27, 1861, 1.

31. *New York Times*, April 27, 1861, 1.

32. John Hay, diary entry, April 24, 1861, in *Letters of John Hay*, 11.

33. Clifford Arrick, diary entry, April 24, 1861, Clifford Arrick Diary.

34. *National Republican*, April 27, 1861, 2; *Philadelphia Inquirer*, May 2, 1861, 1.

35. John A. Dahlgren *Memoir of John A. Dahlgren*, ed. Madeleine Vinton Dahlgren (Boston: J. R. Osgood, 1882), 332.

36. Ibid., 327.

37. Ibid.

38. Abraham Lincoln to Reverdy Johnson, April 24, 1861, Abraham Lincoln Papers, LOC.

39. Barton to B.W. Childs, April 25, 1861 in William E. Barton, *The Life of Clara Barton, Founder of the American Red Cross*, vol. 1 (Boston and New York: Houghton Mifflin, 1922), 110.

40. Nicolay and Hay, *Abraham Lincoln: A History*, 4:149.

41. Frank A. Bond to George P. Kane, telegram, April 24, 1861, Abraham Lincoln Papers, LOC.

42. Scott Daily Dispatch, April 24, 1861, Abraham Lincoln Papers, Library of Congress.

43. Fitz-James O'Brien, "The Seventh Regiment—How it Got from New York to Washington," letter to *New York Times*, April 27, 1861, in *Rebellion Record*, ed. Frank Moore, vol. 1 (New York: G. P. Putnam, 1861), 153.

44. Theodore Winthrop, "New York Seventh Regiment: Our March to Washington," *Atlantic Monthly* (June 1861), 751. A slightly different version appears as "Our March to Washington," in *Oxford Book of American Essays*, ed. Brander Matthews (New York: Oxford University Press, 1914).

45. Robert Gould Shaw to Sarah Blake Sturgis Shaw, April 26, 1861, in *Blue-Eyed Child of Fortune: The Civil War Letters of Colonel Robert Gould Shaw*, ed. Russell Duncan (Athens: University of Georgia Press, 1992), 79.

46. Ibid., 79.

47. Emmons Clark, *History of the Second Comany of the Seventh Regiment*, New York, J. G. Gregory, 1864), 304.

48. Ibid.

49. *Albany Journal*, April 27, 1861, 2.

50. Robert Gould Shaw to Sarah Blake Sturgis Shaw, April 26, 1861, in *Blue-Eyed Child of Fortune: The Civil War Letters of Colonel Robert Gould Shaw*, 80.

51. *Newark Daily Advertiser*, May 1, 1861, 2.

52. Robert Gould Shaw to Sarah Blake Sturgis Shaw, April 26, 1861, in *Blue-Eyed Child of Fortune: The Civil War Letters of Colonel Robert Gould Shaw*, 81.

53. Ibid.

54. Winthrop, "New York Seventh Regiment," 748.

55. Winthrop, "Our March to Washington," 254.

56. Ibid., 257.

57. William Swinton, *History of the Seventh Regiment, National Guard, State of New York, during the War of the Rebellion* (New York, Boston, Fields, Osgood & Co., 1870), 101.

58. O'Brien, "The Seventh Regiment—How it Got from New York to Washington," 153.

59. Clark, *History of the Second Company*, 306.

60. Swinton, *History of the Seventh Regiment*, 99.

61. Ibid., 100.

62. Clark, *History of the Second Company of the Seventh Regiment*, 306.

63. Ibid.

64. Winthrop, "Our March to Washington," 259.

65. Ibid., 258.
66. Robert Gould Shaw to Sarah Blake Sturgis Shaw, April 26, 1861, in *Blue-Eyed Child of Fortune: The Civil War Letters of Colonel Robert Gould Shaw*, 80.
67. Ibid.
68. Winthrop, "Our March to Washington," 262.
69. Ibid.
70. O'Brien, "The Seventh Regiment—How it Got from New York to Washington," 153.
71. Clark, *History of the Second Company*, 308.
72. Ibid.
73. Ibid.
74. Swinton, *History of the Seventh Regiment*, 107.
75. Clark, *History of the Second Company*, 308.
76. Robert Gould Shaw to Sarah Blake Sturgis Shaw, April 26, 1861, in *Blue-Eyed Child of Fortune: The Civil War Letters of Colonel Robert Gould Shaw*, 81.
77. Ibid.
78. Clark, *History of the Second Company*, 309.
79. Clifford Arrick, diary entry, April 24, 1861, Clifford Arrick Diary.

Thursday, April 25

1. John Hay, diary entry, April 25, 1861, in *Inside Lincoln's White House: The Complete Civil War Diary of John Hay*, eds. Michael Burlingame and John R. T. Ettlinger (Carbondale: Southern Illinois University Press, 1999), 11.
2. Helen Nicolay, *Lincoln's Secretary: A Biography of John G. Nicolay* (New York: Longmans, Green, 1949), 226.
3. *National Republican* (Washington, D.C.), April 26, 1861, 2.
4. Theodore Winthrop, "New York Seventh Regiment: Our March to Washington," *Atlantic Monthly* (June 1861): 756.
5. William O. Stoddard, *Lincoln's White House Secretary: The Adventurous Life of William O. Stoddard*, ed. Harold Holzer (Carbondale: Southern Illinois University Press, 2007), 83.
6. *Baltimore Sun*, April 26, 1861, 1.
7. *Baltimore Sun*, April 24, 1861, 1.
8. Andrew Carnegie and John Charles Van Dyke, *Autobiography of Andrew Carnegie* (Boston & New York: Houghton Mifflin, 1920), 100.
9. *New York World*, April 30, 1861, 4.
10. Thomas, remarks to the Seventh Regiment, quoted in William Swinton, *History of the Seventh Regiment, National Guard, State of New York, during the War of the Rebellion* (New York, Boston, Fields, Osgood & Co., 1870), 111.
11. *New York Tribune*, April 27, 1861, 5.
12. *New York World*, April 30, 1861, 4.
13. Ibid.
14. John Hay, diary entry, April 25, 1861, in *Letters of John Hay*, 11.

15. Ibid.
16. Robert Gould Shaw to Sarah Blake Sturgis Shaw, April 27, 1861, in *Blue-Eyed Child of Fortune: The Civil War Letters of Colonel Robert Gould Shaw*, ed. Russell Duncan (Athens: University of Georgia Press, 1992), 82.
17. *New York Tribune*, April 27, 1861, 5.
18. Swinton, *History of the Seventh Regiment*, 112–113.
19. *New York Times*, May 1, 1861, 2.
20. John G. Nicolay and John Hay, *Abraham Lincoln: A History*, 10 vols., vol. 4 (New York: Century Co., 1890), 156.
21. *New York Times*. May 1, 1861. 2.
22. Chittenden, diary entry, April 25, 1861, in Lucius Chittenden, *Invisible Siege: The Journal of Lucius E. Chittenden, April 15, 1861–July 14, 1861* (San Diego: Americana Exchange Press, 1969), 14.
23. *New York Times*, May 1, 1861. 2.
24. *New York Tribune*, April 27, 1861, 5.
25. *National Republican* (Washington, D.C.), April 26, 1861, 2.
26. *New York Times*, May 1, 1861, 2.
27. Ibid.
28. Emmons Clark, *History of the Second Company of the Seventh Regiment*, New York, J. G. Gregory, 1864), 3.
29. Swinton, *History of the Seventh Regiment*, 120.
30. Gen. George H. Steuart to William James Steuart, April 24, 1861, George H. Steuart Papers, Duke University Archives, Durham, North Carolina.
31. Ibid.
32. *Baltimore Sun*, April 25, 1861, 1.
33. *Baltimore American*, April 24, 1861, 1.
34. George H. Steuart to John Letcher, April 25, 1861, OR vol. 51, pt. 2: 34–35.
35. *Evening Star*, April 24, 1861, 2.
36. William Wilkins Glenn, *Between North and South: A Maryland Journalist Views the Civil War: The Narrative of William Wilkins Glenn, 1861–1869*, ed. Bayly Ellen Marksand Mark Norton Schatz (Rutherford, N.J.: Fairleigh Dickinson University Press, 1976), 32.
37. E.W. Bell to George H. Steuart, enclosure in letter, Philip St. Geo. Cocke to Lee, OR, ser. 1, 2:779.
38. Pratt, OR, ser. 1, 2:780.
39. Philip St. Geo. Cocke to Robert E. Lee, April 24, 1861, OR, ser. 1, vol. 2, 777–79.
40. Ibid.
41. Robert E. Lee to Philip St. Geo. Cocke, April 24, 1861, OR, ser. 1, vol. 2, 778.
42. Robert E. Lee to Daniel Ruggles, April 24, 1861, in *The Wartime Papers of R. E. Lee*, ed. Clifford Dowdey (Boston: Little, Brown, 1961), 11.
43. *New York Tribune*, April 27, 1861, 5.
44. Clifford Arrick, diary entry, April 25, 1861, Clifford Arrick Diary,Frontier Guards Records, Library of Congress (LOC).
45. *Daily State Gazette and Republican* (Trenton), April 26, 1861, 2.

46. Lucius Chittenden, April 25, 1861 diary entry, in *Invisible Siege: The Journal of Lucius E. Chittenden, April 15, 1861–July 14, 1861* (San Diego: Americana Exchange Press, 1969), 16.

47. Nicolay, *The Outbreak of the Rebellion* (New York: Charles Scribners, 1881), 104.

48. Nicolay and Hay, *Abraham Lincoln: A History*, 4:156.

49. *New York Tribune*, April 27, 1861, 4.

50. Clifford Arrick, diary entry, April 25, 1861, Clifford Arrick Diary,Frontier Guards records, LOC.

51. Ibid.; Arrick records Lane's remark as "H—l." In 1860s usages "Capitol" was often used interchangeably with "Capital" to refer to Washington.

Epilogue

1. Chittenden, diary entry, April 26, 1861, in Lucius Chittenden, *Invisible Siege: The Journal of Lucius E. Chittenden, April 15, 1861–July 14, 1861* (San Diego: Americana Exchange Press, 1969), 16.

2. Robert Gould Shaw to Sarah Blake Sturgis Shaw, April 26, 1861, in *Blue-Eyed Child of Fortune: The Civil War Letters of Colonel Robert Gould Shaw*, ed. Russell Duncan (Athens: University of Georgia Press, 1992), 80.

3. Clifford Arrick, diary entry, April 26, 1861, Clifford Arrick Diary, Frontier Guard Records, Library of Congress (LOC).

4. Chittenden, diary entry, April 27, 1861, in *Invisible Siege*, 20.

5. Frederick W. Seward, *Seward at Washington as Senator and Secretary of State: A Memoir of His Life, with Selections from His Letters, 1846–1861* (New York: Derby & Miller, 1891), 559.

6. William Howard Russell, *My Diary North and South* (Boston: T. O. H. P. Burnham, 1863), 142.

7. John G. Nicolay, *With Lincoln in the White House: Letters, Memoranda, and Other Writings of John G. Nicolay, 1860–1865*, ed. Michael Burlingame (Carbondale: Southern Illinois University Press, 2006), 39.

8. Quoted in John Niven, *Salmon P. Chase: A Biography* (New York: Oxford University Press, 1995), 250.

9. Winfield Scott, General Order No. 4, April 26, 1861, in OR, ser. 1, 2: 603.

10. "The Lincoln Log: A Daily Chronology of the Life of Abraham Lincoln," April 26, 1861, www.thelincolnlog.org/. National Center for Supercomputing Applications at the University of Illinois at Urbana-Champaign.

11. Winthrop, "Washington as a Camp," *Atlantic Monthly*, July 1861, 108.

12. Robert Gould Shaw to Sarah Blake Sturgis Shaw, April 27, 1861, in *Blue-Eyed Child of Fortune*, 82.

13. Justin G. Turner and Linda Levitt Turner, eds., *Mary Todd Lincoln: Her Life and Letters* (New York: Knopf, 1972), 86.

14. *New York World*, April 29, 1861, 5.

15. Craig L. Symonds, *Confederate Admiral: The Life and Wars of Franklin Buchanan* (Annapolis: Naval Institute Press, 1999), 137–138.

16. "Reminiscences by Janet Chase Hoyt," *New York Tribune*, April 5, 1891, 18.

17. Ibid.

18. Erich Langsdorf, "Jim Lane and the Frontier Guard," Kansas Historical Society Quarterly 9:1 (February 1940): 21.

19. Clifford Arrick, diary entry, April 27, 1861; also in *The Collected Works of Abraham Lincoln*, ed. Roy P. Basler, vol. 4 (New Brunswick, N.J.: Rutgers University Press, 1955), 345.

20. Chittenden, diary entry, April 26, 1861, in *Invisible Siege*, 17.

21. *New York Tribune*, April 27, 1861, 5.

22. Clifford Arrick, diary entry, April 26, 1861, Clifford Arrick Diary, Frontier Guards Records, LOC.

23. *Baltimore Sun*, April 22, 1861, 3.

24. Frederick Douglass, "Hope and Despair in the Cowardly Times," Address, Rochester, New York, April 28, 1861 in John W. Blassingame, ed. *The Frederick Douglass Papers* ser. 1, vol. 3 (New Haven, Yale University Press, 1985), 425.

25. Benjamin F. Butler, *Butler's Book: Autobiography and Personal Reminiscences of Major-General Benj. F. Butler* (Boston, A.M. Thayer, 1892), 220.

26. Russell, *My Diary North and South*, 50.

27. John A. Logan. *The Great Conspiracy: Its Origin and History* (New York: A. R. Hart & Co., 1886), *The Great Conspiracy*, 211.

28. Butler, *Butler's Book*, 200.

29. Henry Villard, *Memoirs of Henry Villard, Journalist and Financier, 1835–1900*, vol. 1 (Boston: Houghton, Mifflin, 1904), 167.

30. *Philadelphia Inquirer*, April 25, 1861, 4.

31. Ibid.

32. Francis W. Pickens to Jefferson Davis, confidential communication, April 16, 1861, in *Papers of Jefferson Davis*, ed. Lynda L. Crist and Mary S. Dix, vol. 7 (Baton Rouge: Louisiana State University Press, 1992), 105.

33. Jefferson Davis to. John Letcher, April 22, 1861, in OR, ser., vol. 2: 773.

34. Theodore B. Gates, *The War of the Rebellion* (New York: P. F. McBreen, 1884), 17.

35. Henry Wise to William Ambler, April 24, 1861, OR, vol. 51, pt. 2: 32.

36. *New York Tribune*, April 25, 1861, 4.

37. *Philadelphia Inquirer*, April 25, 1861, 4.

38. John Slidell to Davis, April 24, 1861, in *Papers of Jefferson Davis*, ed. Lynda L. Crist and Mary S. Dix, vol. 7 (Baton Rouge: Louisiana State University Press, 1992), 122.

39. *Goldsboro Tribune* (North Carolina), April 24, reprinted in *Rebellion Record*, ed. Frank Moore, vol. 1 (New York: G. P. Putnam, 1861), 189.

40. Robert Gould Shaw to Sarah Blake Sturgis Shaw, April 26, 1861, in *Blue-Eyed Child of Fortune*, 82.

41. John G. Nicolay, *The Outbreak of the Rebellion* (New York: Scribner's, 1882), 104.
42. Frederick W. Seward, *Seward at Washington as Senator and Secretary of State: A Memoir of His Life, with Selections from His Letters, 1846–1861* (New York: Derby & Miller, 1891), 560.
43. John Nicolay to Therena Bates, April 26, 1861, in John G. Nicolay, *With Lincoln in the White House: Letters, Memoranda, and Other Writings of John G. Nicolay, 1860–1865*, ed. Michael Burlingame (Carbondale: Southern Illinois University Press, 2006), 40.

PHOTO CREDITS

Page 4: Confederate Broadside Poetry Collection, Special Collections and Archives Department, Z. Smith Reynolds Library, Wake Forest University; **page 16.** Abraham Lincoln Papers, Library of Congress (LOC); **page 18:** LOC; **page 83:** Abraham Lincoln Papers, LOC; **Page 121:** Abraham Lincoln Papers, LOC; **page 144:** Butler, LOC; Lefferts, Emmons Clark, *History of the Second Company of the Seventh Regiment*, (New York, J. G. Gregory, 1864); **page 192,** Civil War Collections, Acton Memorial Library, Acton, Massachusetts; **page 239,** New York Historical Society (NYHS).

Insert page 1: Top: *Topographical Map of the District of Columbia* (Washington, D.C: D. McClelland, Blanchard & Mohun, 1861), courtesy of LOC; Bottom left, Bottom right: LOC; **page 2:** LOC; **page 3:** LOC; **page 4:** Top: LOC; Bottom left, Bottom Right: New York Public Library; Bottom Middle: Egbert L. Viele, "The Seventh Regiment at the Capitol," *Magazine of American History* 14:1 (July 1885):74; **page 5**: Top: LOC; Bottom: Courtesy of John Hoptak; **page 6:** LOC; **page 7**: Top: LOC; Bottom: NYHS; **page 8:** Top left, Top right, Bottom left: NYHS; Bottom right: Courtesy of Patrick Ciccone; **page 9:** NYHS; **page 10:** Top left, Top right: LOC; Bottom: Heber S. Thompson, *The First Defenders* (n.p.: First Defenders Association, 1910), 226; **page 11:** Top, William Swinton, *History of the Seventh Regiment, National Guard, State of New York, during the War of the Rebellion* (New York, Boston, Fields, Osgood & Co., 1870), facing 62; Bottom: Swinton, *History of the Seventh Regiment*, facing 96; **page 12:** Top: NYHS; Bottom: Asher Taylor, "A Tribute to the Seventh Regiment" (New York: n.p., 1871), 259, courtesy of NYHS; **page 13:** Top: LOC; Bottom left: Taylor, "A Tribute to the Seventh Regiment," 261, courtesy of NYHS; Bottom right: Andrew

Carnegie and John Charles Van Dyke, *Autobiography of Andrew Carnegie* (Boston & New York: Houghton Mifflin, 1920), facing 214; **page 14:** Top: LOC [note: the image depicts a parade later in 1861, not the April 26 parade]; Bottom: *Harper's Weekly*, May 25, 1861, 327; **page 15:** *Harper's Weekly*, May 25, 1861, 333; **page 16:** Top: The White House, Washington D.C., at the start of the American Civil War, 1861 by American Photographer, Private Collection, Peter Newark Military Pictures, The Bridgeman Art Library; Bottom: LOC.

INDEX